BANANA WARS

AMERICAN ENCOUNTERS / GLOBAL INTERACTIONS

A SERIES EDITED BY GILBERT M. JOSEPH AND EMILY S. ROSENBERG

This series aims to stimulate critical perspectives and fresh interpretive frame-
works for scholarship on the history of the imposing global presence of the United
States. Its primary concerns include the deployment and contestation of power, the
construction and deconstruction of cultural and political borders, the fluid meanings
of intercultural encounters, and the complex interplay between the global and the
local. American Encounters seeks to strengthen dialogue and collaboration between
historians of U.S. international relations and area studies specialists.

The series encourages scholarship based on multiarchival historical research.
At the same time, it supports a recognition of the representational character of all
stories about the past and promotes critical inquiry into issues of subjectivity and
narrative. In the process, American Encounters strives to understand the context
in which meanings related to nations, cultures, and political economy are
continually produced, challenged, and reshaped.

BANANA WARS

Power, Production, and History in the Americas

EDITED BY STEVE STRIFFLER AND MARK MOBERG

Duke University Press   *Durham and London 2003*

2nd printing, 2005

© 2003 Duke University Press

All rights reserved

Printed in the United States of

America on acid-free paper ∞

Designed by Rebecca M. Giménez

Typeset in Adobe Minion by

Tseng Information Systems, Inc.

Library of Congress Cataloging-

in-Publication Data appear on

the last printed page of this book.

CONTENTS

3 The Caribbean

ACKNOWLEDGMENTS

This book is a collaborative effort that owes much to the contributions and insight of many individuals along the way. They have shaped the contours of this project by guiding and challenging our understanding of how a single export commodity has conditioned society and power in much of the Americas. Steve Striffler, inspired by the work of his mentor, the late Bill Roseberry, on coffee production in Central and South America, conceived of a panel emphasizing recent scholarship on banana production for the 1998 meetings of the American Anthropological Association. For that panel, we invited the participation of an interdisciplinary group of scholars whose areas of research spanned the banana-producing regions of the hemisphere.

From a rich assortment of papers in fields as diverse as history, geography, sociology, and business history, as well as anthropology, there emerged the central themes of power, resistance, and ethnicity around which this volume is organized. To each of the authors herein, we owe a great debt of gratitude for their participation in the conference panel from which this book developed and for their receptiveness to our suggestions and those of the external readers who reviewed their work. Without exception, the patience and good faith of this volume's authors were indispensable to our ability to transform a collection of disparate essays into a cohesive book manuscript. So, too, were the efforts of our editor Valerie Millholland and the staff of Duke University Press. Both deserve our profound thanks for their enthusiastic support of this project. Not the least of their contributions was the placement of the manuscript with two sympathetic yet critical reviewers whose insight forced all of us to clarify our arguments and rethink our preconceptions. We would also like to thank Sarah Mattics of the University of South Alabama Center for Archaeological Studies for preparing the map of banana-producing areas of the Americas. In addition, the editors thank their respective college deans, Donald R. Bobbitt of the University of Arkansas and G. David Johnson of the University of South Alabama, for financial assistance in producing this volume.

Each of us, editors and authors included, owes our greatest debt to the many individuals—from farm workers to growers to government officials and archivists—whose expertise with various facets of the banana trade was essential to the research on which this volume is built. Their experiences are too often hidden from the metropolitan consumer who is the endpoint of that trade. For that reason, we offer this volume in the hope that their voices will be revealed in the pages that follow—in tandem with the hidden history of the commodities that they produce throughout this hemisphere.

BANANA WARS

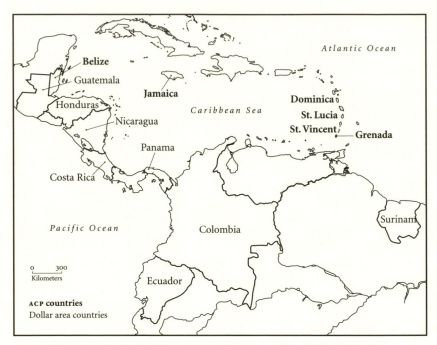

Banana Exporters of the Americas. Source: University of Texas Map Web site.

MARK MOBERG AND STEVE STRIFFLER

Introduction

F rom the "banana republics" at the beginning of the twentieth century to the "banana wars" at its conclusion, one tropical fruit has transformed more of Central America, the Caribbean, and South America than any other commodity. The conversion of much of the Americas into banana-producing enclaves during the last century has also informed North Americans' most popular, and often stereotypical, images of the rest of the hemisphere. In most of the regions examined in this book, the onset of commercial banana cultivation coincided with a broadly similar set of processes: in various diplomatic, military, and economic guises, foreign interests entered Latin American countries, created banana-exporting sectors, and deepened the dependence of regional and national economies on a volatile world market. The expansion of banana production and the further integration of Latin American countries into the world economy necessarily entailed profound ecological, demographic, cultural, and political changes. Settlers and immigrants poured into frontier zones as banana companies carved roads, railroads, and towns from tropical forest. In the process of transforming the physical landscape, the workers, farmers, state officials, and company men also transformed themselves, forging new varieties of political and cultural identity, conflict, and organization. The same themes, processes, conflicts, and actors often reappeared from one banana-producing region to the next, yet their local expression was inevitably conditioned by the histories, cultures, and geographies of each place. It is both the similarities and the variations among banana-producing regions throughout the Americas that give this volume its coherence.

Ultimately, though, this collection stresses variation — the profound differences in social, cultural, economic, and political processes and experiences — because, although the development of various banana-exporting regions did reflect similar historical forces and processes, such transformations took strikingly different forms throughout the Americas. Banana-export sectors have always been situated within distinctive national and regional contexts, yielding significant contrasts in the relations between multinational corporations, workers, contract farmers, and the state. Even where multinational corporations controlled all phases of production in vertically integrated enterprises, such as those in Colombia and Costa Rica, the companies utilized and disposed of land in varying ways. Similarly, while confrontational labor relations seem almost inherent to banana production, labor problems were resolved in quite distinct ways in Costa Rica in the 1920s, Ecuador during the 1940s, and Honduras in the 1990s. Even within a single corporation, such as the United Fruit Company, managers devised varying methods of labor control and recruitment in the company's many spheres of operation. Finally, where multinationals have procured some or most of their fruit through contract farming — in St. Vincent, Ecuador, Belize, and Costa Rica, for example — the practice has taken a wide range of forms and had varied effects on farming communities. Despite their common experience with a particular commodity, then, banana-producing regions developed dissimilar patterns of social relations, labor mobilization, multinational involvement, and political conflict.

This volume describes such differences as they were expressed in particular times and places. Why did different banana-producing regions — even within the same country — develop distinct patterns of property relations and labor mobilization? What effects did these differences have on the class structures and economies of national societies? How did the distinctive political contexts of each nation-state influence the ways in which domestic and foreign producers operated? How were the possibilities for labor mobilization realized or constrained in different regions? In confronting such differences, this volume adds up to more than a collection of "case studies"; rather, it contributes to the comparative and historical analysis of capitalism, state power, and popular struggle in Latin America and the Caribbean. Through the consideration of a single export crop that transformed the physical and social environment of much of the hemisphere, this collection reevaluates the workings of global capitalism.[1]

The ensuing analysis is more nuanced and complex than most popular portrayals of banana-producing nations and banana multinationals. Throughout most of Latin America and the Caribbean, it was rarely possible for even the most powerful and infamous expression of foreign capital — the United Fruit

Company—to simply dictate the terms of its presence. The creation of so-called banana republics was never as simple as the metaphor suggests because the actors themselves were highly complex and differentiated. Companies such as United Fruit and Standard Fruit had the power and resources to move from one country to the next, but while they were there—whether *there* was Belize, Colombia, Costa Rica, St. Lucia, or Ecuador—they had to operate in distinct political-economic contexts. At certain times and in certain places, national governments and domestic elites were fully compliant agents of foreign capital. At other moments and in other locales, multinationals could find themselves in political quagmires as allies became enemies, workers became militants, and peasants became squatters.

A GLOBAL FRUIT IN THE GLOBAL CENTURY

Although small-scale banana production has existed in Latin America since the sixteenth century and bananas were first exported to foreign markets in the nineteenth, the last hundred years have been the century for bananas in many parts of Latin America. It was in the early twentieth century that a handful of capitalists, in an ambiguous relationship with workers, peasants, labor organizations, national governments, and consumers, transformed the banana into a fully global commodity (see table 1). In the process, these entrepreneurs not only transformed themselves into major multinational corporations but dramatically altered the political, economic, cultural, and natural landscapes of numerous Latin American and Caribbean regions.

Throughout the Americas, the introduction of commercial banana cultivation involved daunting tasks for entrepreneurs, engineers, and workers of the late nineteenth century. Tropical frontiers once regarded as impenetrable and disease-ridden required clearing and settlement, to be followed by the creation of a fully industrial infrastructure for the production and transportation of a highly perishable commodity. From region to region, whether Ecuador's coastal plain, the northern coast of Honduras, or the Santa Marta region of Colombia, the cultivation of bananas was intimately linked to processes of nation building, capital formation, and internal and international migration. These processes shifted the primary sites of "economic development" and "national progress" from capital cities to rough-hewn frontier zones. Ironically,

TABLE 1   Growth in World Banana Trade and Multinational Monopoly, 1900–1932

Year	Total Exports in Bunches
1900	19,848,692
1913	50,111,764
1929	97,233,972
1932	87,888,200
United Fruit:	51,600,000
Standard Fruit:	15,559,887

SOURCE: Kepner and Foothill 1935, 37.

while the global banana trade is now popularly associated with the brazen manipulation of national governments by foreign capital, at its inception it was viewed as one of Latin America's most promising mechanisms of economic and social modernization. In large part this was because the banana trade's infrastructural demands brought the first railways, modern harbors, and electrification to the humid tropics. As shown by many of the contributors to this volume, however, such technological progress rarely led to enlightened labor relations or democratic forms of governance.

Wherever the banana trade established itself, it generated broadly similar demands for labor, land, and capital, causing common patterns and themes of development to emerge in otherwise disparate regions. In many places, these included the conversion of tropical forests into monocrop plantations, the construction of railways, ports, and roads, and the integration of frontier zones into world markets, all of which occurred at a huge human cost. In the early years of the trade, banana companies recruited countless workers locally and internationally to secure a foothold in tropical forests rife with malaria and yellow fever. In the process, thousands of lives were sacrificed to establish the estates and infrastructure required of large-scale banana production. While consumers in developed countries came to regard the banana as an exotic and benignly nutritious fruit, few were aware of the abuses that made the banana trade possible. Yet these practices have formed an indelible historical memory on those who reside in the lowland tropics. More than a century after Minor Keith imported West Indian workers into Costa Rica in order to labor on the construction of his first railroad, their descendants still observe that "under every one of those *poleen* [railroad ties] is the body of a colored man" (Purcell 1993, 26). An estimated 5,000 workers died in the construction of Keith's railway through the malarial hinterland of Limón on the Atlantic Coast (Stewart 1964, 43).

Similarities between banana enclaves continued well after commercial production was firmly in place, with yeoman farmers, foreign capitalists, and the state fighting over access to land, export policies, and taxes. Labor unions, communist parties, and individual workers resisted the attempts of foreign companies to impose punitive working conditions and low wages. Already divided among themselves by language, color, and national origin, workers often clashed because of the disparate treatment to which they were subjected by the banana companies (Bourgois 1989; Moberg 1997). The often conflict-ridden ethnic relations that exist to this day along the entire Atlantic coast of Central America owe much of their existence to policies of ethnic and racial discrimination practiced on banana plantations in both the past and the present day.

However, what is most interesting in our examination of banana-producing regions is not their commonalities but their differences — in terms of productive organization, methods of labor control, land tenure, labor and ethnic conflict, state intervention, and forms of political and cultural resistance. This variation becomes most evident when contrasting the hemisphere's three main banana-producing regions: Central America, the Caribbean, and South America (see Raynolds herein, table 3). Foreign banana companies made their earliest forays into the Central American isthmus, where they have exerted their greatest influence over national governments and civil societies. In Costa Rica, Panama, Honduras, and Guatemala, banana cultivation was established on exceptionally large plantations in the early 1900s, a pattern that still persists in some locales. Massive "division" farms operated by both the United Fruit and Standard Fruit companies eventually absorbed entire regions of Central America, creating vast enclaves under foreign control in which national sovereignty was nominal at best. Although smallholders frequently surrounded such enclaves and provided exporters with an important source of fruit, their access to supplies, transportation, and markets was largely under the control of their giant corporate neighbors. To the extent that the banana multinationals dominated the economies of Central America — in particular their sources of export earnings and markets for labor and land — the region's national governments have often found their actions constrained by company policies and their ultimate guarantor, the

U.S. government. Indeed, much of Guatemala's horrific recent history may be attributable to United Fruit's emergence as the country's largest landowner by the 1930s, a pattern that generated intense opposition to the company and culminated in U.S. intervention to topple a government committed to land reform (Dosal 1993; Gleijeses 1993; Schlesinger and Kinser 1982; Forster 1998). Since the late 1970s, the banana multinationals have sought a less prominent (and less risky) political profile by divesting themselves of some landholdings and subcontracting much of their production to local and foreign investors (Bourgois 1989; Moberg 1997; Euraque 1996c; FLACSO 1988; Slutsky and Alonso 1980; Urra Veloso 1975). To this day, however, Central American plantations remain among the largest by the standards of the hemisphere.[2]

At the opposite extreme are the banana-producing islands of the Caribbean, a region where production is centered on diminutive landholdings, often of no more than several acres. A few foreign-owned plantations could be found on Eastern Caribbean islands until the 1980s, but the region's banana industry has always been dominated by small-scale contract farmers. Today nearly all eastern Caribbean banana production is in the hands of small growers, many of whom utilize only household labor. This has not meant that Caribbean economies have been any less dependent on the natural and social vagaries of banana production or that land and income inequalities are absent. To the contrary, the producers and island economies of the Caribbean have been even more vulnerable to the uncertainties of weather and international marketing agreements than have their Central American counterparts. Although they retain nominal control over production, Caribbean banana farmers have historically been at the mercy of two European-based multinationals. After controlling all exports from the four eastern Caribbean banana-producing islands for more than a half-century, Geest Industries sold its Caribbean banana marketing interests in 1999 to a joint venture operated by the parastatal Windward Islands Banana Development and Exporting Corporation (WIBDECO) and Fyffes Limited. The latter Irish-based multinational now exercises total or partial control over all exports from the commonwealth Caribbean. Marketing monopolies of this sort have enabled banana companies to dictate prices as well as the very conditions of production, including fertilizer, other inputs, and harvesting and packing procedures. National governments, in turn, act as enforcement agencies for production routines dictated by multinational corporations, often incurring small-grower resistance in the process. As Lawrence Grossman examines in his chapter on St. Vincent, much of the literature on contract farming centers on the limited autonomy of ostensibly "independent" producers, with some scholars even contending that contract farmers are little more than "disguised proletarians" (see Friedmann 1991; Goodman and Watts 1994; Little and Watts 1994). Yet their ongoing control of land and inputs has also created possibilities for resistance among contract farmers, including the diversion of inputs from bananas to food crops (Grossman 1998, 207). The prevalence of small contract growers, the absence of large plantations and labor forces, and the European market orientation have all contributed to the distinctive political, cultural, and economic milieu within the Caribbean (see Marie 1979; Trouillot 1988; Nurse and Sandiford 1995; Grossman 1998; Welch 1996; Slocum 1996; Thomson 1987).

Located somewhere between our extremes of Central America and the Caribbean are the South American producers of Ecuador and Colombia. At the beginning of the century, United Fruit extended its system of large corporate-owned plantations to the Santa Marta region of Colombia (Botero Herrera and Barney 1977; Posada Carbó 1991; White 1978). By 1930, however, the company not only found itself overwhelmed by labor problems but involved in a massacre that signaled a sea change in the way that foreign banana companies would do business in Latin America (Bucheli 1997; Fonnegra 1980; LeGrand 1984; LeGrand 1998). In the case of Ecuador, United Fruit again led the way, turning its attention to Colombia's southern neighbor in the mid-1930s as agricultural diseases and labor problems plagued its operations in Central America and Colombia. Although Ecuador rapidly became the largest producer of bananas in the world (a position it has held through the second half of the century), the expansion of banana cultivation there took a different route. A number of foreign-owned plantations existed during the 1950s, but Ecuadorian commercial farmers and peasants controlled most direct production. And by 1965 virtually no foreign-owned plantations remained in the country (Larrea Maldonado 1987; Striffler 1999; Striffler 2002). Unlike in Central America, where many plantations continue to operate under the direct control of multinationals, banana production in Ecuador and Colombia is in the hands of domestic capitalists who sell their crops to the major exporters. The operations of contract farmers in Ecuador and Colombia are much larger than the typical holding in the Caribbean but remain smaller than the average banana farm in Central America, whether corporate or independent in ownership.

Broadly outlined, these regional variations help us to make sense of the wide range of cultural, political, and economic forces associated with banana production. Yet, as the following essays make clear, these general patterns do not suggest an invariable regional correlation between land tenure, plantation size, labor control, and local-regional politics. Over the last seventy years, for example, banana production within Belize has shifted from the Central American pattern of large-scale, corporate-controlled plantations geared to U.S. markets to the Caribbean pattern of small-farmer subcontracting oriented toward Europe. Notwithstanding the importance of general regional patterns, then, causation is complicated and a comparative examination allows us to explore the articulation of a variety of factors such as state building, labor struggles, cultural diversity, monopoly practices, ecological constraints, and gender relations. Within Central America, for example, many foreign-owned enclaves were threatened by agricultural diseases and political conflicts by the 1940s, prompting a general shift toward subcontracting in the following decades. Yet within the region, and even within single nations, the ensuing modes of labor discipline, control, resistance, and state involvement varied considerably by locale. Whereas Pacific Coast plantations predominantly employed ladino workers of Central American origin, those of the Atlantic Coast employed many black workers recruited from the anglophone Caribbean, in addition to ladino and indigenous laborers. As Cindy Forster shows in this volume (see also Echeverri-Ghent 1992; Chomsky 1996), the absence of West Indians from Pacific Coast plantations was no accident. Reacting to the often violent resentment of mestizo banana workers and Costa Ricans in general to the recruitment of Caribbean blacks for plantation work, lawmakers imposed restrictions on the internal migration of West Indians, effectively limiting their residence to the sparsely populated Atlantic Coast. On Pacific Coast plantations, the relative absence of ethnic divisions within plantation labor forces lent itself to comparatively confrontational relations between workers and managers, while the more segmented workforce of the Atlantic Coast was frequently beset by ethnic and national antagonisms. In building on a significant body of research across all of the regions of banana production in the Americas, the essays included here strive to contextualize the local and regional variation associated with commercial banana production since its inception a century ago. Our aim here is not to produce a general model that mechanically predicts variations and similarities in banana enclaves regardless of time and place, but to recognize that the global circuits of the banana trade have always been expressed locally, within distinctive geographies, histories, and sociopolitical contexts.

THE BANANA IN HISTORICAL AND
COMPARATIVE PERSPECTIVE

Although the banana originated in the Old World, it is now produced in virtually all lowland tropical regions and supplies a large percentage of the caloric intake for many people in Africa, Asia, and Latin America. In terms of volume, the majority of bananas are produced *and* consumed in highly populated countries like Brazil, India, Mexico, and Indonesia. In this book, however, our concern is with the 20 to 25 percent of the world's bananas that enter the global market (Nurse and Sandiford 1995, 16–18).[3] It was only with the emergence of that market a century ago that entire regions and populations of the humid tropics were transformed to make way for the fruit's production. This collection not only extends through time, examining the world production and trade of bananas at particular moments, but traverses space as well. A number of the contributors explore the relationship between, on the one hand, key production sites in Central America, the Caribbean, and South America, and, on the other, key sites of capital, consumption, and trade regulation in the United States and Europe.

Our global history begins about 150 years ago in Central America and the Caribbean, the two sites from which bananas were first exported to North American markets. In his pioneering work on the banana trade, Charles Kepner (1936) noted that the first yellow bananas exported to the United States arrived from Central America at the end of the Civil War, although small quantities of red bananas were imported from Cuba and the Bahamas before 1850. The success of these initial efforts led a number of people, including sea captain Lorenzo D. Baker and fruit merchant Andrew Preston, to begin exporting bananas from the Caribbean in a more consistent and organized fashion. Together, Baker, Preston, and several other investors formed the Boston Fruit Company in 1885 and expanded their operations in Cuba, Jamaica, and Santo Domingo. At roughly the same time, Minor C. Keith began cultivating bananas in Costa Rica, Panama, and Colombia (Frederick Upham Adams 1914). Keith's banana operations, which began as a humble subsidiary to his railroad construction projects throughout the lowland tropics, were eventually to become one of the most prominent expressions of U.S. capital in the hemisphere. While Keith and a handful of rivals were soon to create today's banana multinationals, they initially operated in a field of considerable competition. As late as 1899, there were 114 firms involved in the importation of bananas to the United States (Davies 1990, 32).

By the turn of the century — when it was rapidly becoming apparent that the export of bananas was a profitable enterprise — two key changes transformed the industry. First, foreign banana companies began direct production on a dramatic scale, shifting away from their earlier role as exporters of fruit produced by independent growers. Requiring large volumes of high-quality produce, the fruit companies could no longer depend on local producers for the majority of their exports and began to establish banana plantations of their own. The entry of foreign companies into direct production — and their resulting need to control systems of transportation, communication, law, land tenure, and labor recruitment — would have a dramatic impact on Latin America as the industry expanded in the early decades of the twentieth century. A second key development took place in 1899, when the Boston Fruit Company combined with Minor Keith's operations in Central America and Colombia to form the United Fruit Company. Within a decade, United Fruit had established a stranglehold over many fruit-producing regions of Central and South America, systematically acquiring or destroying competitors in all its areas of operation (Kepner 1936). Were it not for the resilience of the Vaccaro brothers, who eventually built the Standard Fruit Company (Dole) into one of the largest producers and exporters of bananas in the world, United Fruit's monopoly over the North American banana trade would have been virtually complete (Karnes 1978).

Although Minor Keith and, later, United Fruit attempted to extend their control to European markets as well, their ability to do so was constrained by the speed with which bananas ripened, the distance to markets, and the lack of practicable refrigerated shipping. In the 1890s Keith had attempted to ship bananas from his Costa Rican plantations to Liverpool, but the fruit usually arrived spoiled, and he was forced to suspend the operation after three straight years of losses. The inability of U.S.-based banana companies to enter and dominate markets outside of North America allowed European shipping companies to establish a banana trade of their own. To satisfy growing British demand for the then exotic fruit, Elder Dempster and Alfred Fyffe began importing fruit from the Canary Islands in the 1890s. Their merger, incorporated in 1901 as Elders and Fyffes (later becoming Fyffes Limited), produced a banana company that remains Europe's largest. With the improvement of refrigerated shipping methods at the beginning of the century, Fyffes turned for its primary sources of fruit to the British West Indies, particularly Jamaica. Obligated by a Crown contract to operate mail and passenger steamers between the West Indies and England, the company found that its shipping line often suffered losses when Caribbean banana producers were unable to fill the company's freighters to capacity. There ensued a series of agreements between Fyffes and United Fruit, in which the U.S. multinational agreed to provide full cargoes of bananas for Fyffes steamers in exchange for a 45 percent share of the company's stock. In 1913 United Fruit secretly negotiated for the stock of Fyffes's principal shareholder, securing majority interest in the now nominally British firm. Although Fyffes eventually became a wholly-owned subsidiary of United Fruit, its name and logo persisted independently of the parent company, and it has historically focused on the importation of Caribbean rather than Latin American fruit.[4]

A second European banana multinational was established in the 1950s, and indirectly owed much of its growth to the acquisition of Fyffes by United Fruit. Wary of the possibility that the U.S. firm, through its Fyffes subsidiary, would gain a monopoly over banana exports from the West Indies, the British government assigned a contract in 1948 to Antilles Products for the purchase of fruit from the Windward Islands of St. Lucia, Dominica, and St. Vincent. Geest Industries, a firm founded by a Dutch immigrant family in the United Kingdom, acquired Antilles Products in 1952 as a subsidiary to its horticultural bulb business. When Fyffes's Jamaican exports were devastated by Panama Disease and bad weather in the early 1950s, and as Canary Islands fruit became prohibitively expensive due to growing European protectionism, Geest stood poised to gain the lion's share of the British fruit trade. Relying on fruit cultivated on several company-owned plantations as well as by thousands of small-scale independent farmers in the eastern Caribbean, Geest increased its imports to Britain nearly sixfold between 1956 and 1965. By the late 1970s, as the last large plantations were broken up and distributed by national governments to independent farmers, the region's banana industry rested entirely in the hands of small growers. Notwithstanding its withdrawal from direct production, Geest's capitalization underwent phenomenal growth, its net worth climbing from 100,000 pounds sterling in 1953 to over 23 million in 1980 (Trouillot 1988, 169).

The monopoly that a few multinationals established over the world banana trade was facilitated by the nature of banana production during much of the twentieth century. The opening of new frontiers and the transportation of bananas required capital and labor on a massive scale. Further, the very nature of large-scale banana cultivation until the 1950s necessitated an ongoing process of land acquisition and capital investment, often followed by the relocation and even destruction of infrastructure to prevent its seizure by potential competitors. Until that decade, commercially produced banana varieties had been susceptible to Panama Disease (*Fusarium oxysporum f. cubense*), a highly infectious soil-borne fungus that devastated entire banana-producing regions. As older banana groves fell prey to the disease, growers were forced to open up new plantations in disease-free zones. As a result, the banana companies were continually on the move, shifting their operations from one region, and often from one country, to another as Panama Disease spread. The banana companies often defended their vast operations as "natural monopolies" in that few small-scale producers possessed sufficient resources to start new enterprises, much less the large quantities of land required for each relocation. By 1930, for example, United Fruit owned nearly twenty times the 139,000 acres of land that it then held under cultivation, ostensibly to ensure the availability of virgin lands for future banana cultivation. Company critics claimed that much of this land was acquired simply to deny opportunities for banana production to rivals, whether other banana corporations or independent farmers. Such was the contention of the ill-fated Arbenz government of Guatemala, which was overthrown after attempting to redistribute some of United Fruit's uncultivated land to landless peasants (Dosal 1993). Ironically, each relocation of corporate operations typically spread the disease to newly opened divisions in short order, as workers, tools, and equipment reassigned from infected areas to virgin lands inevitably brought *Fusarium* spores with them.[5]

This continual movement of corporate operations was not, however, random. After United Fruit consolidated its control over much of the banana trade in the first decades of the twentieth century, it decisively shifted most of its operations out of the Caribbean and into Central America (Kepner 1936). Not only were hurricanes less of a problem in Central America, but the region had an ideal combination of cheap land and labor. An additional factor may have been the relative resistance of British colonial governments to direct control by United Fruit, although, as Mark Moberg's essay demonstrates, British administrators occasionally facilitated the company's goals when it was in their interest to do so. The company quickly abandoned production in Santo Domingo, switched from bananas to sugar in Cuba, and began a number of short-lived enterprises in the Windward Islands during the 1920s and 1930s (Nurse and Sandiford 1995). In Jamaica, where United Fruit also had operations at the time of its formation, the company continued to purchase fruit from local producers but did not move further into direct production. In contrast, multinational-driven banana production exploded in Central America during the decades prior to World War II. Although United Fruit's presence in particular countries varied from decade to decade depending on the Panama Disease, the multinational had major investments in Colombia, Panama, Costa Rica, Honduras, and Guatemala, as well as significant influence in Jamaica, Nicaragua, Ecuador, and even Mexico. Standard Fruit, whose operations were concentrated in Honduras for many years, eventually expanded (as a producer and / or exporter) into Mexico, Nicaragua, Jamaica, and Cuba (Kepner 1936, 67).

In sum, the first half of the century was characterized by regionally disparate processes. On the one hand, banana production in Central (and, to a lesser extent, South) America was geared predominantly toward North American markets, and was centered on large corporate-owned plantations. Lacking such economies of scale and Central America's low-cost labor, relatively small producers in the Caribbean struggled to survive through preferential access to European markets. This system, the legacies of which can be seen in the contemporary context, was seriously challenged in the 1930s by political instability, and eventually transformed in the postwar period by, among other things, new disease-resistant varieties of bananas. Indeed, it seems likely that the expansion of labor conflicts and the introduction of new banana varieties were not entirely unrelated phenomena. By the 1930s corporate-owned plantations in

Central America and Colombia were having problems not only with Panama Disease but with workers, peasants, and national governments, all of which were becoming increasingly assertive after the Great Depression.

As Bucheli's piece shows, the system of production and marketing defined by the corporate-owned plantation was coming under attack just prior to World War II. It was increasingly difficult for United Fruit to find areas that were free of agricultural diseases, labor problems, and meddlesome governments. The multinational's solution—to withdraw from direct production and to contract with local producers—was not easily implemented prior to the introduction of the Cavendish strain of banana in the 1950s.[6] Immune to Panama Disease, the Cavendish not only provided planters with a more productive fruit but allowed them to cultivate bananas on the same piece of land for an almost indefinite period. The multinationals no longer needed the large quantities of reserve land that had made them such prominent political targets in the past. At the same time, because the Cavendish is highly susceptible to bruising, drought, and a variety of plant diseases, it requires labor-intensive methods of handling, a more regular supply of water, and the greater application of chemicals. In short, it demands more labor and capital, making it increasingly difficult for small producers to compete with their larger counterparts.

Once introduced, the Cavendish transformed banana-producing zones. Multinationals began to produce fewer bananas themselves, preferring instead to contract with highly capitalized farmers who assumed all of the risks of production and labor control. Although contract farmers in Central and South America still include some small-scale producers in their ranks, the tendency of the banana multinationals to dictate prices, input use, and handling procedures to its suppliers has made it increasingly difficult for small farmers to profitably produce bananas for export markets. Their counterparts in the Caribbean have fared slightly better, but only with a protected European market. At this writing, the complex system of import licenses and tariffs that protected Caribbean producers has crumbled under the challenge brought by the United States before the World Trade Organization (wto). Having just ended in 2002, it remains to be seen whether the region's small-scale farmers will be eliminated or will find a way to survive.

Despite regional variation between Central and South America and the Caribbean, in all their areas of operation, multinational exporters have sought to insulate themselves from the normal risks associated with agricultural production. They have done so by ridding themselves of fixed assets while retaining considerable control over the production process through a monopoly over chemicals, expertise, credit, and, above all, access to the market. As Raynolds demonstrates in her essay, this intense competition for markets fueled trade conflicts between the United States and Europe before the WTO, in which Chiquita successfully challenged market preferences for Eastern Caribbean fruit in the European market.

This collection contributes to an ongoing, and exceptionally rich, body of scholarship whose history is almost as old as the banana industry itself. Not surprisingly, most of the early work on the industry focused on the banana barons themselves. Written during a period of rapid U.S. political and economic ascendance, these corporate histories saw the rise of large banana companies in rather stark terms—as either a classic case of U.S. imperialism or as a fine example of the North American entrepreneurial spirit. Not only did the political perspectives of the early scholars vary—ranging from the anti-imperialist stance of Kepner (1936) to the middle ground of LaBarge (1959) to the pro-United Fruit position of May and Plaza (1958)—but so too did the quality of scholarship and access to sources. Kepner's studies stand out in terms of both their political commitment and their high quality of scholarship. Scholars (such as Karnes [1978]) who have been more sympathetic to the major multinationals have also been able to gain the most open access to corporate archives.

Although histories of particular corporations are still being written (e.g., McCann 1976; Argueta 1989), most recent scholarship has gone in two related directions. Both of these latest trends focus on region, but whereas the first tends to be more comparative, macroeconomic, and sociological, the second emphasizes local history and anthropology. In the former, some of the richness associated with local histories and actors is necessarily sacrificed in favor of the broader comparative analysis of regional and national processes. Ellis (1983), for example, has examined how the relationships between production regimes and multinational corporations change over time and space in the banana-producing regions of Central America. Similarly, an important edited collection, *Cambio y Continuidad en la Economia Bananera* (FLACSO 1988), examines the banana industry in its national dimensions, emphasizing broad trends in productivity, export levels, land patterns, commercialization, and labor mobility in particular countries of Central and South America. It is in these studies that we find some of the most basic information on changing patterns of land tenure, systems of production, and exports across both regional and national borders. There are also a number of national and regional studies within this tradition (Larrea Maldonado 1987; Carías Velásquez 1991; Botero Herrera and Sierra 1981). In the second tradition, the emphasis on particular locales or regions has produced studies that are both well situated within broader political and economic currents and rich in historical detail (i.e., "real people doing real things"). Earlier efforts in this vein (Gaspar 1979; Acuña Ortega 1984) were followed by book-length local histories of banana-producing regions (Trouillot 1988; Bourgois 1989), and then a still-growing body of local-regional histories (Purcell 1993; Chomsky 1996; Moberg 1997; Grossman 1998; Striffler 2002). A spate of recent and ongoing dissertations suggests that this will continue to be a productive avenue of scholarship for years to come (Slocum 1996; Soluri 1998; Putnam 2000; Sanders forthcoming). The latter studies are not, by and large, *comparative* in intent, perspective, or methodology, at least with respect to the banana industry and other banana-producing regions.

This collection brings these scholarly trends together by both deepening our knowledge of corporate history and by placing local and regional histories into comparative perspective. It is important to note that this comparative exercise is only possible because of the wealth of local studies that now exist. In general, we integrate the two traditions of banana scholarship by confronting the differences found in particular banana-producing regions—differences in class, ethnic and gender relations, production patterns, state-capital configurations, and the like. We begin, however, with three broader views of the banana industry as a whole. The first essay, by Laura T. Raynolds, examines the ongoing trade dispute widely reported in the popular press as the "banana wars." This conflict has pitted U.S. and Latin American "dollar bananas" against a number of European countries and their banana-producing former colonies in Africa, the Caribbean, and the Pacific (known as the ACP countries). Even at this macrolevel, however, Raynolds's emphasis is on differentiation and contingency, in terms of the divergent trade geography, state sponsorship, corporate involvement, productive relations, and environmental conditions characterizing the two productive systems. Next, John Soluri's essay examines an underexplored but provocative dimension of the global banana industry: the dialectical relationship between banana production and consumption. How did bananas go from a tropical novelty to one of the most popular and traded fruits in the world? Finally, Marcelo Bucheli's contribution examines the internal workings, strategies, and decision-making processes of *El Pulpo* itself, the United Fruit Company.[7] In so doing, Bucheli helps us understand why and how the multinational pulled out of direct production, transforming itself into a marketing company that contracts with producers of varying sizes in Central America, the Caribbean, and South America.

The remaining essays examine histories of specific locales, regions, and nations where bananas have been and are produced. Rather than providing a general or national history of the politics of banana production in Honduras, Ecuador, Belize, St. Lucia, or Costa Rica, each of the essays examines a particular problem that highlights the uneven development of the global industry as a whole. The first three case studies continue Bucheli's examination of the United Fruit Company, albeit from more local perspectives. Through a display of documents, letters, and photographs, the essay by Philippe Bourgois provides an intimate view of the world of United Fruit, including the company's (not always successful) attempts to dominate both workers and governments. Mark Moberg, in turn, looks at United Fruit's entrance into Belize during the first decades of the century, focusing particularly on the complicated, ambiguous, and changing relationships that the multinational formed with different sectors of the colonial state. Steve Striffler examines United Fruit's tenure in Ecuador during the 1930s, 1940s, and 1950s. Here, the discussion shifts from the state to the role played by peasants and workers in the dismantling of United Fruit's Ecuadorian operations and the origins of contract farming.

The next two essays focus on aspects of the relationships between race, ethnicity, national identity, and political struggle within the context of banana-producing areas in Guatemala and Honduras. Cindy Forster's essay examines the role played by United Fruit's plantation workers in Guatemala's national revolution (1944–1954). She highlights the differing political positions and opportunities that ladino and Central American workers had in comparison to black workers from the Caribbean. Darío Euraque continues this discussion in a slightly different form and from a distinct locale, examining the importance of the "banana enclave" for understanding race, ethnicity, and national identity in the case of Honduras.

The final two case studies bring us to the Windward Islands of the Eastern Caribbean, whose banana industry is much more recent than that of Latin America. While differing greatly from South and Central America in its scale, the eastern Caribbean industry relies exclusively on the contract-farming relationships that are fast becoming the norm elsewhere. In the eastern Caribbean banana production was promoted by island governments during the 1950s as a mechanism for creating a class of "politically stable" yeoman farmers. Since then, however, the multinational that markets island fruit has imposed dramatically increased technical demands and routinization on small farmers. Much of the recent literature on subcontracting examines whether the independence of small growers is in fact illusory, and some scholars contend that farmers' diminished autonomy defines them as "disguised proletarians" of the firms that purchase their fruit. As Karla Slocum documents for St. Lucia, an unanticipated consequence of these processes has been small-farmer resistance against prevailing discourses on globalization, which promote the interests of Geest. Lawrence Grossman deepens this discussion of contract farming, focusing on the critical role played by the state in St. Vincent's banana industry. Recent developments in the eastern Caribbean suggest that a strategy designed to create a stable small-farmer class has instead united many rural producers against the dictates of Geest and the states that enforce those dictates.

In the final, and perhaps most provocative essay, Allen Wells steps back from the individual studies, reflecting on the collection as a whole, including its importance for understanding the global banana industry, regional histories of Latin America and the Caribbean, and processes of capitalist transformation in more complex terms. In so doing, he points to some of the important problems that this book raises and the need for further comparative research along a number of lines.

NOTES

1. Here we take as a point of departure an edited volume (Roseberry, Gudmundson, and Kutschbach 1995) on another of Latin America's important commodities: coffee.

2. Comparing farm size between the three regions is complicated by a number of factors, not least of which is the fact that the surveys were conducted at different times. Nonetheless, it is clear that, on average, Caribbean farms are much smaller than those in Central or South America. In 1992, for example, there were some 27,000 banana farmers in the Windward Islands. Over half had fewer than 10 hectares of land and only 950 had more than 50 hectares. The average farm size was less than 2.5 acres (Nurse and Sandiford 1995, 45, 67). In contrast, the average size farm in Ecuador was around 30 hectares during the 1980s, a figure that has probably not changed dramatically during the intervening years due to the perseverance of small producers. Moreover, although farms of between 100 and 200 hectares are quite common in Ecuador, larger plantations along the lines of those found in Central America (i.e., more than 500 hectares) are fairly rare. For the size of Ecuadorian farms, see Charvet 1987, Larrea Maldonado 1987, and FAO 1986 (17). Colombia is similar to Ecuador, though the average holding is larger and small producers are less predominant. The United Nations Food and Agriculture Organization (FAO) (1986, 12), for example, estimated that farms in the Uraba region of Colombia averaged about 82 hectares in size. For the size of Colombian farms, see Botero Herrera 1988. On average, Central America has the largest farms, due in large part to the continued presence of multinationals in direct production and the advanced nature of the system of associate producers (i.e., large producers who contract with multinationals).

3. In the mid-1980s, Ecuador, the world's largest exporter, sold almost 18 percent of the bananas that were traded on the global market. However, in terms of total production, Ecuador produced only slightly more than 5 percent of the world's bananas. Brazil (17.2 percent), India (11.4 percent), and the Philippines (9.9 percent) all produced more (FLACSO 1988, 25).

4. Fyffes remained a subsidiary of United Fruit until 1986, when the parent company (then known as United Brands and soon to become Chiquita) sold its British subsidiary to raise cash for a series of costly mergers (Davies 1990). At present, as Laura T. Raynolds's essay indicates, Fyffes finds itself in a protracted trade dispute with its former parent company over European market preferences for Caribbean bananas.

5. On the migratory nature of banana production during this period see Kepner 1936, LaBarge 1959, and Bourgois 1989. For a sophisticated look at the relationship between plant diseases and social processes within the industry see Soluri 2000.

6. The Cavendish strain encompasses most of the commercially produced bananas grown in Latin America and the Caribbean, including the Grand Nain, Valerie, Robusta, and Lacatan varieties. All are closely related and share a common resistance to Panama Disease, unlike the Gros Michel variety cultivated until the 1950s.

7. "The Octopus" is the term by which United Fruit is popularly disparaged throughout Latin America for its tenacious control over national governments and independent producers.

A GLOBAL FRUIT

LAURA T. RAYNOLDS

The Global Banana Trade

Bananas represent one of the most widely traded agricultural goods in the world with annual exports valued at roughly five billion dollars (FAO 2001). Though bananas are typically seen as an undifferentiated commodity, historically divergent patterns of trade regulation have defined two distinct commodity systems for this fruit: the dominant Dollar Banana system centered on the U.S. market and the smaller ACP Banana trade between Europe and its former African, Caribbean, and Pacific (ACP) colonies.[1] Using a comparative commodity system approach, I examine the divergent trade geography, state sponsorship, corporate involvement, social relations of production, and environmental conditions characterizing each of these production systems in order to illuminate how Dollar and ACP Bananas have been socially defined as distinct commodities.

The banana trade has historically been forged through global and local forces that simultaneously connect and divide major Latin American and Caribbean sites of production and major North American and European sites of consumption. In recent decades there have been two regimes regulating the trade in bananas: Dollar Bananas have been regulated by "free market" conditions shaped by the oligopolistic power of key transnational corporations, while ACP Bananas have been regulated by preferential market agreements between nations. The conflict between the ACP and Dollar Banana regimes—the so-called banana wars—illuminates historical tensions between these two systems and the emergence of the World Trade Organization (WTO) as the new arbiter of the global market. In the most recent skirmish the United States and its transnational corporations appear to have won, undermining the future viability of the ACP Banana system. But this does not mean that trade conditions will necessarily be homogenized under the Dollar Banana system. Alternative trade systems are developing that could offer opportunities for the survival of displaced ACP Banana farmers and for building a more socially and environmentally sustainable system of banana production, trade, and consumption.

COMMODITY-SYSTEM ANALYSIS

A historically rooted commodity-system approach is well suited to analyzing how bananas have been transformed from a subsistence food in Latin America and the Caribbean into a favorite fruit purchased by consumers in North America and Europe. This approach traces the complex social, political, and economic relationships and institutions created in the movement of a particular commodity from the point of production to its consumption. Research focusing on key agro-export commodities has facilitated analysis of the configuration and reconfiguration of labor forces, production patterns, market ties, and political alliances in export-dependent Latin American and Caribbean countries. Extensive study of the region's coffee economies, for example, has emphasized how the macrodynamics of the coffee trade have converged with local forces to forge strikingly different patterns of production organization (see Roseberry, Gudmundson, and Kutschbach 1995). Mintz (1985) brilliantly demonstrates the role of sugar in shaping social, political, and economic structures in both Caribbean production regions and Europe consumption regions (see also Tomich 1990). The commodity-system approach, however, has been less often applied to bananas (but see Trouillot 1988).

A commodity-system approach grows out of the complementary work of Friedland (1984) and Hopkins and Wallerstein (1986) who, from slightly different vantage points, advocate the analysis of the interconnected processes of raw material production, processing / packaging, shipping, marketing, and consumption that are embodied in a given commodity. One of the strengths of this approach is its ability to locate local production systems within larger networks that span economic sectors, geopolitical regions, and historical periods. As Gereffi (1994, 97) notes, commodity-system analysis focuses on the interlinking of products and services in a sequence of value-added activities; the nature and spatial configuration of enterprises that form production and marketing networks; and the power relations that determine how resources are allocated along the commodity chain. Recent studies in various commodity areas highlight the increasingly critical role of transnational corporations in organizing and transforming current global production systems (see, for example, Gereffi and Korzeniewicz 1994).

Much of the commodity-based literature focuses on production, though trade and consumption form equally important terrains for research. Consumption relations are particularly vital in shaping the networks that supply what we eat, since food is not only a human necessity but a key to cultural identity (Arce and Marsden 1993; Soluri herein). Whereas research on consumption highlights the importance of global, national, and local cultural forces in shaping commodity systems, investigations of agrofood trade often emphasize the importance of political forces operating in intersecting local and global arenas. Recent agrofood studies challenge economic models of comparative advantage, highlighting the importance of political factors in constructing market competitiveness and in regulating trade (McMichael 1997; Raynolds et al. 1993; Watts and Goodman 1997).

THE HISTORICAL DIVERGENCE IN THE BANANA TRADE

Since the 1800s, bananas (along with sugar and coffee) have integrated Latin America and the Caribbean into the international division of labor, forging the region's ties to the United States and Europe.[2] Early mercantilist relationships and successor affiliations between countries of the north and south defined the parameters of the banana trade. The two hands of colonialism — the direct rule of European colonial powers and the indirect rule of the increasingly hegemonic United States and its corporations — created the two systems through which bananas are currently produced, traded, and consumed. As with other key agro-exports, the politics of bananas has been, and continues to be, central to the politics of national development as well as international trade.

The Creation of the Latin American / United States System

Until the late nineteenth century the international banana trade was highly decentralized, involving a number of U.S. and European trading companies that bought produce from independent growers in the Americas, Africa, and the Pacific. At the turn of the century the newly formed, U.S.-based United Fruit Company transformed the banana industry, linking the shipping and distribution of bananas — which characterized the earlier mercantilist trade — to major production enterprises. The vertically integrated United Fruit Company merged large banana operations in Latin America and the Caribbean, major railroad, port, and shipping facilities, and a substantial U.S. fruit distribution network (Davies 1990, 23–36, 96; Bucheli herein).

United Fruit continued to expand its holdings in the early 1900s, consolidating its control over the regional banana industry. In this era company plantations were relocated every ten to twenty years due to the onset of major diseases and the rapid depletion in soil fertility. Although only a small portion was ever planted at one time, United Fruit acquired over three million acres in Honduras, Costa Rica, Nicaragua, Guatemala, Panama, Colombia, Cuba, and Jamaica. By combining this productive base with expanding shipping, railroad, and port facilities, the company was able to take advantage of economies of both scale and scope. Guaranteeing regular supplies of high-quality produce, United Fruit drove most of its regional competitors out of business, acquiring 50 percent of the growing U.S. consumer market (Roche 1998, 37–41).

During the mid-1900s era of rising U.S. hegemony, United Fruit became a significant political as well as economic force in the hemisphere. The powerful banana company was involved in shaping domestic politics within producer nations increasingly dependent on banana revenues. At the same time, the company played an important role in guiding U.S. diplomatic relations toward a region increasingly defined as vital to American interests. In 1954 United Fruit played a critical role in orchestrating and gaining U.S. support for the overthrow of Guatemala's president; in 1974 the company was again implicated, this time in bribing the president of Honduras. United Fruit exerted such influence over the economies and governments of Central America that these countries came to be referred to pejoratively as "banana republics." Given its stranglehold on the region, United Fruit in turn came to be known locally as El Pulpo (the octopus) (Kepner 1936; Langley and Schoonover 1995).

United Fruit's banana monopoly was challenged repeatedly under U.S. antitrust laws, resulting in the creation of two spin-off companies (Roche 1998, 41–49). Standard Fruit, spun off in 1909, became a major producer and shipper of Central American bananas and was purchased in 1964 by the U.S.-based Castle and Cooke, now known as Dole Food Corporation. A 1972 antitrust action against United Fruit precipitated the sale of banana lands to the smaller U.S.-based Del Monte Fresh Produce Company. Trying to shed some of its notoriety, the United Fruit Company was reorganized and renamed, first as United Brands, more recently as Chiquita Brands. Chiquita, Dole, and Del Monte have largely maintained their preeminence in the Latin American banana industry, despite two major recent challenges to their market dominance. One challenge has come from the rise of independent Ecuadorian and Colombian banana producers and exporters. Though Ecuador and Colombia have gained an important share of the banana trade, particularly in Asia, U.S. companies have maintained their market position by buying produce from these countries and expanding their own production in the Pacific (Glover and Larrea Maldonado 1991). The 1974 creation of the Union of Banana Exporting Countries (Union de Paises Exportadoras de Banano) raised a second potential threat to U.S.-based banana company domination, but this group's impact has been largely limited to the imposition of a modest tax on corporate banana exports (ibid.).

The Divergence of the Caribbean / European System

Though initially part of the Latin American trade, the Caribbean banana industry developed along a different trajectory due to the persistence of powerful European colonial administrative structures and mercantilist trade policies. At the turn of the century, the introduction of on-board cooling techniques opened up the transatlantic banana trade (Davies 1990, 74). Seizing this opportunity, the British and French made bananas a central vehicle for continued colonial rule in the region, forging a distinct banana circuit that linked the Caribbean to Europe. In contrast to the Latin American banana industry, the key players in this new Caribbean banana circuit were not large-scale producers, but state administrators and banana shippers.

In the early 1900s, British colonial policies transformed Jamaica — previously a minor source of U.S. and European bananas — into the major supplier of bananas to Britain, the largest market in Europe. Small-scale Jamaican producers were encouraged to grow bananas for export to Britain, where they were guaranteed a market. To counter United Fruit's growing banana monopoly, the British government gave the company known today as Fyffes Limited control over banana shipping and distribution (Davies 1990, 86). Fyffes was guaranteed 75 percent of the British market and an exclusive contract over bananas from Jamaica and, later, Belize and Surinam (Thomson 1987, 80). Since Fyffes was not a banana producer, colonial administrators established an association of growers to coordinate banana production and shipping (Sealy and Hart 1984). After World War II, Britain sponsored the emergence of the Windward Islands as a major supplier of European bananas. Colonial administrators again created a decentralized banana industry, channeling peasant production into the export economy with the help of a powerful state-backed banana growers' association (Thomson 1987, 13–44). Exclusive banana-exporting rights were granted to a major U.K. food company, Geest Corporation (Trouillot 1988, 127; Grossman herein; Slocum herein).[3]

England's colonies in the Caribbean won their independence, but their economies still hinge on the smallholder banana industry established by the British. The former colonies maintain their preferential access to the lucrative British market, with British-based companies continuing to ship most of the area's bananas. Geest's banana division was recently purchased by Fyffes, making Fyffes the largest shipper-distributor in the European banana circuit (Roche 1998, 143–46).

Colonial relationships similar to those of Britain configured other strands of the European banana circuit, creating a network of smallholder production systems in the former colonies that remain linked to the metropolitan centers through preferential trade. Martinique and Guadeloupe, formerly colonies and now departments of France, have traditionally provided the second-largest share of European bananas under a system that mirrors that in the neighboring Windward Islands. Like their British counterparts, French colonial administrators founded a smallholder banana export industry coordinated by a state-supported growers' association. This decentralized banana industry remains critical to the economies of Martinique and Guadeloupe (Welch 1996). While the locus of the European banana circuit has always been the Caribbean, other former colonies in the Mediterranean and Africa also supply this system.

THE DOLLAR BANANA SYSTEM AND
THE ACP BANANA SYSTEM

By the 1960s the political and economic ties between the United States and its Latin American neighbors and European countries and their former colonies had defined two opposing banana systems (see map, below). The Dollar Banana system centers on the U.S. market, long the largest market in the world, which

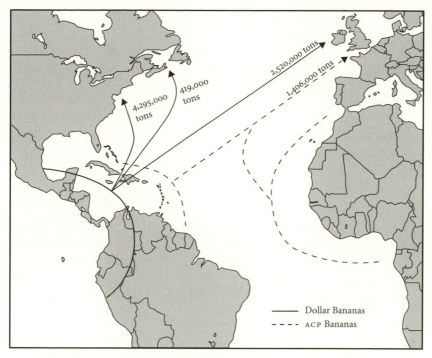

ACP and Dollar Banana Trade Circuits. Sources: Dollar Banana figures from FAO 2001; ACP and Overseas Territory figures from Eurostat 1999, cited in FruiTrop 1999.

currently absorbs 31 percent of total world exports (FAO 2001). Reflecting the historical sphere of influence of the U.S. government and U.S.-based corporations, Latin American exports — from Ecuador, Costa Rica, Colombia, Panama, Guatemala, and other countries — supply most of the U.S. market, as well as the smaller Canadian market. Dollar Bananas currently constitute about 80 percent of world trade. This "open market" trade remains largely in the hands of the big three banana companies.

The ACP system, which links former colonies and offshore territories in Africa, the Caribbean, and the Pacific with the European market, is the world's second major banana circuit. The Lomé agreement between the European Union (EU) and the ACP group of seventy former colonies has upheld the historically rooted preferential trade access and market share of ACP Bananas (Chambron 1995, 2; Sutton 1997, 11). The EU currently absorbs 33 percent of total world banana imports (FAO 2001). ACP countries — including St. Lucia,

Dominica, St. Vincent, and Jamaica in the Caribbean, and Cameroon and the Ivory Coast in Africa—supply 18 percent of the EU banana market. European offshore territories—including Guadeloupe and Martinique in the Caribbean and Madeira and the Canary Islands in the Atlantic—supply an additional 21 percent (FAO 1999a).

DOLLAR AND ACP BANANA-PRODUCTION REGIMES

Bananas move through an intricate set of transnational production, processing, and marketing activities as they make their way from the fields to distant consumers. Distributors play the pivotal role in this commodity system since it is distributors that must guarantee that bananas reach their destination undamaged and ready to eat.[4] To ensure that bananas are not bruised in transit and are delivered in amounts that will be sold before spoiling, distributors must tightly coordinate activities along the commodity chain. While the central tasks of cultivation, washing, packing, local transport, international shipping, ripening, and wholesaling must be smoothly linked, these activities may be carried out by distributors themselves or by associated firms.

The Dollar Banana system is vertically integrated with the biggest corporations—Chiquita, Dole, and Del Monte—which manage most production and distribution activities themselves (figure 1). Dollar Banana cultivation remains anchored in the huge Latin American plantations acquired by the heirs of United Fruit. The big three banana corporations produce roughly 70 percent of their own produce, buying most of the remainder via contracts with large growers. In the event of production shortfalls, Ecuadorian bananas are purchased on the open market (Glover and Larrea Maldonado 1991). Interlocking divisions within Chiquita, Dole, and Del Monte are responsible for intermediary produce handling: preparing and packing the bananas, often in boxes from their own cardboard factories; transporting the produce from field sites to the port, often on their own truck or rail systems; and shipping the bananas internationally, often using their own refrigerated containers, their own boats, and sometimes even their own harbors.[5] Bananas from Chiquita, Dole, and Del Monte subsidiaries around the world are shipped to corporate ripening centers in major North American, European, and Asian markets. These global sourcing networks help balance out regional production variations and guarantee

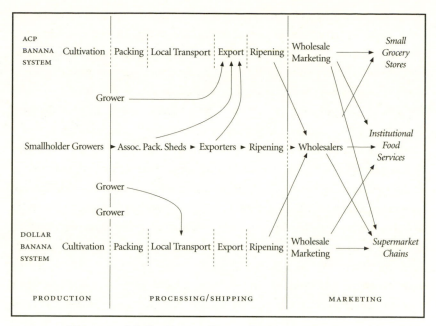

FIGURE 1   The ACP and Dollar Banana Commodity Systems

a consistent supply for sale to supermarkets and institutional food services. Dollar Banana corporations' vertically integrated structure provides important advantages in guaranteeing produce quality and supplies, channeling market information into production planning, and facilitating promotional efforts to expand markets for their brand-name fruit.

Reflecting its strikingly different historical roots, the ACP Banana production system based in the Caribbean is much less vertically integrated than the Dollar system. As highlighted in figure 1, ACP Banana distributors are essentially trading companies with limited involvement in cultivation. Fyffes, the largest traditional ACP firm, has experimented with plantation production and open-market purchases, but the bulk of its produce still comes from contracts with Windward Island smallholders. A number of distributors handle produce from Martinique and Guadeloupe, creating an even more decentralized system. On each of the major Caribbean banana islands, thousands of small-scale banana producers are organized into state-sponsored growers' associations that facilitate production and coordinate banana exports.[6] Banana growers' associations in Martinique and Guadeloupe rent shipping space for their members but leave them to market their bananas individually to various European distributors (Welch 1996). In contrast the Windward Island banana growers' association, in association with the Windward Island Banana Development Exporting Company (WIBDECO), has for decades sold all their export-quality produce to the same shipper-distributor. Fyffes ships the bananas on company and rented vessels to its European ripening centers and then sells the produce to supermarkets, institutional food services, and grocery stores. Under the Windward Island banana contract the distributor does not purchase the bananas prior to shipping, but rather agrees to pay WIBDECO for the produce at a rate fixed in Europe, minus shipping and handling fees. Shipping and distribution costs of ACP Bananas are significantly higher than those for Dollar Bananas, since volumes are lower and vessels must make multiple stops to load their cargo. While ACP distributors have higher costs and less control over produce supplies than vertically integrated Dollar Banana companies, some costs and risks are shifted onto banana growers, either individually or collectively via growers' associations.[7]

DOLLAR BANANA PRODUCTION:
SOCIAL AND ENVIRONMENTAL CONDITIONS

Dollar Bananas are grown primarily on plantations that often exceed 12,000 acres and are operated directly by the major distributors: Chiquita, Dole, and Del Monte. Dollar corporations and their huge plantations dominate Latin American banana production (see table 1). For example, 87 percent of Costa Rica's 2.5 million tons of bananas are currently exported under the Chiquita, Dole, or Del Monte label (Banana Link 1999).

Chiquita, Dole, and Del Monte all have extensive plantations that provide the core of their supplies and allow them to benefit from important economies of scale. These plantations entail substantial fixed investments, though much of the land is leased from local governments. Chiquita, for example, cultivates 17,000 acres of largely rented land on the border of Panama and Costa Rica, producing almost half a million tons of bananas a year (Bourgois 1989, 4). Production on this scale permits the efficient use of human, chemical, and mechanical inputs. Particularly important for bananas is the use of cost-saving,

TABLE 1   Major Dollar Banana Producers, 1999

	Major Exporters*	Acres Harvested	Yield (tons / acre)	Holdings	Workers
Ecuador	Noboa; Dole; Del Monte; Chiquita	477,000	12	100% medium	180,000
Costa Rica	Dole; Del Monte; Chiquita	123,000	20	25% medium 75% large	47,000
Colombia	Uniban; Dole	124,000	16	100% medium	40,000
Panama	Chiquita; Del Monte	47,000	24	25% medium 75% large	10,000

SOURCES: APROMA 1992 (11–14); ECCR n.d. (10–16); FAO (2001); and author's estimates.
* Firms listed in order of export shares.

scale-dependent technologies like the aerial spraying of pesticides and the use of cable networks that transport harvested bananas to packing sheds up to a mile away.

Banana-plantation production remains labor intensive since the fragility of the fruit limits mechanization. Chiquita's Panama–Costa Rica enterprise, for example, employs roughly 10,000 workers. Men are hired in the fields to apply chemicals, prune, wrap the stems with plastic, harvest, and load bananas on the aerial cables. Women are mostly hired in the packing sheds to cut up the banana bunches; select, sort, and wash the exportable produce; apply fungicides; and pack the boxes. Labor demand fluctuates around the banana harvest. To cut costs, corporations typically employ temporary laborers excluded from legal minimum-wage standards, job-security guarantees, and benefits (Foro Emaus 1997; Ransom 1999, 10–13). Further weakening the position of labor, most Central American banana plantations hire ethnic minority workers, often migrants working in the country illegally.[8]

In addition to their own plantations, banana transnationals rely on contracts with large associate growers that supply about 30 percent of their produce.[9] There are two major benefits for corporations in using these typically five-year contracts. First, it allows corporations to avoid increasingly frequent and costly conflicts over the violation of labor, health, and environmental standards.[10] Second, it increases the flexibility of produce supplies. Contracts specify the quantity and timing of banana deliveries, but corporations typically loosen quality standards when supplies are low and tighten their standards to exclude produce when their supplies are high (Glover and Larrea Maldonado 1991).

The plantation-based Dollar Banana system has fostered a number of environmental problems. Banana plantations have fueled deforestation throughout Latin America. The recent expansion of Dollar Banana production has led to the clearing of thousands of acres of Costa Rican jungle (Foro Emaus 1997). Contractions in banana production also harm the forests as hundreds of laid-off workers, unable to find alternative jobs, resort to clearing land for subsistence farming.[11] The preparation of plantation land leads to substantial erosion as the biomatter stabilizing the top soil is removed to facilitate irrigation and make way for banana monocropping. During the rainy season, the soil washes away, silting up rivers and fueling water-borne chemical contamination (Colburn 1997). Pesticide-laced plastic bags used to protect maturing bananas litter the area around large plantations. Discarded banana bags and other plantation run-off often make their way to the ocean, killing fish and destroying entire reef systems.

One of the most critical environmental problems arising from Dollar Banana production derives from intensive pesticide use. The large-scale monocropping of bananas has fostered the rise of pest populations and potentially devastating diseases. To combat these threats, Dollar Banana companies utilize an arsenal of pesticides. Fungicides are applied to control Black Sigatoka, while extremely toxic insecticides, nematocides, and soil fumigants are used to control nematodes (Wheat 1996). Much of the pesticide use is for cosmetic treatments ensuring the uniform size and appearance of brand-name fruit. In Costa Rica, bananas absorb nearly one-third of all pesticides, contributing to the country's dubious distinction as the world leader in per capita pesticide use (Murray 1994). Pesticides, particularly when aerially applied, contribute to both environmental contamination and public-health problems.[12] The use of the nematocide DBCP has led to the sterility of thousands of Central American banana-field workers (Thrupp 1991); extensive chemical exposure in the banana-packing sheds is increasing women's risks of developing cancer and having children with birth defects (Banana Link 1998a).

TABLE 2   Major ACP and Overseas Territory Producers, 1990

	Major Exporters*	Acres Planted	Yield (tons / acre)	Holdings	Growers
Windward Islands	Fyffes / WIBDECO	42,000	8	53% < 10ac 43% 10–50ac 3% > 50ac	27,000
Jamaica	Fyffes; JAMCO	11,000	18	6,000 small 2 large	6,000
Guadeloupe	SICA-ASSOBAG	18,000	12	34% < 10ac 22% 10–50ac 44% > 50ac	1,400
Martinique	SICABAM	19,000	12	29% < 10ac 17% 10–50ac 54% > 50ac	1,300

SOURCES: Addy 1999 (9); Nurse and Sandiford 1995 (45); Welch 1996 (288–93).
* Firms listed in order of export shares.

ACP BANANA PRODUCTION:
SOCIAL AND ENVIRONMENTAL CONDITIONS

In contrast to the large-scale production of Dollar Bananas, the production of ACP Bananas rests largely in the hands of small- and medium-scale producers. In the early 1990s there were about 27,000 growers in the Windward Islands, most of whom cultivated less than ten acres of bananas (see table 2).[13] Land-holdings are slightly larger in Jamaica and the French Caribbean, but production remains decentralized, and even the largest holdings are small by plantation standards.

Small-scale Caribbean banana production is economically tenuous due to its highly dispersed structure and limited grower resources. Local and regional banana growers' associations help to overcome some of these problems, coordinating production and making scale-dependent technologies available. Producer associations may provide research and extension services, bulk input purchases, credit advances, collective aerial spraying, local transportation, and packing facilities as well as joint shipping and marketing services (Welch 1996). Getting the bananas from the fields to the port unharmed remains a major challenge. Most Windward Islands producers prepare and pack bananas in the fields. The bananas are cut into clusters, washed, dipped in fungicide, and boxed (Grossman 1998, 130–32). Banana boxes are then transported to the port by truck.

Caribbean banana production is very labor intensive. To cultivate, harvest, and pack the bananas, small-scale producers rely largely on unpaid household labor, supplemented by hired day workers. Women provide a critical share of the labor in bananas (Cecilia Babb cited in Pantin, Sandiford, and Henry et al. 1999, 34). In St. Lucia, 60,000 people (about one-third of the population) are directly or indirectly employed in the banana industry (Godfrey 1998, 2). The labor-intensive nature of production and relatively high Caribbean wage rates help explain the high cost of ACP Banana production (Nurse and Sandiford 1995, 52,144).

ACP Banana production in the Caribbean is characterized by very different and far less environmentally destructive agroecological conditions than Dollar Banana production (Caribbean Conservation Association 1991; Vandermeer and Perfecto 1995). Most Caribbean banana production takes place on small hillside parcels of land. Rather than being monocropped like Dollar Bananas, banana plants are typically intercropped with fruit trees and ground crops. Banana cultivation has historically caused deforestation in parts of the Caribbean, but the damage to local ecosystems has been limited by the interspersing of small banana holdings with remaining tropical forest areas. This diversified land use pattern also limits soil erosion and river siltation (Caribbean Conservation Association 1991). Given their intimate long-term contact with the land, small-scale ACP banana producers are arguably better land stewards than are plantation managers oriented toward short-term returns.

Pesticide use in the production of ACP Bananas is significantly lower than in Dollar production.[14] The maintenance of agroecological diversity within Caribbean banana regions helps control pests, and fewer fungicides are needed to control Black Sigatoka, which is less prevalent than in Latin America. Although Caribbean banana-growers' associations often recommend high levels of chemical input use, these recommendations are rarely followed. Where bananas are intercropped, growers often resist applying pesticides for fear that it might harm their food crops (Grossman 1998, 201). Pesticide use in ACP Bananas actually declined in recent years, due to producers' budget constraints and the inability of banana growers' associations to finance expensive inputs (Welch 1996, 260). In the Windward Islands costly and hazardous aerial spraying is rare. Though plastic banana bags create litter, they are rarely treated with pesticides (Grossman 1998, 128). In some cases, small-scale Caribbean banana production has become almost pesticide-free.

The divergent social and agroecological characteristics of the ACP and Dollar systems help explain the significantly lower market price of Dollar Bananas while revealing the hidden costs of this system. Vertically integrated Dollar Banana corporations benefit from economies of scale and scope in both production and distribution. Dollar Banana plantations achieve higher yields than smaller ACP producers due to their large-scale, chemical-intensive monocropping system, but these production characteristics fuel substantial environmental and health problems. Latin American Dollar Banana production costs are less than half of that of Caribbean ACP Bananas (U.S.$150–200 per ton f.o.b. as compared to U.S.$400–700 per ton f.o.b., respectively), largely as a result of the lower returns paid to disadvantaged workers (Hallam and Peston 1997, 23). In short, while the ACP Banana production system may be more expensive than the Dollar system, it represents a more environmentally and socially sustainable form of production.

DOLLAR AND ACP BANANA-TRADE
REGIMES AND THE BANANA WARS

Bananas remain the most important internationally traded fresh agricultural commodity. Dollar Bananas account for 85 percent of the 14 million tons of bananas on the world market. Most Dollar Bananas continue to be produced largely in Latin America, with Ecuador, Costa Rica, and Colombia supplying 57 percent of the world's bananas (table 3; see also table 1). These Latin American countries have become more diversified over the years, but bananas continue to contribute from 1 to 10 percent of gross domestic product.

The big three banana corporations — Chiquita, Dole, and Del Monte — have oligopolistic control over the trade in Dollar Bananas, selling huge quantities of their relatively inexpensive, input-intensive, blemish-free bananas. Chiquita,

TABLE 3   World Banana Exports and Imports, 1999

Exports		Imports	
Country	Tons (1,000)	Country	Tons (1,000)
Latin America		*North America*	
Ecuador	3,966	United States	4,295
Costa Rica	2,523	Canada	419
Colombia	1,856		
Panama	593	*Europe*	
Guatemala	536	EC-15	4,681**
Mexico	174	Russian Federation	378
		Poland	348
Caribbean		Czech Republic	131
Windwards	130	Former Yugoslavia	90
Martinique and Guadeloupe	375*		
Dominican Republic	67	*Asia*	
		Japan	983
Africa		China	432
Ivory Coast	215	Saudi Arabia	119
Cameroon	165		
		Latin America	
Asia		Argentina	294
Philippines	1,320	Chile	155
World Total	14,673	*World Total*	14,047

SOURCES: FAO, Banana Statistics, CCP:BA/TF 99/3 Gold Coast, Australia 4–8 May, 1999. Geneva: FAO; FAO "FAOSTAT database results," 2001, *http://www.fao.org/*

* This figure is for 1997.

** This figure includes shipments from EC overseas provinces.

Dole, and Del Monte have stimulated consumption of bananas throughout the world via expensive marketing campaigns, capturing the majority of this growing market for their standardized name-brand fruit. The three corporations have increased their hold over the market over the past thirty years, with their combined share of world trade rising to 66 percent (Hallam and Peston 1997, 44; van de Kasteele 1998, 14).

Conditions in the so-called open market for Dollar Bananas are essentially established by the competitive pressures between Chiquita, Dole, and Del

TABLE 4   Major Corporate Market Shares, 1997 (in percentages)

Corporation	World Market	USA	European Union
Dole	5–26	35	18–19
Chiquita	24–25	35	15–16
Del Monte	16	18	10–11
Noboa	13	—	—
Fyffes / Geest	6–7	—	16–17

SOURCE: van de Kasteele 1998 (table 4).

Monte. Historically the world's largest banana distributor, Chiquita Brands currently controls 25 percent of the world market. Chiquita is the most aggressive company in the industry, with almost half of its U.S.$2.6 billion in annual sales coming from bananas, and it has the largest investments in banana infrastructure (Chiquita Brands International 2000). In recent years Dole Food Corporation has also acquired 25 percent of the world market, challenging Chiquita's position as the foremost banana distributor (see table 4). Dole is more diversified and larger than Chiquita, with sales of U.S.$5.1 billion (Dole 2000). The third major banana distributor, Del Monte has sales of U.S.$1.5 billion (Fresh Del Monte 2000). Noboa has the fourth-largest share of the world market and is the major distributor of Ecuadorian bananas.

Chiquita, Dole, and Del Monte have virtually complete control over the U.S. banana market, which is the largest in the world, accounting for 31 percent of total imports (FAO 2001). Bananas are the leading fruit in the North American diet, with U.S. and Canadian consumers leading the world in per capita consumption (Hallam and Peston 1997, 26). Having largely saturated the North American market, these corporations have had to find new outlets for their growing exports. In recent years Dollar Banana corporations have expanded sales in Japan, the former U.S.S.R., and other countries in Asia and the Middle East (ibid., 24). But the real prize has been the European market.

Since the mid-1980s, Europeans have greatly increased their consumption of bananas, causing per capita imports to rise in eastern and western Europe. The European Union (EU) absorbs 33 percent of world imports (FAO 2001). Unification has made expansion in Europe particularly attractive to Dollar Corporations since it facilitates continent-wide distribution strategies. To capture this growing market, Chiquita, Dole, and Del Monte expanded their Latin American plantations during the 1990s, flooding Europe with Dollar Bananas. Despite hurricanes that devastated a number of Dollar Banana production regions in Central America, the 1990s saw an oversupply of bananas. Excessive production heightened competition and drove down world prices, encouraging Dollar Banana corporations to challenge the position of smaller banana distributors and the ACP Banana system in Europe.

THE EU BANANA MARKET

Until the 1990s, the European banana market was structured around a set of preferential trade agreements granted to former ACP colonies under the Lomé Agreement. In 1993 a single EU banana market was established, consolidating earlier trade privileges under a complex tariff-quota system. The EU modified these regulations in 1995 to settle a charge brought by Colombia, Costa Rica, Guatemala, Nicaragua, and Venezuela that the EU banana regulations restricted their exports. The revised regulations upheld a three-tiered system: (1) bananas from European overseas territories were given free-market access; (2) ACP Bananas were given a tariff-free quota set at the traditional import level of 858,000 tons per year; and (3) Dollar Bananas were given a quota of 2,200,000 tons with a 75 ECU (European Currency Units) per ton tariff.[15] The 1995 complainant countries were assigned favorable shares of the overall Dollar Banana quota.[16] An import-licensing system was also established guaranteeing traditional EU and ACP importing firms access to 30 percent of licenses and allocating the remainder to producer countries (Chambron 1995, 3–4; Sutton 1997, 22; Solidaridad 1995, 48–54).

ACP countries and European overseas territories supported the new banana-trade regulations, which reserved a large share of the EU market for their relatively expensive and variable quality bananas. Bolstered by the new regulations, ACP Bananas saw their share of EU imports rise from 37 to 39 percent between 1992 and 1997 (Banana Link 1998b). The protected EU market has been particularly critical for the Windward Islands. Although the ACP Caribbean countries have often been unable to fill their quotas due to storm-induced losses, the EU regulations have allowed them to market their produce at twice the price of Dollar Bananas (Hallam and Peston 1997, 60).[17]

Traditional ACP Banana importers, like Fyffes, benefited under the EU regulations from their control over supplies of tariff-exempt bananas. ACP firms also profited from guaranteed access to licenses, which they often used to import Dollar Bananas. The EU regulations spurred the concentration of the European banana industry. Fyffes, with its purchase of Geest's banana division, acquired a continent-wide distribution system and now controls 16–17 percent of the EU banana market (van de Kasteele 1998).

Chiquita, Dole, and Del Monte have maneuvered the recent EU regulatory environment with varied success. When the companies flooded Europe with Dollar Bananas in the early 1990s, they reduced their profits but secured their European market position by inflating the base of the subsequent Dollar Banana quota. To expand sales above this quota, Dollar corporations acquired ACP Banana supplies, gaining control of almost a third of all ACP production (Arthur D. Little cited in Southey 1995). Dole has pursued this strategy the most effectively, initiating production in African ACP countries to source tariff-free bananas and purchasing ripening and distribution centers in Europe to facilitate access to EU import licenses. Under the EU banana regime, Dole actually increased its share of the EU market from 12 to 18 percent. Del Monte strengthened its European position, raising its share of the EU market from 7 to 10 percent. Only Chiquita lost out, due to its failure to break into the ACP Banana trade, with its share of the European market declining from 30 to 15 percent during the 1990s (van de Kasteele 1998).

THE BANANA WARS

Claiming that the EU banana regulations cost it U.S.$400 million, Chiquita launched an attack that escalated into a full-fledged trade war. In 1994, Chiquita charged that the EU violated U.S. laws by discriminating against U.S. corporations. Despite the tenuous U.S. national interest in this matter — given that the U.S. neither exports bananas nor has a significant number of jobs at stake — Chiquita was able to use its substantial political clout to ensure that the U.S. Trade Office pursue the case (Larimer 1997). The U.S. government filed Chiquita's complaint with the World Trade Organization (WTO), charging that the EU regulations discriminated against U.S. banana corporations and against Dollar Banana producer countries, which were not given favorable export shares.

Chiquita and the U.S. Trade Office recruited Ecuador, Guatemala, Honduras, and Mexico (countries not given 1995 quotas) to sign the WTO petition. Raising questions about the charge of discrimination against U.S. corporations, Dole and Del Monte refused to sign the WTO complaint. In 1997, the WTO ruled that the EU banana regulations did violate international free-trade agreements both in granting preferential licenses to traditional ACP Banana importers and in allocating preferential quota shares to the Latin American countries that signed the 1995 agreement (de Jonquieres and Urry 1997).[18]

The EU revised the banana regulations in 1999, maintaining existing tariffs and ACP and Dollar Banana quotas but allocating new country quotas for top suppliers and import licenses for major distributors (FAO 1999c). Chiquita rejected the revisions and the U.S. Trade Office took the case back to the WTO. Again the WTO ruled against the EU, authorizing the United States to impose trade sanctions worth U.S.$191 million against European imports (ICTSD 1999b).[19] The WTO also approved Ecuador's request to impose trade sanctions against Europe valued at U.S.$202 million (United Press International 2000). The EU tried again in 2000 to bring the banana regulations into compliance, eliminating country quotas and allocating import licenses on a first-come, first-served basis (ICTSD 2000). After consulting with Chiquita, the U.S. Trade Office again rejected the EU proposal.

In 2001 Chiquita and the U.S. government finally agreed to an EU proposal to modify the banana regime, and U.S. and Ecuadorian sanctions against European exports were suspended (Banana Link 2001). This agreement established a transitional banana regime scheduled to be replaced by a tariff-only system in 2006. The transitional system (designed to be introduced in two phases) eliminates individual producer country quotas. A tariff-quota system exempts 750,000 tons of ACP Bananas from the 75-Euro-per-ton tariff applied to Dollar Bananas. The most dramatic change in the new regulations is in the allocation of import licenses to distributors, which will be based on their share of imports in the 1994–96 reference period. This system cements the historical market dominance of the big three transnational banana corporations and benefits Chiquita most, since it receives licenses based on its earlier, substantially higher, EU market share (Banana Link 2001). The biggest losers under the new system are newer importers, which have gained significant market share in recent years but will now have to compete for access to the 17 percent of licenses reserved for new operators. Ecuadorian distributors have already been promised a substantial share of the new operator licenses in return for their government's dropping of trade sanctions against the EU (ICTSD 2001).

CONCLUSIONS: A NEW ERA FOR BANANAS?

The history of bananas could be read narrowly as a description of the ascendancy of the Dollar Banana system and transnational capital in an era of globalization. But this would be an overly deterministic reading. The dominance of Dollar Bananas is rooted in the intensive exploitation of human and natural resources by transnational corporations and in the success of these corporations in mobilizing national and supranational state institutions for their cause. Historically, an important divergent banana-commodity system was created and maintained by the national regulation of trade between European countries and their former colonies. While the ACP Banana system appears to be on the decline, promising new alternatives to the trade in socially and environmentally destructive Dollar Bananas are emerging.[20]

Recent years have seen a dramatic rise in the trade in organic bananas, produce that is certified as being grown under organic conditions. Bananas are adding to a world market for organic products with sales valued at U.S.$10–11 billion in 1997 (Kortbech-Olesen 1998). This new trade builds on mounting interest in northern industrialized countries for foods that are healthier for both consumers and the environment. The world market for organic products is expanding at a rate of 20 percent annually; sales of organic bananas are growing at a phenomenal 30 percent per year (FAO 1999b). Given their recent introduction, trade in fresh organic bananas is still relatively small, with about 27,000 tons shipped annually (Sauve 1999). Europe is the world's largest importer of organic bananas, buying 10,000 tons each year, followed by the United States, Japan, and Canada in that order (FAO 1999b).

Since the mid-1990s there has been a related growth in the market for Fair Trade bananas, bananas that are produced under socially and environmentally sustainable conditions and traded under more equitable relations (Murray and Raynolds 2000).[21] This new trade in bananas is expanding a world market for Fair Trade products valued at U.S.$400 million per year (Fair Trade Federation 1999). The Fair Trade movement taps mounting consumer concern over the global ethical implications of their purchases—that is, the social conditions of production and the livelihoods afforded to producers—as well as the environmental and health concerns fueling the organic market. The growing Fair Trade market is centered in Europe, with nascent markets developing in the United States, Canada, and Japan. Fair Trade bananas were introduced in Europe in 1996; by 1999 sales had grown to 18,000 tons per year even though they were only available in six countries (Max Havelaar 1999). The prospects for expanding Fair Trade banana sales in Europe appear very promising, with an overall market demand of 300,000–400,000 tons per year (Banana Link 1997b). There is also a small market for Fair Trade bananas in Japan, and plans for introducing this produce in the United States and Canada are under way.

The growing market for organic and Fair Trade bananas may provide important opportunities for threatened ACP Banana growers like those in the Caribbean. The Dominican Republic is already one of the world's major producers of organic bananas (FAO 1999b). Existing production conditions in the rest of the Caribbean are conducive to a move into the organic banana trade, since chemical input use is already relatively low and organic production benefits from the small-scale, labor-intensive intercrop farming already common in the region. There are important agroecological difficulties in producing bananas organically and the transition and certification process are costly, but favorable price premiums are accrued by producers (ibid.). The major impediment to ACP Banana growers' successful entry into the organic trade may well come from transnational corporations, which have in recent years greatly increased their control over this expanding market (Raynolds 2000b). Dole, which has an important stake in the organic market, has recently expanded its production of organic bananas in Honduras and Ecuador. Small-scale ACP growers may begin growing organic bananas only to find themselves contracting or selling their produce to the major Dollar Banana corporations. If this were to happen, organic bananas would become a strand of the Dollar Banana system— a strand with better environmental conditions but similarly exploitative social conditions.

The development of Fair Trade links may provide a more hopeful opening for ACP Banana growers in the Caribbean, whose livelihoods are threatened by shifting world-trade regulations. Fair Trade bananas for the European market have been successfully produced in the Dominican Republic for a number of years (FAO 1999b). The Windward Island Farmers' Association, which represents small banana growers in the region, has also recently begun shipping Fair Trade bananas to Europe (Renwick 1999). Conversion to Fair Trade production would be relatively easy for more small-scale Caribbean banana growers, since their environmental and social conditions of production generally already conform to Fair Trade standards (Banana Link 1997a; Banana Link, 1997b). Fair Trade banana production is likely to be profitable since producers are guaranteed prices well above those paid by transnational corporate distributors, and though there are shipping and marketing difficulties, these are likely to be worked out as the market becomes more established. While Fair Trade's social dimensions limit the ability of transnational corporations to capture this new market, Chiquita has tried to carve off a piece of this new market by repackaging their Dollar Bananas under a new label (Murray and Raynolds 2000). The opening for Fair Trade to create an alternative banana system — one based on the social re-linking of production, trade, and consumption — will depend in large measure on consumers' rejection of the unfair practices that have historically characterized Dollar Banana production.

NOTES

1. To facilitate analysis of the divergent Dollar Banana and ACP Banana systems, I consider Ecuadorian and Colombian production within the context of the Dollar Banana system, although, as suggested in the introduction to this volume, there are some important differences between production conditions in South America and Central America.

2. This section draws on the author's earlier work reported in Raynolds and Murray 1998.

3. Geest was given the contract because United Fruit for a short time owned a controlling share of Fyffes.

4. The importance of banana distributors hinges on the fact that the perishability of this produce increases dramatically as it ripens. Green bananas can be, and are, traded on the open market, but ripe bananas need to be handled as little as possible and sold promptly. Some European supermarkets ripen their own bananas; specialized fruit distributors do the ripening in North America and increasingly in Europe.

5. Of the three big corporations, Chiquita is the most vertically integrated. It has its own railroads and cardboard-box factories in three Central American countries, exclusive rights to a number of the region's deep-water ports, and the world's largest fleet of refrigerated vessels.

6. Welch 1996 outlines the banana-grower association activities, demonstrating that the Windward

Island associations are more involved in coordinating production, packing, and transportation than are their counterparts in Martinique or Guadeloupe.

7. In Martinique and Guadeloupe these costs and risks remain with individual producers; in the Windward Islands, WIBDECO must absorb these costs and risks and determine how they will be distributed among various members.

8. In Costa Rica, many banana-plantation workers are from Nicaragua, Panama, and Honduras (Bourgois 1989; Purcell 1993; Vandermeer and Perfecto 1995, 8); in Belize, 91 percent of workers on one banana plantation were recent migrants from Guatemala, Honduras, and El Salvador (Moberg 1996, 427).

9. In 1978 roughly 25 percent of Dole's and Chiquita's Honduran bananas were produced on contract (Glover and Larrea Maldonado 1991, 98). Currently, 35 percent of Dole's, 50 percent of Del Monte's, and 25 percent of Chiquita's Costa Rican bananas come from contract growers (Fabre 1997, 15). Glover and Larrea Maldonado (1991) estimate that 30 percent of Dollar corporation bananas now come from associate growers. The rising use of contracts is confirmed by corporate reports (see Dole Food Company 2000).

10. By not producing the bananas themselves corporations can escape responsibility for abiding by labor and environmental regulations and discourage increasingly common large-scale strikes (see Hernandez 1997). Companies can also avoid potential lawsuits like that filed by Latin American plantation workers for pesticide exposure that recently cost Dole U.S.$22 million (Interpress News Service 1997).

11. The large numbers of migrant workers hired in Dollar Banana production are particularly unlikely to be able to find jobs off the plantation (Purcell 1993; Vandermeer and Perfecto 1995).

12. One study finds that in the aerial spraying of bananas in Costa Rica, 40 percent falls on the ground instead of on the plants, 35 percent washes off the leaves in the rain, and 15 percent is carried off by the wind or irrigation water (Foro Emaus 1997).

13. The number of Windward Island banana growers appears to have declined precipitously in recent years (Addy 1999). The early 1990s figure is used in table 2 to be consistent with the other data.

14. Though the problems associated with pesticide use in the Caribbean are less severe than in Dollar Banana regions, I do not mean to suggest that there are no such environmental and health problems (see Andreatta 1998; Grossman 1998).

15. Bananas from ACP countries not traditionally exporting to Europe, such as the Dominican Republic, fell under the Dollar Banana quota but were exempt from tariffs.

16. Guatemala refused to sign the 1995 framework agreement and was not granted a preferential quota.

17. Rising ACP banana imports have come largely from West Africa.

18. The dispute panel did not fault the use of tariffs to favor ACP Bananas, since this practice is protected under a previous WTO waiver for Lomé provisions until the agreement's renegotiation in 2002.

19. The WTO cited (1) the license allocation system and the reference period (1994–96) used to determine this allocation and (2) the ACP and country-specific quotas as being the major areas of noncompliance.

20. For a more detailed analysis of these new alternatives see Murray and Raynolds 2000, Raynolds 2000b, and Raynolds forthcoming.

21. To be Fair Trade certified, banana production and marketing must meet set standards: (1) trade must involve as few middlemen as possible; (2) producer prices must be guaranteed and include a price premium; (3) producers must be democratically organized; (4) producers must uphold basic labor standards; and (5) producers must uphold basic environmental goals (Murray and Raynolds 2000).

JOHN SOLURI

Banana Cultures: Linking the Production and

Consumption of Export Bananas, 1800–1980

Grapes may fill the cup in Summer, apples and oranges may make indoor cheer in the Fall and Winter; the watermelon may cool and satisfy the thirst; the pineapple may keep step with the peach and the plum and in serried ranks come forward for our delectation in the Summer time, but the only fruit that comes every day in the year, year in and year out, almost unvarying in price, within the reach of all, nutritious, healthy in its germ proof coat, is the golden ranks of the incoming tide of bananas, 40,000,000 bunches a year, 2,400,000,000 golden satisfiers of American desires. — HARRY WEINBERGER, Secretary, Banana Buyers Association, *New York Times,* 12 July 1913

In 1923 the Skidmore Music Company of New York reluctantly published a novelty tune by two young musicians called "Yes, We Have No Bananas!" By the end of the year the company was selling thousands of copies of the sheet music on a daily basis and dance-hall bands were performing the tune throughout the United States and many parts of Europe. One of the song's composers, drummer Frank Silver, organized a ten-piece "banana band" that toured the United States with a set that included real bunches of bananas and a backdrop that featured a picture of a banana plantation (Wilson 1947). The tune's immense popularity may have been due in part to the series of familiar melodies strung together by Silver, including the "Hallelujah" chorus from Handel's *Messiah* and the last line from "My Bonnie Lies over the Ocean," among others (Silver and Cohn 1977 [1923]). But the music was not the only aspect of the song that struck a familiar chord with listeners; by the early 1920s, bananas were as commonplace as the string beans, onions, and potatoes carried by the immigrant produce peddler who inspired the song.

The banana's transition from novelty item to mass-marketed commodity in the United States was swift. In 1871 the wholesale value of banana imports into the United States was less than $250,000; by 1901, the figure had jumped to $6.5 million. Over the course of the next decade, the value of banana imports almost doubled, increasing to $12.4 million (Adams 1911). Entering the 1910s, per capita banana consumption stood in excess of twenty pounds, far more than the comparable figures for oranges, grapes, peaches, pears, and strawberries and second only to apple consumption. The banana was also widely consumed as a cultural symbol. In addition to Silver and Cohn, other popular composers such as George Gershwin incorporated bananas into hit songs such as "Let's Call the Whole Thing Off" and "But Not for Me." The word *banana* slipped into the popular lexicon via phrases such as "top banana," "banana boat," "to go bananas," and the tragically powerful metaphor, "banana republic."

The dramatic rise in banana consumption was linked to expanding production in the Caribbean. Early export centers included Cuba and Jamaica; by the 1880s, banana production was proliferating along the Caribbean coast of Mesoamerica from Mexico to Colombia. Throughout the nineteenth century, small-scale cultivators grew most of the bananas exported to the United States. They sold their fruit to schooner captains operating in what for a brief period of time was a highly competitive marketplace. However, as the century came to a close, shipping companies began consolidating, a process that culminated in the 1899 formation of the United Fruit Company. Soon thereafter, United Fruit, along with the Cuyamel Fruit Company and the Standard Fruit and Steamship Company, began establishing plantations, transportation infrastructure, and work camps along the Caribbean coast of Central America and Colombia. The unprecedented levels of capital invested in banana-growing regions, combined with expanding markets in North America and Europe, led to a sharp increase in export banana production between 1900 and 1930.

This period also witnessed the emergence and spread of a plant pathogen, popularly known as Panama Disease (*Fusarium oxysporum f. cubense*), that infected export banana farms, reducing yields and lowering profit margins. The U.S. fruit companies responded by abandoning vast amounts of land, a strategy that enabled them to maintain production levels on a short-term basis but virtually ensured the further spread of the disease. Panama Disease has been widely recognized as a critical obstacle to export banana production during the first half of the twentieth century, but seldom has its relationship to banana markets been explored (Marquardt 2001). The history of Panama Disease, and, by extension, the history of the export industry in Latin America, is best understood by adopting a transnational perspective. Consequently, this essay moves back and forth between plantation and marketplace in order to trace the dialectical relationship between banana production and consumption, revealing how entwined biological and cultural processes, operating at local and international levels, shaped the growing and eating of bananas.

FROM NOVELTY TO COMMODITY, 1800–1920

Varieties of *Musa* (bananas and plantains) reached the New World no later than the sixteenth century and possibly earlier (Langdon 1993). The plants diffused quickly throughout the tropical regions of the Americas where they were widely cultivated and consumed. In the sugarcane-growing areas of the Caribbean, the plantain formed a staple of slaves' diets (McDonald 1981). However, banana and plantain plants, which require bountiful rainfall and mild temperatures throughout the calendar year, remained largely unknown to North Americans prior to the nineteenth century. Alexander von Humboldt's description of bananas and plantains in the American tropics was among the first to be circulated widely in Europe and the United States (Pratt 1992). He praised plantains for their productivity, declaring that they yielded far more "nutritive substance" than did grains such as wheat (Humboldt and Bonpland 1852). Humboldt's estimate of the banana's productivity was reproduced in popular sources throughout the nineteenth century. For example, a brief article about the banana that appeared in the 29 September 1832 edition of *Penny* magazine cited Humboldt's figures to highlight the plant's productivity. Significantly, the article's anonymous author considered the banana's bountiful yields to be a mixed blessing: "the facility with which the banana can be cultivated has doubtless contributed to arrest the progress of improvement in tropical regions." A drawing of a dark-skinned human figure standing near a thatched dwelling in a small clearing shaded by banana plants and coconut trees served to reinforce an image of "the poor Indian" who, content with "gathering the fruit of his little patch of bananas," was barely elevated above the "inferior animal."

Thus, even before the banana became a commonplace item in North American diets, it had begun to enter into the U.S. popular imagination as a symbol of exotic, tropical places in which nature's fecundity sapped the initiative of the residents. This view of the banana and its cultural landscape would be re-produced by a later generation of U.S. entrepreneurs anxious to demonstrate the need for Yankee ingenuity (and capital) to tap the potential of the tropics. The racialized lens through which the banana was viewed would also shape the meanings that the fruit would acquire in North American culture as it made the transition from exotica to commodity.

The first recorded bunch of bananas to reach New York arrived in 1804 aboard the schooner *Raymond,* whose captain brought a small quantity of the fruit from Cuba and sold the tropical curiosity for a profit (Rodriquez 1955). Shipments of bananas, primarily a variety known as the Cuban Red banana, arrived sporadically in New York and Boston during the first third of the nine-teenth century (Garcia 1999).[1] By 1850 importers such as the firm of J & T Pear-sall were regularly bringing bananas and other tropical fruits from Cuba to North Atlantic ports. When Irish Catholic bishop James Donnelly was travel-ing in the United States between 1850 and 1853, he tried a banana for the first time, an experience noteworthy enough to make it into a journal entry.[2] Fol-lowing the U.S. Civil War, the number of banana traders increased significantly, and Jamaica began to displace Cuba as the main supply source. The banana re-mained something of a novelty throughout the 1870s. At the 1876 Centennial Exhibition in Philadelphia vendors sold individual bananas wrapped in tin foil for a hefty price. In 1880 the chef at Delmonico's Restaurant in New York City prepared a banana mousse as one of several desserts served at a posh dinner held in honor of General Winfield Scott Hancock (Levenstein 1988).

A few years after the soiree for the general, the U.S. government lifted im-port duties on bananas and customs officials began listing banana imports as a separate item in published statistical reports.[3] More than 12 million stems of ba-nanas passed through U.S. ports in 1892, two-thirds of which entered through New Orleans and New York. Other important regional import centers included Philadelphia, Baltimore, and Mobile. By 1894 the banana, according to one con-temporary observer, was already joining the apple as a "staple article" in U.S. diets (Humphrey 1894).

Late-nineteenth-century sources indicate that more than one banana variety reached United States markets. The text of an 1889 advertisement about ba-nanas stated that "there are two kinds, the yellow and the red. The latter is considered the best, and the season for them is from March to September; the season for the yellow ones continues to the middle of October."[4] The Boston Cookbook's recipe for "Tropical Snow" called for using red bananas, an indication that they were available for purchase and well regarded by epicures. Price sheets distributed by a Portland, Maine-based wholesaler during 1903–1905 indicate that red bananas were carried regularly and sold for double the price of yellow bananas.[5] However, a Jamaica-based observer noted around this same time that the red banana was prized primarily for its decorative value (Fawcett 1902). By 1900 the vast majority of the yellow bananas imported to the United States were Gros Michel (*Musa acuminata*), having traveled from Africa to the Americas in the early nineteenth century (United Fruit Company 1958). In 1837 a single Gros Michel rhizome was carried from Martinique to Jamaica where the variety prospered. From Jamaica, the Gros Michel traveled to Panama in the mid-nineteenth century and subsequently spread throughout Central America. This "creation story" of the Gros Michel should not be taken too literally, but it suggests that the variety's genetic base in the Americas was a narrow one (Rodriquez 1955; Simmonds and Stover 1987). Traders praised the Gros Michel's relatively thick, bruise-resisting skin and its symmetrical, tight bunches that facilitated packing in the holds of ships. The Gros Michel's flavor, aroma, and peel color also received high marks, but as the prevalence of recipes calling for red bananas suggests, aesthetic values alone did not account for the Gros Michel's popularity in export markets.

During the first decades of the trade, bananas exported to the United States were probably grown in home gardens and / or small patches cultivated for local markets. In Jamaica home gardens generally consisted of polycultures in which an array of crops were cultivated. As late as 1886, observers noted that precise figures on banana acreage in Jamaica were unknown due to the frequency with which the fruit was intercropped with coffee, cacao, and vegetables.[6] In Cuba, where plantains formed a central part of an emerging regional cuisine in the nineteenth century, small-scale growers cultivated several varieties of *Musa* in their *conucos* (home gardens) (Dawdy 1999). Thus, for growers in the Caribbean and elsewhere, the emergence of the export banana trade did not initially bring about radical transformations of local agricultural landscapes and livelihoods.

However, as the market for the fruit expanded and traders sought both to increase their profits and to lower their risk levels, cultivation practices began to change. Traders not only encouraged the cultivation of specific varieties of bananas, but they also increasingly shaped grower practices. For example, British colonial officials urged Jamaican growers to time the planting of their bananas in order to maximize yields between the months of March and June when demand for the fruit peaked in the United States. They also encouraged growers to adopt pruning strategies that increased the likelihood of having plants "shoot nines," that is, produce large, nine-handed stems of fruit, which fetched the highest prices in export markets ("Timeing of Bananas" 1905).

The discourse about producing quality bananas that emerged in the final decades of the nineteenth century reflected the rising quantity of fruit produced throughout the Caribbean. Exports from Jamaica rose from 1.5 million stems in 1885 to 8 million stems in 1900; that same year, Costa Rica and Honduras combined to export more than 6 million stems (Rodriquez 1955; Blaney 1900; Soluri 1998). As growers and national governments alike began to sense the growing international competition in the banana trade, they strengthened their efforts to promote the quality of their fruit in order to attract shipping companies. Traders often rejected fruit that was judged to be unmarketable due to defects in quality. In Honduras growers concerned about fruit rejections lobbied for the building of railroad lines capable of transporting bananas with both speed and care, objectives that were hard to accomplish when hauling fruit in ox-drawn carts over bumpy, muddy roadways. In 1893 the Honduran government passed legislation that created fruit inspectors charged with monitoring transactions between growers and shippers (*La Gaceta,* 17 October 1893). The law also provided subsidies to steamship companies in order to ensure consistent shipping schedules.

Transporting highly perishable bananas from farms to retail markets with minimal fruit losses was among the most important challenges facing nineteenth century traders. By the early 1880s steamships had all but replaced the schooners that had once dominated the banana trade.[7] Although costly to operate, steamships offered a couple of key advantages over schooners: they were capable of carrying larger cargoes, and they were less likely to be delayed by weather conditions than wind-powered vessels. Thus, steamers greatly reduced the risks of having a shipment of fruit reach North Atlantic ports in an unmarketable (overripe) condition due to delays in transit. Recognizing the advantages offered by steamships, the longtime schooner captain Lorenzo Dow Baker merged his company with the Standard Steam Navigation Company and the Boston Fruit Company in 1885 (Rodriquez 1955). The resulting entity, also named the Boston Fruit Company, enjoyed considerable success; by the mid-1890s, the company was loading five steamers per week during the peak months of the season. However, the company was only one of several commercial ventures shipping large quantities of bananas to U.S. ports (Wilson 1947, 92–97). In 1899 the Boston Fruit Company merged with several other entities to form the United Fruit Company, capitalized at $20 million. Among other advantages, the merger generated the large sums of capital needed to maintain the "Great White Fleet" that would become one of the company's most visible symbols.

The development of inland railroad networks in the United States further expanded the potential market for fresh fruits of all kinds. For example, the production of California citrus crops for national markets became possible following the completion of the transatlantic railroad in 1869 and the subsequent development of refrigerated railcars in the 1880s (Tyrell 1999). Similarly, bananas acquired access to inland markets following the expansion of railways and the development of ventilation systems that circulated warm air through fruit cars during the winter and cool air in the summer. The banana quite possibly was the first seasonless fresh fruit widely available for consumption in the United States. Both steamships and locomotives required a relatively compact fuel (coal), and in this light, the banana trade reflected the possibilities created by the rising use of fossil fuels to power steam engines.

But, technological changes alone cannot account for the banana's immense popularity. Economic, social, and cultural forces at work in the late nineteenth century transformed North American diets and help to explain the rapid rise in banana consumption. When bananas first began to appear in Atlantic ports, most North Americans did not consume a great variety of fresh fruits. One of the few fruits of mass consumption at the time was the apple. Orchards were commonplace, and cooks baked, sauced, and dried apples. Other popular seasonal fruits in the mid-nineteenth century included strawberries, peaches, and melons. As the century came to a close, a growing number of fresh fruits, including varieties of citrus, became available on a regular basis, particularly in urban markets and rail centers. Doctors, public health officials, and nutritionists increasingly promoted fresh fruit as an important component of daily diets.

Authors of cookbooks and home economics manuals also promoted fruit consumption. For example, Hester M. Poole's 1890 housekeepers' manual,

Fruits and How to Use Them, began with a chapter praising the value of fruits in an age when society was threatened by "too great concentration — whether it be found in social life, in wealth, or in food" (10). Citing scientific data related to "food values," Poole noted that a diet based on fruits and grains was superior to one based on animal proteins and fats. She also criticized the "smothering" of fruit with sugar and cream as unhealthful and instead urged an appreciation for the "natural flavors skillfully compounded by the Great Chemist in nature's own laboratory" (10). The metaphor of God as a scientist is not surprising during an era when both the internal systems and external surroundings of the human body were increasingly subject to analyses by the techniques of reductionist science. Home economics brought scientific rationality into the kitchen via recipe books with precisely measured ingredients, nutritional information about foods expressed in terms of chemical "building blocks," and labor-saving techniques related to food preparation.

Advocates such as Poole declared that fruits gave strength and could help to cure a number of maladies. One source went so far as to recommend bananas for any disease accompanied by a fever. Fruit was also praised as a blessing for housewives since its preparation generally required labor that was less demanding and more agreeable to a "refined woman" than was the handling of greasy animal products. Nonfermented fruit juice, such as grape juice, was touted as a means to help reduce alcoholism, and the cultivation of berries and other fruits was put forth as a viable livelihood for destitute women.

Fruits and How to Use Them included a section on bananas, which in the eyes of the author were "among the most important of all fruits." Poole praised the banana plant's productivity and the fruit's reasonable retail price, ease of preparation, and year-round availability before providing about a dozen recipes featuring bananas. The majority of the recipes featured the banana as either a breakfast food or sweetened dessert. Poole's recipes for banana fritters, baked bananas, banana pudding, and banana pie all called for sugar. The author's concern about "heavy foods" notwithstanding, most of the recipes also called for fat-laden dairy products such as cream and butter (Poole 1890). An 1897 edition of *Boston Cooking School* magazine included a recipe for a dessert called "Banana Charlotte." Other issues of the magazine recommended that bananas, along with fruits such as dates, figs, and prunes, be served with cereals for breakfast. Mary J. Lincoln, principal of the Boston Cooking School, published recipes for banana ice cream, banana fruit salad, and a dessert called "Tropical Snow," whose ingredients included oranges, coconut, sherry, lemon juice, powdered sugar, and red bananas. Five banana recipes found in the *Twentieth Century Cookbook* all involved some combination of sugar, eggs, and / or dairy products such as butter and milk. A 1911 collection of fruit recipes contained twenty-six banana recipes, nearly all of which were sweetened desserts.[8]

Banana recipes continued to proliferate during the first half of the twentieth century, but the most popular form in which to eat the banana — raw — seldom appeared in cookbooks. Although early-twentieth-century nutritionists often compared the banana to the potato in terms of nutrient content, the notion of cooking green bananas or plantains as starchy foods did not take hold in the United States. In contrast to its place in Caribbean cuisines, where *Musa* were consumed both green and ripe, the banana found a niche in U.S. diets as a mildly sweet fruit.

Some late-nineteenth-century cooks warned against eating raw bananas: "in countries where the banana is indigenous, only the most delicate varieties are eaten uncooked; the bananas that are brought to our markets cannot be eaten safely until they have been cooked" (Boston School of Cooking 1898). Another source urged that children be fed bananas that had been cut or mashed to facilitate digestion. The idea that bananas could be difficult to digest was sufficiently widespread to prompt the United Fruit Company to compile and publish numerous studies demonstrating that the banana, when properly ripened, was easily digested. In 1917 the company issued a compendium of papers written by "leading medical and scientific authorities" about the nutritional value of bananas. Dr. Albert H. Hoy took up the question of digestibility and argued that many people tried to eat the fruit "too much in a raw state; that is when the skin is simply yellow. . . . [A]s a fact, the skin should begin to darken and shrivel before the fruit is in its proper edible state" (United Fruit Company 1917, 15). Samuel Prescott, a microbiologist on the faculty of the Massachusetts Institute of Technology, acknowledged that unripe bananas could be indigestible but provided data indicating that a thoroughly ripened banana was one of the easiest foods to digest (Prescott 1917, 10). The American Medical Association concurred, noting in a 1912 editorial that consumers should be educated to avoid eating "green" bananas in much the same way that "green" apples were eschewed.[9]

The banana's germ-resistant peel further pleased public health officials concerned about the spread of infectious diseases in poor, densely populated urban areas. Once again, the American Medical Association offered its endorsement and published a study demonstrating that bananas, even when immersed in pathogen-laden fluids, did not absorb bacteria into their fruit pulp. The nutritious fruit could thus be given to children with confidence, "even if purchased from the pushcart in congested streets" (United Fruit Company 1936, 10). Such endorsements from the increasingly influential medical establishment likely made for great advertising copy in the early twentieth century, but banana consumption had begun its meteoric rise well before the United Fruit Company began promoting the fruit as a healthy food. The slew of early-twentieth-century medical publications addressing the nutritional aspects of the banana was therefore more a reflection than a cause of the fruit's popularity.

The banana possessed another quality that contributed to its popularity: a comparatively low retail price. In a 1913 editorial entitled "Apples and Bananas," the *New York Times* called on apple producers to adopt the methods of the "trusts" (i.e., the United Fruit Company) that "have brought exotic products within the reach of those who cannot eat domestic fruits because they are dear and inaccessible." Scolding the apple industry for its "inefficiency," the editorial concluded, "there is much need for an apple trust as 'bad' as the fruit trust." Although it is difficult to compare wholesale prices for apples and bananas because of differences in the units of sale, limited evidence indicates that bananas often retailed for prices lower than that of apples.[10] A number of studies estimated that the banana provided nearly as many calories per pound as the potato and considerably more than apples and oranges. The commissioner of the New York City Department of Health stated that the banana was "used in almost all racial and social groups in this city," a claim supported by the findings of a study that examined the diet of an African American woman living in New York (United Fruit Company 1917, 33). Margaret Byington's 1910 study of households in Homestead, Pennsylvania, indicated that steel-mill workers' fruit consumption included apples, bananas, and grapes (76).

The low retail price of bananas goes a long way toward explaining their popularity among working people, but other factors, such as dwindling amounts of time available for meal preparation, also shaped late-nineteenth-century working-class diets. As more women and men became urban wage earners, the time and energy available to prepare meals for children and spouses dwindled. In an era when the protein- and fat-rich farm breakfast was giving way to prepared breakfast cereals, breads, and jams, it seems probable that one factor contributing to the banana's popularity was its ease of storage and preparation (Levenstein 1988). In contrast to most domestically grown fruits available in the United States, bananas could be eaten throughout the year without any need of canning, drying, or other method of preservation. Also, the banana's relatively high carbohydrate content provided considerably more calories for growing bodies than did apples and oranges (Rose 1918). The banana, then, was an affordable, nutritious, self-packaged "fast food" during an era when working people in the United States were becoming both more health-minded and more harried.

In 1910 over 40 million bunches of bananas entered the United States (Franklin Adams 1911). Four years later imports neared the 50 million-bunch mark, and per capita consumption was around twenty-two pounds (Bitter 1922). Banana consumption was rising concurrently in Europe, but the European volume of imports paled in comparison to that of the United States; England, the largest European market for bananas in 1914, imported some 6 million bunches that year. For the United Fruit Company, this translated into rising wealth. The company's cash reserves increased from $11.2 million in 1899 to more than $50 million in 1918. Net profits soared to more than $33 million in 1920, a six-fold increase over earnings in 1913 (ibid.). Shipping restrictions during World War I led to a short-term decline in per capita banana consumption, but by the mid-1920s per capita consumption of bananas had soared to about twenty-four pounds.[11] Although the dollar value of banana imports paled in comparison to that of coffee, the fruit had unquestionably become one of the most important trade commodities in the Americas.

Perhaps the most convincing evidence of the banana's popularity is found not in data on per capita consumption or corporate profits but in the records of a political controversy triggered by a proposal to establish an import duty on bananas. In 1913 the U.S. Senate Finance Committee, arguing that the banana fit the legal definition of a luxury import, proposed levying a duty of five cents per bunch on all bananas entering the country. However, when word of the proposed "banana tax" became public, a number of organizations representing growers, importers, retailers, and consumers protested vociferously. In an editorial letter, Byron Holt, representing the Reform Club, claimed that the banana was one of a few food commodities that had not been subject to dramatic price increases and consequently was the most widely consumed fruit among the urban poor (*New York Times,* 2 July 1913, sec. A., p. 8). Shortly thereafter, the *New York Times* published an editorial praising the Housewives' League and "all who follow their example" for protesting the proposed banana tax. If the banana was a luxury item, the editorial reasoned, it was an "exceptional kind" since it was within the reach of nearly everyone: "Cheap starch and sugar in finer combination are hardly to be found in the vegetable kingdom, and the wonderful extension of the banana trade that has marked recent years has been nothing less than a national blessing" (*New York Times,* 12 July 1913, p. 6). At a rally in Cooper Union organized by the Banana Buyers Protective Association, speakers drove home the fact that the banana was both inexpensive and widely consumed (*New York Times,* 12 July 1913, p. 3). A follow-up editorial in the *New York Times* noted that "people who count their pennies do not live on basic articles of food alone. They are entitled to their little luxuries exactly because they are poor, and their luxuries are few" (*New York Times,* 30 July 1913, 6).

Diplomats representing several banana-producing nations, including Jamaica, Costa Rica, Guatemala, and Panama, presented President Woodrow Wilson with official letters of protest. In the face of this onslaught of domestic and international opposition, the proposed duty was removed from the tariff bill, and bananas remained on the duty-free list. Clearly, many of the highly vocal critics of the proposed duty on bananas perceived a direct threat to their economic self-interest. Still, the uproar over the proposal revealed that the banana, while meeting the legal definition of a "luxury" import, had acquired very different social and political meanings. Affordable, nutrient-bearing, and pleasing to most palates, the banana was the "poor man's luxury." Two decades later in the midst of the Great Depression, some roadside stands continued to sell bananas alongside apples (Schremp 1996, 65).

THE BANANA AS CULTURAL ICON

In the final scene of William Faulkner's 1929 novel *As I Lay Dying,* the children of the deceased Addie Bundren eat bananas while awaiting their father in the family's mule-drawn buckboard that is parked on a street in Jefferson, Mississippi. Not only is Faulkner's decision to incorporate bananas in this scene further evidence of the fruit's popularity across class and regional lines, but the appearance of bananas at such a crucial moment in the novel is hardly gratuitous: Faulkner appropriated the banana as a symbol of the social and economic changes taking place in the New South that lay at the center of many of his other novels. The Bundren's journey from country to city can be read as a metaphor for the rural-to-urban migrations that transformed the nation during the interwar years. The visit to the city exposes the children to the wonders of mass consumer society: electric trains, graphophones—and bananas. The rural poor might not be able to attain the levels of power, wealth, and prestige enjoyed by the North's industrial bankers and industrialists, but they could—on occasion—enjoy a taste of the tropics and other "fruits" of economies of scale. Sharecroppers could only dream about cruising the Caribbean aboard United Fruit's Great White Fleet or attending an evening at a concert hall, but the mass production of bananas and recorded music enabled poor folk to partake of what had previously been exotic and elite. However, *As I Lay Dying*'s final scene reveals the author's unease about the commodification of desire. When Vardaman, the youngest member of the family, implores his older siblings to explain the meaning of their mother's death, his sister responds, "Wouldn't you rather have a banana?" The banana as commodity is offered as a substitute for the painful knowledge of the transition that the family (and southern sharecroppers) would endure in the future (Willis 1987).

Faulkner was not the only novelist to use the banana to symbolize the social and economic transformations taking place in the United States. A vacationing Edith Wharton pointed to banana consumption as a sign of national decline: "I have been spending my first night in an American 'summer hotel' and I despair of the Republic! Such dreariness, such whining callow women, such utter absence of the amenities, such crass food, crass manners, crass landscape! And, mind you, it is a new and fashionable hotel. What a horror it is for a whole nation to be developing without a sense of beauty and eating bananas for breakfast" (Edith Wharton to Sara Norton, 19 August 1904, in Wharton 1988, 92–93). Wharton's despair over banana consumption appears to have stemmed from the fact that the act of eating a banana was accompanied by none of the aristocratic traditions associated with the consumption of other tropical commodities such as tea, coffee, and chocolate. Instead, the banana was associated with the "crass" popular culture of the United States, shaped by both mass consumerism and democratic ideals. Even after sugar, tea, and coffee became central to working-class diets in the late nineteenth century, social elites continued to consume these products in exclusive social spaces and contexts. However, the banana had little or no association with social exclusivity or cultural refinement; indeed, what seems to have bothered Edith Wharton so much was the idea that an article of popular consumption could find its way into the fashionable playgrounds of the wealthy.

The celebrated poet Wallace Stevens apparently shared Wharton's distaste for the banana. In "Floral Decoration for Bananas," Stevens contrasts the severe elegance of well-to-do Anglo culture with the raw sensuality of tropical people and places (Stevens 1972, 84):

Well, nuncle, this plainly won't do.
These insolent, linear peels
And sullen, hurricane shapes
Won't do with your eglantine.
They require something serpentine.
Blunt yellow in such a room!
You should have had plums tonight,
In an eighteenth-century dish,
And petifogging buds,
for the women of primrose and purl,
Each one in her decent curl.
Good God! What a precious light!
But bananas hacked and hunched.
The table was set by an ogre,
His eye on an outdoor gloom
And a stiff and noxious place.
Pile the bananas on planks.
The women will be all shanks
And bangles and slatted eyes.
And deck the bananas in leaves
Plucked from the Carib trees,
Fibrous and dangling down,

Oozing cantankerous gum
Out of their purple maws,
Darting out of their purple craws
Their musky and tingling tongues.

By juxtaposing the images of bananas piled on planks with plums "in an eighteenth-century dish" Stevens emphasized the banana's less-than-noble background. The poem associates elegantly served plums with women "of primrose and purl" in "decent curls" but linked the "hacked and hunched" bananas to female prostitutes. The eroticized image of the oozing, tingling-tongued banana plant created by Stevens both echoed nineteenth-century constructions of the tropics as primitive and anticipated the association of bananas with sensual women that would be exploited by the United Fruit Company's immensely successful 1940s advertising campaign featuring "Miss Chiquita."

Elite Anglo-American writers were not the only ones to use the banana for its symbolic value. Popular musicians and songwriters of the 1920s and 1930s often deployed the banana to evoke laughter and lewdness. Following the international popularity of "Yes, We Have No Bananas!" folk-blues musicians appropriated the banana as a phallic symbol. For example, the Happiness Boys performed "I've Never Seen a Straight Banana" in 1926, Bo Carter recorded "Banana in Your Fruit Basket" in 1931, and Memphis Minnie sang "Banana Man Blues" in 1934. In 1943 Busby Berkeley's Hollywood musical *The Gang's All Here* scandalized viewers with its Freud-inspired dance number that featured Carmen Miranda singing "The Lady in the Tutti-Frutti Hat" while showgirls straddled oversized strawberries and bananas.

Miranda, dubbed the "Brazilian Bombshell" by the popular U.S. press, took both Broadway and Hollywood by storm.[12] She brought exoticism to the North American stage and screen through her highly stylized versions of Bahian market women's headwear, the samba rhythms played by her Brazilian musicians, and her often amusing (and calculated) mix of Portuguese and English. The bananas that frequently dominated the sets for Miranda's musical numbers provided a visual link between her "hot" rhythms and a sensual — yet never quite locatable — tropical region. However, as some recent studies of Miranda have argued, numbers such as "The Lady in the Tutti-Frutti Hat" possessed an "over the top" quality that hinted at self-parody. The humor worked to dissolve the sexual tension and remove the possibility that either Miranda or the banana would threaten the moral standards of the era. Both Carmen Miranda and the banana were simultaneously sexy and comic, a combination that does much to explain their widespread popularity.

Of course, neither Miranda's nor the banana's commercial successes can be understood outside of the geopolitical contexts in which they took place. The dramatic increase in banana consumption coincided with the rise of U.S. imperialism in Central America and the Caribbean. Although few U.S. interventions during the first third of the twentieth century were directly linked to the interests of U.S. banana companies, the omnipresence of Yankee marines and warships indirectly facilitated capitalist investments in places like Cuba, Honduras, and Panama. Similarly, Carmen Miranda's popularity reflected not only her own onstage talents but also the U.S. government's promotion of the Good Neighbor policy. After three decades of U.S. interventions in Central America and the Caribbean, the rise to power of New Deal Democrats along with the exigencies of World War II led to a reorientation of U.S. foreign policy (Coatsworth 1994). Anxious to neutralize German influence in the Americas and secure strategic raw materials such as rubber, quinine, and manila hemp (*abacá*), the U.S. government encouraged Hollywood to produce motion pictures capable of "spreading the gospel of the Americas' common stake" in the struggle against Nazi Germany (Roberts 1993, 5).

For Fox Studios, Carmen Miranda became the star of films designed to portray harmonious relations between the United States and its hemispheric neighbors to the south. In films such as *Down Argentine Way, Weekend in Havana,* and *That Night in Rio,* the Portuguese-born Miranda portrayed a generic Latin American woman. Regardless of the imagined setting, the music and dance steps were always what Carmen had learned during her youth in Rio de Janeiro (a fact that did not escape the notice of Argentine and Cuban film critics). In the opening scene of *The Gang's All Here,* quintessential Latin American export products (sugar, coffee, and fruit) are unloaded from a freight ship, the S.S. *Brazil,* followed by Carmen Miranda, who proceeds to perform the "Uncle Sam-ba" (ibid.). The cultural and geographic distance between Central American banana plantations and Rio de Janeiro notwithstanding, Hollywood's wartime productions seamlessly united Miranda and bananas as icons of "Latin Americanness."

The United Fruit Company did not hesitate to take advantage of the Carmen Miranda craze. Prior to the 1920s, the company's advertising budget was small and directed toward the production of recipe books, short histories of the banana, and information about the fruit's nutritional content and ripening qualities. As late as 1925, some company executives expressed skepticism about the merits of investing in advertising (Fruit Dispatch Company 1925). However, by the 1940s, United Fruit was eager to advertise through new forms of mass media such as radio and films. The company created a banana-woman cartoon character named Chiquita whose "tutti-frutti" hat unmistakably conjured Carmen Miranda. In 1943 United Fruit's advertisers produced a radio commercial song, "I'm Chiquita Banana," that was heard coast to coast, marking the second time that a banana tune acquired hit status. By the end of World War II, then, the banana was a part of everyday life for most people in the United States. If they did not actually eat the fruit for breakfast or as a midday snack, they symbolically consumed the banana through words spoken or sung.

BETWEEN FARM AND MARKET: FRUIT JOBBERS AND THE DISTRIBUTION OF BANANAS

Historically, the movement of commodities from point of production to place of consumption has often involved complex layers of shippers, brokers, wholesalers, retailers, and others. The banana was no exception despite its minimal processing needs and the industry's vertical integration. The Fruit Dispatch Company, a subsidiary of United Fruit, coordinated the distribution of the majority of bananas that entered North American markets. Founded in 1900, Fruit Dispatch established offices in Boston, New York, and in a number of railway centers such as Chicago, Kansas City, Pittsburgh, and Richmond (Wilson 1947, 170). Company employees traveled with the fruit, ensuring its proper storage and handling and lining up sales with wholesalers located along the route. If the fruit was not sold in one market, it was rerouted to another. By 1925 Fruit Dispatch had offices in more than fifty U.S. and Canadian cities. The only other companies with significant market share were Banana Sales (a subsidiary of Samuel Zemurray's Cuyamel Fruit Company) and Standard Fruit.

Because most fruit jobbers purchased bananas through brokers, they had little direct contact with the fruit companies and generally did not express much loyalty to particular companies. However, the very limited competition among importers meant that jobbers often had little opportunity to shop around. For example, only United Fruit imported bananas into Boston. A jobber in Massachusetts could purchase bananas in New York City from another importer, but this would mean subjecting the delicate fruit to additional jostling as it traveled overland by rail.[13] The result was a de facto regional monopoly for United Fruit.

Fruit jobbers in the northeastern United States surveyed in 1929 voiced some complaints about prices set by importing companies, but they perceived a bigger threat from seasonal jobbers who entered the market during periods of peak demand and sold low-quality fruit (called "deck ripes") below market cost. For example, "Nick, the Banana Man," a jobber in Worcester, Massachusetts, who claimed that he bought "mostly nines" from United Fruit, said that the purchase price was fair as long as all of the jobbers were offered the same price. He explained that "little fellows" sometimes bought up the "lower quality" fruit in order to undersell other dealers.[14] One of Nick's larger competitors, the Tsones brothers, agreed that United Fruit's practice of selling deck ripes at lower prices allowed jobbers to undercut each other. In fact, the Tsones offered Nick as an example of a jobber who tried to undersell: "He gets decks, Jamaicas and some sevens. He never buys first quality fruit." The Tsones, who sold most of their fruit to A&P chain stores, asserted that they only traded nine-handed stems. Nearly all of the jobbers interviewed in a Fruit Dispatch-sponsored marketing survey expressed similar complaints about small-time dealers, but just who the "little guy" was seemed to depend on who was doing the underselling. Small profit margins, the absence of purchase contracts, and the perishability of the fruit all tended to foster a climate of highly competitive commodity dealing.

Virtually all jobbers interviewed in 1929 talked about "fruit quality," but ideas about the perfect banana varied in relation to jobber perceptions of market demand. For example, Joseph Fielding, a longtime dealer in Lowell, Massachusetts, said that "everyone" in town bought "sevens" (i.e., seven-handed bunches of fruit) because brokers charged higher rates for eight-handed stems for which Fielding could not get "a penny more."[15] However, in the neighboring town of Lawrence, a jobber whose large operation serviced several chain stores sought out brokers who "always used nines (nine-handed stems). . . . [T]he customers like large fruit."[16] Another Lawrence-based banana dealer, George Lampros, concurred with Fielding that stores retailing bananas by the pound sold sevens and eights at the same price, but added that he generally bought "eights" since they "showed up better" and because "people don't buy sevens."[17] Thus, jobber perceptions and strategies varied even within the same local market. However, on one point, the jobbers in the economically depressed Lawrence–Lowell area were in agreement: "when the mills die, bananas die." Thus, patterns of banana consumption in the United States were subject to geographical variations resulting from changes in local economies as well as consumption habits shaped by culture and agroecological possibilities.

By the late 1920s the repeated complaints about the "little guy" notwithstanding, the retail food market was beginning to consolidate with important implications for the marketing of bananas. Street vendors and peddlers continued to serve working-class clientele in urban areas such as Cleveland and Atlanta, but middle- and upper-class markets were increasingly served by chain stores such as A&P and Kroger. In 1929 about two-fifths of all consumers "usually" purchased fruit from chain stores; one-third frequented independent grocers; the remainder bought from fruit markets and peddlers.[18] The chain stores' mass-market strategy enabled them to move huge quantities of fruit. A fruit buyer for Kroger stressed that volume sales were crucial to the chain's success and represented a mutual interest between his company and the banana importers. In the late 1920s Kroger began purchasing its fruit directly from the importing companies. The A&P also operated on volume dealing and often used bananas as a "leader" item, selling them at cost in order to draw customers away from competitors.

The social, economic, and cultural transformations symbolized by the rise of chain supermarkets were captured by the divergent images contained in the 1920s pop tune "Yes, We Have No Bananas!" and United Fruit's 1940s radio jingle "Chiquita Banana." In the former, Silver and Kahn's lyrics describe a peddler hawking his produce in city streets, his unconventional English an allusion to the largely immigrant workers who inhabited urban landscapes. In contrast, the Chiquita Banana jingle's oft-quoted couplet "But bananas like the climate of the very, very tropical equator / So you should never put bananas in the refrigerator" conjured images of middle-class homes adorned with electric appliances such as refrigerators that changed the way that people (mostly women) bought, stored, and prepared food. What changed very little during the turbulent years between 1923 and 1944 was the banana's popularity. The fruit continued to hold its own against a slew of new food products that became available to U.S. consumers in the postwar era. However, entering the 1950s, the export banana itself began to change as a result of ecological transformations in banana-producing regions.

THE AGROECOLOGY, GENETICS, AND AESTHETICS OF THE EXPORT BANANA

In the 1940s and 1950s, the United Fruit Company cultivated its image as a modernizing influence on Latin America that helped to transform disease-ridden "jungle wastelands" into productive agricultural complexes complete with railroads, telegraph lines, hospitals, and schools. In one sense, this image was undeniably true: the process of vertical integration undertaken by United Fruit and other U.S. fruit companies dramatically transformed tropical landscapes and livelihoods. Thousands of immigrant workers felled and burned forests, drained wetlands, laid railroad tracks, and built work camps and other infrastructure. One result was a sharp increase in banana exports. In Honduras the large capital investments made by three U.S. banana companies (United, Standard, and Cuyamel Fruit) between 1912 and 1929 led to a tripling of exports, from 8.4 million stems to a world-record 29 million stems.

A second result was the transformation of regional landscapes. In 1928, when U.S. botanist Paul Standley visited an export banana zone in Honduras, he remarked that "practically all of the land within this area that is fit for the purpose is covered with banana plants which, however beautiful when standing alone or in moderate quantities, become exceedingly monotonous when massed in plantations many miles in extent" (Standley 1931, 12). But the impact of changing landscapes was not merely aesthetic; the resulting interconnected system of densely planted monocultures helped to trigger disease epidemics by providing high densities of genetically similar hosts (Mundt 1990; Stover 1962).

The most important disease epidemic to affect the export banana industry during the first half of the twentieth century was Panama Disease. Between 1899 and 1930, the soil fungus reached virtually all of the major growing regions of Latin America. United Fruit enlisted a number of soil scientists and plant pathologists in order to find a way to control the disease's spread. As early as 1910, researchers studying Panama Disease recommended that growers adopt banana varieties that displayed resistance to the pathogen (McKenney 1910). However, this approach was complicated by the fact that United Fruit Company executives and fruit jobbers remained wary of bananas that did not possess physical characteristics similar to the Gros Michel. Both fruit company and government researchers initiated banana-breeding programs in the 1920s, but both biological and cultural processes slowed progress.

A shared characteristic of most varieties of edible bananas is the absence of seeds in the fruit pulp. Growers established new banana farms by planting pieces of budded rhizomes into the soil. Once established, individual plants self-propagate by sending out lateral shoots (*hijos*) that, in the absence of pruning, mature into adult plants, thereby eliminating the need to replant annually. Thus, some of the consequences of the banana's asexual reproduction have been viewed favorably by producers and consumers alike. However, the absence of seeds created problems for those trying to breed a Panama Disease-resistant variety, the irony of which did not escape United Fruit researcher J. H. Perman: "This character of seedlessness naturally is the valuable feature of the fruit; but it is also the feature that retards and reduces the possibility of prompt and successful development of new types" (Perman 1929, 1). Reports of breeding programs carried out by United Fruit in Central America and the Imperial College of Tropical Agriculture (ICTA) in Trinidad during the 1920s indicate that the process was both tedious and full of uncertainty (Wardlaw 1935, 116).[19]

Biological stumbling blocks were not the only challenges involved in breeding a new export banana. Another major problem, in the words of one United Fruit scientist, was the development of a "marketable variety" (Johnston 1923, 32). For example, ICTA's breeding program eventually yielded a variety that demonstrated resistance to Panama Disease, but that quality alone by no means guaranteed future commercial success. Claude W. Wardlaw described some of the new variety's other important qualities: "The colour when ripe was excellent, the flavour pleasing but probably an acquired taste while the texture was noticeably delicate" (1935, 118). He added that the new banana's ripening behavior and shipping qualities were similar to that of the Gros Michel. The major "commercial disadvantage" was that the fruit occasionally bore seeds when grown under "ordinary banana-field conditions." A 1929 United Fruit Company bulletin on banana breeding reveals that the company confronted problems similar to those faced by ICTA researchers. United Fruit began collecting resistant varieties in Panama in 1920, and ten years later had accumulated some 157 samples (Stover 1962). Breeding projects carried out by the company between 1925 and 1928 yielded fourteen varieties with edible, seedless fruit pulp. However, these hybrids were considered to be of little economic value since, "in no case is their quality equal to the fruits that are generally recognized by the public as 'bananas'" (Perman 1929, 13).

United Fruit's competitors in Honduras also tried to find a banana that possessed both Panama Disease resistance and market appeal.[20] The Standard Fruit Company began searching for new banana varieties in the mid-1920s. Standard's general manager in Honduras, A. J. Chute, directed the collection and propagation of numerous varieties of Cavendish bananas that at the time formed the bulk of the banana trade between Europe and the Canary Islands (Wardlaw 1935; Sanchez n.d). Standard Fruit also encouraged small-scale cultivators to grow a variety known as Lacatan (Hord 1966). However, the Lacatan fruit did not ripen at the same temperature as the Gros Michel. Exposing the green fruit to ethylene gas improved the Lacatan's ripening color, but few U.S. jobbers were willing to adopt the new procedure. Even when ripened under ideal conditions, the stem of the Lacatan tended to break when hung up for display due to a fungal rot (most retailers did not begin to sell fruit in precut units until the 1940s).

The reports written by banana breeders indicate how entwined biological, economic, and cultural processes shaped efforts to create and recreate the export banana. Breeding for disease resistance was merely one of the challenges facing plant breeders, since any new variety would have to compete with Gros Michel fruit, which continued to be cultivated and marketed on a large scale. Indeed, the myriad varieties of *Musa* cultivated in tropical regions did not exist in the minds of most twentieth-century U.S. fruit brokers, jobbers, and consumers, whose image of a banana consisted of little more than the large, "golden yellow" Gros Michel.

Given both the perceived risks involved in marketing a new banana variety and the abundance of suitable lands for cultivation, the fruit companies adopted a strategy of shifting plantation production from disease-infected soils to locations with no recent history of banana cultivation. The United Fruit Company claimed to have abandoned more than 100,000 acres in Central America during the first half of the twentieth century (United Fruit Company 1955). This figure is probably a conservative one. In Honduras the company abandoned more than 40,000 acres between 1939 and 1953 (United Fruit Company Annual Reports 1939–53).[21] In the late 1940s Standard Fruit reported that it was annually losing 10 to 15 percent of its productive lands in Honduras.[22] The strategy of abandoning diseased soils enabled the companies to maintain production levels, but the social and ecological costs were considerable. The expansion of railroads and monocultures into new areas resulted in widespread deforestation and alterations of local hydrological systems while all but ensuring the eventual spread of Panama Disease. Residents of areas abandoned by the companies faced the vexing task of finding new livelihoods, often without the aid of the fruit-company rail service that had given economic life to many a village. Thousands of workers migrated to active banana zones; others turned to the cultivation of crops for local markets (Soluri 2000).

The practice of abandoning diseased farms could not be sustained indefinitely. By the 1940s fruit companies operating in Honduras faced the reality of diminishing quantities of prime banana land. Standard Fruit embarked on an aggressive policy of buying up land in the middle and upper Aguan Valley, but nearly all of these lands required heavy irrigation that taxed the region's water resources and elevated production costs.[23] In the Sula Valley United Fruit also began running out of disease-free soils suitable for banana production. Company managers and engineers turned their attention to "reclaiming" the area's wetlands. These projects, which involved draining and filling thousands of acres of swamp, were costly to create and maintain. United Fruit scientists also experimented with "flood fallowing," a process that flooded diseased soils with water for several months in order to "drown" the fungus. By 1953 some 14,000 acres in Honduras had been flooded and replanted with disease-free Gros Michel rhizomes. However, enthusiasm for flood fallowing faded when United Fruit researchers observed Panama Disease reinfecting treated fields in as few as five years (Stover 1962).

Running low on both disease-free soils and the capital needed for large-scale flood fallowing, Standard Fruit's management decided to phase out the Gros Michel in favor of a disease-resistant banana plant. After experimenting with three different varieties during the 1940s and early 1950s, company executives settled on the Giant Cavendish (Hord 1966). The name "Giant Cavendish" was something of a misnomer; the plant was much shorter than the Gros Michel, making it less susceptible to wind damage. Standard Fruit officials praised the variety for its "fine, large bananas" that ripened "very nicely" with proper temperatures and exposure to ethylene gas.[24] The company marketed the new banana under the name "Golden Beauty." In 1956 Standard Fruit discontinued flood fallowing; two years later, the company completed its conversion from Gros Michel to Giant Cavendish.

United Fruit continued to export Gros Michel fruit throughout the 1950s. By 1957 flood-fallowed lands accounted for about 50 percent of the company's Honduran production, but company researchers considered the process to be "extremely expensive," and the short productive life of the farms "narrowed the profit margin" (United Fruit Company Annual Report 1957, 13). That same year, United Fruit scientists called for a revival of the company's long-neglected banana breeding program. Two years later, company-sponsored expeditions to New Guinea, Indonesia, and the Philippines collected more than 400 different cuttings of *Musa,* which were shipped to Honduras for future breeding experiments (Rowe and Richardson 1975). As late as 1960, United Fruit executives remained reluctant to drop the cherished Gros Michel on which the company had been built (Arthur et al. 1968; McCann 1976).[25] However, the conjuncture of increased rates of Panama Disease, rising labor costs, political unrest in certain producing regions, and legal troubles at home produced a sharp reduction in United Fruit's annual earnings and stock value. Between 1950 and 1960, earnings fell from $66 million to $2 million and share prices plummeted from $70 to $15 (Arthur, Houck, and Beckford 1968). Following a shake-up of top-level management, new chief executive officer Thomas Sunderland quickly authorized the replacement of Gros Michel bananas with Cavendish varieties (ibid., 146). In the early 1960s the company test-marketed the Valery banana in the U.S. Midwest and received a favorable consumer response. An independent panel found both the flavor and aroma of the Valery to be "distinctly superior" to that of the Gros Michel (ibid., 151). United Fruit initiated a swift conversion process and by 1965 virtually all of its Central American production consisted of disease-resistant varieties.

The high-yield, disease-resistant Cavendish varieties had one drawback: they were very susceptible to bruising. During their journey from farm to market, bananas had to be handled about a dozen times. In addition, despite careful packing, fruit stems jostled against one another during their journey at sea. As the 1950s came to a close, Standard Fruit's non-Gros Michel exports suffered a high rate of rejection and discounting (Arthur, Houck, and Beckford 1968). Wholesalers complained about the appearance, shape, and ripening character- istics of the new variety. Standard Fruit officials maintained that sales of Giant Cavendish fell sharply when there was an abundance of Gros Michel fruit on the market (*Correo del Norte,* 12 February 1958). In 1957 the company constructed an experimental boxing plant in Honduras where workers removed bananas from their stems and cooled them in a water bath before packing them into corrugated boxes of uniform weights. After two years of trial marketing, Stan- dard executives deemed boxed bananas "the greatest innovation in the history of the banana industry" and began commercial shipments of boxed fruit under the trade name "Cabana."[26]

United Fruit conducted its own trials with boxed fruit shortly after the com- pany began converting its farms to Cavendish varieties. By July 1961 the com- pany reported that it was "moving ahead" with banana boxing (United Fruit Company 1961). One year later, United Fruit had forty packing plants in Hon- duras alone. Company executives, like their counterparts at Standard Fruit, ag- gressively promoted boxed bananas as a marketing tool: "Boxing has cleared the way for developments in merchandising which have never been possible before in the banana business. We are now ready to consider changing our busi- ness from the sale of a commodity item to the sale of a branded, identifiable item, which, if adopted, will enable us to advertise *our* bananas, instead of ba- nanas generally" (Arthur, Houck, and Beckford 1968, 151)

By transforming the banana from a commodity to a retail product distin- guishable by a brand name the companies sought to create demand for a higher- priced, "premium" export banana (ibid.). In order to ensure consistent quality, United Fruit created an executive position, director of quality control, that was responsible for establishing and maintaining new standards of quality. The company's advertising department revived the Chiquita icon first introduced to consumers in the mid-1940s. Marketing material produced by the company for supermarkets in the 1960s featured oversized Chiquita-brand stickers bearing a Mirandaesque icon of a woman bearing a fruit-topped hat and the phrase "this seal outside means the best inside."[27]

In 1969 United Fruit continued to exploit the memory of Carmen Miranda (who died in 1955) by sponsoring a search in Latin America for two women to be "Señorita Chiquita USA" and "Señorita Chiquita Europe" (United Fruit Company 1969, 4–5). The winners, Ximena Iragorri of Colombia and Ana Maria Gonzalez of Guatemala, were young and petite and had prior experience working in television and modeling. As United Fruit promotional material noted, "Just as another famous Chiquita — Elsa Miranda — became known for her exotic hats, the inheritors of her title are expected to attract lots of attention with their mod banana-looking outfits." Not surprisingly, yellow dominated a wardrobe that included a "short, flippy little petal dress," a "floating chiffon dress," a "banana-kini," and a "sleek jumpsuit." However, if company publicity portrayed Iragorri and Gonzalez as sexy Latin singles, both the cosmopolitan backgrounds of the two women (the trilingual Iragorri had attended a French school in the Hague while Gonzalez learned English in a California high school) and the contest prize — a college scholarship — hinted at the changes in women's status that had occurred since World War II. In fact, United Fruit explicitly linked the popularity of its Miss Chiquita revival to consumer nostalgia for an era when antiwar protestors, feminists, hippies, and civil-rights activists did not threaten social order and ideas about morality (United Brands 1972, 7).

The Chiquita brand and image redefined what constituted a quality banana by emphasizing features such as bunch symmetry, the fullness of individual bananas, and blemish-free peels that ripened uniformly. In order to bear the Chiquita label in 1970, a bunch of bananas had to be a minimum of eight inches long and free of a long list of "defects," defects that primarily affected the visual appearance of the fruit rather than its flavor or nutritional quality (United Brands 1970, VI–6). Standard Fruit also based its quality ratings on the number of "outward defects" and the "fresh appearance" of the peel. As one former Standard Fruit employee noted, the destemming, washing, and boxing process virtually eliminated "in-farm defects" and enabled the company to export "essentially blemish-free" fruit (Muery 1984, 46).

The goal of improving quality by cutting down on in-transit bumping and bruising was by no means a new one. Banana companies had experimented with crating and bagging "select" fruit in the tropics as early as the 1920s. Some fruit jobbers in the United States began destemming the fruit and packing it in boxes for shipment to retail outlets prior to the 1940s. In the early 1950s jobbers tried placing colored bands bearing the name "Chiquita" around "consumer-sized units" of bananas (United Fruit Company Annual Report 1948; United Fruit Company Annual Report 1950). United Fruit's 1951 annual shareholder report noted that selling banded bananas was "particularly suited" for self-service supermarkets that increasingly dominated the grocery business in the United States (United Fruit Company Annual Report 1951; United Fruit Company Annual Report 1954). Thus, the emphasis on quality that accompanied the shift to boxed Cavendish varieties represented less of a sharp break in marketing strategies than an evolution of preexisting ones.

The new banana varieties and changing quality standards introduced in the 1960s altered production processes. Both United Fruit and Standard Fruit began applying heavy doses of nitrogen-rich fertilizers to their farms in order to boost yields. They also incorporated a host of other agrochemicals, including insecticides, herbicides, fungicides, and nematicides designed to increase output of premium quality fruit (Bourgois 1989; Soluri 1998). Company research agendas, after devoting decades of attention to Panama Disease, now shifted to finding controls for fungi and insects that discolored and / or scarred peels "in view of the importance of unblemished fruit in the Chiquita quality program" (United Fruit Company Annual Report 1966). In 1969 United Fruit's annual research report noted that fruit-spot diseases caused greater losses of bananas and "reduction in quality scores" than all other diseases and pests combined. The company's fruit-spot control program included fungicide treatments and the use of polyethylene bags to protect stems of maturing fruit (United Fruit Company Annual Report 1970). Threats to the delicate Cavendish peel did not end with harvesting. The cardboard boxes in which destemmed bananas were packed created an environment favorable to a variety of bacteria and fungi capable of rendering the fruit commercially unacceptable (United Fruit Company Annual Report 1960). In the mid-1960s the fruit companies addressed this problem by bathing cut bananas in fungicidal solutions (United Fruit Company Annual Report 1963; United Fruit Company Annual Report 1965; United Fruit Company Annual Report 1968).

For workers, the Cavendish era brought new opportunities and risks. Large numbers of women found employment in packing plants. Fieldwork remained largely a male domain, but new production techniques altered daily and seasonal tasks. For example, harvesting became less arduous due to the introduction of dwarf varieties and mechanized means of transporting fruit from fields to packing stations. The tedious work of weeding with machetes gave way to the less-taxing task of applying chemical herbicides with backpack sprayers. The application of herbicides and other agrochemicals brought workers into regular contact with a number of toxic substances capable of producing both acute and long-term health effects. The thousands of male workers who became sterile following prolonged exposure to the nematicide DBCP on Standard Fruit plantations in Costa Rica and Honduras during the late 1960s and 1970s are the most widely publicized, but by no means the only, workers who suffered health problems linked to chemical exposure (Thrupp 1991).

CONCLUSION

Consumers in the United States shaped landscapes and livelihoods in export banana zones both by creating a market demand (i.e., quantity) and by demonstrating preferences for certain kinds of bananas (i.e., quality). North Americans have eaten billions of bananas over the past century, but not just any old variety satisfied them: the banana trade was built around a very particular notion of what constituted a banana. However, "consumer preference" is at best an imprecise term and at worst downright misleading. To judge by the evidence, intermediaries—brokers, wholesalers, jobbers, and a wide range of retailers— played a key role in defining what constituted a quality export banana. Preferences among these dealers varied somewhat by region, season, and individual idiosyncrasies, but there was little debate about what constituted a premium banana during the first half of the twentieth century: the nine-handed stem of Gros Michel fruit was the U.S. market standard. The historical explanation for the variety's popularity lay in both nineteenth-century traders' desire for a thick-skinned fruit capable of withstanding the rigors of transportation and the emergence of the United Fruit Company, whose domination of the industry enabled it to limit the range of consumer preference.

The evolution of the Gros Michel banana from novelty to a commodity of mass consumption shaped, and was shaped by, changing production practices. The rapid expansion of vertically integrated Gros Michel monocultures in the early twentieth century dramatically increased the quantity of low-cost fruit reaching U.S. consumers but accelerated regional rates of deforestation and created agroecosystems highly conducive to the spread of plant pathogens such as Panama Disease. The historical meanings of the disease are best understood in the context of the U.S. banana companies' unwillingness to replace the Gros Michel with a disease-resistant variety. The fruit companies continued to clear forests and drain wetlands in order to maintain production levels throughout the first half of the twentieth century. The practice could not be maintained indefinitely, and between 1956 and 1965, both Standard Fruit and United Fruit converted their farms entirely to disease-resistant Cavendish varieties. This innovation in production prompted changes in marketing strategies: the banana became a branded, retail product.

The reinvention of the Chiquita banana reflected broader changes in banana production and consumption trends. The rapid rise of Ecuador, the world's leading banana exporter by the close of the 1950s, combined with the major companies' adoption of technological innovations (high-yield varieties and fertilizer inputs), precipitated an era of chronic overproduction that would continue to affect the industry throughout the latter half of the twentieth century. Under such conditions, the heightened emphasis on quality standards can be seen as an effort to cultivate consumers' ability to recognize and desire "premium" fruit. Finally, the dominance of self-serve supermarket chain stores created a retail environment that tended to favor heavily marketed, uniform products.

The banana's life as a commodity was not limited to the breakfast table; over the course of the twentieth century, the banana served as a ubiquitous symbol in U.S. popular culture. The banana's cultural meanings were (and are) multiple, but the fruit has most often been linked to humor, zaniness, and sexuality. Since at least as far back as the 1870s, comedy sketches have deployed bananas in a variety of ways to amuse audiences. Songwriters and poets have played with the word's phonemic qualities; comedians and musicians have exploited the fruit's physical qualities to conjure everything from a penis to antidemocratic political regimes. The banana's association with humor (it is hard to imagine a serious connotation for the fruit) can be explained in part by Anglo-American perceptions of the tropics as culturally backward. From the early nineteenth century to the late twentieth, U.S. popular discourses have linked the fruit to dark, sensuous, bumbling, lazy, non-English-speaking people. The enduring use of the term *banana republic*—which first appeared in an overtly racist text—suggests that the banana continues to be a metaphor deployed in order to distance the United States from the tropical neighbors with whom it has been intimately connected for a century.

U.S. consumers witnessed a tremendous increase in the variety of tropical fruits and vegetables available in their local supermarkets during second half of the twentieth century, but none have come remotely close to approaching the banana's widespread and enduring popularity. Entering the twenty-first century, the export banana industry continues to be threatened by plant pathogens and saturated markets. In the tropics growers maintain a tenuous control over diseases by applying expensive and potentially hazardous chemical controls, but the export industry is hesitant to adopt disease-resistant varieties that may fail to be the next "golden satisfier" of consumer desires.

NOTES

1. Personal communication from Alejandro Garcia, Cuban historian, July 1999.

2. Personal communication from David W. Miller, Carnegie Mellon University, February 1999.

3. Prior to 1884, bananas were classified as "dutiable fruits and nuts" (United States Division of Statistics to Boston District Office, 12 November 1925, United States National Archive, U.S. Foreign Agricultural Service, Record Group 166 [hereafter USNA RG 166], Narrative Reports, 1904–1939," entry 5, box 343, folder "Fruits–Bananas–General, 1922–1937").

4. "Subjects on Cooking, No. 26," 1889, National Museum of American History, Washington, D.C., Warshaw Collection, "Food," box 1, folder "Arbuckles coffee."

5. Hannaford Brothers Company (Portland, Maine) price sheets, 1903–1905, National Museum of American History, Washington, D.C., Warshaw Collection, "Food," box 8, folder "Hannaford Bros. Co."

6. Louis D. Beyland, "Report on Agriculture in Jamaica, 1884–1885," 10 September 1886, United States National Archive, U.S. Department of State, Record Group 59 [hereafter USNA RG 59]. "Dispatches from U.S. Consuls in Kingston, Jamaica, British West Indies, 1976–1906," microfilm edition T 31, vol. 29.

7. George E. Hoskinson, "A Report on the Fruit Trade of the Island of Jamaica," 24 July 1884, RG 59, "Dispatches from U.S. Consuls in Kingston, Jamaica, British West Indies, 1796–1906," microfilm edition T 31, vol. 28.

8. For recipes, see "Banana Charlotte" 1897 (47–48), Lincoln 1900 (391), Moritz and Kahn 1898, and Berry 1911 (250–59).

9. The rising rates of banana consumption in the early twentieth century indicate that fears of indigestion did not diminish the fruit's popularity. However, United Fruit continued to provide consumers with advice about the proper stage of ripeness for eating bananas as late as the 1950s.

10. A 1915 article praising the United Fruit Company's accomplishments noted that for the price of one "decent" eating apple, a consumer could buy three bananas (Thompson 1915, 17). A study conducted in 1917 on the Upper East Side of Manhattan found that bananas sold for about four cents per pound, comparable in price to cooking apples and less expensive than "fancy" eating apples (Prescott 1917, 8).

11. U.S. Department of Agriculture 1957, 16; Harvard University Graduate School of Business Administration, exhibits presented for the Harvard Advertising Awards, Baker Historical Collections, "Report and Recommendations on Field Survey for the Fruit Dispatch Company" [hereafter "Field Survey for Fruit Dispatch"], vol. 8, pt. 1, ms. div. SPGD H339a. I thank Catherine LeGrand for bringing this fascinating study to my attention.

12. Miranda achieved widespread fame in Brazil before being spotted by Broadway producer Lee Schubert at a nightclub in Rio de Janeiro. Her Broadway debut in *Streets of Paris* received rave reviews in the popular press. My discussion of Miranda is based on the following sources: Enloe 1989 (chap. 6), Roberts 1993, and Solberg and Meyer 1994.

13. "Field Survey for Fruit Dispatch," vol. 8, pt. 2, pp. 14–15.

14. "Field Survey for Fruit Dispatch," vol. 8, pt. 3, p. 49.

15. "Field Survey for Fruit Dispatch," vol. 8, pt. 3, p. 18.

16. "Field Survey for Fruit Dispatch," vol. 8, pt. 3, p. 21.

17. "Field Survey for Fruit Dispatch," vol. 8, pt. 3, p. 24.

18. "Field Survey for Fruit Dispatch," vol. 8, pt. 1, p. 34.

19. In the absence of seeds, desirable varieties such as the Gros Michel had to be pollinated with seed-bearing "wild" varieties. In one experiment some 20,000 pollinated flowers yielded fewer than 200 seeds. Only seventeen seeds germinated and a mere five survived to the fruit-bearing stage (Wardlaw 1935, 116).

20. The Cuyamel Fruit Company under the leadership of Samuel Zemurray tried to export resistant varieties, but the new cultivars were "less marketable" than the Gros Michel (Ray Fox, U.S. Consul at Puerto Cortés, "Report on Commerce and Industry for the Year and Quarter Ended December, 1925," 10 February 1926, USNA RG 166, "Narrative Reports, 1904–1939," entry 5, box 343, folder "Fruits").

21. United Fruit Company, *Annual Report to the Stockholders,* 1939–53. I am grateful to Robert H. Stover for making the United Fruit Company Annual Reports available to me.

22. Graham S. Quate to State Department, 28 October 1948, USNA RG 166, "Narrative Reports, 1946–1949," entry 5, box 743, folder "Finance–Fruits."

23. A. J. Chute, to P. C. Rose, 21 February 1941, "Standard Fruit and Steamship Company Papers,"

box 8, folder 12; and John Miceli, La Ceiba, to Mr. Salvador D'Antoni, 20 October 1945, "Standard Fruit and Steamship Company Papers," box 8, folder 18.

24. A. J. Chute, La Ceiba, to P. C. Rose, New Orleans, 6 May 1944, "Standard Fruit and Steamship Company Papers," box 8, folder 15.

25. See also Hobson 1959, 2–3; United Fruit Company Annual Report 1951, 5; and United Fruit Company Annual Report 1957, 2.

26. Photocopy of Joseph S. D'Antoni to All Employees, Standard Fruit and Steamship Company, 20 April 1960, Baker Business Library, Henry B. Arthur Papers, "Banana Study: Retailing and Demand 1964–65."

27. United Fruit Sales Corporation, "Branded P.O.P Material Makes Variety of Displays," Baker Business Library, Henry B. Arthur Papers, "Banana Study: Unifruitco info / pamphlets, 1816–1968."

MARCELO BUCHELI

United Fruit Company in Latin America

During the first half of the twentieth century the United Fruit Company created a global network for producing, distributing, and marketing bananas.[1] This undertaking required substantial investments in infrastructure in Latin America and the Caribbean, including plantations, hospitals, roads, canals, docks, telegraph lines, railways, and ships. United Fruit's attempt to control all stages of the production process reflected a general shift toward vertical integration within the American economy during the late nineteenth century and early twentieth century.[2] In the post–World War II period, however, this trend—both globally and within the banana industry—has gone the other way, toward vertical *disintegration*. United Fruit has gradually pulled out of direct production, preferring to contract with domestic planters and concentrate on the global marketing of bananas.

Although several studies have examined United Fruit's emergence as a vertically integrated company, its subsequent transformation into a marketing company during the post–World War II period has received less attention. When one examines the company's history over a long period of time, from its establishment in 1899 until its transformation in 1970 into a food conglomerate, the picture looks substantially different from standard accounts. In the first half of the century, Central American military dictatorships and U.S. intervention created a safe environment for the company to engage in direct production. However, in the decades following World War II, the company faced quite a different political-economic environment, one characterized by increased labor union activity, higher taxes on exports, growing nationalism, competition from "independent" producers in Ecuador, and a technological transformation that made vertical integration less important. Well aware of these changes, the company, its shareholders, and representatives of American capitalism slowly transformed the multinational from a direct producer of bananas into a marketer of tropical fruit.

Most studies of United Fruit have focused on the company's political and social impact, and not on the company's business itself or on how it adapted to a changing political and social environment, which requires a unique set of sources and methodology. Herein, the information on the general consolidated balance of the company is taken from the United Fruit Company's *Annual Report to the Stockholders* for the years between 1900 and 1970. Data on dividends and stock prices come from the *Wall Street Journal.* The yields of other industries in the American economy during this period and some analyses (when quoted) of the company are taken from the Moody's Investors Service *Stock Survey* for the years between 1945 and 1970. Together, these sources reveal the inner workings of El Pulpo, as United Fruit was commonly called, and help explain the motives, perceptions, and forces that drove changes in its corporate strategy during the postwar period.

THE UNMAKING OF THE BANANA EMPIRE

The drive toward vertical integration within the banana business was given a gigantic boost when American entrepreneurs Minor Keith, Andrew Preston, and Lorenzo Baker merged interests and formed the United Fruit Company in 1899. In addition to banana plantations in Colombia, Keith controlled a railway network in Central America and dominated the banana market in the southeastern United States. Preston and Baker owned a steamship fleet (that would eventually become the Great White Fleet), possessed land in the Caribbean, and controlled the market in the U.S. Northeast.

Early studies viewed United Fruit's move toward vertical integration as a triumph of civilization over nature (Frederick Upham Adams 1914) or as the latest stage of imperialism (Kepner and Soothill 1935). More recent scholarship has seen the company's shift as part of a broader trend toward vertical integration within corporate America during the late nineteenth and early twentieth centuries (Robert Read 1983; Wilkins 1970; Wilkins 1974). For these authors, the reasons behind vertical integration are purely technical: ships were not fast enough, agriculture was / is uncertain, and bananas are a perishable fruit that cannot be grown in the principal places where they are marketed. Companies who wanted to market bananas had to ensure a smooth flow of fruit from production sites in Latin American to consumers in Europe and the United States.

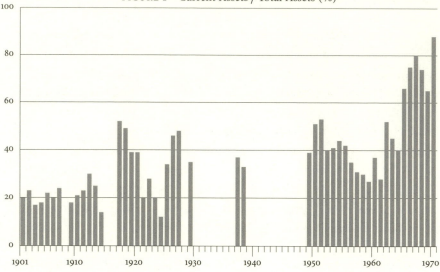

FIGURE 1 Current Assets / Total Assets (%)

The best way to reduce uncertainties was to control all stages of the production process from plantation to market. By so doing the company was—during the first half of the twentieth century—able to coordinate the entire process.

Nevertheless, three indices point to a shift—from a production company to a marketing company—in the internal structure of United Fruit during the decades after World War II: (1) when the company's current assets are weighed in relation to its total assets, it appears more and more like a marketing company during the period after 1951, and particularly after 1961 (see figure 1); (2) the importance of land and railways as a percentage of the company's tropical fixed assets decreased significantly during the same period (see figure 2), which suggests that the multinational was shifting its assets out of direct production; and (3) most important, the company was getting rid of its landholdings (see figure 3).[3] Land became less and less important as a percentage of the company's total assets. The proportion of land to total assets reached its highest point in 1902, the first year in which this measure was recorded (see figure 4). Between 1900 and 1935 the company increased its landholdings from a starting point of around 200,000 acres to a peak of 3,500,000 acres. After the forced slumber of World War II, the total number of acres decreased to levels that had been unseen

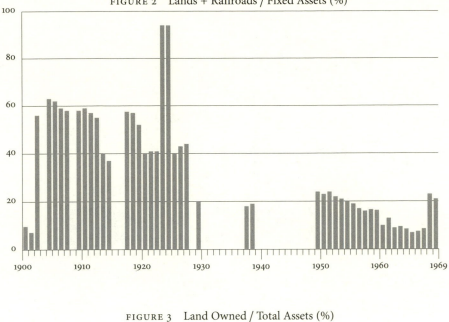

FIGURE 2   Lands + Railroads / Fixed Assets (%)

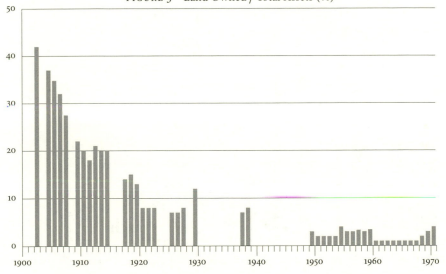

FIGURE 3   Land Owned / Total Assets (%)

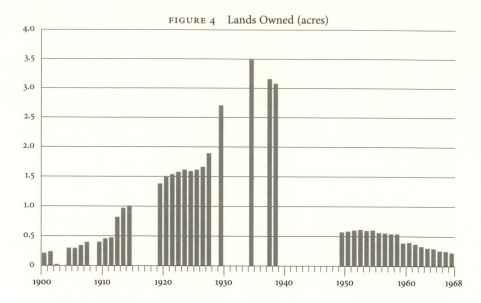

FIGURE 4   Lands Owned (acres)

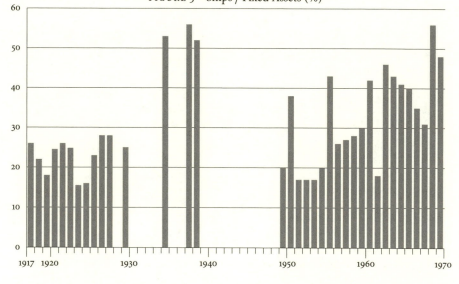

FIGURE 5   Ships / Fixed Assets (%)

since 1915, totaling around 600,000 by 1948 (see figure 3). The company further reduced its landholding in the 1950s, and in a much more aggressive way after 1960. Interestingly, the only fixed asset that did not decrease in importance during the post–World War II period was the steamship fleet — a strong indication that United Fruit was turning into a marketing company (see figure 5).

PROFITABILITY OF EL PULPO'S OPERATIONS

Given United Fruit's image throughout Latin America as El Pulpo (the octopus), one would expect to find exorbitantly high profit rates. Indeed, in some years, especially early in its history, the company did very well. However, the company's return on equity and return on assets reveal a somewhat more complicated picture characterized by declining profits, especially after World War II. *Return on equity* indicates how much income the company created from the amount of capital received from investors. *Return on assets* establishes the relationship between net income and total assets, indicating how much profit the company earns from its assets. The higher each of these ratios is, the better the company is doing.

The company's return on assets shows a variable rate for the pre–World War II period but a decreasing tendency in the postwar period. In the late 1910s, it reached levels of 30 percent, falling to around 5 percent just prior to World War II. After the war, the return on assets began at levels of around 25 percent, then fell below 5 percent in the early 1960s. In short, the return on assets peaked in the 1920s and declined dramatically in the postwar period (see figure 6). The return-on-equity ratio demonstrates a similar pattern, reaching levels of more than 20 percent in the early 1920s, then decreasing thereafter (see figure 7). During the postwar period it fell dramatically, actually having a negative value in 1970.[4]

United Fruit's profitability ratios suggest that the earlier period of the company's history, one defined by vertical integration, was actually more profitable. Why, then, did the multinational switch to a system that appears to have been less profitable in the long run? Was this decision simply a strategic miscalculation, or were there other factors that compelled the company to divest itself of landholdings and production?

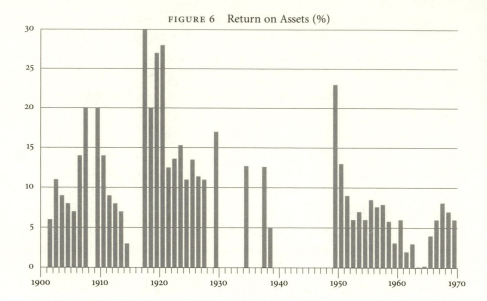

FIGURE 6   Return on Assets (%)

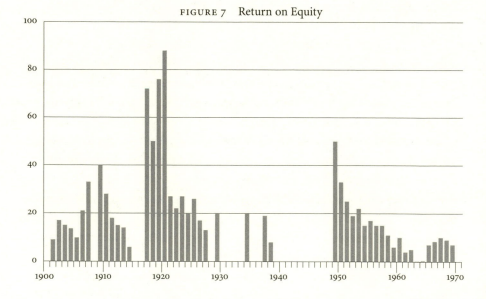

FIGURE 7   Return on Equity

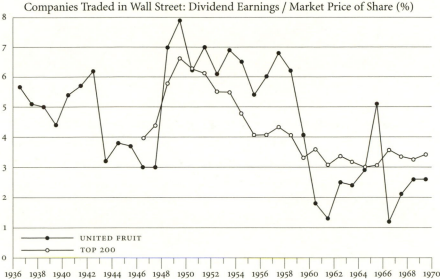

FIGURE 8   Comparative Yield on Common Stock, United Fruit vs. Top 200
Companies Traded in Wall Street: Dividend Earnings / Market Price of Share (%)

UNITED FRUIT
TOP 200

UNITED FRUIT'S RISKS AND SHAREHOLDERS FEARS

Why did the company continue to divest, that is, pull out of direct production and switch its resources into marketing, despite the fact that the strategy
resulted in decreased profit rates? Part of the explanation has to do with the
expectations of investors. One of the most accepted ratios that investors use in
order to analyze the risk of an investment is the yield on common stock. The
higher the yield, the riskier the investment is considered.

A comparison of the yield on common stock for United Fruit and the average yield calculated by the Moody's Investors Service for the top 200 companies traded in Wall Street reveals relative risk ratios.[5] If the company's risk ratio
is higher than those of the top 200 companies, it is considered a riskier investment than these companies, and vice versa. The results of this calculation
clearly show that before 1949 United Fruit was considered less risky by investors
than after that year (see figure 8). Perceived risk increased from 1950 until 1959.
From 1960 on, however, the company was considered a less risky investment
because it announced that it would pull out of direct production and depend

more heavily on contract producers (United Fruit Company Annual Report 1960; United Fruit Company Annual Report 1961).

The more involved the company was in direct production, the riskier it was perceived to be by the market. Where did this risk come from? Why this perception? Why this close relationship with the internal transformation of the company? Answers to these questions emerge through analysis of the company's own views of its problems as revealed in its annual reports and as balanced by the perception of independent financial analysts such as Moody's Investors Service. Moody's is (and was) one of the two most important analysts in the United States. Because negative evaluations from Moody's can prove fatal to a company's share prices, no publicly traded American corporation can afford to ignore Moody's recommendations. This was especially true during the period under consideration, when the stock market was dominated by major institutional investors.

Before 1949, Moody's considered United Fruit a fairly good investment option. As late as 1946 the company was even included among Moody's "Recommended Investment Stocks." By 1949, however, doubt about the company's activities emerged, and although Moody's still considered United Fruit a good option, it attributed the company's decreasing profits to rising social and political problems in Central America. In its April 1949 stock survey Moody's warned that "future political developments remain an uncertainty" (528). This year coincides with a gloomy letter from United Fruit's president to the stockholders: "Whereas at the beginning of the year the Company had expectations of exceeding 1948 both as to tonnage of bananas marketed and sales volume, conditions arose during the year which made this impossible. Labor trouble in Guatemala interrupted shipments from that country for six weeks; labor trouble in Colombia and Costa Rica of shorter duration also resulted in the loss of some fruit from these countries" (United Fruit Company Annual Report 1949, 7).

The market reacted to the company's situation by raising its risk ratio (see figure 8). Moody's overall concern emanated from labor unrest in United Fruit's Central American divisions. These concerns were highlighted in the opening statements of three analyses from 1950 and 1951. In March 1950 Moody's wrote, "The lower earnings last year were caused by abnormal weather conditions and labor troubles in several important Latin American areas" (561). In the following two years Moody's saw conflicts with the Guatemalan labor movement as an important issue affecting the company's stock. In its November 1951 stock survey, for example, Moody's assessed United Fruit's prospects as follows: "Outcome of the company's wage dispute with Guatemalan labor could have longer term effects than the mere reduction in earnings this year. If United Fruit were to abandon production there, other companies would probably move in and develop a competitive position. Or, if the company compromises the issue, labor in other countries would probably demand similar concessions" (133). Moody's November 1952 survey noted, "The 25% price decline of this stock from its 1951 all-time high can be attributed primarily to the impact upon earnings of a hurricane and a six month work stoppage at the company's Guatemala plantations" (157).

The company's report to its stockholders was no more optimistic:

During recent years banana production in Guatemala has been declining due to frequent windstorms, inroads of disease, and the absence of conditions conducive to the planting of new cultivations. At the same time labor costs have been rising sharply. The company has always paid wages far greater than those paid by others in Guatemala for similar work, and up to the last few years its labor relations have been most satisfactory. During recent years, however, extremists who are not employees of the Company have kept the laborers in a constant state of unrest. . . . To date the Company's offer to negotiate participation contracts with Guatemala similar to those negotiated with other countries has not been accepted. (United Fruit Company Annual Report 1951, 9–10)

Moody's suggested that problems in Central America were not limited to labor but were related to potential difficulties that United Fruit could have with local governments. Moody's proved prophetic. United Fruit faced its most infamous problem in 1951, when Jacobo Arbenz was elected president of Guatemala. With United Fruit in mind, Arbenz developed the Agrarian Reform Law and expropriated some of the company's uncultivated lands in 1953. The company considered its conflict with Arbenz serious and gave a long explanation of it in its annual report, but company president Kenneth Redmond was unable to assure the shareholders that the company would prevail.

The Company has filed with the Department of State, for presentation to the Government of Guatemala, a claim for just compensation for the expropriation including the appraised present value of the lands and improvements expropriated, and the damage caused to the Company by depriving it of its reserve banana lands and greatly shortening the useful life of its expensive facilities on the west coast. Since the lands have actually been expropriated, the acreage has been dropped from the records. . . . Under the present conditions the Company is not planting additional acreage in Guatemala, and the acreage of banana cultivations in production will become less each year. . . . As long as the political atmosphere remains inimical to American enterprise, the Company must of necessity follow a policy of retrenchment. (United Fruit Company Annual Report 1954, 4)

But Moody's was worried about the broader implications, as its March 1953 survey made clear: "This is not a question of immediate crucial importance to the company's earning power. More important is whether Guatemalan events are indicative of what may happen elsewhere in Latin America where United Fruit operates" (561). Arbenz was eventually thwarted by opposition from certain sectors of the Guatemalan Army, the U.S. Department of State, the Organization of American States, and Guatemalan large land owners. Colonel Castillo Armas, who took power after the coup, overturned Arbenz's social reforms and returned the expropriated lands to United Fruit. The company reported the change with great relief to its shareholders and highlighted the new negotiations it was holding with other Central American governments regarding taxes and welfare: "The overthrow of the Communist-dominated government of Guatemala, while causing a cessation of shipments from that country for a period of about three weeks, was a decidedly favorable development which will have far-reaching effects in the future" (United Fruit Company Annual Report 1954, 3).

The company also reported its cooperation with the new government in land distribution and welfare policies, and highlighted the negotiations it was holding with other Central American governments regarding taxation, land, and labor. However, despite the company's optimism, Moody's was skeptical. In 1954 it published an article—"United Fruit's Prospects Under Political Pressures"—that suggested that problems in Guatemala reflected United Fruit's general inability to manipulate Latin American governments in the postwar period (as an unfavorable tax policy in Costa Rica quickly confirmed). Three years after Arbenz's overthrow, Moody's still warned, "Further political disturbances in the Caribbean area can never be ruled out" (March 1955, 589). Similarly, in its December 1956 stock survey Moody reported that "United Fruit has finances that are proportionately among the strongest of any United States corporation. . . . Unfortunately, however, the company's operations are subject to natural and foreign political hazards beyond its control" (75).

The political risks were not limited to Central America. In 1954 the United States Department of Justice filed a lawsuit against United Fruit for violating antitrust legislation. As a result, the company had to sell its holdings in the International Railways of Central America (IRCA) in 1956. In 1959 the company also reported bad news from the Caribbean. First, the Cuban revolutionary government was expropriating land.[6] Second, in Costa Rica (a country with a very different political regime), United Fruit clashed with the government around labor legislation and was rewarded with a massive strike by workers.

> In November the Congress of Costa Rica passed, over the President's veto, a law requiring all employers to pay labor a year-end bonus. As some of the terms of the law were clearly discriminatory and in direct violation of the company's operating contracts with the Government, the company refused to comply with these improper and discriminatory provisions. Certain elements used this as a means to provoke an illegal strike and by threats and intimidation prevented labor from continuing to work. (United Fruit Company Annual Report 1959, 6)

Following these events, Moody's began to advise investors to look elsewhere, as is clear from its August 1959 survey: "United Fruit has been hurt by political troubles in several Latin American countries and periodic weather damage to its banana crops. . . . Management is currently attempting to combat its problems . . . but any appreciable effect will be far in the future. . . . We therefore see no reason to hold the stock, and would switch into U.S Rubber for better prospects" (354–55).

The company also faced competition from the rapid emergence of a fairly "independent" banana industry in Ecuador, which grew to be the world's largest producer by the mid-1950s (see figure 9; Larrea Maldonado 1987, 46). Ecua-

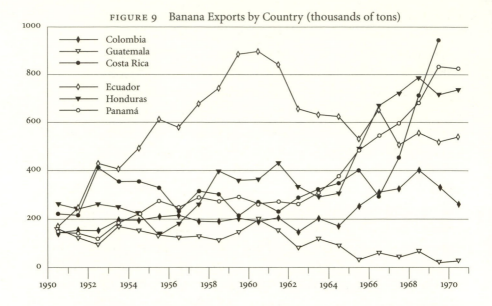

FIGURE 9 Banana Exports by Country (thousands of tons)

dor was unique in the sense that the government helped to maintain the industry in the hands of domestic planters. The dramatic increase in exports from Ecuador threatened United Fruit by leading to a general decrease in international banana prices (United Fruit Company Annual Report 1959, 5; United Fruit Company Annual Report 1960, 2).

Ecuador had a tremendous comparative advantage in terms of production costs and was seen as a real problem by United Fruit's president.

> [In Ecuador] the local growers were not required to furnish housing, schools, hospitals, the necessary access roads, port facilities, as United Fruit had to at its own cost [in Central America]. . . . Wages of banana workers in these areas were also far less than United Fruit paid its workers in other producing countries. The small compensatory tax put on export bananas in Ecuador was insignificant compared with the costs to United Fruit elsewhere. . . . Large quantities of bananas became available at costs less than United Fruit's costs. (Thomas Sunderland quoted in Arthur, Houck, and Beckford 1968, 147)

A study made by Harvard Business School also pointed to the rise of Ecuadorian production as one of the most worrisome issues faced by United Fruit in the early 1960s. According to this study, the company had just two options:

TABLE 1 Comparative Costs of Banana Production

	Ecuador	Central America
Cost of opening a banana plantation ($ / hectare), 1958	120	2,000–3,100
Workers / hectare, 1964	0.5	0.60–0.75
Cost of harvested bananas (cents), 1958	1.16	1.98
Share of total freight plus unloading of the CIF Price, 1964	36%	32%

SOURCE: Statistics drawn from Valles 1968 (115, 117, 119, 123, 136, 137).

(1) to get rid of all its Central American production and associate producers and buy only from Ecuadorian producers in the open market; or (2) drastically reduce its costs and increase its productivity in the areas it operated (ibid., 148). The company could only survive if a radical change was made.

THE BANANA EMPIRE STRIKES BACK

It was under these circumstances that United Fruit appointed Thomas Sunderland president of the company. In his 1960 letter to shareholders Sunderland announced that the company was going through a long-range readjustment program. The main transformations included a switch from the Gros Michel to Cavendish banana varieties, a growing reliance on contract producers, an increase in purchases from Ecuador, and a general diversification of operations (United Fruit Company Annual Report 1960, 2). Due to the company's withdrawal from direct production, the total income from sales of tropical properties increased dramatically from $2,871,094 in 1960 to $16,483,492 in 1961 (United Fruit Company Annual Report 1961, 1). As a result, the company was perceived as much less risky after 1960 (see figure 8). Indeed, as a Harvard Business School study noted, although United Fruit could produce bananas more cheaply on its own, it made sense to get out of direct production for a number of reasons that were not strictly economic in nature.

By encouraging the nationals to enter the banana industry, Sunderland believed, United Fruit could contribute to the development of stable conditions in the tropics (i.e., aid in the creation of a growing middle class), gain partners who would be valuable allies in the development of joint interests, and reduce the frequent attacks by "trouble makers" against United Fruit as a large land owner and employer, despite the fact that as a straight matter of production United Fruit could probably produce bananas at less cost on its own (Arthur, Houck, and Beckford 1968, 148).

Despite United Fruit's positive outlook, Moody's remained only cautiously optimistic about the company's prospects, writing in March 1962, "Symbolic of management's innovations is its policy of selling Latin American land holdings to local interests while contracting to take their produce. This defense against possible expropriations has had mixed success, but it has aided in a 37% cut in the number of 'tropical' employees in the last four years" (669). A year later, in January, Moody's maintained a similar attitude: "Fourth quarter earnings were hurt by windstorm damage last summer, and the continuing longshore-men's strike. This may cool near-by investor enthusiasm for the stock, but with the price still well below book value, and the longer range outlook brighter, we would hold it" (772). Nevertheless, once the company presented a plan (in 1966) that emphasized ongoing withdrawal from direct production, Moody's opin-ions improved. In 1967 Moody's viewed United Fruit's future with optimism and advised investors to hold the stock because of its potential growth.

The replacement of the Gros Michel strain of banana with the Cavendish also proved to be successful, improving productivity (now mostly under the asso-ciate producers' control) and (from 1966) return on equity. The increase of the Central American productivity thanks to Cavendish was enough to counterbal-ance the low production costs in Ecuador such that by the late 1960s that coun-try had lost its comparative advantage (Glover and Larrea Maldonado 1991, 95). Central American production increased after 1965, quickly reaching levels similar to those of Ecuador (see figure 9 and table 2).

In the late 1960s the company's management made it clear to shareholders that it was aware of the social and political changes happening in Latin America and that the company had no other choice than to adapt to them. In a retro-spective analysis of United Fruit's operations, company president Herbert Cor-nuelle wrote, "No matter how successful we are in this process, we still will be perceived, however, I am sure, as a threat to national independence and sover-eignty. The fact that we are domiciled in a foreign country and that we are big assures that" (United Fruit Company Annual Report 1968).

Two years later, Eli Black, president of the renamed United Brands, wrote:

TABLE 2   Productivity of the Central American
Banana Industry, 1947–1970 (tons per hectare)

	Costa Rica	Guatemala	Panama	Honduras
1947	621.9	870.1	939.9	870
1948	762.5	860	1,163	860
1949	957.4	513	1,196	513
1950	878.9	712	1,051	712
1951	841.1	515	1,030	515
1952	955.3	252	810	252
1953	849.3	796	825	796
1954	919.1	811.1	904	811
1955	878.2	646.6	1,043	646
1956	663.2	664	909	663
1957	1,045.4	627	1,071	627
1958	1,111	528	930	528
1959	756.4	595	985	595
1960	964.7	829	839	829
1961	756.8	830	917	830
1962	843.2	552	867	552
1963	764.5	948	852	948
1964	928.9	1,734	984	1,734
1965	1,082.9	738	1,082	739
1966	1,253.1	1,275	1,262	1,275
1967	1,339	1,763	1,598	1,763
1968	1,546.9	2,330	1,652	2,330
1969	1,982	2,351	1,952	2,351
1970	2,203	2,561	2,386	2,561

while these operations are in stable countries with enlightened governments, the fact is that all Latin American countries are being swept by strong winds of nationalist aspiration. [The company] knows that it must adjust to change in Latin America. It is adjusting. . . . One of the most sensitive areas is that of land use policies. . . . Since 1952 the Company has divested itself of 65% of its holdings in the four countries. Many thousand acres have been given to the governments for distribution; the remainder has been sold to individuals and firms. . . . In several countries land has been given to unions to build low-cost housing financed by the company. (United Fruit Company Annual Report 1970, 35)

The 1970 merger of United Fruit with AMK to create United Brands Company was the event that definitively marked the end of the transformation process. The company became part of a giant food conglomerate that included processed foods and meat packing. The 1970 letter to the shareholders in the company's annual report emphasized that this was not a banana company anymore. The new company was not free of political conflicts, however. In 1974 it faced a so-called banana war around taxation policies (see Raynolds herein). This marked the beginning of a new era of local governmental participation in the banana export business and led to the establishment of the Unión de Países Exportadores de Banano (UPEB).

CONCLUSIONS

The grasping and ever expanding "Banana Empire" that Kepner and Soothill described in their 1930s classic has had its counterparts in the political and literary imaginations of Latin Americans throughout the twentieth century. From the leaf storm that swept through García Márquez's Macondo to the sinister interests that installed Asturias's Green Pope, United Fruit has been perceived by scholars, activists, and writers alike as an implacable and overwhelming force throughout the hemisphere. Yet even as these images were being fixed firmly in the minds of the company's opponents, the conditions that had given rise to United Fruit's unrivalled control over land and national governments were rapidly changing. By the mid-twentieth century altered conditions in Latin America obliged the company to transform itself or die. In Guatemala, Honduras, and Costa Rica, where national governments had once virtually surrendered sovereignty over the company's areas of operation, the company found itself confronting increasingly assertive workers, less compliant national officials, and growing demands from would-be landowners. More ominously for the company, by midcentury similar pressures were growing throughout the hemisphere, all of which threatened United Fruit's ability to marshal the quantities of land and labor necessary to maintain production on a large scale.

These events and their relationship to investors' perceptions of the company are summarized in table 3, which compares yields on the company's common stock with the average yield calculated by Moody's for the top 200 companies traded in Wall Street while relating the events reported by United Fruit's management as major issues affecting the company's earnings.[7] The yield on common stock measures how risky the market perceives an investment to be; the higher the yield, the higher the risk perception.[8] A calculation of the yield in itself does not say much, as investors need to know if a stock is more or less risky than other stocks in which they could invest their money. When United Fruit's yield is compared with that of the top 200 companies, it becomes possible to know whether the company was considered more or less risky than other investments (see table 3).[9] The data show clearly that the risk perception of United Fruit decreased when the company diminished its direct operations in Latin America and, therefore, reduced its labor and political problems in the region.

As labor unions grew more powerful, as governments sought more revenue from exports, and as local elites became less reliable agents of foreign capital, the company witnessed an erosion of the political and economic control on which its vertical integration rested. Simultaneously, at home, the company could no longer count on the unconditional support of the U.S. government, at least where direct military intervention was concerned. All of these developments contributed to a perception among investors in midcentury that the political and social environment in Latin America was an increasingly risky place to do business. Examination of the data demonstrates how United Fruit adapted to these perceptions, eventually choosing to withdraw from direct production and become a marketing company. These changes were made possible in part by the technical improvements of the post–World War II period in the banana industry. However much nationalist politicians and labor leaders created the conditions leading to the company's disinvestment from Latin America, these corporate policies were intended not as concessions to company adversaries but as strategies to please both financial analysts and investors. The "octopus" that created the "Banana Empire" in the early twentieth century consciously dismantled that empire in later years, largely to ensure itself a continued place on top of the banana world.

TABLE 3   Comparison of the Yield on Common Stock for United Fruit
and for the Top 200 Companies Traded on Wall Street

Year	Yield: United Fruit	Yield: Top 200	Issues significantly affecting United Fruit's earnings
1946	3.0	3.95	
1947	3.0	4.38	
1948	7.0	5.98	
1949	7.9	6.62	Labor problems in Guatemala, Colombia, and Costa Rica decrease production and interrupt shipments
1950	6.2	6.27	
1951	7.0	6.12	Labor unrest in Guatemala plantations. The company has problems solving the conflict.
1952	6.1	5.50	Slow recovery of the Guatemalan operations after the strike.
1953	6.9	5.49	Expropriation of some of the company's lands in Guatemala under Jacobo Arbenz. The company reports problems in the negotiations.
1954	6.5	4.75	The U.S. Department of Justice files an antitrust lawsuit against United Fruit. The company faces a ten-week strike in Honduras.
1955	5.4	4.06	Big losses due to weather problems.
1956	6.0	4.07	Heavy windstorms provoke new losses.
1957	6.8	4.33	The company loses a lawsuit from a group of International Railways of Central America shareholders.
1958	6.2	4.05	The company announces the change of banana from Gros Michel to Cavendish to decrease potential losses from windstorms and Panama Disease.
1959	4.1	3.31	Conflict with the new Costa Rican government over "discriminatory" labor legislation, followed by big strike in the fields.

TABLE 3   Continued

Year	Yield: United Fruit	Yield: Top 200	Issues significantly affecting United Fruit's earnings
			The Cuban Agrarian Reform Law makes virtually all the company's lands subject to expropriation. The company has little hope of succeeding in a conflict with the revolutionary government.
1960	1.8	3.60	The company announces a long-term plan for restructuring, a plan that assigns a much larger role to associate producers.
1961	1.3	3.07	The company reports no labor problems parallel to the larger participation of associate producers.
1962	2.5	3.37	Losses due to windstorms.
1963	2.4	3.17	
1964	2.9	3.00	
1965	5.1	3.06	The company announces that it will lose about 15 percent of its gross revenue when the antitrust legislation consent is implemented.
1966	1.2	3.57	
1967	2.1	3.35	
1968	2.3	3.25	
1969	2.6	3.42	

SOURCE: Yields calculated with information taken from the *Wall Street Journal* and the *United Fruit Company Annual Reports*. Information on earnings issues taken from United Fruit Company annual reports.

APPENDIX: CALCULATION OF UNITED FRUIT'S RISK LEVEL

The risk ratio of United Fruit is measured by calculating the yield on common stock, a widely accepted ratio. The ratio is calculated by dividing the share's dividend earnings by its market price, and it indicates how much of a return an investor would have if he / she purchased a share of the company. The higher this ratio is, the riskier the investment is considered. To calculate United Fruit's risk ratio, I proceeded as follows: First, I took the information on the stock price and dividends from the *Wall Street Journal* as published on the last day of each month for the years between 1936 and 1970. Even though this information is published daily, this method is considered a good proxy. Second, I calculated the year's average stock price and dividend using the mentioned monthly information. Third, I calculated the company's annual yield using those averages. Fourth, I compared these yields with the annual yields calculated by the Moody's Investors Service for the top 200 companies traded in Wall Street. In the years of 1947, 1949, and 1968 Moody's published not an annual but a monthly yield for the top 200. For those three years I calculated a year average with the monthly information.

NOTES

1. The author wishes to thank Zephyr Frank, Avner Greif, Stephen Haber, Claudia Linares, Noël Maurer, Luis Fernando Medina, the anonymous referees, and the editors for very useful comments on earlier versions of this paper. The usual caveats apply.

2. Between 1895 and 1899 more than 1,800 firms disappeared into consolidations. More than half of those consolidations absorbed more than 40 percent of their industries and nearly a third absorbed in excess of 70 percent (see Lamoreaux 1985, 2).

3. During the period before World War II the company did not include depreciation on fixed assets in its annual report. I took the market value of those goods for these years.

4. This trend holds true despite the fact that the company tried to diversify its holdings during this period. Bananas remained the main source of income / profit for United Fruit prior to 1970, representing more than 60 percent of its sales of products and services.

5. For an explanation of how I calculated this yield, see the appendix at the end of this essay.

6. In that year's annual report the company's president wrote, "The estimated present value of these [expropriated] properties is two and one-half million dollars. Occupation of these lands has not been carried out in conformance with the terms of the law. The company is taking every legal recourse open to it under the laws of Cuba against these illegal occupations, but thus far without results" (United Fruit Company Annual Report 1959, 8).

7. Opinions about the company did not change only among investors or within the company itself; a recent study shows that the American media, as represented in the *New York Times,* also changed their perception of United Fruit throughout the twentieth century. Before the 1940s, the company was portrayed as "civilizer" of the Caribbean and as an important ally in World War II, whereas after the war the media became more concerned with the way the company managed its labor conflicts (see Ian Read 2000).

8. For a detailed explanation of how I calculated United Fruit's yield on common stock see the appendix at the end of this essay.

9. The comparison between United Fruit's and the top 200 companies' yields is also shown in figure 8.

CENTRAL AND SOUTH AMERICA

PHILIPPE BOURGOIS

One Hundred Years of United Fruit Company Letters

T he United Fruit Company is the quintessential model for the institutional form of the multinational corporation that changed the face of
the world during the twentieth century. Legally established in 1899 in
New Jersey through the merger and acquisition of several different banana production and import companies operating in Central America and the Caribbean, it was a pioneer of capitalist globalization. Through vertical and horizontal integration, the United Fruit Company consolidated the monopoly of
both production and commercialization within a global free-market capitalist
context. At the same time, it was buttressed by the political, military, and economic might of the U.S. government. It replaced the predecessor international
corporate form, which had dominated the colonial era through government-
sponsored international trade monopolies.

The following selection of internal archival documents of the United Fruit
Company, dating from 1914 to 1970, provides an intimate view of day-to-day
interactions and concerns at the highest, most confidential levels of United
Fruit Company management. The documents consist of discussions, reports,
and directives by managers, lawyers, accountants, undercover informants, and
lobbyists documenting strategies for reducing taxes, increasing labor discipline,
consolidating landholdings, and maximizing political influence. The documents make the bureaucratic logic of monopoly capital during its era of height-
ening consolidation come alive in intimate detail. They also provide vibrant
testimony to the repeated and diverse attempts by workers (and occasionally
host-country governments) to organize in defense of their rights on the plantation.

Some of the letters and reports from the archives reproduced here make
the United Fruit Company appear to be an omnipotent total institution — à
la Erving Goffman (1961) — capable of controlling not just political and eco-

nomic outcomes but even the basic tenor of social and psychological relations. Other documents reveal that the company, no matter how powerful and effectively organized, was often unable to achieve its will unilaterally whether it be through bribery, interpersonal cajoling, direct threat, manipulation of data, physical violence, or more impersonal economic institutional might. The archives demonstrate that management was often divided over strategy and, more important, that company policies were frequently inconsistent with the pursuit of long-term corporate interests and even short-term bottom-line profits. The archives provide a bird's-eye view into the ideological blinders worn by company officials. By demonstrating the social, political, and even cultural considerations that drove technical management decisions, they complement Marcelo Bucheli's essay in this volume, which analyzes United Fruit Company production-versus-commercialization restructuring strategies based on the financial statistics published in annual reports. They reveal the impetus for confrontational action generated by what Pierre Bourdieu (and Wacquant 1992) would call the company's "field of power," from debates in Boston boardrooms to bullets in Central American drainage ditches. Michel Foucault (1978) could have used these documents to describe the process of "governmentality" on corporate plantations, had the shaping of Latin American worker struggles in the context of the rise of multinational corporations in the twentieth century been one of his political and intellectual concerns.

Often company managers reveal themselves to be trapped in bizarre and often zealously abusive policies because of their ideological blinders and because of the force of the pathways shaping their actions and beliefs. In particular, the documents that focus on managerial manipulation of the ethnic composition of the labor force provide an especially rich display of the pseudoscientific racialist theories upheld by the elite of the United States with respect to how best to administer "natives" or "tropical laborers." In its attempts to jockey for advantage the company drew from a wide repertoire of strategies operating at very different social levels: from the macropolitical economic such as the manipulation of the size of the local labor supply, the killing of labor union organizers, and the expulsion of leaders of ethnic-rights movements, to the micropsychological, including subtle evaluations of the intelligence of "communist agitators," profiles by confidential informants of the vanity and drinking habits of clandestine union organizers, and the promotion of sports events and popular movies to distract workers from working and living conditions.

I WAS NOT TRAINED in archival research when I sought access to the plantation to conduct fieldwork for my dissertation. As a cultural anthropologist, I assumed the bulk of my doctoral dissertation research data would be participant-observation fieldwork notes supplemented by a dozen or so oral-history tape recordings and maybe one basic questionnaire. This is indeed what I collected during most of the eighteen months (from mid-1982 through 1984) that I spent living in the workers' barracks of the Chiriqui Land Company, a United Fruit Company subsidiary that spanned the borders of Costa Rica and Panama. I conducted my interviews in the context of relaxed, free-flowing conversations. Much of the time I simply hung out and made friends—although, admittedly, often strategically—with whoever was willing to talk to me.

Ironically, this purposefully subjective anthropological style of interaction for obtaining research data resulted in my fortuitously stumbling into full access to a century of United Fruit Company archives containing management's most confidential documents. At the time, approximately one year into my fieldwork, I had become an almost mascotlike figure to management and workers alike. The managers both on the plantation and at United Fruit Company headquarters in New York City and San José, Costa Rica, granted me permission to live on their property and interview their workers. The Costa Rican subsidiary headquarters even provided me with a formal letter of introduction to facilitate fuller access to their plantations. Consequently, they encouraged me to browse through their filing cabinets after hours without any supervision and even to hand copy into notebooks data from their current labor relations files and production statistics. Local managers liked me and were comfortable with my presence in their offices and homes. They became bored, however, by my constant questions on every aspect of the minutiae of management activities.

My primary research topic was a history of the ethnic composition of the plantation labor force, but I was politically and theoretically committed to the call put out by anthropologist Laura Nader (1972) to study the rich and powerful in order to better understand the lives of the poor. Consequently, I sought ethnographic information on the local political economy of ethnicity and culture both from the workers and from the local and international power-holders. Although I lived in the laborers' barracks, I intentionally spent long hours socializing with all levels of management, which involved activities that ranged from visits to the luxurious quarters of what was then officially called the "White Zone" (an exclusive residential neighborhood at the heart of the plantation, complete with air-conditioned club, bowling alley, and nine-hole golf course) to drinking sessions in back-alley bars. It also included home-cooked meals with foremen and day laborers in company-built dormitories, as well as in the tin- and thatch-roofed shacks of unemployed migrants, peasant squatters, and petty criminals. Most of the high-level managers were either U.S. citizens or U.S.-educated members of the upper class of Costa Rica and Panama. They were so ethnocentric and class-bounded in their worldview that they could not imagine that a polite, white, university-educated North American could be anything but racist and pro-management.

In requesting permission from company officials for access to their confidential archives I was conscientiously precise about my research interests: a history of plantation culture from its founding at the turn of the century to the present day. Labor relations during the early 1980s, when I lived on the plantation, were tense and violent. One worker was shot to death and his five-year-old daughter wounded by the rural guard during a strike three months before my arrival on the plantation, and approximately a dozen more workers were shot—several fatally—during strikes on other banana plantations during the two years that I lived in Costa Rica. To my surprise, however, my research priorities were judged to be appropriately anthropological and nonthreatening. I serendipitously obtained access to the company's historical archives precisely because of the relaxed, trusting quality of my relationship with managers, which was spawned out of the participant-observation methods of anthropology.

During the early months of my fieldwork, managers informed me that they had several years earlier received orders from central headquarters to destroy all historical archives. This was reconfirmed to me in interviews at corporate headquarters in New York and San José. By a quirk of disorganization—or perhaps because of a subversive appreciation of history by an unsung lower management hero—this did not occur on the plantation subsidiary where I was conducting fieldwork. By sheer dumb luck, I had befriended an aging warehouse foreman who one day led me to the damp, steaming attic of his semi-abandoned warehouse and told me, "You might find these old papers interesting, because you like to ask so many questions about the old days."

Tens of thousands of pages of letters and memoranda had been stuffed into four to five dozen unnumbered, mildewed, and rodent-eaten cardboard boxes. The warehouse manager told me to take whatever documents might be useful for my work since they were all meant for destruction anyway. He simply had not yet "gotten around to throwing them out." Unfortunately, there is no longer any trace of this unique archive. The warehouse was damaged in a major earthquake in 1991 and the structure was leveled. On my last visit in 2000, the foreman had passed away and his former warehouse was the site of a vacant, muddy lot.

Space constraints allow us to publish full copies of only a tiny selection from the almost 2,000 pages of letters I salvaged from that mass of decaying papers. They were selected to provide examples of management concerns and concrete corporate strategies as well as cultural styles. They are organized around three major themes: (1) the development of monopoly power relationships with host-country governments; (2) the organization of ethnic-specific strategies to increase labor control; and (3) the repression of labor discontent and labor-union organizing. The last two themes provide a contextualized meaning to the often abstract term "class struggle," demonstrating in full detail its actual practice. When I salvaged materials from the archive, I was determined as an anthropologist to go beyond the limits of the economic reductionist analysis that stunted many Marxist approaches in Latin America at that time. Simultaneously, however, I wanted to maintain at the center of my data collection the creative ways in which struggles for human dignity and economic rights shape everyday social relations—from grassroots workers organizing around economic and ethnic rights to high-level corporate power plays geared to flooding regional labor markets, lowering tax rates, acquiring inexpensive land, and promoting pro-management political values.

In the section titled "Monopoly Power" I present the correspondence of company lobbyists in the capital cities of Central America. They speak of direct, usually friendly access to presidents, generals, and dictators as well as to local-level labor inspectors and military officials. They brag about lowering taxes and changing labor laws. They even joke about misrepresenting corporate profits to elected officials. The pièce de résistance in this section is a personalized thank-you letter mentioning an enclosed $25,000 personal check written to General Torrijos of Panama by Eli Black, the CEO of the United Fruit Company in the 1970s. Four years later, Black committed suicide when it was revealed that he had paid a $1.25 million bribe to the president of Honduras, General Lopez Ariano, in order to lower banana taxes and break the power of the Union of Banana-Producing Countries (UPEB), which was founded by General Torrijos.

The core of my participant-observation project was published as a book analyzing the history of the company's ethnically based divide-and-conquer labor-control strategies (Bourgois 1989). Materials addressing ethnic policies are presented in the second section, "Ethnicity of the Labor Force," and include examples of correspondence addressing: the Bribri Amerindians whose land the Company expropriated at the turn of the century; Afro-Antillean immigrants who comprised the bulk of the labor force through the 1930s, with special emphasis on the way the company initially repressed and then accommodated Marcus Garvey and his Universal Negro Improvement Association movement; the Cuna Amerindians, with whom the United Fruit Company developed a patron-client relationship, including a paid position for a major traditional elected leader (Sahila) as labor recruiter, disciplinarian, and union buster; the Ngöbe Amerindians (referred to in these documents as the Guaymi or the Cricamola), who entered the labor force in the 1950s under extremely vulnerable conditions and at the turn of the twenty-first century constituted the majority of banana workers; and Latino laborers from all over Central America, who were recruited aggressively in the 1940s because the Afro-Antillean population was increasingly rejecting the exploitive conditions on the plantation by emigrating or by becoming small farmers on homesteaded land. In this "ethnic divide-and-conquer section" I also included letters that outlined the company's more or less conscious manipulation of ethnic and nationalist sentiments in order to promote immigration from neighboring countries and thus augment the supply of more docile labor.

In the final section, "Labor Relations," I selected a range of documents depicting the repression of labor-union organizing and strikes as well as more generic descriptions of the company's intentional flooding of regional labor supplies. These materials complement the valuable original source material on the United Fruit Company's violent repression of workers in Guatemala presented in Cindy Forster's essay in this volume. I included an urgent circular accompanied by photographs distributed by Boston headquarters to "All Tropical Division Managers," which identified labor "agitators" and "Anti-American" "red Bolshevists," as they were called in the 1920s, and "radical communists" as they were framed in the 1950s. A letter from 1958 reveals Cold War politics in full tilt, with the U.S. government pressuring the company to recognize the anticommunist Inter-American Regional Labor Organization (ORIT) labor movement following World War II. Correspondence during the 1950s confirms that the company had begun organizing pro-management unions to weaken the appeal of the socialist labor movement.

Once again, the overall purpose of this brief selection of confidential corporate documents is to make jargon-laden terms such as "field of power," "total institutions," the "governmentality of corporate capitalism," and the "practice of class struggle" come alive in a concrete case study of one of the most powerful institutional forms to have emerged during the twentieth century: the multinational corporation, which has continued to achieve ever-greater global power during the early part of the twenty-first century.

MONOPOLY POWER

[On letterhead]

UNITED FRUIT COMPANY

BOCAS DIVISION

J. M. KYES — MANAGER

J. O. POSEY — ACCOUNTANT

GENERAL OFFICES: 131 STATE STREET, BOSTON, MASS.

CABLE ADDRESS: UNIFRUITCO, BOCAS

ALMIRANTE, R. P.,

At Panama, January 3, 1919.

Dear Mr. Kyes:

This afternoon I received your letter of the 24th acknowledging mine of the 17th relative to the Records Building. This and other letters arrived in Panama on December 30, but it seems the Company's messenger has not come to the Panama Post Office for FOUR days. I think, after what I told him and the Agent here he will come daily hereafter.

The President this afternoon called my attention to the B/40. per share dividend on United Fruit Company stock, notice of which was published here the other day and seemed to think that we could easily have stood a cent additional tax per bunch. I assured him that this was all sugar and freight profits and explained in a lot of details, mostly made up at the moment, how much sugar lands we had planted and the profit thereon, that we had paid no extra dividends for several years to my knowledge, but we had made little of the $40. on bananas. He seemed rather relieved after receiving this information and said he was anxiously awaiting our decision on the Records building. He never forgets anything. I told him that I understood from your letter that you had recommended the project to the Boston office. Mr. Cutter seems to think the bank here would oppose the loan. To the contrary they seldom make loans, except in special cases, for more than six months and at 9%. The slaughterhouse loan, signing of which was completed yesterday, rund [*sic*] for five years, but the income from this is much larger than from the building, and the building is better security.

Sincerely,
[Signed]
E. C. McFarland

[Not on letterhead]

January 7th, 1919.
Mr. E. C. McFarland,
Asst. to Manager,
At Panama City—

Dear Mr. McFarland:—

I acknowledge receipt of your letter of January third and note that the President called your attention to the $40.00 per share dividend on U. F. Co. stock, and that he seemed to think we could easily stand a cent additional tax per bunch. I also note the line of conversation you gave him, and hope that you will be able to stave this question off.

A good long while ago he promised Mr. Schermerhorn he would not increase the duty on bananas, and this year he has virtually promised you the same thing. It might be mentioned to him that at least two-thirds of our bananas come from Costa Rica side of the river where we not only pay Costa Rica duties but are also paying Panama duties, and that if Panama raises the duty we will be compelled to ship these bananas out by Limon, or construct a wharf at Gandoca. This would cut Panama revenues down very much indeed. As a matter of fact, if it becomes necessary I think we could probably take this matter up with the State Department at Washington and they would compel some settlement of the question.

Yours very truly,
[Unsigned]
Manager.

[On letterhead]

UNITED FRUIT COMPANY

GENERAL OFFICES, 131 STATE STREET, BOSTON, MASS.

STEAMSHIP SERVICE

M. C. O'HEARN — GENERAL AGENT

E. G. FESSENDEN — AGENCY ACCOUNTANT

AGENTS FOR:

COMPAÑIA SUD AMERICANA DE VAPORES

ELDERS & FYFFES CO., LTD., S. S. SERVICE

EAST ASIATIC COMPANY, LTD.

CRISTOBAL AGENCY,

CANAL ZONE

January 22, 1924.
Mr. H. S. Blair,
Manager, United Fruit Company,
Almirante, R. P.

Dear Sir:

The situation in the Gatun Lake Region is day by day getting more complicated with the future danger of new buyers entering the field paying new prices to ship direct to New York and San Francisco. In accordance with your instructions that I should do all possible to control all fruits produced in this territory, I am doing all in my power to comply with same, and if it is in order, I would like to make the following suggestions:

To start with it is absolutely necessary that the Company organize and do the buying direct from the producers, as I am sure that most of them would rather do business direct with us rather than have an intermediate man, for as you no doubt know, these people are very suspicious and they are in the belief that Mr. Walker makes a large profit out of their earnings, and it is more plainly impressed on them when the other Companies pay 75¢ for what Mr. Walker pays 60¢. These natives discuss this question among themselves after comparing the difference and wonder why the other companies pay 75¢ and Mr. Walker only pays 60¢.

I being aware of the difficulties we will encounter on entering the territory above mentioned as direct buyers and knowing the propaganda most likely to be used by the agents or the other companies in trying to keep us out, I would suggest that in order to bring their shipments to the lowest figure so as to force them to disorganize, we should accept three quarter fruit for the English market, as well as full three quarter for the New York market. The natives would be very glad to give us three quarter fruit for the following reasons: First that they would receive their money ten days prior to the time if they were to give us full three quarter grade instead. Second, that the load would be much lighter for them to bring from their patch to the edge of the Lake (this is the part of the work they hate to do), as all the carrying is done by shoulder, fruit being transferred in this way half a mile to three quarters of a mile, to their Cayucas and from there on by water to the receiving stations or lighters which in many instances are located three and four miles. This distance by water is always taken into consideration by the natives, and although time with them is no object, they hate to part with a part of their earnings in such cases, as when they own only one cayuca that may hold approximately fifty stems and they have seventy stems to bring they then are obliged to hire an extra cayuca, which certainly breaks their hearts at the time of paying for the extra cayuca. Now if we were receiving three quarter fruit in all probability the same cayuca could carry instead of fifty stems seventy.

These natives are very ignorant, but when it comes to counts dollars and cents they are as smart as any other so, therefore, knowing them as well as I do (as well as their weak points), is the reason for which I suggest that we accept fruit for the English market until such time as the other companies have been routed. There are also many other reasons to the advantage of the fruit seller in giving us three quarter fruit, which I do not make mention of, as you are well familiar with them, but which nevertheless I will certainly bring to the attention of the native producers.

My reason for accepting fruit for the New York market is that in all probabilities for the first few months the fruit brought in by the natives will be of a mixed grade, and being aware of the delicate proposition of shipping fruit to England, I would no doubt after separating same have fruit of a full three quarter grade. I am sure that by buying the two grades we can keep the Lake Region cut down to where it would not pay anybody to waste time and money for securing a few stems.

With reference to Mr. Walker: I should [note] that he controls between 1200 to 1500 stems of fruit per week, that is, part of it produced by squatters on the land he lately bought from President Porras, and from a tract of land known as the Cespedes land, the other part being obtained through small loans which he makes to the small producers in the Lake. You are no doubt very well aware that the natives do not comply with their promises, and regardless of who goes there to do the buying, just as long as there is some advantage over the other, they will always give him some fruit, so you can readily see that it is out of the question for Mr. Walker to control the production in the Gatun Lake Region.

These suggestions are made by me with the view of urging the Company to go openly in the Lake as I have heard rumors that Mitchell at one time a partner of Mr. Walker, wishes to establish himself here and ship fruit to San Pedro, California, where I understand he has made arrangements with Henry & Company of Los Angeles, to take all the fruit delivered there. I also understand that Juan Diaz, at one time an agent for Perino (American Banana Corp), expects to buy sometimes in the near future and ship to New York. This man has already purchased a first class gasoline launch and is getting equipment.

Trusting that this report contains all the information desired by you, I remain,

Respectfully,
[Signed]
D. O. Phillips

cc Mr. M. C. O'Hearn,
    Mr. E. C. McFarland,

[Carbon copy, not on letterhead]
Chiriqui Land Company
[Handwritten note] *Hank, note & return.*
[Initialed] — *H. F.*
[Handwritten note] *Mr. Spence: Please note. Also Mr. Spence please initial.* — *M. N. 1/2/51*

Panamá, R. P.
December 12, 1950
Mr. G. A. Myrick — Armuelles
Mr. G. A. Myrick — Almirante

Dear Mr. Myrick:

With further reference to my letter of December 9th regarding minimum wage scale, etc., and our telephone conversation yesterday, I called on the President this morning and discussed the situation with him.

The President told me that he had heard about this report from one of his deputies and that he had made it very clear to him that Assembly could not establish minimum wage for our Company without making it general throughout the country and that no agriculturist could afford to pay any such wages. That if they tried to make it effective only against our Company or only in the Provinces of Chiriqui and Bocas del Toro it would be inconstitutional [sic]. Also that he did not want any publicity given this matter as it would only tend to drive foreign capital away from the country when his Government was trying to encourage foreign capital to invest here.

I told him that I hoped [the] matter would be killed in the commission because if it came up for discussion in the Assembly, it was going to cause a lot of discussion, even though I felt sure that it would be defeated there. He said he was going to take care of that.

I then told him that as far as appointment of Labor Inspector / Judge in Armuelles and Almirante that we would be glad to see this happen as it would save both Company officials and labor time and money. I also told him that if Assembly approved appointment of Labor Inspector / Judge in Almirante that his Government could save money by eliminating similar position in Bocas. He thanked me very much for this suggestion and said that he agreed there would be no need for Inspector in Bocas if there was one in Almirante.

During our conversation and, again, just as I was leaving, he asked me to tell you not to worry as he could guarantee that no minimum scale would be established.

While waiting to see the President "Tito" Arias, who is now owner of LA HORA, came in and sat next to me and told me that he was very sorry about the manner in which LA HORA had been attacking us but that we could expect it to continue until end of this month. That when he took over this paper there were some employees who were very unfriendly but whose contracts did not expire until end of this month, and that he would not have full control of this paoer [*sic*] until after January 1, 1951. He said that he hoped we would not pay any attention to these attacks.

I thanked him for the information and pointed out to him that we had not tried to defend ourselves by publishing anything in the other newspapers so he could be sure that we were not taking these attacks too seriously although we did not like to see them.

[Illegibly signed]
Copy Messrs Pollan, Turnbull, Baggett

[On letterhead]
UNITED BRANDS COMPANY
PRUDENTIAL CENTER
BOSTON, MASS. 02199
(617) 262–3000

6 November 1970
Brigade General Omar Torrijos
Commander of the National Guard
Panama, Republic of Panama

My Dear General Torrijos,

It was a pleasure for me to receive your personal letter through the conduit of the Honorable Shlomo Gliksberg.[1]

A check for $25,000 is the object of this package to you from our Honorable Vice President, Harvey Johnson, and from our managers in Panama, in the name of the United Fruit Company and its subsidiary, the Chiriqui Land Company, as a gift to the children of Panama.

The cause that you and your wife defend is truly of great merit and we are pleased to be part of your efforts. This present is a symbol of our mutual cooperation and good will toward the government and people of Panama and its companies.

Please convey my warmest respects to His Excellency President Lacas, whom I had the pleasure of meeting during his recent visit to New York.

I beg you to accept my best wishes for your good health.

Attentively,
[Signed]
Eli M. Black, President of the Board

ETHNICITY OF THE LABOR FORCE

[Not on letterhead]

Limon, January 17th, 1914.
E. Mullins,
San Jose.

Dear Sir:—

At Corona, Talamanca I have two pieces of land which for a long time have been cultivated with cocoa and other products, which I acquired with my wife by will of her father, the King of that region Sr. Francsco [*sic*] Saldaña. Now I am prohibited to work those lands by the representatives of the United Fruit at that place alleging that the Company owns the land. Apart of the rights which since immemorial times I have acquired, due to the possession of the first cultivators of the lands which I have continued for so many years, I cannot see how the United Fruit Company can have acquired a cultivated land in those conditions and much more than it considers itself with a right to exact from me the ejection from legitimately belongs to me, in such a manner that the act they are trying to exercise is out of order and gives me the right to exercise procedures which I am trying to avoid. —

For this reason I refer the matter to you in order that in future I be not despoiled of what I have and belongs to me or I am indemnified for the cultivations and damages and prejudices corresponding to me.

I trust you will issue your orders and that you will favor me with a prompt reply addressed in care of don Juan Rafael Alvarado at Limon.

[Unsigned]
Sgd. William Smith.

[Not on letterhead]

April 28, 1919
Colon,
R. de Panama.
155 D. Street
c/o United Fruit Co.
Cristobal.
Mr. J. M. Kyes
Gen. Manager, Bocas Division
Unites [*sic*] Fruit Company.

Sir:

I am sending you under separate cover a newspaper published and printed in Panama called the "Workman" which you will see contains an outrageous publication regarding the past strike in Bocas. This from some malicious view to injure the Company's interest has been widely circulated throughout Panama, and if I understand correctly said information came through Shaw Davis, Winter and Samuder all of Bocas.

Owing to this malicious publication I find it very hard to get the right kind of men here. I am therefore asking your permission and authority to proceed to Jamaica where I am sure I can do twice as much work, in getting a better selection of hard-working men, within the reach of pay. I can have it so arranged to bring my men to Colon and connect them with the Moter [*sic*] Schooner to Bocas.

Sir, all this I can have done without the slightest trouble or unnecessary expense to the Company, my reason for suggesting this trip to Jamaica, is that some of the men who have returned to Panama claim that they are arranging another strike very soon, and I am sure the seeing of the new Jamaicans from the country parts of Jamaica who know nothing about strikes would be of great help and control the situation, hoping this will receive your approval, while, I await your instructions to proceed.

There is also here in Panama, a man by the name of Benito Charmingo, one of the old farm hands of Bocas, who is a native of Chiriqui and is desirous to return to Bocas but wants to bring, he says about a hundred machet [*sic*] workers along with himself, all these men are natives, shall I give them transportation? Please advise.

I am,
Respectfully,
[Signed by A. F. Coombs]

[On letterhead]
UNITED FRUIT COMPANY
BOCAS DIVISION

GENERAL OFFICES
131 STATE STREET, BOSTON, MASS.
SIXAOLA PLANTATION
OFFICE OF SUPERINTENDENT

Guabito, June 26th, 1919.

Mr. H. S. Blair,
Manager,
Almirante.

Dear Sir:—

I return herewith your file on the subject of Indian reservation in Talamanca.

I believe that we should get some definite ruling on this question before buying anymore Squatter cultivations in Talamanca and it is most desirable that we proceed with these purchases as rapidly as possible.

In a short trip through the eastern end of the Valley last week I found several people, whose cultivations in another part of the valley have been purchased, who had signed an agreement to make no more cultivations on Company property. In every case they told me that they had cultivated their present holdings because the land had been pointed out to them as part of the Indian Reservation.

Among these cultivations were those of Samuel Levy which is by far the biggest and best in the valley at present and of Solomon Paddyfoot. Levy sold his former holding to the Company on January 26th, 1917 for $400. and Paddyfoot sold on the same date for $75. Both these men claim that the land on which their cultivations are now located was pointed out as Indian Reservation by Alejo Jimenez who at that time was Jefe Politico in Talamanca.

In order to settle this question definitely I suggest that some kind of Official ruling be obtained from San Jose and that, with this in hand, a Costa Rican Lawyer who is also a Notary Public come over to assist us in drawing up the contracts of sale. It should also be determined whether Jamaicans not naturalized citizens of Costa Rica can acquire titles in a reservation supposedly set aside for Talamanca Indians.

Alejo Jimenez is still in the country and if we could employ him to aid in making these purchases his assistance might be of considerable value. On the other hand he might be antagonistic and make it much harder to come to an agreement with the squatters. Is there not some one who knows him by whom he can be sounded?

Yours very truly,
[Signed by G. S. Bennett]

Superintendent Agriculture.

GSB/R

[On letterhead]

UNITED FRUIT COMPANY

GENERAL OFFICES, 131 STATE STREET, BOSTON, MASS.

G. P. CHITTENDEN, MANAGER

D. C. TAYLOR, ACCOUNTANT

CABLE ADDRESS: UNIFRUITCO, SAN JOSÉ, LIMÓN

COSTA RICA DIVISION

LIMÓN, COSTA RICA.

December 21st, 1919.

V. M. Cutter, Esq.,

Vice-President, United Fruit Co.,

Boston, Mass.

Dear Sir:

On December 17th, Wednesday, Mr. Fred Gordon, the Acting British Vice-Consul of Limon, told me that he had been informed by Fowler, a Jamaican, who is in charge of affairs of the Negro Improvement Association here, that Henrietta Vinton Davis, the international organizer of the Negro Improvement Association, had just landed in Colon, and that she intended shortly to visit Bocas and Limon.

A perusal of the attached file will show you the steps taken by me, and will show you the steps taken by Mr. Blair at Bocas. Mr. Blair's letter of December 19th, was written before receiving my letter of the same date. We arranged by guarded conversation on the telephone to inform each other fully in writing, and the two letters are the result.

We have two courses open to us:

First. To do everything we can to prevent her admission to this country, or to Bocas.

Second. To wait a little while before acting, in the hope that Miss Davis will overstep herself on the Canal Zone and so act as to give the Canal Zone authorities cause for arrest; furthering at all times any action of the British authorities or the Costa Rican authorities to prevent her landing. In other words, keeping ourselves as much in the dark as possible, in order to be in a position to make the best of it should she finally land at either port.

The Jamaicans here state openly her arrival will start a strike and that they are just awaiting her arrival in order to so start. Her action so far on the Zone, and the action of her agent in Bocas, as reported by Mr. Blair, would tend to show that the main object is the sale of stock. Stock can only be sold to those who are earning money. Miss Davis is probably intelligent enough to realize this and I believe there is a chance that she will encourage the goose to lay the golden eggs, rather than advocate a strike, which would stop the purchasing power of the Jamaicans.

I am figuring that this letter will reach you before she leaves the Canal Zone. You have our policy expressed in these letters, and there will be plenty of time for a change in such policy if you so instruct.

We are taking a chance to allow her to land at all if it is in our power to stop her, as she has only to lift her finger when she gets here to start trouble that it might take months to smooth over.

There is a great difference between our Government allowing such a woman aloose on the Canal Zone, where the presence of 20,000 troops in itself is sufficient to brake any uprising, and our Government allowing such a woman to enter a Central American country inadequately policed, and where the respect for the British Government on the part of the Jamaicans is the only real control that exists over them. At a final show-down the Costa Rican Government can be counted on to do its best for law and order, but its best will only manifest itself after trouble has started and probably after many of both races, African and White, have been killed. If Washington can be persuaded to stop her progress through these countries, I believe it should be done.

Very truly yours,
[Unsigned, from G. P. Chittenden]

UNITED FRUIT COMPANY
GENERAL OFFICES, 131 STATE STREET, BOSTON, MASS.

G. P. CHITTENDEN
MANAGER

A. A. CATTERALL
ACTG. DIVISION AUDITOR

CABLE ADDRESS
UNIFRUITCO | SAN JOSÉ | LIMÓN

COSTA RICA DIVISION
LIMÓN, COSTA RICA

April 22, 1921.

V. M. Cutter, Esq.,
Vice-President,
Boston, Mass.

Dear Sir:

Marcus Garvey sailed for Bocas Thursday morning after three days of speaking in Limon and vicinity. The result of his speeches will be in general, favorable to our business. The meetings were largely attended but there were not so many people as was expected originally. Three or four Jamaicans, resident in Costa Rica, had been groomed by their followers to attack Garvey in the meetings, demanding financial statements of his various enterprises and show him up in general. The best one of these lasted five minutes.

After all Garvey was the most conservative man of any attending the meetings. He told them they should not fight the United Fruit Company, that the work given them by the United Fruit Company meant their bread and butter and that they would not only deserve but receive the same respect as the United Fruit Company, once they had farms, railways and steamships of their own and showed that they could operate them. He said that in order to operate such an enterprise they must have money and that in order to get money they had to work. I know that at one meeting two scrap baskets and one suit case full of United States gold notes were collected (Garvey announced that he would receive nothing but U.S. currency in contributions). I know that at another meeting he stood beside a pile of gold notes which reached above his knees. It is impossible to estimate the amount collected but it might easily be as much as $50,000.00, all of which he took away with him in cash.

Mr. Barnett of the Federacion de Trabajadores, endeavored to start a counter attraction during Garvey's stay here. He made no impression on the populace. All together we are very well satisfied with the results of the visit and can only wish the Panama Division the same luck as walked with us. I enclose Mr. Barnett's circular covering his counter attraction.

Very truly yours,

cc H.S.Blair, Esq.

FIGURE 1   Internal memo, United Fruit Company.

[On letterhead]

UNITED FRUIT COMPANY

GENERAL OFFICES, 131 STATE STREET, BOSTON, MASS.

G. P. CHITTENDEN, MANAGER

A. A. CATTERALL, ACTG. DIVISION AUDITOR

CABLE ADDRESS: UNIFRUITCO, SAN JOSÉ, LIMÓN

COSTA RICA DIVISION

LIMÓN, COSTA RICA

April 22, 1921.
V. M. Cutter, Esq.,
Vice-President,
Boston, Mass.

Dear Sir:

Marcus Garvey sailed for Bocas Thursday morning after three days of speaking in Limon and vicinity. The result of his speeches will be in general, favorable to our business. The meetings were largely attended but there were not so many people as was expected originally. Three or four Jamaicans, resident in Costa Rica, had been groomed by their followers to attack Garvey in the meetings, demanding financial settlements of his various enterprises and show him up in general. The best one of these lasted five minutes.

After all Garvey was the most conservative man of any attending the meetings. He told them they should not fight the United Fruit Company, that the work given them by the United Fruit Company meant their bread and butter and that they would not only deserve but receive the same respect as the United Fruit Company, once they had farms, railways and steamships of their own and showed that they could operate them. He said that in order to operate such an enterprise they must have money and that in order to get money they had to work. I know that at one meeting two scrap baskets and one suit case full of United States gold notes were collected (Garvey announced that he would receive nothing but U.S. currency in contributions). I know that at another meeting he stood beside a pile of gold notes which reached above his knees. It is impossible to estimate the amount collected but it might easily be as much as $50,000.00, all of which he took away with him in cash.

Mr. Barnett of the Federacion de Trabajadores, endeavored to start a counter attraction during Garvey's stay here. He made no impression on the populace. All together we are very well satisfied with the results of the visit and can only wish the Panama Division the same luck as walked with us. I enclose Mr. Barnett's circular covering his counter attraction.

Very truly yours,
[Signed by G. P. Chittenden]
cc H. S. Blair, Esq.

[On letterhead]

UNITED FRUIT COMPANY

GENERAL OFFICES, 131 STATE STREET, BOSTON, MASS.

G. P. CHITTENDEN, MANAGER

A. A. CATTERALL, ACTG. DIVISION AUDITOR

CABLE ADDRESS: UNIFRUITCO, SAN JOSÉ, LIMÓN

COSTA RICA DIVISION

LIMÓN, COSTA RICA

April [Date illegible] 1921.
PERSONAL

Dear Blair:

Referring to letters between you and Mr. Doswell, dated April 16th and 17th, in the matter of Marcus Garvey. Mr. Garvey made a long call on me in San José the day before yesterday. If he keeps his word he will make no trouble; but the policy originally initiated by you of not entering into any discussion, is beyond doubt the best one to follow.

Garvey impressed me as something mean to debate with. He has no rules at all. However, if you play up to his vanity a little, and talk to him the way you would talk to one of your own laborers with whom you were on extra good terms, you will have no trouble with him. This is said long before he leaves, and I may be wrong, but it is the way I size up the matter right now.

He states that he too is an employer of labor, understands our position, is against labor unions, and is using his best behavior to get the negro race to work and better themselves through work.

Supposing you take this as my final size-up. If I have anything else to add I will send it by special messenger.

Garvey expects the "Antonio Maceo," his yacht, to arrive in Bocas on Sunday and will, therefore, not require transportation back to Limon. That is, he has not engaged transportation here and therefore will have to come after anyone else in case he changes his mind.

I confirm what Mr. Doswell said on the 17th, to the effect that it would be well to handle him on the "Preston" if you can possibly see your way to do so. We have made him pay for all train service here at special rate which covers the cost of handling, and a bit over. Do you want us to collect in advance for the "Preston?" If so, how much?

Very truly yours,
[Signed]
G. P. Chittenden

cc V. M. Cutter, Esq.
[Handwritten note] *We shall expect you to cancel ball game anytime you see fit. Are you coming over and is Mrs. B coming* [referring to a social gathering]. *We expect you both are.*

[On letterhead]

UNITED FRUIT COMPANY

GENERAL OFFICES, 131 STATE STREET, BOSTON, MASS.

G. P. CHITTENDEN, MANAGER

A. A. CATTERALL, ACCOUNTANT

CABLE ADDRESS: UNIFRUITCO, SAN JOSÉ, LIMÓN

COSTA RICA DIVISION

LIMÓN, COSTA RICA

August 4th, 1922
H. S. Blair, Esq.,
Division Manager,
Almirante, R. P.
PERSONAL

Dear Sir:

Recently Santiago Chamberlain made a trip to Puerto Castilla on the Semper Idem, a rather appropriate ship for such a man. What is the reason for the fatal attraction you and Bennett seem to feel toward him?

Anyway, he went to Puerto Castilla as I stated above, and while there made tentative arrangements to run Jamaican laborers from Limon to that point. This, as you may know, is against the law of Honduras. As soon as he made the arrangements he seems to have dropped over to Truxillo and spilled all the beans in every saloon in town. Naturally those left out of the arrangement are now laying for Santiago. He then returned to Limon,—he and his partner, killing his partner's wife on the way down by neglect and sea-sickness, and as soon as he got here made himself conspicious [sic] and objectionable to everybody, talking along the lines of his having made arrangements with the Truxillo Railroad Company that was shortly going to make him a millionaire, and that Julio Acosta could go to Hell, etc. etc. This rather sets the stage for any preventive measures the Costa Rica Government may care to take.

The day before yesterday I received the following telegram from Mr. Brown:

"Albert should arrive at your port 8th for birds,—refer to your telegram July 29th, ship 20,000 pounds coffee; if unable to fill entire order substitute black beans, ship 100 pounds honey, 50 Gonzalez cheese."

to which I replied as follows:

"Refer to your telegram of August 2nd. Loose talk of Chamberlain here makes bird traffic absolutely dangerous for the present. Am positive consequences would be serious for you and embarrassing to me. Will take care of your merchandise orders if you decide to send schooner."

[End of page 1 of letter]

UNITED FRUIT COMPANY

GENERAL OFFICES, 131 STATE STREET, BOSTON, MASS.

G. P. CHITTENDEN, MANAGER

A. A. CATTERALL, ACCOUNTANT

CABLE ADDRESS: UNIFRUITCO, SAN JOSÉ, LIMÓN

COSTA RICA DIVISION

LIMÓN, COSTA RICA

August 4th, 1922

H. S. Blair, Esq.,
(#2 Cont.)

Yesterday I sent him the following telegram:

"Do you own schooner Albert? If I can arrange for birds trip Bocas to Puerto Castilla, am considering putting De Leon in charge of collecting birds. Would this be acceptable to you? How many birds can schooner carry in one trip conveniently? Can you make all necessary arrangements at your end?"

It occurs to me that you and I might be able to assist the Truxillo Railroad Company by making it easy for De Leon to recruit men around Almirante or Bocas and take them up, saw twenty or thirty at a time. I think that De Leon would be able to pull several men away from here to Almirante, and then pull them through Almirante onto his schooner and thence to Puerto Castilla. I also think the available supply might be increased if you became a little more active in your recruiting on the Canal Zone.

I am coming down to see you next week and want to go into this matter very fully in order that we may help them out at Puerto Castilla. Their labor situation seems to be indeed serious, and I imagine they need all the help they can get. The cost of doing this work does not need to scare you or me. I remember that I was once in the same position, and the cost per head of a Jamaican landed in the port was the smallest consideration of all. Naturally any expense that we go to can be charged against the Truxillo Railroad Co.

Very truly yours,
[Signed]
G. P. Chittenden

[Handwritten note] *The big idea would be to let DeL* [labor contractor De Leon] *appear to be doing this for his own account*

c.c. V. M. Cutter, Esq.
   W. E. Brown, Esq.

[Carbon copy, not on letterhead]

Almirante, Panama
March 11, 1954

Mr. Franklin Moore
Boston

Dear Mr. Moore:

I refer to your letter of March 2nd, about getting some labor from Honduras to speed up the development program and at the same time stabilize our labor force.

I do not know if you had seen my letter of February 27th, about Mr. Holcombe's talk with the President when you wrote your letter of March 2nd, but presumably you had not. I do not think there is a chance of importing labor into this country at the present time. Bill Mais is on the YAQUE, returning from vacation and gets in here Saturday. I will talk to him about this and ask him to inquire discreetly when he gets back to the city but I feel pretty sure he will confirm my opinion.

For some time now we have been bringing in San Blas Indians in groups of twenty five and at the present time have approximately 225 of them working. The drawback with these Indians is that they can only remain six months and must then return and be replaced by a new group. This arrangement was made with one of the principal "caciques" and he would not permit that any one group remain for more than six months. They are good workers, are well disciplined and have helped to relieve the shortage of the labor very considerably. They have been exceptionally good in railway section gangs and of the groups here now about half of them are working in the section gangs, and the other half are split between bananas and cacao on the Panama side. They are quick to learn and cause absolutely no trouble. Even though they are obligated to return after six months, I feel that a lot of them will eventually work their way back as they are making good money here and from appearances, at least, seem to be contented.

In addition to the San Blas Indians we are getting some labor from Chiriqui.

As usual, we are very short of housing and even though a permit could be obtained we could not handle any sizable group of Hondurans and I do not want to cancel the arrangement for the San Blas labor, as they are working out exceptionally well and eventually I believe we shall have a good number of them here on a permanent basis.

Within the last couple of weeks we have brought in some 150 laborers from Guanacaste for the Costa Rica side cacao farms and are getting these farms cleaned up nicely. We are also getting in touch with a construction foreman who worked for Mr. Bishop in Quepos, and hope to have a good sized construction gang located on the Costa Rica side shortly to start work repairing the camps which have been crying for attention.

We are in better shape for labor today than we have been for a long time.

Very truly yours,
[Signed]
G. D. Munch
cc: Mr. Hartley Rowe
    Mr. J. R. Silver
    Mr. V. T. Mais

[On letterhead]

REV. E. S. ALPHONSE

SUPT. METHODIST CHURCH

BOCAS DEL TORO AND VALIENTE MISSION

BOCAS DEL TORO

REP. DE PANAMA

[Initialed by UFC officials]
[Handwritten note] *I talked a long time to him and he is quite cooperative.*

The Management C. L. Co.
July 26th 1954

Sir,

I have just drawn up a plan of Campaign to take place among the Guaimie Indians working along the lines. This Campaign I intend to carry out with Jesse the Indian we have at Base Line under my guidance. I shall be depending on you for transportation in order to do an effective work. I take with me my lantern or Projector so that I can have visual aid in order to inculcate in their minds the things we want them to know. To use this effectively I must take my 12 volt battery to places such as Dos Caños where there is no electric current. I write this in duplicate so that Mr. Flores can arrange through you to put a car at my disposal to reach the Indians and bring me back to my base night after night. I also ask that the foremen be notified to make them aware of the time of gathering together especially for the mass meeting to be held at Guabito on Sunday Aug. 8th at 2 P.M.

Plan of Itinerary
Wed. Aug. 4th.: Elena & Dos Caños Indians to meet at Dos Caños (Using flat car and trailer ?) Subject to your existing plan of organization.
Thurs. " 5th: Nievecito and Baranco
(Time for all these _7.P.M.)
Friday " 6th: Guabito and Long Range
Sat. " 7th: Base Line
Sunday ": Indians from Almirante, Rubber tree, Empalme Base Line, Elena, Dos Caños, Nievecito, Barranco, etc. etc. all to converge on Guabito to meet at 2 P.M. for a mass meeting.

I will come to Almirante early Wednesday the 4th to take up Projector and battery to Elena and Dos Caños. Travelling by my own launch to Almirante.

Points to Discuss with them
1. The damage licor [*sic*] is doing to them

2. The inconvenience to the Co. caused by their changing of their names as they go from farm to Farm.

3. The need to have a fixed name and if needs be fix up certificates for each one which must be kept and presented each time he is to be paid and when he asks for work.

4. To make complaints when they arrive only through the correct channel & at the Labour Office _ Where I take it that they will be patient enough to have the Indian grievance or case properly translated to him and to the Office. I now refer to Indian accidents, and death on the job whereby he leaves perhaps a young wife and children in the mountains orphaned and unprovided for a long time. Matters of this kind I venture to suggest are best dealt with through me interpreting _ And I shall be willing to give freely my services in their interest.

5. The harm that is done to the machinery of productive labour caused by Strikes. To Avoid Communist agitators.

6. Sanitation . . . . . Recreation. . . . . . (Organizing of an Indian Base ball team) To ask the Mangement [*sic*] to withold [*sic*] part of their earnings til they are leaving for home. To specify a shorter period for releasing them to go home to attend to their crops since the country becomes impoverished by the diminishing Indian Crops . . Corn, Yams, Rice, etc. The cream of labour being harnessed at this end.

Yours sincerely,
[Signed by E. Alphonse]

[Not on letterhead]

Guatemala, Guatemala
12 December 1957

Mr. G. D. Munch
Almirante. —

Dear Mr. Munch:

During my recent visit to Almirante I discussed with Mr. Richards the necessity for preparing a monthly earnings report on the daily and tarea workers, showing average daily and monthly earnings, days lost and days worked. I believe such statistics are vitally important to your supervisors to keep them informed monthly of the earnings and time lost of their employees.

Mr. Richards makes up a monthly report showing the total payroll figures by departments which I do not think is adequate.

I understand that in the near future, the Accounting Department will be receiving a new IBM unit on which a very detailed report on earnings, days lost etc. can be prepared. When this machine arrives and the report is prepared, copies should be furnished to all your department heads. I would appreciate receiving copies also.

The so-called unrest among your Indian labor which you told me about and that you say does not exist should be closely watched as you say there are some unscrupulous outside labor leaders who are endeavoring to gain control of the Indians. On two occasions, I tried to talk to the Indians on the farms but I was not very successful and could not get them to answer my questions. If the Padre who has the confidence of the Indians and whom you requested to visit the banana zone to investigate the so-called Indian unrest develops anything on his trip, I would like to hear what he had to say.

I was very favorably impressed with the Secretary General of the Union, although as I advised you having a Union officer in an important position in your Labor Relations Department does not look good as people will not be able to understand how such a person can look after the interests of the workers and the Company. The Union is doing a good job in running night schools for the workers and I was told by the Secretary General with whom I had a long talk that the Union was paying for the teachers out of Union funds.

I was very much impressed with Jorge Rivera, the Labor Conciliator, who appeared very energetic, capable and had a very good knowledge of all phases of the operation. He apparently gets along well with the labor and the supervisors, which is a good sign.

We visited several of the schools, commissaries and dispensaries. The rice being sold in the commissaries was of poor quality and badly broken and deteriorated. The dispensaries were well stocked and the people in charge were neatly dressed. Supplies were adequate and good reports kept of the patients. [End of page 1 of letter; page 2, not transcribed, is signed by F. Moore.]

[Not on letterhead]

Medical Department
Almirante, Panama

December 18, 1957
Mr. G. D. Munch
Almirante

Dear Mr. Munch:

This is to advise that Chali Villagra Chio, 47 years, Guaimi Indian of Farm 61, was found to suffer from progressive blindness due to an extensive chorioretinitis in the left eye. The right eye has been blind for years.

He is no longer able to work. He was advised to return to Cricamola.

Yours very truly,
[Signed]
Dr. Gustav Engler

cc: Mr. D. K. Linton
    Mr. J. Rivera
    File 3.2.0

GE/lw. —

LABOR RELATIONS

[Carbon copy, not on letterhead]
[Handwritten note] *Strike—labor troubles*
Bocas del Toro,
April 16, 1920

Mr. H. S. Blair,
Manager, U.F.CO.
Panama Division
Almirante.

Dear Sir:

In compliance with your request to render you an accurate account, re the part played by E. Glashen, in connection with the labor disturbances which occurred amongst some of the people of the United Fruit Company in this division, beginning on December 2nd 1918, I respectfully beg to state as follows:

In the first place I have to inform you that Glashen, even to the most casual observer, would appear to belong to that class of people who suffer from the disease known as "cacoethes loquenti," men who always want to say something, who profess to know all, except the proper thing, viz: a knowledge of how much they really do know.

There cannot be the slightest doubt that the disturbance in reference, spread and flourished through Glashen's agitation and predomination. The occurrence to every right minded person was looked upon, not as a labor strike, because strikes generally are an organized affair, having as its definite aim the amelioration of conditions, etc. but as a violent disturbance, an uproar, calculated to throw into a state of confusion the Company's operation here, while, from the many criminal acts committed, embarrassing the Governments and their own diplomatic representatives, finally embarrassing their own selves, because the majority of them had not [one] cent to go by two days after the thing began. On the morning after the first day of the disturbance a large number of these soi-disant strikers from the one mile camps, armed with sticks marched down to the Company's machine shop, located at Half Mile, and violently introducing themselves therein, they at once started to throw water on the different engines that were in operation at the time, and also attacking the few men who did not join them and were at work. Later on the same day, about 9 A M a dense crowd, about 400 men, again armed with sticks and stones was formed on the railroad track at One Mile, and they were determined not to allow any Company's vehicles to pass through. An attempt at wrenching out the rails was made, and it was right there that the Panama Police made the first arrests. About 40 men were taken up and 40 sticks collected from them too.

The shooting of white men with buck shot from guns from behind, the beating of foremen, the chopping down of the Company's young cacao trees, the burning down of the Commissary and camp, the opening of railroad switches, etc. etc. continued with unabated fury, while Glashen kept on particularly busy;

conducting mass meetings, which took place almost daily at Guabito; and despatching [sic] here and there his agents to carry the news of his determination to conquer. Glashen's agents were chiefly persons like himself who did not work for the Company, but meddlesome outsiders, Gamblers, speculators, impostors and all such who love to stay at home and maliciously plan as to how to live on the hard earned wages of the workingman. Some of the agents in reference were, Forbes, Alais sugar well known gambler — Jack Collins, professional gambler at the time, Samuda, Gambler, Jeweller, and so forth.

At a mass meeting, held in the open air at Guabito, about 8 PM December 12th of the same year above mentioned it was indeed sorrowful to hear some of Glashen's utterances. I say sorrowful because he was simply leading a poor unfortunate people, his own race and my own race too, astray. Converting an empty barrel into a platform, or pulpit, and mounted like a hero he addressed the crowd, among which he distinctly said:

"Friends, countrymen, I am your leader, and God has sent me to rescue you. Do you remember what the white man told us during the war that we were fighting for democracy, equality[,] and therefore to become free subjects? Do you realize your present position, which is a white man is getting four to five hundred dollars per month? Do you get that much in cents in a week? Is this equality? I ask you all to stand by me and consequently we will get what we want. I expect you not to go back to work. The white folks here are but a handful, and if they won't come to us, we shall compel them to fly away from here. If we could have given a good account of ourselves in the bloody war, why not here too. Why must we be afraid of the few white parasites around here. we will teach them a lesson for life, etc. etc."

The crowd accordingly clapped him up, waved their handkerchiefs and in an unmistakeable [sic] tone it resounded from them, "We shall murder them, we shall kill them" (Persons who can bear testimony to the fact are Emiliano Selles, Adam Arias, E. Thomas).

This sort of meeting at which Glashen presided, and with his characteristic inflamatory [sic] speeches incited the people to violence, went on for days. The arrival of the Governor of Port Limon to Bridgefoot (Costa Rican Territory) put an end to the matter because Glashen crossed over and demanded an interview with him, at which he spoke so very much, saying so many incriminatory things, that the Governor thought he was the fittest man to have taken to Port Limon, reinvestigation of the atrocities that were being committed by the people on the Costa Rican side, he was conducting.

A certain letter signed by Glashen and Samuda addressed to Mr. J. M. Keyes, the then Manager, was also handed over to the Governor. This letter was self explanatory. It contained such incriminating passages that only a madman would thus write.

On the whole I find that Glashen's conduct was of the most perverse nature, he deliberately lent a deaf ear to the good counsel of respectable people, such as, Ministers of the Gospel etc. He persisted in doing wrong, he proclaimed a consistent policy and did not deviate, he sowed the seeds of whirlwind and he could not conscientiously expect, but to reap the fruits of whirlwind. In conclusion as the information might reach further, and as it might be said that nothing else could be expected of me, an employee of the Company, I wish to call attention once more to my motto, which I hold is based on truthfulness, straightforwardness etc. This being so, either I should have no fear to [t]ell you Mr. Blair, (My boss) that to a certain extent, I.E. so far as I sympathized with the people but could not for a minute close my eyes and deny the Company what is expected of me. Here again I must follow my identical course and every word herein said I feel it would never act as a remorse of conscience on me.

Very respectfully.
[Unsigned]

[Carbon copy, not on letterhead]

MEMORANDUM

March 8, 1929

The attached photograph shows five of the principal leaders in the recent disturbances in the Colombian Division. Their names are as follows:

[Check mark] No. 1. Bernadino Guerrero
No. 2. Nicanor Serrano
No. 3. P. M. del Rio
No. 4. Raúl Eduardo Mahecha
[Check mark] No. 5. Erasmo Coronel

FIGURE 2 Photograph accompanying internal memo, United Fruit Company. The numbers marked on the photograph reference the identities of the labor leaders discussed in the memo. The check marks indicate that Guerrero had been imprisoned and Coronel had been killed; note also that over Guerrero's and Coronel's images is written the word *out*.

[Check marks indicate that Guerro had been imprisoned and Coronel had been killed; see figure 2.]

No. 1 was secretary to Mahecha, the leader, and is now serving a term of fourteen years, seven months in the federal penitentiary in Tunga. No. 5 was killed in the fighting at Sevilla. Nos. 2 and 3 were simple laborers and were practically only figureheads in the organization.

No. 4, Mahecha, was the brains of the entire outfit and is one of the most dangerous communistic leaders in this country. He fomented the oil field strike in 1924 and last year was the leader of a bad strike in the coffee region in the interior. He came to Ciénaga about August of 1928 and immediately started fomenting the movement which culminated in the disturbance of December 6th. He is an ex-army captain, has a remarkable personality and an undoubted genius for organization. At the time the strikers were fired on in Ciénaga he fled and it is known that he was wounded in one leg. Since then he has disappeared completely and it is now reported in the press that he has escaped to Costa Rica.

Att. — photograph

[On carbon copy letterhead]

UNITED FRUIT COMPANY

GENERAL OFFICES, ONE FEDERAL STREET

BOSTON, MASSACHUSETTS

ARTHUR A. POLLAN, GENERAL MANAGER

TROPICAL BANANA DIVISIONS

CIRCULAR NO. B-21

November 15, 1929

TO BANANA DIVISION MANAGERS

I am attaching a photograph for the purpose of familiarizing you with the appearance of Manuel Calix Herrera. He is the figure outlined in the center. This man is an agitator of the worst type; anti-American, extremist, given to writing and preaching Red, Bolshevist, and Communistic propaganda. He has recently been the principal organizer of a Bolshevist move originating on the north coast of Honduras. It is possible that as his activities have been restricted in that country, he will move to other fields, and you should be on the lookout for him.

His description is as follows:

Single
24 years of age
Native of Olancho, Honduras
Height about 5′10″
Weight, about 125 lbs.
Very slightly stooped
Eyes, grey
Color, white

UNITED FRUIT COMPANY

GENERAL OFFICES, ONE FEDERAL STREET

BOSTON, MASSACHUSETTS

ARTHUR A. POLLAN
GENERAL MANAGER
TROPICAL BANANA DIVISIONS

CIRCULAR NO. B-21

November 15, 1929

TO BANANA DIVISION MANAGERS

        I am attaching a photograph for the purpose of familiarizing you with the appearance of Manuel Calix Herrera. He is the figure outlined in the center. This man is an agitator of the worst type; anti-American, extremist, given to writing and preaching Red, Bolshevist, and Communistic propaganda. He has recently been the principal organizer of a Bolshevist move originating on the north coast of Honduras. It is possible that as his activities have been restricted in that country, he will move to other fields, and you should be on the lookout for him.

        His description is as follows:

                Single
                34 years of age
                Native of Olancho, Honduras
                Height about 5'10"
                Weight, about 125 lbs.
                Very slightly stooped
                Eyes, grey
                Color, white
                Hair, dark brown
                Smooth-shaved
                Small mouth
                Complexion, pale, as if suffering from some ailment
                Is quick and alert, and rapid in his movements
                Usually dresses without coat or necktie, and a straw
                   hat, with one side turned down in a rakish fashion.
                Personal habits: drinks occasionally, sometimes to
                   excess, given to frequenting low resorts.

            Yours very truly

Enclosure

A. A. Pollan

FIGURE 3   Internal memo, United Fruit Company.

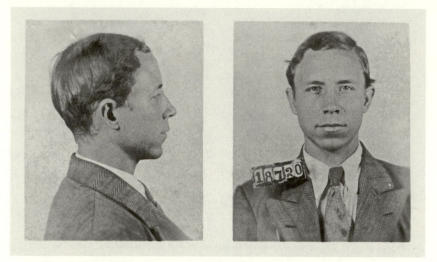

FIGURE 4   Photograph of Manuel Celix Herrera, accompanying internal memo, United Fruit Company.

Hair, dark brown

Smooth-shaved

Small mouth

Complexion, pale, as if suffering from some ailment

Is quick and alert, and rapid in his movements

Usually dresses without coat or necktie, and a straw hat, with one side turned down in a rakish fashion.

Personal habits: drinks occasionally, sometimes to excess, given to frequenting low resorts.

Yours very truly,

[Signed by A. A. Pollan]

Enclosure

[Not on letterhead]

Almirante, Panama

June 18, 1957.

Mr. G. D. Munch:

Attached please find memorandum from Rene Du-Bois, president of the "Sindicato de Trabajadores de la Chiriquí Land Company División de Bocas."

The annual meeting was held at the Empalme Stadium to elect the new board of directors for 1957. There was an attendance of approximately 800 members of the syndicate. The same board of directors was re-elected unanimously. The only changes were two directors who resigned for personal reasons.

The syndicate under the guidance of Rene De-Bois and Modesto Guerra did a fine job during the past year. This division has not had any labor trouble and this is at least due to close cooperation with the syndicate.

During the year they spent out their own funds over $1500.00 in sports equipment which was turned over to the labor teams in all farms. Sport programs have been started and are giving good results. All farms have base-ball, soft-ball, boxing and volley-ball teams.

On June 6th 1957 night classes was started at Farm 21 school for indian labor with an attendance of 25 pupils. Teachers and school material is being furnished by the labor syndicate.

The Governor from Bocas has been trying to sometime to form an indian syndicate. On the syndicate election day they tried to boycott the meeting by having one at the Catholic Club at Base Line, sponsored by the Rev. Dogorthy and two indians from Chiriqui. I have been informed that these two indians Vicente Palacios and Salinas were expelled from Armuelles three years ago for agitating [an] indian strike. As I do not have definite proof that these are the same men I am still investigating and will inform you of new developments. This syndicate is supposed to collect two dollars monthly from each indian and claim they are going to use these funds in the construction of churches and schools in the Cricamola area. I do not believe they will prosper but all precautions are being taken by the Du-Bois organization to try and break it up.

Very truly yours,
[Signed]
J. Rivera

[Carbon copy, not on letterhead]

80 Federal Street
Boston 10, Massachusetts

December 12, 1958

CIRCULAR NO. T-44

CONFIDENTIAL

All Tropical Division Managers:

On Tuesday, December 9, Mr. Redmond, Al Giardino, Jasper Baker and I had a long conference with State Department Deputy Under Secretary Robert Murphy and other high officials in the State Department.

The State Department representatives were obviously disturbed by the bad relations between ORIT and the United Fruit Company and stated that they considered the free labor movement, as well as American business itself, to be essential arms in the fight against communism. Several examples of indiscreet acts on the part of Company employees were given. One was a statement by a "company official" that "our fight with ORIT is a fight to the finish." Another was an episode wherein a member of our Costa Rica public relations department sent a set of clippings to Salvador on the reaction to the McClellan incident with a suggestion of action.

In this short letter I cannot give the details of all of the matters discussed, but our case was adequately presented. Giardino properly summed up our objection to ORIT as due to the complete irresponsibility of ORIT leaders. He listed many speeches, published articles, and acts by these people which have bitterly antagonized our people. The State Department people were told that being accused of favoring communism evidently causes resentment and anger on the part of United Fruit Company personnel and we were surprised that there were not many more intemperate statements and acts.

However, the key of the matter, as explained by Mr. Redmond, is the desire on the part of the State Department and the United Fruit Company for a period of labor peace. We hope ORIT shares the view.

With that in mind, kindly instruct those of your employees concerned to be careful not to further aggravate matters by careless and antagonistic acts and statements, noting that even private and "off-the-record" remarks when made to Embassy personnel are repeated.

The period of negotiation is over for the time being, and with it should pass the pressure tactics to which we have been subjected.

Yours very truly,
[Signed by A. L. Bump]

Copy to: Mr. A. A. Giardino
         Mr. L. S. Greenberg
         Mr. R. V. Howley (12)

NOTE

1. This letter from E. M. Black to General Omar Torrijos was originally written in Spanish:

Mi querido General Torrijos:

Fue en placer para mí recibir su carta personal por conducto del Honorable Shlomo Gliksberg.

Un cheque por $25,000 está siendo objeto de entrega a usted por nuestro estimado Vice-presidente, Harvey Johnson, y por nuestros Gerentes en Panamá, en nombre de la United Fruit Company y su subsidiaria, la Chiriqui Land Company, como regalo a los niños de Panamá.

La causa que usted y su esposa defienden es en realidad de gran mérito y nos sentimos complacidos de ser parte en el esfuerzo de ustedes. Este regalo es símbolo de mutua cooperación y buena voluntad del Gobierno y pueblo de Panamá y las compañías.

Ruégole comunicar mis calurosos saludos al Excelentísimo Señor Presidente Lakas a quien tuve el placer de conocer durante su reciente visita a Nueva York.

Le ruego acepte mis mejores votos por su buena salud (translation mine).

Black committed suicide in 1975 when the press revealed that he had paid the president of Honduras, General Oswaldo Lopéz Arellano, $1.25 million to lower the banana export tax in 1974.

NAMES CITED IN THE CORRESPONDENCE

Alphonse, E. S., Methodist minister, Bocas and Valiente division, 1950s.
Alvarado, T., administrator, farm 8, Bocas division, 1956.
Arias, H., attorney, UFC; subsequently president of Panama, 1919–1920s.
Baggett, S., vice-president, UFC, Boston, 1930s–1950s.
Bennett, G. S., superintendent of agriculture, UFC, Guabito district, Bocas division, 1910–1920s.
Black, E. M., president and owner, UFC, Boston, 1970–1975.
Blair, H. S., manager, UFC, Bocas division, 1910s–1930s.

Chittenden, G. P., manager, UFC, Limón division; subsequently responsible for all southern Central American operations, then vice president, Chiriqui Land Company, Boston, 1916–1940s.

Coombs, A. F., agent, UFC, Panama City, 1919.

Cutter, V. N., general manager, UFC, Central and South American department; subsequently vice president, UFC, Boston, 1915–1920s.

De Leon, [first name unknown], labor contractor, Central America, 1920s.

Diebold, C. W., assistant manager, UFC, Bocas division, 1949–1954.

Engler, G., director of the medical department, UFC, Bocas division, 1950s.

Garvey, M., leader of the Universal Negro Improvement Association, New York and Jamaica, 1910s–1920s.

Holcombe, R. A., manager, UFC, Armuelles division, 1950s–1960s.

Kyes, J. M., manager, UFC, Bocas division, 1912–1919.

McFarland, E. C., assistant to manager, UFC, Panama City, 1910s–1920s.

Mais, V. T. ("Bill"), agent, Chiriqui Land Company, Panama City, 1950s–1960s.

Moore, F., senior assistant vice-president, UFC, Boston, 1950s.

Mullins, E. attorney, UFC, San José, Costa Rica, 1910s.

Munch, G. D., manager, UFC, Bocas division, 1950s.

Myrick, G. A., manager, UFC, Armuelles division; subsequently manager, UFC, Bocas Division, 1940s–1950s.

O'Hearn, N. C., general agent, UFC, steamship service traffic department, 1910–1920s.

Pollan, A. A., general manager, UFC, Tropical Banana divisions, 1929; executive vice-president, UFC, Boston, 1943–1950s.

Phillips, D. O., agent, UFC, Cristobal Agency, Canal zone, 1924.

Richards, R., superintendent, UFC, Sixaola district, 1954.

Rivera, J., manager of labor relations, UFC, Bocas division, 1950s–1960 strike.

Smith, W. P., son-in-law of Bribri King (Francisco Saldaña), small farmer in Coroma, Talamanca, 1914.

Torrijos, O., general and commander, National Guard, Panama, 1960s–1970s.

Turnbull, W. W., manager, UFC, Tela Division, Honduras, 1950s.

MARK MOBERG

Responsible Men and Sharp Yankees:

The United Fruit Company, Resident Elites,

and Colonial State in British Honduras

The former British colony of Belize is widely regarded as a cultural and political anomaly among the states of Central America.[1] Known as British Honduras until 1973, the country claims a cultural and linguistic affinity for the anglophone West Indies that sharply distinguishes it from the rest of Central America. Colonial-era and even many contemporary narratives portray the British influence in the colony as a benign force, one that ostensibly produced an "island of democracy" within a region otherwise marked by oppressive class structures and political institutions. Recent historiography has revealed that such claims, when not openly nostalgic, greatly exaggerate the political and economic freedoms enjoyed by most residents during the colonial period. Throughout much of the colony's history, a close-knit oligarchy of timber companies and expatriate merchants ruled the territory as a virtual fiefdom, often in defiance of the Colonial Office in London. As British Honduras grew almost totally reliant on mahogany exportation in the early nineteenth century, resident elites simply apportioned most of the territory's land among themselves. For more than a century after the abolition of slavery in 1838, a majority of the colony's workers were bound to the timber industry through a system of debt servitude that left them "virtually enslaved for life," according to the colonial secretary in 1890 (Ashcraft 1973, 36).

By the late nineteenth century, colonial administrators from London regularly clashed with the resident "forestocracy" (Grant 1976, 36), whose voracious demands for land and labor conflicted with government plans for diversifying the colonial economy through agricultural development. Seen as a means of averting the catastrophic "booms" and "busts" of the mahogany trade, the promotion of export agriculture inevitably heightened antagonisms between British administrators and timber elites whose control of land and labor had rested on the exclusion of agriculture from the colony. Such policies also drew the colony into closer integration with the region's agricultural export markets of the time, which, then as now, centered on the North American banana trade. This essay examines the often-strained relationship between the colonial state, traditional elites, and the United Fruit Company, which was invited to operate in British Honduras at the beginning of the twentieth century. Seen by colonial governors as an ally in their quest for agricultural development, United Fruit promised a ready market for the colony's nascent agricultural exporters, a farming class that administrators had consciously created through land and shipping reforms. In their pursuit of alternative export markets, however, administrators subjected the colony to a costly and humiliating dependence on the corporation that dominated those markets.

By 1910, United Fruit had emerged as the largest North American banana importer, in large part by systematically excluding all competition from its areas of operation. The company was already infamous throughout Central America for employing bribery and threatening U.S. intervention to further its interests. Colonial-era historians often distinguished British Honduras from the venality and *caudillismo* of the region's banana republics, so-called because of their political and economic domination by United Fruit. Yet communications between the territory's governors and the Colonial Office in the early twentieth century reveal an eager accommodation of the U.S. banana company, one that prompted indignation among traditional elites as well as official concern in London. Contrary to the accusations of their local critics, British officials acted on behalf of United Fruit neither from corruption nor from fear of U.S. intervention. Rather, their actions were dictated by agricultural development policies tied to export markets, which compelled them to deal with the corporation that controlled those markets.

Over the two decades that United Fruit operated in the colony, a succession of colonial governors proved unable to negotiate a relationship with the company that benefited local agricultural producers. Despite the cultural and political differences between Britain's only Central American colony and its neighboring nation-states, ultimately British Honduras was as crudely manipulated by United Fruit as were the governments of Honduras and Guatemala. The common dependence of Central American nations on North American capital during this period highlights the limited sovereignty of states whose economic power is dwarfed by that of the corporations that export their primary products. In this sense, this case study offers lessons for nation-states embarking on neoliberal development strategies in the globalized economy a century later. Under such policies, the provision of land, tax, and wage concessions to multinational investors is viewed as a central mechanism for agricultural and industrial development. Similarly, developing societies are encouraged to specialize in the export of commodities produced under their comparative advantages of climate, agricultural resources, and labor costs (Deere et al. 1990; Watson 1994). The concessions offered by the colonial state in exchange for investment and the machinations by which United Fruit exacted them are all too familiar to critical observers of neoliberal economic policy in the contemporary developing world. From the account that follows, it is evident that such strategies, rather than benefiting most residents of developing societies, serve instead to deepen their dependence on corporations that control their access to world markets.

THE STATE, COLONIAL ELITES, AND UNITED FRUIT

Many historians of the postemancipation Caribbean regard British colonial governments of the time as intermediaries between local elites and the newly freed rural working class. When Parliament voted in 1833 to abolish slavery throughout the British Empire, the Colonial Office and the governors it appointed to the West Indies were charged with enforcing the mandate, invariably over staunch resistance by local planters. Accordingly, governors of the post-slavery West Indies often developed antagonistic relationships with the former slave-owning elite, whom they frequently accused of reintroducing new forms of servitude. Writing of the sugar-producing colonies, W. A. Green argued that "the imperial government . . . assumed a middle position," mediating between planters and former slaves to secure "a fragile industrial peace" (1984, 116). By seeking compromise among the conflicting interests that cross-cut Caribbean society, the functionaries that populate such accounts (e.g., Waddell 1961) appear as unbiased "responsible men" interested more in the general welfare of Britain's imperial holdings than in accommodating elite interests.[2]

Following the designation of British Honduras as a Crown colony in 1862, governors and local elites clashed repeatedly over colonial policy and its enforcement. Until then, the resident forestocracy had administered the territory with minimal interference from the Colonial Office. On gaining Crown-colony status, however, the territory was to be administered by appointed governors whose executive powers could, in theory, override elite interests. Policy making in the colony was vested in a legislative council consisting of the governor and five "unofficial" members whom he or a previous governor had selected from the local population. Invariably, the unofficial legislative appointments were drawn from a list of nominees representing the timber industry and mercantile concerns. This system of governance nearly collapsed in the late 1880s, when Governor Goldsworthy announced a labor-law reform ardently opposed by all of the unofficial members, who responded with a boycott of legislative council meetings. The Colonial Office was forced to curtail the power of governors that it appointed to the colony before the unofficial appointees agreed to rejoin the council and drop their demands for an elected government. In 1892 unofficial members were granted a voting majority in the council (in effect a veto over the governor), thereby weakening executive powers to an extent unprecedented among Britain's Caribbean colonies (Ashdown 1980, 59). After their appointment to the council, many unofficial members served for the duration of their lifetimes. As a result, governors enjoyed little ability to wholly reshape the council during their own terms of appointment, which rarely lasted more than six years.

It did not follow from the occasionally contentious relationship between colonial administrators and local elites that the former used their powers impartially within the local economic and political arenas. Some governors, notably Sweet-Escott (1904–1905) and Swayne (1905–1911), openly opposed the unofficial majority as "a bar to the good government of the Colony in the interests of its various classes and races" (Clarion, 1 September 1910, p. 267). When Governor Swayne filled a Council vacancy with an appointee sympathetic to labor reform, he gained a voting majority on an ordinance curtailing debt servitude, then the primary mechanism of labor control in the timber industry. The appointment provoked a storm of protest among the other councillors, who condemned the passage of the bill as "unprincipled and autocratic" (ibid.). As a bastion of elite opinion, the Clarion, the colony's major newspaper, mounted strident attacks against Swayne that continued until the end of his term, when

it greeted the departure of the "derelict sordid-minded" governor with jubila-
tion (20 March 1913, p. 411).[3] Apart from such confrontations, however, most
governors rarely challenged the elite majority in the legislative council. As has
been noted elsewhere in the Caribbean, colonial governors "discovered a local
white society whose members were eager to welcome [them] as their ceremonial
head. . . . To join with them meant a pleasant tour of duty, to fight them meant . . .
political conflict and social ostracism" (Gordon K. Lewis 1968, 104). More criti-
cally, the assertion that administrators were autonomous of elite interests ne-
glects their actions on behalf of powerful metropolitan-based actors in the
British Caribbean. Metropolitan interests, represented first by British timber
firms and later by North American investors, enjoyed consistent support from
colonial administrators, regardless of their attitudes toward local elites. Indeed,
both governors who opposed resident elites, as well as those who enjoyed con-
genial relationships with them, differed little in their accommodation of foreign
capital. By the early 1900s, North American investment had eclipsed British
economic power throughout the Caribbean. Foremost among North American interests at the time was the United Fruit Company, which had acquired
control over the region's primary export commodity.

From its incorporation in 1899, United Fruit became known for its relentless
pursuit of a monopoly in the banana trade. In its first years of operation, the
company refined a formidable array of tactics that it continues to employ even
today to restrict competition from other importers. United Fruit frequently
secured marketing monopolies over independent Central American growers
by paying them higher prices than its competitors could afford, thus depriving rivals of marketable fruit (Thomas C. Holt 1992, 354). Short-term losses
from this strategy were offset by profits generated in other markets where the
company's monopoly was secure. United Fruit's attractive producer prices remained in effect only until its rivals had withdrawn from the market, after
which it could dictate prices and marketing conditions to its suppliers. United
Fruit also used similar means to thwart marketing efforts among independent
growers. In the late 1920s Jamaican smallholders formed a cooperative that developed a shipping line and marketing organization rivaling United Fruit's.
The company retaliated by raising its Jamaican producer prices far above those
of the co-op. By 1935, the cooperative was appealing to the colonial government for intervention to stave off collapse and an ensuing United Fruit mo-

nopoly control of banana exports. Neither the colonial governor, members of the Jamaican legislative council, nor the Colonial Office in London answered the cooperative's pleas. Eventually it was forced to surrender to United Fruit's demands, among which were an insistence that it reorganize as a shareholding company, that it cease exporting fruit to the United States, and that it pay its suppliers prices no greater than those offered by United Fruit for Jamaican bananas (ibid., 365).

United Fruit further enhanced its monopolistic advantages as it developed plantations of its own. By 1930, the company had procured over twenty times the amount of land it held under actual cultivation, a strategy designed, according to company critics, to limit the availability of land to competitors (McCann 1976, 39–40). The company defended its acquisitions in terms of its need to relocate production due to Panama Disease and soil exhaustion. To contend with the disease, United Fruit established "division" plantations of tens of thousands of acres, only to abandon them as they succumbed to the disease. Despite the virulence of the disease, small-scale producers often remained in production by adopting labor-intensive methods of quarantine. However, with each relocation, the company "systematically destroyed the infrastructure it had constructed (railroads, bridges, telephone lines, etc.) in order to prevent competitors from being able to renew production on a smaller scale" (Bourgois 1989, 8). Once United Fruit withdrew its infrastructure from an infected division, small farmers usually lost their only marketing outlets, forcing them to suspend production as well.

Finally, United Fruit enlisted national and colonial authorities to secure company interests over those of their local constituents, while invoking U.S. diplomatic and military pressure against recalcitrant governments. By the early twentieth century, the company was brazenly manipulating Central American officials through bribery and intimidation (Dosal 1993). More subtly, the company played national governments against each another when negotiating land acquisitions and taxes. Much as United Fruit prevailed in price wars by compensating with profits from regions where its monopoly was secure, it used its geographically dispersed holdings to extract concessions. Profits earned from Central American operations, for example, enabled the company to sustain higher producer prices than the Jamaican producers' cooperative. Meanwhile, the company threatened to suspend investment in British West Africa to prevent the Colonial Office from supporting Jamaican growers (Thomas C. Holt 1992, 356). Bluff and misrepresentation played a significant role in such strategies, company negotiators often emphasizing to local officials that other countries produced fruit less expensively and under more favorable conditions (Bourgois 1989, 21). Such claims implicitly threatened that the company would abandon operations in any country that failed to meet its terms.

Although United Fruit secured an effective monopoly over banana exports from British Honduras by 1904, the company did not resort to the bribery or threatened intervention that it employed with some success in Honduras and Guatemala. Rather, its influence increased in tandem with the colony's new-found orientation to North American markets, which left it particularly vulnerable to the demands of U.S. capital. By 1903, British Honduras was directing the majority of its exports to the U.S. market, following a decade of declining trade with the United Kingdom. As the orientation of the colony's trade shifted between 1890 and 1900, bananas accounted for, on average, 71 percent of the value of its exports to the United States (AB Colony of British Honduras 1890–1903). In that decade the banana sector grew in importance due to a depression in the mahogany trade—the colony's traditional mainstay—and the government's gradual recognition that agricultural development was essential to overcoming the colony's chronic economic stagnation.[4] During this period, then, British Honduras became more fully integrated with the circuits of trade that had earlier tied the rest of Central America to the United States. While the U.S. market became critical to the colonial economy at this time, banana exports from British Honduras were, as Governor Eyre Hutson admitted, but "a minute part" (1925, 176) of the U.S. fruit trade as a whole. Even at its peak, the output of the colony's banana industry constituted no more than 3 percent of United Fruit's total banana imports to the United States (ibid.). This trade imbalance points as well to an imbalance in power relationships. While colonial trade was increasingly tied to the banana market, United Fruit could easily dispense with British Honduran bananas if need be. Having acquired a marketing monopoly over the colony's primary export, the company dominated not only the colony's economy but its officials as well.

Although the Stann Creek and Toledo districts of southern Belize are climatically well suited for banana production, the growth of a banana industry in the region during the late nineteenth century was not a simple outcome of its natural endowments. Belize Town timber and mercantile elites had long resisted expansion of any local farming activity, which was seen as a competitor for the colony's scarce labor. They succeeded in blocking agricultural development until 1879, when a newly appointed governor, Frederick Barlee, lowered the price of Crown lands to $1.00 per acre to promote their sale to smallholders. Further antagonizing the local oligarchy, the governor shifted colonial mail subsidies from a Kingston-bound steamship line to a New Orleans route to promote the shipment of bananas to the U.S. market. Barlee's reforms earned him the "almost unanimous opposition of the colony's commercial community" (*Colonial Guardian*, 15 August 1911, p. 2), who relied on access to British goods through Jamaica. Colonial merchants and the timber industry aggressively lobbied the Colonial Office for his recall, a demand that it finally obliged in 1884. Land prices were eventually raised to their earlier level, but during Barlee's administration thousands of former timber workers acquired land where the forestocracy had not yet consolidated its control. Most acquisitions by small-scale farmers were limited to the sparsely settled Stann Creek district in the southern part of the colony, where only 12 percent of the land was under private control as of 1880 (Ashdown 1979, 25).

During the 1880s, newspapers recorded an exodus of labor from the timber industry, "as many captains and labourers from mahogany gangs . . . have been able to invest their earnings on banana plantations instead of spending them in Belize [Town] in riotous living" (*Colonial Guardian*, 1 January 1887, p. 2). Census figures of 1880 and 1890 indicate a steady shift of the colony's population to banana-producing areas of the south (Cal 1991, 315). Most population growth was centered in places such as the Stann Creek valley and Monkey River, a village whose size increased from 250 residents in 1881 to nearly 700 ten years later. Most of the new settlers were Creoles and Garifuna, the Afro-Caribbean segments of the population that had historically dominated forestry work. Former timber workers were joined by Mestizos and Maya migrating from neighboring countries, and even Bahamians and black and East Indian Jamaicans who were brought to work on several of the colony's larger farms (*Colonial Guardian*, 9 March 1901, p. 2). Family-operated smallholdings coexisted with much larger estates, several of which exceeded 1,000 acres. The largest farm in the region, the 14,301-acre Melinda estate, operated a five-mile-long mule-driven tramway to transport its fruit to port. By the mid-1890s, some 6,000 stems were being shipped weekly from the towns of Stann Creek (now Dangriga) and Monkey River. At both places, bananas were carried in paddle dories and rowboats to offshore steamers.

Until 1897, the government subsidized a local steamship line to carry the colony's mail and fruit. When the contract was reassigned to a New Orleans-based firm in that year, the so-called fruit clause, obliging steamers to carry all marketable bananas produced in the colony, was deleted at that company's insistence (AB Colony of British Honduras 1901, 21–31). Thereafter, when steamers called weekly along the colony's southern coast, their holds were frequently filled with Honduran and Guatemalan fruit. Colonial newspapers reported occasions when more than 4,000 stems were discarded when the steamer refused to ship them, causing enormous losses to growers (*Colonial Guardian*, 9 March 1901, p. 2). Within a year of its incorporation, United Fruit stealthily acquired majority ownership of six shipping lines operating along the Caribbean coast of Central America, dramatically expanding its control of the region's banana trade (Kepner 1936, 42). Among these was the Belize Royal Mail and Central American Steamship Company, the aforementioned holder of the colony's subsidized mail contract and primary exporter of its bananas. Over the next three years United Fruit would undermine all rival lines serving British Honduras to emerge as the sole exporter of the colony's bananas.

Within several months of United Fruit's acquisition of the mail contract, several Stann Creek planters invited the shipping branch of the Vaccaro Brothers Fruit Company to arrange regular port calls in the colony to purchase their bananas.[5] The new line was welcomed by both growers and merchants as a source of competition with United Fruit. As soon as the Vacarro steamers arrived at Stann Creek, however, United Fruit tripled its fruit prices to colonial producers, a tactic that the *Colonial Guardian* termed a "ridiculously transparent stratagem" (1 January 1902, p. 3) to deprive the Vaccaro Line of business.[6] Within a year, United Fruit had forced its rival from the colony and emerged as its only carrier of mail and bananas. The company promptly exercised its newfound monopoly by raising charges for freight and lowering the payment price for bananas purchased in the colony (*Colonial Guardian*, 1 January 1902, p. 2). On the expiration of its mail contract several months later, United Fruit informed the government that it would suspend steamship service entirely unless granted an annual subsidy of $14,500. Its request was nearly 50 percent greater than the subsidy previously provided under the Belize Royal Mail line's contract with the government (BPRO CO 123 240 1902a).

Governor Wilson responded with a proposed $12,000 subvention, which the company accepted after some negotiation. The unofficial members of the legislative council promptly vetoed the governor's proposal, proposing a lower subsidy of $10,000. United Fruit immediately ended steamship service, a decision that represented "a great calamity to the Colony," in the governor's words (ibid.). Henry Keith, manager of the company's Honduras Division, imperiously informed Governor Wilson of the suspension in these terms: "I am now instructed to withdraw all previous offers relating to the Mail Contract, and I now beg to advise you that the Company will only accept a Mail Contract on the conditions of the one that has just been proposed — namely — $14,500, subsidy per annum. . . . I am also instructed to inform you that these terms are final with my Company and if not accepted, all negotiation may be considered closed" (BPRO CO 123 240 1902b).

After a month without mail or scheduled freight service to the colony, the governor reopened negotiations with Keith while seeking a renewed opportunity to pass his proposed contract. When one unofficial member failed to appear at a council meeting, the governor suspended the rules of order requiring prior notification of agenda items and cast the deciding vote on the $12,000 subsidy (*Colonial Guardian*, 8 March 1902, p. 3). Unofficial members and the press were outraged at the governor's "high-handed and undignified maneuvering" (ibid.) to pass the subsidy, while a fruit grower in Stann Creek charged that Wilson had "cringed to the Trust and betrayed the fruit industry of the Colony to [its] tender mercies" (*Colonial Guardian*, 26 July 1902, p. 3). In a written protest to the Colonial Office in London, the unofficial members recited a litany of abuses suffered by the colony since United Fruit had acquired the contract in 1900: "The freight rates were increased: Discrimination was introduced against supporters of other [shipping] lines: Fruit was rejected without reasonable cause in large quantities, on more than one occasion because the subsidised mail steamers had filled up with fruit from the Southern Republics" (BPRO CO 123 240 1902c).

Finally, Benjamin Fairweather, the council's only "coloured" member, decried the racial discrimination that already permeated all aspects of United Fruit's operations in Central America: "Black passengers though paying first class fares were prevented from sitting at table with the other passengers and were otherwise treated as a class apart" (ibid.). In subsidizing such treatment, the councillors claimed, the government had not only exhibited bad judgment but betrayed local interests: "Too many sacrifices have been made and the Government has gone too much out of its way to retain the Services of the United Fruit Company" (ibid.). Responding to both Wilson's dispatches detailing his negotiations with United Fruit and the unofficial members' protest of his actions, Colonial Office staff in London penned comments for internal circulation. The final, anonymous notation on a minute paper from 1902 best expresses the colonial government's predicament in dealing with the company: "Nothing else to be done, but the Govt. has been completely bluffed by these sharp Yankees" (BPRO CO 123 240 n.d.).

If United Fruit found a consistent ally in colonial administrators of the early twentieth century, it also cultivated ties with wealthy expatriate planters in Stann Creek. As members of the nascent agricultural bourgeoisie favored by British policy in the Caribbean, several planters were well positioned to influence governors in matters of agricultural policy. One of the largest growers at the beginning of the century, Bede Ormsby, was a white expatriate who served as district commissioner for Stann Creek under Governor Wilson. In 1903 Ormsby intercepted a letter from the Canadian shipping firm of Marsh and Marsh that proposed a direct fruit trade between the colony and Canada's maritime provinces, in effect establishing a marketing alternative independent of United Fruit. Although the letter had been addressed to the Stann Creek postmaster, Ormsby confiscated the letter and replied in his official capacity that all colonial growers were already under contract to United Fruit. In fact, the company had offered contracts only to nine large planters or firms (Ormsby among them), but the estimated 500 to 600 small growers of the time were not committed to sell exclusively to United Fruit. Ormsby's efforts to deter competition in the colony's fruit trade led to considerable unrest among the small growers of Stann Creek. Following a series of rallies in the town, ninety smallholders formed a Native Fruit Growers Union of "people whose complexions are too lowly to merit recognition from so exalted an individual as a District Commissioner" (*Colonial Guardian*, 19 March 1904, p. 3), as one supporter described the group. According to its members, most of whom were Garifuna, United Fruit had issued preferential contracts to the region's largest growers, all of whom were white, while subjecting small farmers to far more unpredictable marketing conditions (*Colonial Guardian*, 26 March 1904, p. 3). Subsequently, little is heard of the growers union, although Ormsby's reply to Marsh and Marsh defused the final threat to United Fruit's monopoly over the colony's banana exports.

THE STATE AT THE SERVICE OF UNITED FRUIT

United Fruit established its presence in British Honduras on its terms and extracted concessions even more favorable than those it obtained from other Central American governments. Following the precedent of the firm's founder, Minor Keith, United Fruit obtained many of its Central American landholdings for token sums or free of charge, albeit in exchange for the construction of railroads. Although the resulting railroads remained under United Fruit's ownership, such arrangements were encouraged by national governments lacking the resources or expertise to lay track through heavily forested tropical lowlands (Kepner and Soothill 1935, 154). In tandem with vast holdings of virgin land on which to cultivate bananas, railroads provided United Fruit with a transportation and marketing monopoly. Unlike most of Central America, in British Honduras the company secured such a monopoly without having to assume the costs of railroad construction. Within months of United Fruit's incorporation, Governor Wilson proposed to the Colonial Office that the government itself build a railway to promote banana production and encourage the company to invest in the colony: "The future action of the great Fruit Combine . . . will be greatly influenced by the decision whether there is, or is not to be a railway . . . with a pier for loading fruit direct from the railway trucks. If a railway is decided upon, they may introduce much capital here to grow fruit for themselves, or buy it from producers here. If on the contrary there is to be no railway, they will probably devote their energies and their capital to obtaining their supplies of fruit from the Honduras Republic and further South" (BPRO CO 123 233 1899).

The governor's next sentence reveals that his support had been secured through the sort of cross-national manipulation for which United Fruit was to become infamous: "As an instance of the possibilities in this direction, Mr. Walsh, the future manager in Central America of . . . the United Fruit Company, informed me at an interview which I had with him . . . that he was at the present moment in doubt whether he would establish his head-quarters at Belize or at Puerto Cortés [Honduras]" (ibid.). Such "doubt" implied that the company's decision would hinge on the government's provision of a railroad and land for its use. Notwithstanding the colony's willingness to extend such concessions, all company operations in British Honduras were soon to be directed from its Bananera Division headquarters in Guatemala.

While both governors and local elites concurred on the desirability of a railway, they differed sharply on the route to be adopted. Belize Town elites favored a line extending from the capital to the Guatemalan border, a route that, not coincidentally, improved access to timberlands and to Guatemalan and internal markets. Most of the unofficial members would benefit materially from such a route, and several were financially involved in planning the venture (Ashdown 1979, 125). In contrast, Governor Swayne envisioned the railway as an inducement to agricultural development in the Stann Creek valley, a route ridiculed by the Clarion as "leading from a small coast town to the hills — from nowhere to nowhere" (26 July 1909, p. 123). Swayne went to some length to persuade the Colonial Office that local opposition to the Stann Creek route was far from disinterested. Eventually, London pledged financial support for a railway from Commerce Bight, a port south of Stann Creek Town, to a parcel of land then under consideration for purchase by United Fruit at Middlesex, twenty miles inland. While the line would transport the produce of all growers along its right of way, the railway was also intended as an incentive to United Fruit for the development of a plantation in the colony. Rhetorically, colonial officials rationalized such concessions as investments that would one day generate freight and tax revenues from a flourishing industry. As will be seen, such expectations proved unrealistic, due to severe underestimates of construction costs and a naive belief that the company would uphold its obligations in exchange for the railroad.

After receiving government assurances of the railroad project, United Fruit began negotiations for the purchase of land at Middlesex. Correspondence reveals that the governor avidly represented the company's arguments and interests to London. The Colonial Office originally directed Swayne to price the Middlesex estate at rates equal to banana-producing land in Jamaica (about $7.50 per acre). In response, Swayne argued that the company was unwilling to pay more than one dollar per acre, in addition to the cost of the land survey, due to the presence of abundant inexpensive land in the neighboring countries: "Comparing British Honduras with Guatemala, I find that the United Fruit Company paid nothing for their large plantations in Guatemala. The land belonged to the Railway Company which made them a large concession, on the simple condition that they should plant a certain number of bananas" (BPRO CO 123 255 1907). Should the government fail to offer an attractive sale price, Swayne warned, United Fruit would "extend their operations in Guatemala, where they already work large blocks of land, and have invested money in local railways and tramways, and where conditions are in so many respects more favourable; and having once given up their idea of establishing themselves in the Colony, their interests in the future are not likely to coincide with ours" (ibid.). By conveying United Fruit's threat to abandon operations in the colony after construction had already begun on the railroad, Swayne left the Colonial Office little choice but to accept the company's offer for the Middlesex estate.

An agreement setting forth the conditions of United Fruit's operations in British Honduras was signed between company president Minor Keith and the colonial government in 1909. The company received the 7,549-acre estate for one dollar per acre, plus $1,500 in surveying costs. It also specified that United Fruit would plant out the estate in increments of at least 250 acres per year. In exchange, the contract limited the land tax at Middlesex to ten cents per acre per year, exempted bananas from export taxes, and excused the company's agricultural implements and machinery from import duties (BPRO CO 123 261 1909). Although the agreement required United Fruit to operate the plantation for twenty-five years, it provided no penalties in the event that the company broke its commitment. Nor did it allow the government to increase its freight rates or require the company to renegotiate fruit prices to private growers over that period (BPRO CO 123 295a 1918). These terms entailed lavish concessions when compared to the conditions under which other growers acquired land in the Stann Creek valley. Much to the government's embarrassment, an issue of the official *Government Gazette* juxtaposed the United Fruit contract with an advertisement for Crown lands available to residents of the colony wishing to settle along the railway. Smallholders who purchased land in the area were required to pay up to $8.00 per acre and held to stricter cultivation standards than the company (*Clarion,* 22 July 1909, p. 94). Further, unlike the company, smallholders were not exempted from duties or the standard land tax rate of fifty cents per acre.

This double standard prompted colonial newspapers to respond with populist indignation, notwithstanding the elite interests that they represented. The *Clarion* sarcastically "congratulate[d] the Trust on its easy victory over a weak Government ready to respond to the wishes of the rich and powerful" (22 July 1909, p. 98). The *Colonial Guardian* went further in describing the government as "amongst the worst we have had. . . . Just think of the contrast this policy presents—a wealthy foreign trust . . . is granted land at one eighth the price that taxpayers of the Colony . . . are allowed to purchase it at, although the profits made by the latter would remain in this country to the benefit of the Colony generally—No wonder people living in the Stann Creek District believe that the Government have [*sic*] constructed the railway for the United Fruit Co." (11 December 1910, p. 3).

"If this were the United States, one would look for graft," P. S. Woods commented facetiously in the *Clarion,* "but of course such things are unknown in a British colony" (20 March 1912, p. 303). In the face of such criticisms, the government later announced that all banana farmers along the railway would pay a final price not exceeding one dollar per acre (ibid., p. 329). To become eligible for such prices, farmers were required first to purchase the land at the advertised price of $8.00 and were later granted a $7.00 rebate for each acre planted in bananas. This policy revision did little to assuage critics, who noted that many small farmers lacked the ready cash or credit necessary for the initial land purchase. Further, the clause requiring that farmers plant their lands in bananas was, according to the *Clarion,* "tantamount to a declaration that the available lands were . . . granted to the Trust to be exploited solely in its interests, since the Trust had killed competition in bananas and held a monopoly of the commodity" (20 March 1912, p. 303).

Although envisioned as a self-supporting venture, the construction and operation of the Stann Creek railway proved to be a massive colonial subsidy to the company. Initially planned as a twenty-mile-long, narrow-gauge line, the line was approved by the Colonial Office in 1906 at a cost of $280,000. By the time the railroad was completed four years later, its gauge had been widened to accommodate heavier rolling stock and its length increased by five miles due to an initial surveying error. So, too, had its final cost more than tripled, to more than $841,000. By 1911, the project's deficits had come to the attention of several members of the House of Commons in London, who demanded an explanation of such substantial expenditures on behalf of a non-British firm (BPRO CO 123 271 1911). Yet the railroad's construction and operating losses only strengthened the company's hand in dealing with the colony. British authorities realized that the railroad's financial success depended on United Fruit's willingness to supply it with freight. Knowing of the government's need to recoup its construction costs, the company was able to wring still further concessions from the Colonial Office, overcoming even parliamentary opposition.

Soon after the railroad was completed United Fruit sought to establish a radio telegraph station, the colony's first, to communicate with its ships and other divisions in Central America. After entertaining the request, a parliamentary committee in London ruled that a foreign company should not control the colony's only direct telegraphic links abroad. Acting on the advice of Governor Swayne, the Colonial Office pleaded with the committee that it reverse its decision, anticipating retaliation if it failed to do so.

> The United Fruit Company is very important to British Honduras as a buyer and exporter of fruit, and it would be a serious thing for the Colony if the Company's operations were discouraged. . . . It is not too much to say that if [it] were to suspend its operations in and about Stann Creek, the [rail] line would be . . . a hopeless failure. For this reason, therefore, it is important to maintain good relations with the United Fruit Company. . . . This appears to be a justification for the unusual proposal to place telegraphic communication in the hands of a foreign company. (BPRO CO 123 267 1909)

Remaining resolute before such pleas, the parliamentary committee upheld its rejection of the company's request. United Fruit lost little time in responding; within a month it withdrew its passenger steamers from service to British Honduras, substituting smaller vessels that carried exclusively mail and fruit. The suspension of the colony's only passenger service to the United States caused, in the governor's words, "a good deal of dissatisfaction in the Colony"

(BPRO CO 123 268 1911b). Responding to the governor's request for a resump-
tion of service, C. H. Ellis, United Fruit's New Orleans manager, wrote, "It
would greatly assist me if I could be assured that we could get our Wireless Station established there, and a small increase in the passenger rate there on the
large steamers. . . . I need not tell you that our experience with operating the
large steamers to Belize was very unprofitable and unsatisfactory" (BPRO 123
268 1911a).

The governor forwarded Ellis' correspondence to the Colonial Office with an
added appeal on behalf of the company: "A wireless station is peculiarly necessary for a large Fruit Company, and I am convinced that without one we cannot
hope to have the 5,000 ton steamers calling here. . . . I trust, therefore, that
you will be able to see your way to permit the station to be established" (BPRO
CO 123 268 1911b). In June 1911 Parliament relented, granting the company permission to operate a radio station in the colony. Not coincidentally, passenger
steamship service resumed the following month.

CRISIS AND COLLAPSE

In the decades after the 1880s, banana cultivation rapidly expanded along the
Stann Creek valley. After 1911, the railway significantly boosted banana exports
by making new farms accessible to transportation. The entire colony exported
140,000 stems of fruit in 1893, but by 1917, 621,000 stems were shipped from
the Stann Creek valley alone. By 1920, an estimated 10,000 acres of land in
the colony were under banana cultivation. Yet a series of natural and climatic
disasters following the construction of the railway were soon to prevent these
newly opened lands from realizing their potential.

Heavy rains in June 1911 washed out two bridges on the railway and isolated
the United Fruit plantation. Until the bridges were replaced later that year, more
than 90 percent of the farm's output could not be shipped to market. Expansion of the farm soon resumed, and by 1914 United Fruit claimed over 1,800
acres under cultivation at Middlesex. The estate's recovery was to prove short-
lived, however, as a hurricane leveled more than 75 percent of the Middlesex
farm in 1915 and caused an estimated loss of 300,000 stems of fruit throughout
the valley (BPRO CO 123 284 1915). Bad weather returned in 1917, when heavy
flooding destroyed an additional 115,000 stems on area farms. As the governor

noted when explaining the railway's continuing deficits to London, "the volume of business with Middlesex is reduced owing to blow-downs, floods, etc. This farm has had much misfortune" (BPRO CO 123 291 1918).

The industry's decline was much in evidence by the end of the decade, but it was disease, rather than weather, that provided the fatal blow. As early as 1914, United Fruit workers had detected Panama Disease on some portions of the Middlesex estate. The disease is caused by a highly infectious fungus and may be transmitted from plant to plant during periods of flooding or even through contact with workers or tools that have been exposed to *Fusarium* spores. The colony's agricultural officer, W. R. Dunlop, inferred that Middlesex had been infected by United Fruit workers transferred there from its Guatemalan division. Initially, the disease was limited to the United Fruit holdings, but in 1918 it appeared throughout the Stann Creek valley, apparently borne downstream by the floods of the previous year. As Dunlop grimly reported after a 1920 inspection of the Stann Creek valley, the heady optimism that greeted the railroad's construction had evaporated by decade's end. All along the railway, he had observed the "ghostly, grave-yard appearance" of farms abandoned to Panama disease, "the brown headless trunks [of banana plants] still standing as they died" (BPRO CO 123 300 1920a). After 1918, the most heavily affected farm, Middlesex, underwent no further expansion, and United Fruit announced plans to abandon production there in 1920.[7]

Postmortems of the banana industry claim that its demise was only partly the result of disease and adverse weather, for the effects of natural disasters were aggravated by poor cultivation techniques. Observers of the time condemned the "primitive . . . milpa-style" methods (Samspon 1929, 23) and "fugitive crop-taking" (BPRO CO 123 329/2 1928) employed by the colony's small-scale banana growers. The government's agricultural officer largely concurred that the industry was "doomed" by its reliance on *milpa* (shifting) cultivation. Yet where others had blamed such techniques on the supposed ignorance or indolence of small farmers, Dunlop observed that cultivation practices simply reflected the conditions under which colonial banana growers sold their fruit: "It all comes back to the agreement with the United Fruit Company. [An intensive] system of production should have been insisted upon in the agreement, and the price paid for fruit should have been higher . . . to meet the increased cost of production under the intensive methods. It is highly probable, in fact certain, that the

United Fruit Company would never have signed such an agreement" (BPRO CO 123 300 1920a).

In hindsight, colonial officials came to realize that the contract with United Fruit had been, as one dispatch noted with characteristic understatement, "a very one-sided one" (BPRO CO 123 292 1918). Under the terms of its contract, the company purchased fruit from the colony's growers for less than it paid elsewhere in Central America while enjoying hugely subsidized rail rates.[8] Ten years after United Fruit had signed its contract with the colonial government, during which time its prices to farmers had remained unchanged, growers in British Honduras urgently petitioned for an increase in fruit prices. The company's response was a price increase of two cents per stem in June 1919. The colonial secretary appealed directly to the company's Boston headquarters for a much greater increase, reflecting the substantial rise in supply and labor costs over the preceding war years: "Your Company has never failed to bring to this Government's notice the increased cost of conducting the service of the fruit ships, a representation which has been recognised by this Government, but . . . His Excellency has never understood why the price offered by the Company for bananas in British Honduras should not be more in accordance than it has with the prices offered and paid in Jamaica" (BPRO CO 123 300 1920b).

United Fruit, whose role in the colony was now reduced to that of a marketing outlet for independent growers, responded to the appeal with a set of revised marketing procedures. While growers could, in theory, earn more under these revisions, the governor noted that "the conditions imposed by the Company provide for strict grading of the bunches, and if they carry out thorough inspection the gain to the planters is questionable" (BPRO CO 123 300 1920d). Indeed, for stems of seven hands, the growers would be paid a full third less than they had previously. Further, while introducing more uncertainty about producer prices, the new contracts now explicitly prohibited growers from selling their fruit to any other buyer.

United Fruit's abandonment of Middlesex did not strengthen official resolve in dealing with the company, despite the growing indignation expressed at its practices. The company's decision to close its estate flouted its contract with the government, which mandated that it cultivate "bananas *or other agricultural produce*" there for not less than twenty-five years (BPRO CO 123 295a 1919). In 1919 Governor Hutson appealed to company officials to substitute other crops at Middlesex "with a view to meeting their moral obligations under their agreement with the government" (BPRO CO 123 295b). These suggestions were rejected by the company's visiting division manager, who noted simply that United Fruit had "already lost a considerable amount of money on the plantation" (ibid.). Yet, even as United Fruit completed its withdrawal from the colony, the government continued to scrupulously observe its own contract obligations. The governor vetoed a recommendation to raise freight rates on the railroad in 1920, for example, because it "would be construed as an invitation to [United Fruit] to vary the Agreement" (BPRO CO 123 300 1920d). More astonishing was the government's offer to refund the purchase price of Middlesex, rather than insist that United Fruit comply with the contract. In 1921 United Fruit rejected the offer of a refund and put the estate up for sale at $15,000, nearly twice its purchase price (BPRO CO 123 316 1923). Colonial officials not only acquiesced to United Fruit's attempt to sell Middlesex at a 100 percent profit after breaking its contract but recommended two years later that the government itself buy back the estate on these terms (AB MP 3121–23 1923).

If the colonial government's stance toward the company in the early 1920s bordered on self-abasement, its unwillingness to confront United Fruit should be seen, at least in part, in terms of the company's continued control of the colony's banana exports. Governor Hutson had debated whether to hold the company to the contract in 1919 but soon recognized that the agreement with the company "is one without penalties [and] is of no value whatever to the Government . . . in saving the railway" (AB MP 1148–19 1919). After meeting with several influential Stann Creek banana growers, Hutson decided against any confrontation with the company: "I was considering whether the government should take any action in the matter [but] I hesitated to do so, at present, because I wished to do nothing which may prejudice the position of banana planters in the District" (BPRO CO 123 302 1921).[9] As long as United Fruit remained the sole buyer of bananas in the colony, Hutson understood that confrontation might invite a costly retaliation against those producers who remained, including an emergent agricultural elite that the government itself had nurtured through policy reforms. Yet the government's continued overtures to United Fruit seemed to draw equally from a naive optimism and a well-founded fear of company retaliation. Months after the closure of the Middlesex estate, the governor inexplicably boasted before a government commission that "the banana industry in the colony is valued very highly by the United Fruit Company" and that "there are large coastal districts immediately available for banana cultivation, which so far have not been touched" by Panama Disease (*Clarion,* 25 November 1920, p. 613). Claiming that the spread of the disease had been checked, Hutson predicted that production levels would improve and that United Fruit would return to the colony as a direct investor.

In fact, banana production in the colony continued to dwindle through the 1920s as farm after farm was abandoned to Panama Disease and the discouragement of United Fruit's producer prices. From 1917 to the 1931 closure of the colony's last remaining large estate, Riversdale Farm at South Stann Creek, annual production fell from a peak of 886,881 stems to just 78,867 (AB Colony of British Honduras 1937). In the succeeding decade, some small farmers remained in the Stann Creek valley, and United Fruit steamers continued to periodically call at Stann Creek to purchase their fruit. The fate of these growers was sealed in 1937 when the government, computing the railroad's cumulative losses at over two million dollars, declared it an intolerable burden on the colony's finances (AB MP 2091–33 1933; AB DO 123 1937). The following year, the railroad was dismantled and its rolling stock sold off to Jamaica, closing export markets to those Stann Creek valley producers left unscathed by the disease.

CONCLUSION AND POSTSCRIPT

The history of the United Fruit Company in British Honduras highlights the complex interactions of local elites, colonial administrators, and foreign capital in a region of rapidly ascending North American economic power. As the colony's economic fortunes shifted from British toward North American markets, administrators extended preferences to U.S. firms, often favoring them over the interests of timber and mercantile firms based in Britain. To supplant a declining timber industry, colonial governors also advanced the cause of agricultural development, one of whose goals throughout the British Caribbean was the creation of a politically conservative sector of small and medium farmers (Gordon K. Lewis 1968; Lobdell 1988).

While the governors of British Honduras were increasingly independent of timber and mercantile interests, this autonomy scarcely implied the impartiality before all sectors of colonial society that some imperial historians

have suggested. Governors who promoted labor reforms in the timber industry rarely professed comparable concern for agricultural or rail workers whose
labor was critical to the expansion of banana production. Governor Swayne,
for example, incurred the anger of timber barons by his frequent criticisms of
abusive working conditions in forest camps, pointedly rejecting their request
for the importation of indentured Indian workers with the observation that
"imported labourers . . . will [not] receive any better treatment than is given
to the native labourers of the Colony" (*Clarion*, 15 September 1910, p. 346).
Yet, Swayne had earlier called out an armed militia "in overwhelming force"
to suppress a strike by railroad construction workers in the Stann Creek valley
whose wages were lower than what had been promised by government recruiters (Ashdown 1979, 116). Similarly, his successor, Sir Eyre Hutson, endorsed the
Fradulent Labourer's Act in 1917 at the direct request of Stann Creek banana
planters and managers of the United Fruit Middlesex plantation. Passage of
the bill, which fined or imprisoned agricultural workers who broke contracts
with their employers, was accelerated to coincide with the onset of that year's
labor recruitment on the colony's banana farms (AB MP 3424–17 1917). The
government's advocacy of labor reforms in the timber sector and new sanctions against agricultural laborers demonstrated a conspicuous administrative
favoritism toward rising agricultural elites over traditional timber interests. For
governors locked in policy struggles with traditional elites in the colony's legislative council, workers' rights were to be upheld but only to the extent that the
cause of labor reform challenged those elites.

The response of colonial elites to the government's policies shifted dramatically during this period. At the outset of United Fruit's operations in the colony,
the press and unofficial members of the legislative council condemned virtually
all government efforts on behalf of the company. Despite the populist flavor
of their criticisms, their opposition to the company reflected a short-lived alli-
ance between the merchants of Belize Town and the nascent elites committed
to banana production in Stann Creek. Both sectors suffered from United Fruit's
growing control over shipping and were indignant at the generous concessions
made by successive governors on behalf of its steamship operations. In 1901
Belize Town merchants had made common cause with Stann Creek's planters in
petitioning for the assignment of the mail contract to a firm other than United
Fruit (AB Colony of British Honduras 1901, 21–31). Criticism of the government

reached a fever pitch during the term of Sir Eric Swayne, who presided over the construction of the railway and sale of Middlesex. Curiously, after several scathing editorials on government support for the United Fruit subsidy in 1912–1913, the press and legislative council fell nearly silent on the company's activities in the colony. Indeed, references to United Fruit in the ensuing years indicate a near-total reversal of elite opinion. A 1914 *Clarion* editorial described United Fruit's request for a steamship subsidy as "well within our means and . . . by no means excessive" (9 March 1914, p. 322). A month later the same P. S. Woods who had once regularly denounced the company in his editorials now praised its Middlesex plantation "as an object lesson of what can be done by large capital rightly applied. . . . How unlike other land-owners who simply do nothing with the vast tracts of land they hold which neither enrich the possessor nor the Colony" (*Clarion*, 16 April 1914, p. 439). In 1916 the *Clarion* fawned over United Fruit's management as "Gentlemen and Scholars" and claimed that "the people of the Colony are the direct beneficiaries of [their] improvement work" (3 July 1916, p. 13). At no point in the remainder of the decade, even as United Fruit suspended its contract to grow fruit in the colony, did the press's earlier indignation reassert itself.

The reversal of elite opinion toward the government and United Fruit may be attributable to a shifting local political context in which the composition and metropolitan orientation of elite classes themselves changed. After United Fruit secured a monopoly over the colony's banana exports in 1902, Stann Creek planters became much less outspoken about the company and government policies that favored it, recognizing that company retaliation for such criticism would leave them with no marketing outlets for their bananas. The later outbreak of World War I witnessed a complete collapse of the mahogany export trade with Britain and its replacement by trade ties to the United States, further strengthening the position of planters and U.S.-oriented merchants relative to traditional elites. Finally, by the end of United Fruit's presence in the colony the support of colonial governors for U.S. investment had significantly reconfigured the legislative council. By 1920, most of the unofficial seats were held by merchants and professionals with ties to the United States who consistently supported government efforts on behalf of North American capital (ibid., 181). Among several unofficial members appointed by Governor Hutson was W. A. Bowman, who as a banana planter had once urged the governor not to antagonize United Fruit by holding the company to its contract obligations. If the gradual change in elite opinion toward United Fruit reflected changes in the composition of elite classes, then the government itself must be credited with remaking those elites. Elites in Belize have always been *comprador* in outlook, or complicit with foreign capital, but the shift in their dependence from British to North American capital required decades of concerted government action on behalf of agricultural development.

The crash in banana production and withdrawal of United Fruit after the outbreak of Panama Disease do not suggest merely another abortive episode in a colonial history rife with booms and busts. Rather, the colonial government's efforts during this period definitively reoriented the economy from timber extraction to agriculture and established an agricultural elite that continues to be politically and economically dominant in southern Belize. Many banana farms afflicted with Panama Disease in the Stann Creek valley were subsequently planted with citrus, which remains to this day the valley's primary export. Several now powerful citrus-growing families of the region, such as the Bowmans, originally entered agriculture as banana producers a century ago. For some smallholder and elite families, this episode has come full circle in recent decades. During the 1950s, several privately owned farms in southern Stann Creek district drew heavily on the banana-growing expertise of Monkey River residents and briefly resumed banana exports to the United States. Those efforts came to an end because of transportation difficulties and shortages of investment. In 1969, however, the now self-governing colony once again promoted the development of large-scale banana production, this time under the direct ownership and management of the state (Moberg 1997). When government-owned plantations were privatized in 1985, most of these lands were acquired by families whose members had been involved in the banana boom of the early twentieth century.

Currently, the banana industry comprises the country's third largest legal agricultural sector and generates the primary source of rural wage employment in southern Belize. As a former British colony, Belize is now integrated into the European market as one of the ACP banana-producing countries. With nearly 5,000 acres of land under production in the Stann Creek and Toledo districts, the country currently claims the most productive banana industry in the anglophone Caribbean. In 1996 Belizean growers exported some 65,000 metric tons of fruit to the European Union through Fyffes, the Irish-based multinational that purchases all export-grade fruit from the country. As other essays in this volume show, banana industries throughout the anglophone Caribbean are threatened by the recent World Trade Organization suit initiated at the behest of United Fruit's successor, Chiquita. In Belize few growers believe that they can survive the effects of the WTO ruling, which will end the tariff quota system under which ACP fruit is exported to the European Union. If their fears come to pass, one of the greatest ironies of the ruling is that United Fruit will have dismantled a banana industry that played a major role in the company's own growth at the dawn of the twentieth century.

NOTES

1. Research for this chapter was conducted in the National Archives of Belize in 1993 and 1995 and the Public Records Office of Great Britain (Kew) in 1994, with support from the National Science Foundation and the National Endowment for the Humanities. I would like to thank Charles Gibson, Margaret Ventura, Marvin Pook, Louis Avila, and Elsworth Genus of the Belize Archives Department for their assistance. I also thank Sarah Mattics of the University of South Alabama Center for Archaeological Studies for producing the map at the beginning of this volume and Tawnya Sesi Moberg for her valuable comments and suggestions. Archival sources are abbreviated as BPRO (British Public Records Office) and AB (Archives of Belize). Materials utilized from the former collection consist of dispatches between governors appointed to British Honduras and the Colonial Office in London. Most of the archival materials consulted in Belize consisted of legislative minutes and communications between colonial governors, residents, and the United Fruit Company.

2. Bolland (1984) provides an extensive critique of this traditional historiography.

3. The paper was owned and edited by P. S. Woods, whose brother represented mercantile interests as an unofficial member of the legislative council between 1898 and 1907 (Ashdown 1979, 123).

4. Mahogany recovered its position as the colony's primary export by 1905, but thereafter most mahogany was shipped to the U.S. market. At no point after 1903 did Britain regain its former role as the colony's primary trading partner.

5. By the late 1920s, the Vaccaro Brothers Company was to become incorporated into Standard Fruit, later to become Dole.

6. The company successfully repeated the same tactic two years later when the Southern Steamship Line of Mobile began calling at fruit-producing areas of the coast (*Colonial Guardian,* 26 March 1904, p. 1).

7. Despite the size of United Fruit's land acquisition in the colony, no more than 2,000 acres of its Middlesex estate was ever under cultivation.

8. In 1920 the railroad operated at an annual loss of $77,320, which the superintendent attributed to freight charges that "are and always have been ridiculously low for the service rendered" (BPRO CO 123 330).

9. One of the two planters mentioned in the dispatch was W. A. Bowman, who was later to establish the Stann Creek citrus industry and who became the district's largest private landowner by the end of the decade.

STEVE STRIFFLER

The Logic of the Enclave: United Fruit, Popular Struggle, and Capitalist Transformation in Ecuador

On purchasing Hacienda Tenguel in Ecuador's southern coast in 1934, the United Fruit Company immediately initiated two activities. First, the multinational set up banana groves at the *core* of the property, a massive undertaking that involved building ports and railroads, constructing towns, clearing land, and recruiting thousands of workers into a largely undeveloped frontier zone. Although the process was uneven, and partially halted by World War II, the hacienda was producing more bananas than any other holding in Ecuador by the 1940s (at a time when Ecuador itself was becoming the largest producer in the world). Second, the company attempted to gain control over *marginal* areas in or just outside the hacienda's boundaries. This also required a major effort; boundaries were poorly defined and peasant-squatters inhabited large portions of this "uncultivated" land. Ultimately, however, the long-term survival of Hacienda Tenguel depended not only on the large-scale production of bananas at the core of the property but on United Fruit's ability to control and retain reserve land. Once Panama Disease destroyed banana groves at the core, as it inevitably did, the company had to expand production into uncultivated areas where the disease was not yet present, thereby turning the margins into the core. This logic — of shifting production and the continual need for large tracts of reserve land — proved to be a fatal flaw that was exposed by land conflicts with neighboring peasants.

United Fruit's attempt to reproduce a banana enclave in Tenguel was partially disrupted by Panama Disease and thoroughly thwarted by peasants and plantation workers. The process through which multinational corporations have withdrawn from direct production and turned to contract farming has been driven in large part by class conflict in places like Tenguel.[1] As numerous sources suggest, including Bucheli's contribution to this volume, the foreign-owned enclave had become politically untenable by (at least) 1960 and multinationals were forced to explore alternative forms of production and marketing.

I analyze Hacienda Tenguel's dismantling by first describing how it came to be, including some of the factors that pushed the multinational to Ecuador in the first place, as well as the political, economic, and geographic milieu in which both United Fruit and the workers were situated. I then trace the progression of peasant-worker attacks on the property, beginning first with a relatively minor land conflict in the mid-1930s and ending with the invasion and takeover of the entire property by workers in 1962.

The first conflict, between United Fruit and a small group of neighboring peasants living in Mollepongo, forced the company to cede nearly three thousand hectares of land, marginal land that meant little at the time of the conflict but that became increasingly important in the 1950s as Panama Disease spread and the company looked to expand production into disease-free areas. The second invasion was carried out by former workers in a marginal zone of the hacienda known as Shumiral. Ironically, this group of former workers had been fired because United Fruit's need for labor had diminished as Panama Disease spread and possibilities for expanding banana production were closed off by the Mollepongo peasants. The final invasion was a different beast altogether and brought an end to the multinational's operations in Ecuador. From 1934 until about 1960 — or roughly the same period in which United Fruit was bogged down in conflicts with neighboring peasants — the multinational had relatively few difficulties with plantation workers in Tenguel. The contrast between a politically relentless peasantry and a relatively docile labor force was due not only to socioeconomic differences (i.e., access to land) but to the radically different ways in which the two groups were received by state power (for a similar case see Chomsky 1998). In the end, however, the peasantry's success at controlling the margins of the property forced the company's hand and broke its paternalistic hold over the workers. Because the peasant-squatters made it impossible for United Fruit to expand cultivation into marginal areas of the property, the company was forced to lay off plantation workers at the core once the Panama Disease destroyed large sections of the hacienda (thereby reducing the need for workers). Fired and threatened with eviction from their company-owned homes, the workers turned political and finished off the process begun by the peasants. In March of 1962 the workers took over Hacienda Tenguel, forced United Fruit out of direct production, and ushered in agrarian reform on the national level. In so doing, they relegated the Central American model of foreign-owned enclaves to Ecuador's past and paved the way for contract farming. By the mid-1960s American, Swedish, Panamanian, German, and Chilean corporations had all pulled out of direct production, and a decade later Standard Fruit (followed by other multinationals) implemented a system of contract farming that has restructured power relations and property patterns along Ecuador's coast (Larrea Maldonado 1987).

A MULTINATIONAL ARRIVES

To a certain extent, United Fruit was pushed into Ecuador during the 1930s. Not only was Panama Disease devastating banana production at traditional sites in Central America, but the company was having increasing problems with workers, peasants, governments, and communist parties throughout Central America and Colombia during and after the Great Depression. From United Fruit's perspective, Ecuador seemed ideal. Labor unions were weak (to the point of being nonexistent in rural areas), and the coastal region's primary export crop, cacao, had collapsed during the 1920s. Elites were desperately searching for an export alternative, and large quantities of cheap land and labor were available in a region that was both free of Panama Disease and ideal for banana production.

Nevertheless, although Ecuador appeared relatively tranquil when United Fruit arrived on the scene in the late 1920s and early 1930s, the collapse of cacao and the resulting economic crisis had shaken the political landscape. At the precise moment when United Fruit made its first real commitment to Ecuador (1934), purchasing vast tracts of land and initiating exports, a wave of popular support brought Velasco Ibarra to the presidency for the first of five times. As the first president brought to power by popular forces, Velasco — including his populist rhetoric and sharp attack on elites — reflected the growing power of the lower and middle classes, the fracturing of the dominant class, and a broader crisis of authority. Popular organizations exploded onto the scene and labor organizations began to sharpen their teeth as the political crisis opened up key organizational spaces for workers and peasants.

As company correspondence demonstrates, United Fruit was well aware that the Ecuadorian political climate was deteriorating in the 1930s (from the company's perspective). Indeed, a number of factors, including the general political turmoil and the company's own history in Central America and Colombia, help explain why the multinational worked so hard in Ecuador to avoid negative attention from labor groups and populist sectors within the press and government. As a result, when confronted with squatters, United Fruit opted to go through state authorities instead of using its own police force. Similarly, company administrators did not flagrantly mistreat plantation workers, preferring benevolent paternalism to physical discipline.

Although the company's relatively restrained approach in Ecuador managed to enhance its public image (or at least keep the muckrakers at bay), it had a different impact on peasants and workers. On the one hand, when it came to dealing with neighboring peasants, the company's reluctance to use force, and its resulting dependence on the state, proved disastrous. The state's presence in rural areas was weak, and its internal divisions proved fertile ground for a relentless and increasingly savvy peasantry. On the other hand, the company's paternalism succeeded in attracting and controlling several thousand workers for almost three decades. The high wages and benefits offered by United Fruit proved effective not only in seducing migrant families into a frontier zone but in reproducing a relatively docile labor force until Panama Disease spread and the company was forced to lay off workers in the late 1950s.[2]

STRIKE ONE: THE PEASANTS OF MOLLEPONGO

Almost immediately after purchasing Hacienda Tenguel in 1934, United Fruit became embroiled in a conflict with peasants who lived in an area known as Mollepongo. The peasants, both in documentation at the time of the conflict and in interviews conducted decades later, claim that they bought "shares" from the owners of Hacienda Mollepongo, an immense property on the eastern boundary of Hacienda Tenguel.[3] The shares gave the peasants the right to occupy a certain amount of land anywhere within the poorly defined boundaries of Hacienda Mollepongo. United Fruit's representatives did not dispute the peasants' claim; rather, they argued that the peasants had mistakenly occupied sections of Hacienda Tenguel, not Mollepongo. More importantly, in 1938 an Ecuadorian court agreed and the peasants were forced to sign contracts for the lands they had cultivated. By turning squatters into tenants United Fruit thought it had achieved its primary purpose—the legal and de facto control over a portion of its property. As long as they could be removed at a later date, the peasant-tenants were welcomed by the multinational because they produced much of the food needed by the hacienda's labor force (UFC March 1940–July 1945).

The Mollepongo conflict tapped into different sets of conflicting goals and ideals that proved difficult for state authorities to navigate. On the one hand, sectors within the central government wanted to uphold property rights and support United Fruit as a source of national progress and development. This was particularly true during the 1930s and 1940s; the Great Depression had conspired with the collapse of cacao exports, leaving the Ecuadorian economy in a state of crisis. In theory, the development of a banana industry would revive coastal agriculture, produce a major export, and provide the central government with a new source of income. On the other hand, there were populist sectors within the state that saw United Fruit as a political problem, or at least as an opportunity to garner additional support from prolabor and pronationalist sectors within Ecuadorian society. This sentiment was complemented by the growing belief that uncultivated areas should be brought into production by appropriating land from large landowners and redistributing it to peasants. In short, both United Fruit *and* the peasants were able to mobilize factions of state power at the national level in order to strengthen their hand in Tenguel.

Despite signing the contracts, the peasants did not accept United Fruit's claim or the court's decision. Rather, they organized, attempted to form a commune, contacted labor organizations, and began to maneuver through different sectors within the state. The Mollepongo peasants proved exceptionally skilled at negotiating the political terrain on both national and local levels. On the national level, the attempt to form a commune gave the peasants a *legal* presence before the central government in Quito. Communes were a form of organization created by the Ecuadorian state in 1937; they were designed to put small population centers of at least fifty people onto the geopolitical map (Barsky

1988). Because a commune, much like a town or city, assumed that the inhabitants owned the land upon which the commune was located, the peasants' appeal was an effective way of reinitiating their claim through another branch of the state (in this case, the Ministry of Social Welfare). On the local level, the attempt to create a commune gave the peasants a *political* presence by forcing them to come off their individual plots and form a community on the exact spot where the land conflict was taking place. From this point on, the peasants would confront the company's thugs as a community struggling for its land.

United Fruit quickly pointed out that the Mollepongo peasants were perfectly free to form a commune; they just could not do so on property that did not belong to them. Although logical, this argument did not prevent the Ministry of Social Welfare from examining the peasants' claim and conducting a series of "impartial" studies (a task that United Fruit insisted had already been completed by the courts). Because the ministry did not have any representatives on the southern coast, it asked the local *teniente* (deputy mayor) to conduct what turned out to be the first of many studies.[4] The teniente, in turn, immediately handed the task over to Victor Veléz, a "disinterested" expert on the boundary dispute. In reality, Veléz not only belonged to the Mollepongo commune but was the same person who had lost the 1938 court case to United Fruit regarding the same piece of land. Needless to say, Veléz's study did not favor the multinational (UFC 5 September 1945, April 1940; Llivichusca 1996a).

On becoming aware of Veléz's conflict of interest, the ministry decided to carry out another impartial study in order to resolve the conflict. The second study, this time carried out by United Fruit's allies, favored the multinational. Nevertheless, the company's representatives were slow to celebrate. As United Fruit's lawyer wrote, "The report has been there for awhile sitting around—once the legal dept gets the report a decision will be made in favor of [United Fruit]. This Ministry is a tough babe, I mean they don't know how to decide on anything and matters just lay there for months and months without any decision" (UFC 18 October 1945).

All company officials could do was complain. As the general manager of United Fruit's operations in Ecuador later wrote, "The Ministry has studied [this dispute] from all sides many times. Barros and [the other peasants] have demonstrated themselves to be unscrupulous people that only want to bother us, and it appears as though each time there is a change in the Ministry they are going to renew their unfounded claims" (UFC 12 September 1946). Toward the end, the company's lawyer was simply frustrated: "At this time the situation is completely confused. . . . If you go to a Ministry one finds a communist or fascist. It is divided between socialists, who in this country are the same as communists, and conservatives, who are fascists and just as confusing as the communists" (UFC 19 November 1947).

The peasants' efforts on the national level ensured that an already divided (and often incompetent) central government would (or could) not take a strong, unified stance against them on the local level. This peasant-induced confusion in Quito gave local state officials in Tenguel considerable leeway with respect to deciding when and how to deal with the conflict; this, in turn, created a crucial space in which the peasants could maneuver on the local level. The peasants quickly moved beyond the initial petitions and began to engage in a series of more aggressive actions that ranged from fencing off land and expanding their subsistence crops to destroying banana trees and threatening company employees. Among the small group of extended peasant families, the Barros, Illescas, Llivichusca, and Guerrero families led the fight. In one incident, the company's superintendent reported that José Illescas had confronted a company work crew in the disputed sector. Telling the field boss that he did not believe the company's lies, Illescas (with machete in hand) was quickly backed up by José Llivichusca, Aurelio Illescas, and the Guerrero brothers, one of whom had a shotgun (UFC 6 May 1947).

A month later, a similar confrontation involved the same bunch. This time the company's work crew was immediately surrounded by Llivichusca, Illescas, Barros, Sinche, and four of the Guerreros brothers (now with two shotguns and machetes). Llivichusca quickly informed the work crew that United Fruit had no bananas or land in the sector. Illescas added that not only had state officials from the Guayas province agreed to stay out of the conflict, but authorities from the province of Azuay had told the peasants that they could arrest anyone sent by United Fruit. The peasants had convinced authorities from Guayas that the land in question did not belong to the Guayas province; at the same time, they had convinced provincial authorities from Azuay that United Fruit was trying to steal land not only from the peasants but also from the province of Azuay. Although the peasants did not arrest the workers (because, as they noted, the workers were just poor folk like themselves), they made it clear that any future attempts to work the land would be met with arrests and possible violence (UFC 5 June 1947). As José Llivichusca remembers,

> The company had its own police force in Tenguel and friends in [the province of] Guayas. We knew that neither province was sure where this land belonged [in Azuay or Guayas]. And since most of us were from [the highland province of] Azuay we knew [state officials] there and tried to get help. The problem was that [the province of] Azuay had no real force in the area. It was difficult to send authorities from the highlands because there were no real roads. But we had a priest who helped us make contacts [with the state officials in Azuay] and they said they supported us. And then we got Guayas to stay out. As long as the Civil Guard was not sent, we knew the company could not get rid of us. (Llivichusca 1996a)

The peasants had no qualms about confronting United Fruit either in the offices of state power or on the ground in Tenguel-Mollepongo. As the documentation confirms, they had made contacts with not only labor organizers and sympathetic clergy but with a range of local, regional, and national state agencies in the Ministries of Social Welfare, Government, and even Defense. In this particular instance, the peasants were skillfully manipulating authorities from two different provinces. Whether or not provincial authorities in Azuay actually told the peasants to arrest the company's employees is difficult to determine, but the confusion nonetheless highlights the fact that the multinational could not depend on the state to evict the squatters.[5]

For their part, United Fruit's representatives were every bit as persistent as the peasants in pursuing different avenues of state power. At one point, they even met with President Velasco, who promised to send an order and have the peasants evicted. To no avail. Velasco's communications with the various Ministries became confused and the order was not carried out (UFC 21 May 1947, 15 May 1947). Not only could the central government not take a coherent or decisive stance on the issue (and probably did not want to), but it could not get local and regional authorities to complete even the most basic of orders (in large part because local authorities received such conflicting messages from Quito). More important, the peasants controlled the land. The irony, from the company's perspective, was that the multinational could no longer use its own police force to evict the squatters. The conflict was simply too involved.[6]

Faced with the state's refusal to enforce property rights, and confronted with an increasingly assertive group of peasants, the company backed down. Although the Mollepongo peasants would not acquire legal ownership over the disputed property until the mid-1950s, they had de facto control over approximately 3,000 hectares by 1950 — the exact year in which Panama Disease made its appearance at Hacienda Tenguel.

STRIKE TWO: THE EX-WORKERS OF SHUMIRAL

The loss of land in Mollepongo meant little to United Fruit at a moment when production from Hacienda Tenguel was propelling Ecuador to the top of banana world. The company had no serious problems with labor in the early 1950s, and production expanded throughout much of the hacienda. For more than ten years, from the late 1940s until the late 1950s, the plantation was the largest single producer in Ecuador, employing close to 3,000 workers and exporting some 80,000 stems of bananas a week at its peak (Sylva Charvet 1987).

The company's most visible obstacle during this period was the emergence of Panama Disease. Although the disease had barely made an appearance at the time of the Mollepongo conflict, it began to spread to different sectors of the hacienda in the early 1950s. A variety of measures were taken, including flooding and burning banana groves, but the disease could not be contained. By the mid-1950s the company was forced to surrender whole sections of the property; by the late 1950s production levels were plummeting as the cultivation of new trees failed to keep pace with the loss of old ones. In order to keep exports flowing, the company had to either expand its own production or contract with local producers. Both strategies were adopted with limited success in the late 1950s.

Expanding production into disease-free areas essentially meant going east toward the Andean foothills (because the property ran up against the ocean to the west and large landowners to the north and south). Unable to expand directly to the east because of the Mollepongo peasants, United Fruit turned to the southeast, extending the rail system, building roads, and constructing two new towns from scratch. Hundred of workers were moved from older sections of the hacienda into what became known as the zone of Brasil. Although United Fruit was able to plant several hundred hectares in this area, it once again found itself embroiled in a land conflict with a small group of peasants. Using methods that were remarkably similar to those adopted in Mollepongo, the peasants of Brasil prevented the company from expanding its operations at a particularly crucial moment.

Stopped by peasants in Mollepongo (to the east) and Brasil (to the southeast), United Fruit looked to the only other area of the hacienda where large tracts of disease-free land existed: the northeast section of Shumiral. By this time (1955–1957), however, Panama Disease had forced the company to begin layoffs. Entire sections had been completely destroyed, and the hacienda no longer required such a large labor force. Consequently, many of the fired workers left the zone in search of better opportunities; others remained, refusing to leave their company-owned houses; and a large portion took over the company-run labor union and invaded the entire property in 1962.

It was, however, a small group of ex-workers who struck the first (worker-induced) blow by staking a claim in Shumiral in the mid-1950s. As Sergio Armijos remembers: "When I got fired I didn't know what to do. We were not the first to be fired, but the massive lay-offs had not yet begun so there was no real support [from other workers]. So I talked to some friends and we decided to go and live in Shumiral. We were not sure who the land belonged to, but we knew it was probably owned by United Fruit. This was the dream that had brought us to Tenguel in the first place: la tierra" (Armijos 1996).

Shumiral was not, as in the case of Mollepongo and Brasil, a community formed by smallholders who were trying to retain properties they had been working for years. Shumiral was imagined and developed by United Fruit's own workers—or, rather, former workers the company had been forced to lay off because production was down and expansion made difficult by the peasants in Mollepongo and Brasil. As such, the conflict in Shumiral—inasmuch as it occupied a *transitional* space between the peasant conflicts in Mollepongo / Brasil and the workers' invasion of the hacienda in 1962—was important for a number of reasons.

First, the former workers intentionally invaded an uncultivated portion of Hacienda Tenguel. There was a dispute, but it was not over boundaries. Former workers in Shumiral built on the political traditions and body of knowledge developed by peasants in Mollepongo and Brasil.[7] But the conflict in Shumiral was of a slightly different variety. It was one of the first explicit land invasions during the period immediately preceding a nationwide agrarian reform and thus posed a much greater symbolic threat to the company's enterprise. The invasion was a sign of things to come. Second, in 1960, after five years of struggle, the former workers of Shumiral could claim victory against a major multinational. Forced to sell over 2,500 hectares for a token price, United Fruit found itself with dying banana trees, nowhere to expand, and an increasingly disenchanted labor force. Finally, because it was orchestrated by a small group of former workers and a relentless lawyer, the victory in Shumiral provided plantation workers at the core of the hacienda with a dramatic example of the possibilities opened up by organization and unity. No one had ever imagined that the company could be beaten by workers; Shumiral demonstrated otherwise. Encouraged by the example of Shumiral, workers in Tenguel would invade the heart of the hacienda less than two years later.

Although the small group of former workers would ultimately achieve great success in Shumiral, the initial stages of the struggle were anything but smooth. To begin with, they were unable to acquire the kind of external support that the peasants in Mollepongo had depended on. Although they obtained outside help from Lautaro Gordillo, a Quiteño lawyer with experience in peasant land struggles and labor conflicts, the former workers never received any real support from the state. This was due in large part to the fact that — unlike the peasants in Mollepongo and Brasil — the former workers were not making a legal claim based on property titles. They were simply invading land that did not belong to them. Their argument — that as landless nationals they should be given access to land that a foreign company was not even cultivating — fell on deaf (state) ears.

For its part, United Fruit had learned from its mistakes in Mollepongo and Brasil. In the case of Shumiral the company never bothered turning to state authorities, preferring to treat the conflict as an internal problem between the hacienda and its workers. The results, as Sergio Armijos remembers, were predictable. "The company kept sending police. I got arrested a couple of times as did others. Once they even sent a bulldozer to plow our houses and crops. But they could not be here all the time. They would go to the houses and we would stay in the fields or move up to the mountains" (Armijos 1996).

It was the relative isolation of the zone that gave the former workers room to maneuver and forced United Fruit to adopt a new strategy. Much as they had during the early stages of the Mollepongo conflict, United Fruit's representatives offered the former workers tenancy arrangements. In exchange for signing the contracts and recognizing United Fruit's dominion over the disputed property, the peasants would be given access to ten hectares of land for a period of five years. The company would also assist the former workers in the production of bananas. Who better to produce bananas than United Fruit's own former workers?

The plan nearly worked. The overwhelming majority of former workers signed, reasoning that the company, with all of its economic, political, and legal resources, could not be beaten by a bunch of unemployed workers and a Quiteño lawyer. It was, after all, the company's land. As Rafael León noted, "This just left the crazy ones" (León 1996). Of the thirty or so families that had originally colonized Shumiral, fewer than ten remained. The majority signed contracts and began to work the plots demarcated by the company. Within a week, allies became enemies as the company transformed an emerging community into something resembling the Hatfields and McCoys.

The rental agreements, signed by the majority of former workers, remain a fascinating read, as do the comments written by those who did not sign: "Señor Alvear . . . cut another 4 hectares of underbrush and grew pasture, making it 7 hectares of work destroyed by this man"; "Señor Montaleza possessed the land of Julio Ochoa . . . in 1959 and prevented him from growing crops."[8] Others stole corn, destroyed crops, or put fences on the land. Both groups were involved in similar practices as the battle for possession intensified. Their goals, if not their strategies, were remarkably similar. The *arrendatarios* (tenants) had reasoned that they would have to wait for another opportunity in order to become legal owners. They signed five-year contracts with United Fruit that could be renewed only if both sides agreed. The company would not reimburse improvements they made to the land, and permanent crops other than bananas were expressly forbidden. In other words, the rental contracts were temporary arrangements to be terminated at the company's whim. Significantly, all bananas had to be sold to the company if and when the company so desired. United Fruit, which actively encouraged the arrendatarios to produce bananas, dictated the terms of the contract and the sale.

Exactly why the company eventually gave in and abandoned the arrendatarios is unclear. One would like to attribute the victory entirely to the former workers' quite remarkable efforts. Their persistence clearly played a role. After the majority of former workers signed contracts with United Fruit, the remaining minority recruited new allies and harassed the tenants. Similarly, Dr. Gordillo proved more than a match for the company's lawyers. Yet the timing of the victory — 29 April 1960 — suggests that other factors were also at work. Most of the original contracts were signed in 1957 when Hacienda Tenguel was still relatively strong. By 1960, however, the company must have known — given the deteriorated state of the hacienda — that it might not be in a position to renew the arrendatarios' contracts. United Fruit thus faced the possibility of having to confront two (now larger) groups of peasants, each of which possessed cultivated lands. Pressed by the former workers, an expanding disease, a militant union, and an unsupportive state, the company decided to sell the marginal section of Shumiral. Actually, by the time Dr. Gordillo was done, United Fruit nearly gave the 2,500 hectares away. Rafael León recounts the final episode.

The last meeting with the company was a real triumph. A bunch of gringos came here to Shumiral to negotiate. Yes, here. Our lawyer, Dr. Gordillo, wouldn't go to Tenguel. They all sat down and started talking. Dr. Gordillo never sat, he just paced. They talked for a bit and then Dr. Gordillo said he was leaving. He said he was a busy man with people waiting. Can you imagine? The gringos got real nervous. They wanted to end this matter and didn't like being in Shumiral. They would offer a price and he would reject it and say he was leaving. He said it was an insult that Ecuadorians were paying for our own land. Finally they agreed on a price and asked where they could write up the contract. Dr. Gordillo said we would have to go to Tenguel because we were only poor people here and didn't even have a typewriter. So we walked a bit and then got in the trucks with the gringos. Everyone came. The arrendatarios were following on their horses. That was a sight.

We got to Tenguel and a gringo began to write up the agreement but Dr. Gordillo disagreed with every sentence. Finally they just gave him the typewriter and he typed it out in five minutes. The gringos signed and we had won. We left the offices and no one in Tenguel could believe us. They thought they had brought us here to put us in jail. And there we were leaving as landowners. That was a great day. (León 1996)

If the peasants confronted United Fruit from day one, the workers did not. A number of factors contributed to the absence of organized political activity at the core of the hacienda, not the least of which were exceptionally high wages, considerable benefits, and working conditions that compared remarkably well with other places in rural Ecuador during this period. As one former worker recalled, "Workers came from all over [Ecuador] because the company provided everything. We were paid really well, there was lots of work, and we had things like schools and electricity. There was even a hospital here. Rich people from Guayaquil came for treatment. And the company did not abuse workers as in the past. If a worker did not conform, the company simply fired him. Most recognized the benefits and conformed" (Sanchez 1996).

This is not to suggest that the company was above using more repressive methods of labor control, methods that it had perfected in Central America. Hacienda Tenguel had its own police force; fiestas, gambling, and the consumption of alcohol were all strictly regulated;[9] and workers could be fired at will. However, this was not Central America at the turn of the century; United Fruit was under the continual scrutiny of populist sectors within Ecuador during the 1940s and 1950s. As a result, in Tenguel the company opted for more paternalistic methods of labor control, preferring the carrot to the stick in an effort to create the image of a benevolent father. As long as the male worker came with his family and conformed to the work discipline, he was guaranteed a well-maintained house, access to the company store, cheap food, schools, and a range of other benefits. The company, in effect, offered economic security in exchange for political quiescence.

United Fruit also adopted more subtle methods of labor control. Clubs and sports teams, for example, allowed the company to regulate social and cultural occasions while appearing to be the benevolent provider of services. By reinforcing distinctions between laborers, field bosses, administrators, railworkers, carpenters, and the like, the social clubs strengthened and extended work-based divisions into the realm of daily life. On the more insidious end of things, United Fruit also created a labor union (much as it had done in Central America (Bourgois 1989; Moberg 1997). The company-run labor union served as a preemptive effort to prevent workers or outside groups from creating a more authentic form of labor organization. From the company's perspective, a labor union was fine as long as it was in the right hands.[10]

Company officials rarely expressed any concerns about labor control. They worried that a range of external forces, including the spread of communism, the instability of Ecuadorian governments, and the growth of labor unions, would infiltrate Hacienda Tenguel and disrupt operations. Within the hacienda's boundaries, however, the administrators felt that they were in control of the labor force and asked for little state assistance during the 1940s and 1950s (and preferred to handle problems internally). This relative security with respect to the workers is in stark contrast to the repeated appeals regarding the peasants in Mollepongo and Brasil.

Ultimately, it was Panama Disease, the company's inability to open new groves in peasant-occupied areas, and the resulting layoffs that served to radicalize the labor force at Tenguel. Although United Fruit had been reducing its labor force since the mid-1950s, it was only after 1960 that the massive layoffs were initiated. By 1961 only a skeletal staff remained; more than 2,000 workers were fired within less than a year. Many had been living in Tenguel for decades, and the company's insistence that the workers leave their (company-owned) houses had a politicizing affect. As one former worker remembered, "I could understand why the company had to lay off the workers. The disease had destroyed most of the hacienda and there was just no work. But I couldn't understand why the company was forcing the workers from their homes and not letting us have access to the land. We could have worked the land, produced subsistence crops, and then the company could have returned when the disease was gone. Many of us had lived here for 20 or 30 years and could not leave. This is when I joined the union" (Hernandez 1996). Consequently, the workers wrested control of the labor union from United Fruit and confronted the company on a range of issues, including the pace and nature of the firings, the withdrawal of services, and access to land on a semiabandoned hacienda.

Despite rapidly deteriorating conditions and a rejuvenated labor union, the workers' decision to invade Hacienda Tenguel came slowly and was delayed by a number of factors. At various times during the two years prior to the invasion, most former workers hoped that United Fruit would either return or sell the hacienda to the state and / or workers. By mid- to late 1961 the company was allowing the labor union to work part of the hacienda. Although insufficient to meet the former workers' basic needs, the agreement fueled the hope that the company would negotiate the sale of the hacienda to the workers. State-controlled agrarian reform was still several years away and the idea of a worker-owned and -managed hacienda did not seem unreasonable; nor did it fall outside the parameters of the ongoing debate over agrarian reform. In addition, the workers had developed contacts with sympathetic state officials who were involved in negotiations with United Fruit over the sale of Hacienda Tenguel.

In short, the workers' grievances had been met by official and unofficial statements that a meaningful land reform was about to occur and that Hacienda Tenguel would be the centerpiece of the state's project.[11] From the workers' perspective, there was no need to take action because the state was going to resolve the entire mess. The problem, however, was that United Fruit was actively experimenting with a variety of arrangements in which the company itself would no longer be involved in direct production. Each of these experiments directly threatened the workers' access to land and / or employment.

First, the company was giving contracts to anyone who would produce bananas. This included not only peasants in Mollepongo, Brasil, and Shumiral, many of whom were now cultivating bananas for their old foe, but larger landowners to the north and south of Hacienda Tenguel. These producers hired fewer workers, paid lower wages, and offered none of the benefits associated with Hacienda Tenguel. Second, the company turned the overwhelming majority of the hacienda over to four or five former administrators who worked the land with a drastically reduced and poorly paid workforce. In a system that, eerily, resembled the form of contracting that dominates the banana industry today, the administrators were essentially renting the land and then selling bananas back to United Fruit. Third, there was a small minority of former workers who were also renting plots from United Fruit. Here, the tenant was little more than a well-paid guard. The company would finance and organize the production of different crops while maintaining complete control over technical decisions. The tenant, in turn, would oversee the laborers and maintain security. Fourth, Gala, an eighty-man cooperative comprising United Fruit's favorite former workers, was renting about 3,000 hectares of the most disease-ridden sections of the hacienda.

Finally, and most important, United Fruit sold sections of the hacienda to four or five large capitalists who provided the former workers with little employment and poor wages. While the sales included only a small fraction of the hacienda, the workers feared that they represented a sign of things to come. As national capitalists, the buyers did not face the same political constraints as United Fruit. They began to harass the workers and train a private police force on Tenguel's soccer field. When direct intimidation failed, they tried other tactics, including the placement of spies in the labor union and a smear campaign suggesting that the leaders were connected to Fidel Castro. Yet, it was their final ultimatum that provoked the invasion: they threatened to physically remove the workers from the hacienda and set the date of eviction for 30 March 1962. That the workers invaded the hacienda just several days prior to their scheduled departure was hardly a coincidence.

In order to navigate this constantly shifting terrain — characterized by agrarian-reform debates, state declarations, local thugs, and United Fruit's machinations — the workers transformed their labor union into Cooperative Juan Quirumbay. Once fired, most members of the union simply joined the cooperative. The name change was a strategic move by which the workers placed themselves within a national discussion regarding land reform. As Jacinto Lozano pointed out, "For a short time both the union and [Cooperative] Quirumbay existed together but we knew that the future was in the cooperative. We were trying to encourage the government to buy the hacienda and deliver it to the workers. Few people knew what a cooperative was, but we felt that some sort of organization would show the state we could run the hacienda" (Llivichusca 1996b).

At the time of the invasion, the influence of Cooperative Juan Quirumbay was indisputable. As the direct heir to the labor union, the cooperative had a membership of over 600 families, six times more than the five cooperatives supported by United Fruit. Juan Quirumbay's strength grew as threats to the former workers' lives and homes increased. In response to the growing visibility of armed thugs, Cooperative Juan Quirumbay organized its own brigades and made appeals to student groups, unions, and political parties — any group with even remotely democratic pretensions. The workers knew, however, that they stood little chance against the armed forces that were mounting against them. The few allies they had within the state had little influence with the local police and military. In the end the workers were largely on their own and concluded that a preemptive invasion was preferable to their own eviction.

The workers' takeover of Hacienda Tenguel brought an end to the enclave and forced United Fruit from the country. The invasion, along with other similar events in banana-producing regions of Central and South America, also helped usher in a new system of banana production based on contract farming—a system that had been evolving unevenly throughout the Latin American banana industry during the first half of the century. Frustrated by problems with labor, agricultural diseases, and Latin American governments, foreign banana companies such as Chiquita (United Fruit), Dole, and Del Monte have increasingly withdrawn from direct production, preferring instead to contract with domestic capitalists who employ a poorly paid labor force and assume all of the risks associated with direct production.

EPILOGUE

It is tempting to conclude this story with the series of successful land invasions, carried out first by neighboring peasants in Mollepongo and Brasil, followed by former workers in Shumiral, and finally concluded by the plantation workers themselves. Upbeat histories in which the downtrodden are victorious—if only for a day—are both pleasant to read and write. Moreover, the political activities of peasants and workers in Tenguel-Mollepongo did matter. They not only had a decisive impact on United Fruit's operations in Ecuador—forcing the multinational out of direct production and the country—but shaped the very way in which bananas would be produced in Ecuador. By 1965 all multinationals operating in Ecuador had experienced similar problems with peasant-workers and pulled out of direct production.

At the same time, although peasant-workers were able to effectively dismantle one system of banana production, they were never in a position to determine the broad contours of the subsequent system based on contract farming. In the trenches of what was essentially a class war, the peasants and workers were simply outmatched. The monopoly that multinationals had over shipping, capital, and access to markets ensured that they—and not workers—would construct the foundation upon which the subsequent system of capital accumulation would rest. Indeed, after long and bitter land conflicts with United Fruit, it is more than a bit ironic that the peasant victors in Mollepongo and Shumiral almost immediately began to produce bananas for the multinational (under contract, no less). Similarly, although the workers carried out one of the most courageous land invasions in Ecuador's history and ushered in agrarian reform on both the local and national levels, they have little to show for it. Most own little land and now work on domestically owned plantations in conditions far worse than those found on Hacienda Tenguel in the 1950s. New forms of dependence were woven before old ones had been fully broken.

Yet, the peasants and workers tried. They formed organizations, petitioned the state, denounced their oppressors, and invaded the property of a large multinational corporation. Regardless of their relative success and almost inevitable (long-term) "failure," such actions and organizations mattered, both individually and collectively. They formed through struggles that not only shaped state power and transformed processes of capital accumulation along the southern coast, but provided the basis on which subsequent popular organizations emerged and continued to struggle for a more equitable existence during the postwar period.

NOTES

1. There are, however, numerous sources that speak to the difficulties that foreign-owned plantations (and multinationals in general) were having during this period. Bucheli's article in this volume, as well as his earlier work (1997), speaks directly to this issue. More generally, United Fruit was having considerable problems with both labor and states throughout Latin America during this period. See, for example, Chomsky 1996, Moberg 1997, Bourgois 1989, Acuña Ortega 1984, and Dosal 1993.

2. Although workers and their families migrated to Hacienda Tenguel from all over Ecuador, most were from either the province of Guayas in the coast or the southern highlands near Loja and Cuenca. Moreover, they were almost exclusively mestizo; few Indians from the highlands or blacks from the northern coast came to Tenguel.

3. The documents dealing with this conflict include correspondence between two United Fruit officials (the company lawyer and the manager of Ecuadorian operations), as well as written materials that they forwarded to each other in the course of their conversations regarding the conflict (i.e., reports from the superintendent at Hacienda Tenguel). These documents are clearly biased but nonetheless provide an interesting window into the operations of United Fruit and the problems that the company had with peasants and the Ecuadorian state. I would like to thank Manuel

Chiriboga for making these documents available to me. They are referenced by UFC followed by the date.

4. The teniente was based in Balao, a town just to the north of Tenguel. According to peasants, workers, and former administrators of Hacienda Tenguel, the tenientes in Balao almost never intervened in United Fruit's affairs as long as the company's problems remained within the boundaries of the property (where the teniente allowed the company's own police force to operate). However, boundary disputes were another issue, and here the tenientes seemed more than willing to stand up to United Fruit. This was made possible by the fact that Quito-based government ministries and agencies were forced to work through the teniente (there was no one else). As a result, the teniente had some leeway in deciding *which* state agency he would listen to.

5. Again, such maneuvering was made possible by the fact that the peasants had tacit, and at times overt, support from provincial authorities in the province of Guayas—authorities who were reluctant to intervene at the core of Hacienda Tenguel but occasionally demonstrated some courage when dealing with United Fruit outside of the property's immediate boundaries.

6. Company officials initially turned to the state to evict the peasants because they felt it was an open and shut case and did not want to attract unwanted publicity. Concern for the company's reputation—particularly at a time when it was constantly under attack by populist sectors in the press, the government, and the left—was a guiding factor in the decision to go through proper state channels. At the very least, company officials wanted to get approval from the state to use its own police force to evict the squatters.

7. The links between the peasants in Mollepongo and workers on the eastern edge of the hacienda were considerable due to the fact that they lived right next to each other.

8. I thank Rafael León for sharing these documents.

9. In contrast to enclaves in Central America, where drinking, prostitution, and the like were tacitly encouraged by the company, United Fruit took a different strategy in Ecuador. For a more detailed understanding of the system of labor control employed at Tenguel, as well as some of the reasons why United Fruit adopted a different approach in Ecuador, see Striffler 1999 and Striffler 2002.

10. The decision to create a company-controlled union was probably motivated by a number of factors. First, by the mid-1950s, the labor force at Tenguel had reached close to 3,000 workers (about 75 percent of whom had families), and the social clubs were no longer a sufficient way of controlling the workers. Second, Ecuadorian labor unions—which had only really emerged in urban areas in the late 1930s—were extending their reach and had begun to organize on a number of the coast's larger plantations.

11. In some sense, this thinking was not so far off since Hacienda Tenguel would eventually become the centerpiece for a national agrarian reform. The problem was that agrarian reform did not occur until 1964, and then it was imposed from above by a military government.

CINDY FORSTER

"The Macondo of Guatemala": Banana Workers and National Revolution in Tiquisate, 1944–1954

"I'll tell you this: the thing was good. The government under Arbenz wanted to help us, it wanted the poor to be free. They were giving out land, and money, all so that the campesinos could help themselves." —ANONYMOUS, May 1990

Workers on U.S. plantations in Guatemala were famous for labor unrest during that country's only genuine period of democracy in the twentieth century, the ten years of reform from 1944 to 1954 known as the October Revolution.[1] This essay examines the rural labor history of the revolutionary period in Tiquisate, a township where the Pacific coast plantations of the United Fruit Company sprang up in the late 1930s. Within weeks of the revolution's start in 1944, the banana workers of Tiquisate were holding mass meetings and had decided to go on strike to lay claim to the declarations of justice that were being broadcast from the capital. Over the next ten years, Tiquisate became a locus of sustained and powerful labor activity. Workers there repeatedly struck and were locked out in their struggle to win a collective agreement. They formed the grassroots base most instrumentally engaged in the design of the agrarian reform that was finally passed by President Jacobo Arbenz, two years before the end of the revolution. The banana workers of this former banana republic were exceptionally well organized and effective in their demands from the very first flush of the revolution, a fact not lost on their enemies who targeted the region for repression in 1954. The record of events in Tiquisate during Guatemala's national revolution uncovers the critical role of United Fruit workers in making the larger national and international histories.[2]

In many ways Tiquisate stands as a powerful metaphor for the revolution. Rural inequality lay at the root of class oppression in Guatemala, and the desperate poverty of the rural majority was perpetuated by an agro-export econ-

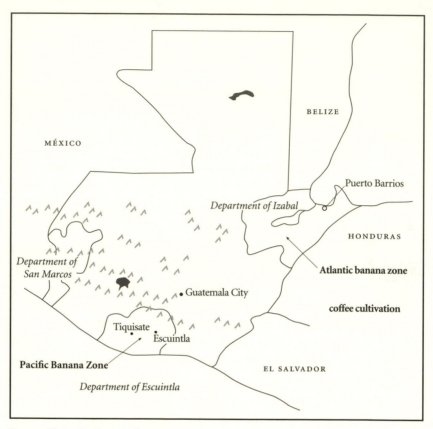

Banana Zones in Guatemala, 1944 to 1955

omy in which coffee ranked as the largest export earner, followed by bananas. By the mid-1940s the Guatemalan banana plantations accounted for more than one-quarter of United Fruit Company's entire Latin American production (Immerman 1982, 72–73; Guerra Borges 1986, 275). Fruit Company officials claimed that their modern plantations raised the standard of living for rural workers. Banana workers recognized their relative good fortune but nonetheless challenged the extreme imbalance of wealth on company plantations. Their organizing, for all its modesty, inspired the United Fruit Company to lobby for the intervention of the Central Intelligence Agency, which responded favorably. Yet the company's animosity began long before the Agrarian Reform Law of 1952, which is often cited as the chief reason for company opposition to the revolution. The evidence suggests that as early as 1944, United Fruit had covered its flank by laying plans to undermine the national government.[3] During the following ten years, the struggles of banana workers poisoned their government's relationship to the company. United Fruit, for its part, increasingly acted as a proxy for the U.S. government; revolving doors between business and the public sector created close, even familial loyalties. In the end U.S. intervention proved the decisive factor in the 1954 coup that forced out Arbenz and ushered in four decades of state terror.

The interventionist role of the United Fruit Company in Guatemala is well documented. Bitter competition between United Fruit and the Cuyamel Fruit Company rankled through the 1920s, then burst in 1928 into a boundary war between Guatemala and Honduras, which was ultimately resolved by the merger of the two companies in 1929 (Dosal 1993, 141–59; Schlesinger and Kinser 1982). The conflicts between Arbenz's government and United Fruit some twenty years later have been singled out as a critical turning point in U.S. dominance in the hemisphere (Jonas 1991; McClintock 1985). By contrast, however, the labor struggles of the banana workers during the revolution have never received in-depth attention even though their militancy lay at the vortex of the national confrontation. Events in Tiquisate unleashed the fury of the company because the workers demanded—and won—the protection of the Guatemalan president in defense of constitutionally guaranteed labor rights. Following a series of labor conflicts, the high-water mark of the October Revolution in Tiquisate was the 1952 Agrarian Reform Law, enacted with special vigor on the Pacific plantation coast. For the "banana barons," these transformations threatened the entire edifice of subservience and power upon which their commercial empire was constructed, or so they thought. Banana workers, for their part, were national protagonists in the struggle for labor rights, yet they never defined themselves as a strict proletariat or surrendered their identification as people who work the land. The "view from below" thus lays equal claim to collective identities both as wage workers and as campesinos struggling for land rights.

The urban and national context of organizing in Tiquisate began in June of 1944 with street protests and a general strike in the capital to protest the fourteen-year dictatorship of General Jorge Ubico, which held its grip through torture, thousands of secret police, and routine murder. The people who risked their lives to unseat Ubico were inspired by the global battles against fascism, as well as democratic movements in other Central American countries. Mass civil unrest forced Ubico to resign at the end of June, but he installed a puppet regime led by one of his generals, Federico Ponce Vaides. By October popular momentum across the country exploded in an insurrection that removed the dictatorship root and branch. The ten years that followed, called the October Revolution, unfolded with tremendous passion. Middle- and working-class reformers sought popular support in their bid to end the economic stranglehold of the coffee elite, as well as that of the three U.S. corporations that had monopolized transport, energy, and banana export by the 1940s.

Juan José Arévalo's presidency from 1945 to 1951 destroyed the political hegemony of large landowners. He presided over the political incorporation of urban middle-class sectors, a modest campaign of literacy and school-building, and the passage of social-security legislation and a progressive labor code. National politics were fought out in Tiquisate from the start. Young revolutionaries descended from the capital to the banana plantations in the "department" or province of Escuintla, where Tiquisate is located, sometimes every weekend. They came and went like birds in flight but left in place functioning party and union structures. Many of the most energetic and committed of these organizers gravitated toward the newly formed Communist Party, which bound Tiquisate's labor history to the fate of the communists. In fact, the militancy of workers on the banana plantations so alarmed the revolution's first president that he responded by sending in the army. Despite repression at the hands of the state under Arévalo and from landowners throughout the period, workers in Escuintla sent socialists and communists to Congress.

Arévalo was a professor, and he envisioned a schoolteacher's revolution that was unapologetically assimilationist. He was eager to transform a rural Indian society into a modern, non-Indian nation-state. Arévalo's successor, Jacobo Arbenz, dropped much of Arevalo's paternalism and took an abrupt shift left with the enactment of agrarian reform. In effect, Arbenz legislated a new social order, so that political democratization might take place among people who for centuries had been divided by deep fissures of race and class. In June 1954 the revolution was destroyed by an invading force that called itself the Liberation Army. This army was trained and funded on orders from President Eisenhower and supported by large numbers of the petty bourgeoisie, whose democratic instincts had by that point been overcome by their racism toward the indigenous majority.

Escuintla is one of the larger of Guatemala's twenty-two provinces or departments and lies in the center of the country, bounded by five smaller departments on three sides and the Pacific Ocean on the fourth. The Pacific coastal plain that was home to the banana plantations stretches about thirty miles in width. It lies at the foot of a volcanic chain that rises at the Mexican border and continues into El Salvador. Human habitation has been continuous in the region for millennia, and various Mayan peoples still make up the majority of the population in the piedmont and highlands.

The region provides ideal conditions for hot-weather crops. The sheer wall of mountain that rises out of the coastal plain creates cloud masses that burst in torrential afternoon downpours every day during the rainy season from May through October. During the dry season, irrigation is required. Since colonial times, Escuintla has been the heartland of cane-sugar production and home to some of the nation's largest sugar mills, as well as a major source of grazing land (Guerra Borges 1986, 24–25, 255; Toussaint, 305, 319; Solórzano 1977, 350). Over the centuries planters in Escuintla tapped highland indigenous populations for their labor needs. The town of Escuintla became the commercial hub for tropical and cattle products and today it ranks as the second largest industrial center after the capital. Long before the arrival of mass banana production under foreign ownership, the region was the country's most active lowland commercial center with thriving plantations geared toward domestic consumption. On the edges of this activity United Fruit carved out a private empire. By contrast the Atlantic-coast company plantation axis was a genuine enclave, created by the company far from existing production centers and devoted exclusively to banana production.

The *municipio* or township of Tiquisate is located just a few miles from the sea and about forty miles west of the town of Escuintla. Before United Fruit arrived, the area was given over to cattle with scattered corn plots farmed by campesinos (a term that embraces peasant owners, sharecroppers, renters, and day laborers who make their living from the land). Foreigners had already purchased large tracts for banana production. In 1930 and again in 1936, the dictator Ubico signed exceedingly generous contracts with United Fruit, which gave it unprecedented powers in Tiquisate, where it owned 180,000 acres by the dawn of the revolution (Immerman 1982, 72–73). Ubico's virtual giveaway outraged many urban professionals and students, as well as working people subjected to the arrogance of U.S. managers, yet such sentiments were too dangerous to express openly during the dictatorship.[4] United Fruit's sister company, International Railways of Central America, proceeded to build rail lines to the township of Tiquisate. The two companies slashed rates to the Atlantic port of Puerto Barrios (hundreds of miles across the country) to ensure that United Fruit's own Great White Fleet would move the cargo, rather than its competitor, Grace Steamship Lines, which serviced the nearby Pacific port (Toussaint 1988, 422; Handy 1984, 84).

In its search for labor, United Fruit obeyed its own social Darwinist inclinations in the belief that the Maya were physically weak. The company did not hire indigenous laborers from the nearby piedmont municipios that for centuries had provided cane workers, nor did they send recruiters a day's walk farther up the mountain face to the cold-country indigenous towns that since the 1870s had been drained of workers, often at gunpoint, for the coffee *fincas* or plantations in the piedmont above the sugar plantations. On the Caribbean side, the company had recruited Afro-Caribbean labor, but anti-immigrant laws targeting black West Indians precluded this option by the time Tiquisate went into banana production. Instead, the company put out the word on their Atlantic-coast plantations that thousands of new jobs would be opening up. They also sent labor contractors to the overpopulated, drought-bitten departments of the east that had provided earlier generations of ladino banana workers for their Atlantic-coast plantations (the term *ladino* defines people acculturated to the dominant culture who identify as nonindigenous). Ladino banana workers (many of them children of West Indians), peasants, ranchers, and day laborers poured into Tiquisate to make fast money. They all considered themselves campesinos. Further, as ladinos they viewed Tiquisate as a frontier in much the same way as their employer did.[5] Despite rapid proletarianization, they never abandoned their identity as campesinos after they went on the Fruit Company payroll.

By the late 1930s Tiquisate was bursting at the seams with laborers. Wages were the greatest drawing power for the workers, while housing was always provided free of charge as part of the wage. The company complied with Ubico's request to lower the wage, out of consideration for competing Guatemalan land-owners (Handy 1984, 90), but even so, the higher wage on the banana fincas won the gratitude of the workers (Interviews 1 and 2 1990). Employment as a banana "peon" paid twice as much as the prevailing wage for the largely in-digenous labor force on coffee and sugar plantations. One thirty-eight-year-old company worker, for instance, averaged 96 centavos a day from 1945 to 1947, while coffee workers during these years were lucky if they earned half as much.[6] However, the company hired on a contract basis and reserved for itself the right to lay off workers at the end of each task or season. The company also trans-ferred workers whenever it pleased.[7] The excellent wage thus compensated for the often temporary and transient nature of the work, which meant that with-out leaving a trace, the company could stifle worker organizing and dismiss troublemakers.[8]

Alongside the influx of new jobs another process unfolded: dispossession of people already on the land. Thousands of people were displaced, hamlet by hamlet, to make way for the new banana plantations (a fact that the frontier my-thology denied by promoting the fiction of uninhabited tropical forest). The vil-lage of Guizicil, Santa Ana Mixtán, offers a glimpse of how the company swept out peasant populations who were farming soils that it coveted. Around 1942, some 200 settlers "through much labor and sickness" cleared and planted lands twelve kilometers distant from Finca Zunil, a Company plantation.[9] The land apparently lay within the boundaries of a large cattle ranch also owned by the company, most of which was left empty. The area that the campesinos of Guizi-cil chose to plant lay only two kilometers from the sea. In theory their location protected them because by law the coastal strip that ran from the Pacific five miles inland was national patrimony and hence could not be claimed by the company.[10] United Fruit, however, viewed the law as malleable and some years after the settlers' arrival, it launched a campaign of "ill treatment and continual harassment" against them.[11] The villagers at this point exercised their rights under the new democracy. They complained to their congressman, who asked the company for clarification, and the company in turn went straight to Presi-dent Arévalo. An agreement was reached that permitted the campesinos to stay on the condition they did not chop down any of the valuable hardwoods. The company in effect usurped the right to log the forest. Soon thereafter United Fruit reneged on its promise and tried to force the villagers to sign usufruct contracts. To hasten the outcome, the company destroyed the houses of thirteen families on the pretext that the structures were too dangerous to inhabit. The Guizicil settlers were lucky to possess any recourse at all; entire generations before them had been removed from the land without a trace entering any official record.[12]

Once the land was cleared of its former inhabitants, United Fruit erected company housing for banana workers. Usually this consisted of blocks of two-story wooden barracks like apartment complexes, built facing each other across open yards like the two sides of an "H." They were called *yardas* after the English usage. These long barracks were divided into separate rooms for each family or for groups of single men in bunkhouses. Communal water pumps and outhouses were usually located in the center of each yard while sheds directly in front of each subdivided unit were used for bathing and cooking. During heat waves it was virtually impossible to bear the humidity in the enclosed buildings, and the workers and their families would move outside to the open space with chairs, tables, and hammocks.

The housing compound for management was located just outside the town of Tiquisate and sprawled beneath the palm trees, constructed around a huge central lodge with a swimming pool on the grounds. All the management housing stood on stilts with screen windows and doors to protect against malarial mosquitoes and the abundant reptilian life that crawled through the grasses (in contrast to the worker housing down the road, which was built squarely on the ground and without screens). Management's quarters were for the most part a foreign compound, though midlevel Guatemalan employees often lived within its fences. (On outlying plantations, resident management was mostly Guatemalan.) Most of the housing in the foreign compound at Tiquisate was built for families, while single men on the company's managerial payroll shared dwellings. An army of Guatemalan attendants cleaned the homes, kept up the grounds, and staffed the commissary and recreational facilities, but most of these people left the compound each evening for homes in the town of Tiquisate.

Tiquisate sprang up overnight. By 1950 some 30,000 people swelled the township's population, where "no more than 300 [had] lived in that place when, in the month of April 1936, the Company first started its activities" (*Censo* 1950, 13; Presidencia de la República 1954, 316). Overwhelmingly the new arrivals were young men. From the start, questions of social control and immorality troubled the literate public. The banana fincas, or plantations, were reputed dens of iniquity. Women allegedly changed partners at whim within a generalized culture of prostitution that existed alongside less clearcut arrangements such as the expected exchange of sexual favors for promotions or better housing (Interviews 1 and 2 1990; Interview 3 1990; Pellecer 1990). Most women of course were not prostitutes. Many came to the area drawn by the opportunities for petty commerce opened up by the new export boom (Interview 61 1990). Even so, "there was a lot of prostitution in Tiquisate, *a lot*. In the town, on its outskirts, everywhere there were *salones,* and each salon or *barra* was full of women. At the very least there were 25 cantinas or barras. They would be packed with men drinking beer and *guaro*" (Interview 1 1990).

Prostitution on United Fruit Company plantations can be attributed to the transience of the population and the extreme imbalance in the sex ratio. Only rarely did women accompany men who came from the eastern provinces. Teenage girls were transported—by independent businessmen—from El Salvador with the promise of respectable work, then delivered to dozens of cantinas, or saloons, that housed prostitutes in the town of Tiquisate. The women on arrival were usually fourteen to sixteen years old. Every Saturday afternoon, workers descended on the profusion of cantinas in the town center. The popular insistence that most of the prostitutes were Salvadoran may have been a fiction created to distance the consumers from the victims of the traffic in women. El Salvador's chronic overpopulation and lack of work did, however, make the country a convenient recruiting ground, with the added advantage of a national boundary to block communication with the girls' families.[13] After several years of prostitution, the women would typically marry workers. The women encouraged their clients to treat them like sweethearts as the fastest route out of the profession, and constant fights and occasional murders erupted over women.[14] In fact, fights at the end of every workweek alleviated the backbreaking monotony of labor in the groves.

My friends would invite me. We wouldn't ask each other out for lunch or to have a drink, no, we'd go together to the barras. We'd go there and ask for a drink. The girls were very beautiful, pure dolls, because there was a lot of competition between the salones to get the most beautiful women since this is what their business was based on. The young woman would bring a drink and if you liked her, you'd make a sign. The danger for the man was that another might arrive who knew her and wanted to marry her, and then there'd be a fight, they'd get mad, right. They'd pull out their knives. Sometimes they'd cut them up from behind and no one would ever know who did it, just because the other one was drinking or talking with the wrong woman. There were many people who died there over women in fights. All the bar owner would do is drag the body out and leave it in the street, then someone would pick them up and bury them in the cemetery like they were dogs, since no one knew their family, and there it would end. (Interview 1 1990)

Men fought over women, and after marriage — which was usually common-law according to the custom of the poor — women fought over men.[15] Wives resorted to violence to defend their income as well as their honor, because the sole company job open to women in significant numbers was that of domestic servant, of whom there were only several hundred. For most women, financial security lay in their ability to gain access to a man's paycheck. Female labor after marriage was unpaid and limited to the home (unlike women in other plantation sectors who joined men and children in the fields to achieve "a family wage").

Prostitution and fighting of course escalated in direct proportion to the intake of alcohol, which the company treated as a necessary social escape valve. At Tiquisate the company facilitated lavish spending on liquor by transporting workers to the town center as soon as paychecks were disbursed (Interviews 1 and 2 1990). Across the country, the drunkenness of plantation workers prompted the constitutional prohibition of 1945 against the sale of alcohol within the boundaries of a plantation. The drafters of the law clearly saw the issue in political as well as moral terms. They believed drinking was a diversion of energies that could be better spent elsewhere; it crippled lower-class organizing potential. Plantation workers for their part chafed against the revolutionary government's efforts to protect them from alcohol consumption.

When convenient, the company shared the government's zeal to modify the drinking habits of the laboring poor, habits they tolerated and in fact promoted on other occasions. Strains of prohibitionism among company managers were accompanied by a distaste for the flesh trade. United Fruit even instituted codes of conduct governing acceptable behavior in the yardas, in effect invading the privacy of the home with standards of morality as a condition of housing. In one example, the company fired a married worker for bringing home a woman other than his wife.[16] In another example of company efforts to police behavior, a worker was accused of urinating one night inside Club Tiquisate. The worker so feared the bosses' moralism that he went straight to the union for protection, "Since in this Company, private matters customarily have repercussions on the job, [and] it could be that any moment they will harass me and make my life miserable at work and for this reason I am troubling you, so you might take due notice if there should arise a case of unjust dismissal."[17]

Management's efforts to encourage domesticity were in any case ambiguous, driven by attempts at worker control as well as by morality, and complicated by the less-than-moral behavior of some company managers. One factor encouraging "libertinism" was the absence of traditional community and religious pressures that existed in the settled towns and ranches the workers had left behind. Religious observance, for example, was largely limited to the feast days of the different towns in honor of their namesake saints, while the priests tried without much success to curb the practice of spending Holy Week in parties at the seashore nearby, when plantation workers joined middle-class vacationers from all over the country and paraded about in the latest beach fashions.[18] Further, considerable transience from one plantation to another in search of better working conditions perpetuated the uninhibited character of popular culture and gender relations in Tiquisate. The company exacerbated this tendency by hiring new people rather than renewing the contracts of those already employed (thereby undermining its stated paternalist intention to promote more stable communities).

Though paid relatively well, banana production was bone-jarring and back-breaking labor for the men who worked in the groves. The work routine began with the clearing of the land. In 1947 the company required a thirteen-hour day for this task, which yielded one hectare (about two-and-one-half acres) per worker in each week of six days.[19] Next, irrigation ditches were dug in rows, and the branchless trees (which are not really trees but rather related to the lily plant and called *matas*) were planted at even intervals on raised mounds.[20] The matas, about ten feet high, reached maturity after a year, when the bunches of fruit had fully formed on the single stem growing from the stalk, which bent like a cane toward the ground, heavy with bananas. The speed of growth of the banana plant is a botanical marvel. Workers constantly pruned the trees so that just one offshoot, or "child" (*hijo*), sprang from the root, allowing all the plant's nutrients to flow instead to the fruit. The matas reached maturity year-round in the unremitting heat; management tried to time the groves to ripen successively. Aside from harvesting, the main work in the groves entailed weeding, maintaining the irrigation ditches, and applying fumigants and pesticides.[21]

Harvesting called for tremendous physical strength since the stem of about 100 bananas grown on a single stalk was the unit of production. Bananas for U.S. consumption averaged eighty-eight pounds a stem, and the smaller fruit destined for Europe averaged about sixty pounds a stem (*Octubre,* 17 January 1952, "La Frutera obtiene," p. 7). The need to repeatedly heave and haul this weight through the course of a twelve-hour day meant that United Fruit never allowed women to work in the banana groves.[22] At the command of the boss, work crews would harvest the stems with one man climbing the tree, sometimes with a ladder and sometimes not, to slice the stalk which then plunged several feet onto the bent back of another man, who would jog with his load to a waiting railroad car if the mata were near the track that formed the lifeline of the plantations. Mules and carts were provided when the grove was too distant from the track, and a second runner would relieve the first. Back injuries were frequent and virtually unavoidable across the span of a normal worklife. Knife wounds were also frequent from various tools used to hack back the jungle growth and sever the banana stem from the tree. The stems were packed directly into the railroad cars, then transported to the Atlantic port of Puerto Barrios, where longshoremen loaded them into the holds of the Great White Fleet that sailed for Boston and New Orleans.[23]

Chemical exposure posed another health threat to all the workers who came in contact with the fruit, since the company's zeal for scientific management and its quest for the perfect banana to market to the U.S. public required generous use of toxins. Another incentive toward overuse of chemicals was fear of the fungi and insects that had wiped out the crop in other zones, such as Sigatoka and Panama Disease.[24]

In addition to labor in the banana groves, company workers farmed subsistence plots awarded in usufruct as part of their wage, following the custom on plantations throughout the land. The company said they gave a *manzana* (1.7

acres) of land when enough was available.[25] Many laborers also kept farm animals that grazed in company-owned pastures. Banana workers clung to their peasant roots — symbolized in the usufruct plot — and insisted on calling themselves campesinos, in spite of the company's exceptionally rapid proletarianization.[26]

In sum, the harshness of the day's labor and the boomtown atmosphere of United Fruit operations created a distinct working-class culture in Tiquisate. Work as a company plantation laborer tested the limits of human endurance, with long days working through torrential rains that cut visibility to several feet and churned the ground to a sea of mud, and heatwaves so intense they transformed the coastal *tierra caliente* into a pressure cooker. It was a regimen that devoured workers, which was also true of the coffee and sugarcane harvest. But to a degree unparalleled in other Guatemalan plantation economies, the United Fruit workers related to each other as a single workforce and subculture, subject to powerful company rules and whims disguised as corporate necessity. The higher United Fruit wage obscures the fact that this labor force was controlled by the employer to an unprecedented degree. In this sense banana workers were arguably less free than the hungrier and poorer permanent workers of other plantation sectors in Guatemala. The workers' will to protest had to surmount exhaustion and fear, the distractions of drink, and the company's facile manipulation of temporary contracts with individual workers. Significantly, the removal of the threat of state coercion in the figure of Ubico played havoc with United Fruit's regime of labor control. Like waters breaking a dam, union loyalties surged forward at the dawn of the revolution. Only a powerful collective identity of shared injustice can explain the extraordinary speed of labor mobilization among banana workers after Ubico fell. More broadly, Escuintla became one of "the most fruitful departments" for organizing in the judgment of the Communist Party (*Octubre*, 24 July 1952, 91, "Vida del Partido," p. 5). While daily life on the banana plantations over the next ten years continued much the same, a more stable work environment took shape as a result of steady union pressure. The boomtown imperceptibly aged, with a growing community of families alongside the culture of prostitution. "Modern" union and anti-imperialist sentiments coalesced alongside a powerful campesino identity and "pre-industrial" attachment to the land, forming a marriage of loyalties that is readily apparent in the history of labor struggles from 1944 to 1954.

"The Macondo of Guatemala" 203

The battle lines emerged quickly in the months between June, when Ubico left office, and October, when several days of street fighting removed Ubico's handpicked successor Ponce. The banana workers did not wait to test the waters of freedom. Male office employees founded the Union of Tiquisate Workers, and they were joined by thousands of agricultural workers. Both clerks and campesinos shared a profound commitment to stand together against United Fruit managers, even though the risk was great since the country was still governed by the repressive machinery of the dictatorship. Only the dictator had fallen, while his mayors and police remained. Yet in late July, Tiquisate erupted into strike to demand pay hikes and an end to long-frozen wages. Meanwhile political parties were forming in towns and villages across the land in preparation for the first genuine presidential elections in fifteen years. The nation was gripped by feverish political and labor struggles, and when the Tiquisate strike seized the headlines, enthusiastic support poured in from other quarters. For sixteen days the workers stayed out, at which point United Fruit agreed to their central demand for a 15 percent raise. Yet the outcome of the Tiquisate strike was mixed. The caretaker regime of General Manuel Ponce, put in place by Ubico when he stepped down, jailed the union leadership, then shipped them off to the northern jungles. General Ponce in his election campaign literature counted the "suppression" of the Tiquisate strike as one of his most important achievements (López Larrave 1976, 38; Levenson-Estrada 1994, 5, 128).[27]

Even before the strike, United Fruit went on the offensive. It was accustomed to subservience and viewed with alarm the fierce anti-U.S. anger that was erupting after decades of enforced silence. The company did not limit its compass of action to the banana plantations. United Fruit was plotting its advantage long before the dictatorship officially ended with the insurrection of October. The Mexican ambassador, Romeo Ortega, told his superiors in secret cables and hand-delivered, coded letters that the company was aiding General Ponce's propaganda machine behind the scenes. Ortega accused United Fruit of planting rumors that Mexico was manipulating the street protests of June and providing funds for Arévalo's candidacy, with the aim of annexing all Central America to Mexico. Several months later in December 1944, Ortega reported home that United Fruit was scheming with the dictators of Honduras, Nicaragua, and El Salvador to stir up public disorders in Guatemala that would furnish the pretext for U.S. intervention. The charge was credible given the company's historical practice of installing and removing Central American presidents at will. Ambassador Ortega said the Guatemalan secretary of foreign relations had begged him "in anguish" for arms to defend the new revolution, which the ambassador refused to furnish.[28] United Fruit from the very start was a sworn enemy of reform and willing, moreover, to resort to violence.

From 1944 onward, banana workers protested persecution at the hands of their supervisors and at the hands of the state, which often used soldiers to break strikes. On the most elementary level, the fall of Ubico allowed banana workers to report incidents that contradicted the company's self-promotion as a corporate utopia in the tropics. Their channels of communication were many. Through the union, workers enjoyed immediate access to the national press since United Fruit was such an important political player on the national scene. The organizing grapevine overlapped with the networks of railroad employees, who made up one of the first and largest union sectors in the country and who came into daily contact with company employees. Rural workers in Escuintla also knit together organizing networks that bridged the sugar, cattle, and banana sectors, and that joined campesinos who owned their land with those who farmed the land of others. Such was the situation when the uprising of October finally swept out the dictatorship. Tiquisate's reputation for militancy is somewhat misleading insofar as other rural workers were behaving in exactly the same manner and risking their livelihoods to make identical demands. The difference lay in the peculiar situation of banana workers as direct employees of the "imperialist" Yankees. The sheer mass of Tiquisate workers amplified their demands. Further, unlike the Atlantic-coast plantations, their proximity to the capital meant that revolutionaries who were directly engaged in crafting national reform could drop in at a day's notice.

These factors conjoined to create strong socialist leadership in the department of Escuintla. In the first place, socialist theory led its practitioners to focus their energies on United Fruit workers for the fact they were more proletarianized than other rural plantation workers and presumably educated by experience to an anti-imperialist consciousness. Workers throughout the department of Escuintla were probably more heavily courted by urban revolutionaries than any other plantation workers in the republic. Banana workers in Tiquisate responded readily. They elected outspoken congressional representatives who took the lead in shaping egalitarian legislation for the poor. These leaders were often born outside Escuintla, yet their talk of rights and liberties joined seamlessly with the aspirations of rural workers who produced their own local, midlevel leadership. National organizers would arrive for a weekend, convene meetings, then return to the capital to attend to a host of other local and national issues, leaving in their wake local structures and leadership to carry on the work. In Tiquisate, for instance, the union found an energetic and committed general secretary in Juan Gabino Pérez, who was thirty-seven years old in 1948 and a company mechanic.[29]

The class distance that lay between national leaders and local workers was mirrored within the union itself. Internal tensions were inescapable. Even so, labor unions were genuinely participatory during the revolution and in fact more democratic than political parties since party structures waxed and waned with the rhythm of elections and promoted individual leadership rather than collective decision making. Campesino leadership grew more cosmopolitan over the course of the revolution. Many banana workers who became trade union militants received some training in organizing strategies, which gave new form to their social analysis but which of course did not mean that they ceased to identify as campesino organizers. Judging from what survives in Labor Ministry records, discord between the different classifications of workers arose in the normal course of organizing, especially between the guild of the captains and foremen and that of the field workers under their direct supervision. Apparently, calls for harmony within the union won peace.[30] Yet the company tried to declare these supervisors confidential employees, as it had done with *mandadores* (who supervised large areas of production) and timekeepers (who clocked the workers' hours). The union argued that, in fact, captains and foremen "are the most exposed [of anyone] to the injustices of the Mandadores."[31]

Among the national agrarian leaders who were active in Escuintla was the social democrat congressman Augusto Charnaud MacDonald, who was allied with the national peasant association, founded in 1950 to serve the needs of campesinos with no access to unions. Another radical was Ernesto Marroquín Wyss, a company office employee who died prematurely after years of organizing and successfully running for Congress on a platform of "Agrarian Reform, Better Wages, Working-class Housing and Guaranteed Freedom."[32] A third was Carlos Manuel Pellecer, a silver-tongued congressman who also represented Escuintla. He was born to a patrician family, exiled in Mexico during the 1930s, where he worked as a rural schoolteacher, then allowed to return home when Ubico fell (Pellecer 1990). During the revolution, Pellecer joined the Communist Party and became one of its national spokesmen. He later turned on his former comrades to cast his lot with the anticommunists in the late 1950s. Another confusing figure was cut by the lawyer Arcadio Chévez, a populist who formed national labor federations and represented Tiquisate workers from 1945 onward while doing what he could to derail communist organizing. Socialist labor leaders vilified Chévez because of his close association with the Ubico dictatorship and his alleged opportunism (López Larrave 1976, 32; Obando Sánchez 1978, 122).[33]

Labor rights were made law in March 1945 with the ratification of the constitution, which protected the right to organize and strike and honored the principle of collective contracts. Even so, by that point it was apparent that the Arévalo administration was fearful of communism and annoyed by confrontational worker tactics.[34] In short, the militancy of Tiquisate workers represented a political threat in the eyes of the new administration. Arévalo believed in gradual "dignification of the workers" through measures handed down by the state, rather than grassroots or workplace democracy.[35] One of Arévalo's earliest efforts to pave the way for major social reform was the First Regional Economic Congress in Escuintla on 27 May 1945, which aimed to design strategies to achieve "harmony" between labor and management.[36] Participants were designated by government decree, which precluded proportional representation of workers. Yet the event was remarkable for the fact the poor enjoyed any representation at all. Landowners and rural workers received equal weight, including two delegates from the Tiquisate branch of the United Fruit Company and another two from the Tiquisate union. The most striking outcome of the Escuintla congress was the stream of testimony from workers describing the depth of their poverty and the extent of their humiliation—it shocked the conscience of the newspaper-reading public and gave new momentum to rural organizing.

Ominously, labor rights in the countryside grew more fragile as the months passed because the agrarian elite went on the offensive to block worker mobilization. In September 1945 President Arévalo bowed to elite pressure and forbade rural unionization, though he spared Tiquisate. In this prohibition, Arévalo declared rural labor organizing a criminal offense but exempted unions with more than 500 members, which in practice covered mainly United Fruit workers. In effect, company employees were the *only* rural workers whose unions could participate as political actors in the battles leading to the passage of the 1947 Labor Code. By contrast, rural workers without unions could try to sway national policy through their votes, but they were denied more substantial participation by the absence of democratic worker organizations. The banana workers slowly won legitimacy in the eyes of the state and became the "elder statesman" among rural unions. But all the while, "UFCO acted as though the new Labor Code were not applicable," according to Alfonso Bauer Paiz, later the head of the Ministry of the Economy, who said that "the Company behaved as though it had the freedom to direct its business with absolute autonomy since its contract with the government predated the Constitution" (Bauer Paiz 1989).[37]

By 1947, the first year of the Labor Ministry's operations and hence the first year of surviving documentation, the union in Tiquisate was collecting more than $800 a month in dues from well over 3,000 members.[38] Since the Octopus, as Guatemalans termed United Fruit, was divided into two corporations, one on the Atlantic coast and the other on the Pacific, the law required two distinct unions. All the workers on the Pacific coast belonged to a single union called the Sindicato de Empresa de Trabajadores de la Compañia Agricola de Guatemala (SETCAG), while the workers in Izabal belonged to another called the Sindicato de Empresa de Trabajadores de la United Fruit Company (SETUFCO). Each plantation laborer paid approximately 25 centavos per month while midlevel employees paid higher dues. The Tiquisate fincas with the largest union membership at that time were Jutiapa, Verapaz, and Izabal, which each counted hundreds of employees.[39] The remaining plantations collected dues from about 100 workers apiece. These numbers were matched only by workers on the Atlantic Coast United Fruit plantations (in SETUFCO) and those on the National Fincas, which were state farms created by massive expropriations from German coffee planters during World War II. (The German colony had dominated coffee, the country's primary export, since the turn of the century.) Yet National Fincas, unlike the banana plantations, were segmented into individual units each with its separate union. Government restrictions prohibited a single union from representing more than one workplace, which meant that hundreds of thousands of plantation workers in Guatemala were fragmented into unions that never numbered more than several hundred members each. The state was willing to countenance large unions under foreign management but made certain that no similar mass of workers organized under its own managerial direction. All told, the numerical strength of the Tiquisate and Izabal unions gave the banana workers exceptional political weight, as well as resources in union dues that allowed them to provide financial assistance to needy members, purchase a small truck, and send a steady stream of union commissions to the capital and different fincas (ibid.). As a result, United Fruit workers formed the most powerful rural constituency in the country from the first flush of the revolution.

A tide of worker claims entered the written record for the first time ever in Tiquisate when the Labor Code became law on 1 May 1947. The code mandated the establishment of a labor ministry with local inspectors, which dealt a crushing blow to planter autonomy. Yet in many ways the code also hampered or hobbled worker organizing; for instance, it restricted the right to strike through the legal principle of "tutelary" state intervention, by which the government took a protective stance toward labor that in practice often functioned as corporatist control. By law every strike was subject to government scrutiny on a case-by-case basis because official approval was required to declare a strike legal. On 9 June 1947 the government conferred legal recognition on the first union in the land, at United Fruit Company (López Larrave 1976, 31). The only other unions in Guatemala that matched the size, and hence the political strength, of United Fruit employees were the railroad and teachers unions. Major labor conflicts erupted in the Pacific banana zone in 1948, 1951, and 1952, some of them legal and some of them not, while more minor conflicts were continuous.

Worker complaints from 1947 forward gave the lie to company claims of paternalism. On a regular basis, in the labor records, United Fruit vehemently denied charges that were later proved true. Workers said, with some exaggeration, that the only time the company ever obeyed labor law was when employees filed a complaint and the government ordered redress.[40] One interesting perspective on company paternalism appeared in the petitions of domestic servants who worked in the homes of company managers. With the support of the union, about 230 maids waged a struggle during the revolution to demand recognition as United Fruit employees. The company, however, insisted they were the employees of individual housewives and subject to whatever working conditions those individuals provided, even though United Fruit paid their managers a stipend to cover the cost of maid service. Many domestic servants said they received only a fraction of the designated stipend.[41]

In general, labor abuses on the banana plantations differed in degree, rather than kind, from the violations commonly practiced by Guatemalan planters. Employment as a United Fruit worker was less exploitative with regard to wages, but to little else. And the real wage fell steadily. Four years after the 1944 strike, banana workers had not seen a raise even though "on multiple occasions we [the union] have solicited such a raise, but you [United Fruit] have always evaded the issue with subterfuges that are more or less legal."[42] Forced and unpaid overtime was also common in Tiquisate as elsewhere. The company did not depart from the general practice among planters when it hired and fired at will or used layoffs to get rid of so-called troublemakers. Layoffs also occurred to circumvent the payment of benefits. As late as June 1950, the Tiquisate union asserted to the head of the Ministry of Labor that the company systematically fired workers on "the pretext of scarcity of work," usually just before the workers reached the one-year period that would entitle them to vacation time. In a letter the following month, the union protested that timekeepers, foremen, and other midlevel supervisory personnel were ordered to play the role of supposedly impartial witnesses to these layoffs.[43] In addition, the company gouged paychecks by making illegal discounts in order to avoid payment of the seventh day's wage, which had been mandated by law but was honored in the breach in the Guatemalan countryside. And without warning, United Fruit would switch back and forth between payment by the day or by piece-rate to cut labor costs for workers clearing the land for new plantations. Workers also reported that they were denied enough land to sow corn, which echoed one of the most common complaints received by the Labor Department from other plantation sectors.[44]

Healthcare was central to the company's image-building efforts, and here as well, the new freedoms of speech and protest revealed the unsightly underbelly of company practice. One "peon," employed by the company in Tiquisate for more than a decade, started coughing up blood, and when he went to the company doctor he was forced to sign a document without knowing or understanding its contents. As it turned out, he had signed away healthcare rights for his wife, their three-year-old child, and their baby.[45] Another worker, Catalino Garcia Flores, had been on the company's payroll since 1938 in Guatemala and before that in Honduras, yet in 1951, at the age of seventy-six, he was laid off with no financial support. He went blind shortly thereafter. On appeal, he finally won retirement benefits.[46] A company sawmill worker who had given fifteen years to the company was denied compensation for an accident on his job.[47] The family of another laborer, who had died in a work accident, was refused any financial compensation because United Fruit claimed the underlying cause of death was malaria rather than the workplace injury.[48]

While the protests of United Fruit suggest it was facing a kind of dictatorship of the banana workers, the record of labor-management disputes shows otherwise. The union in Tiquisate won the workers some room to maneuver, but the union could not always compel United Fruit to obey the new laws. On Finca Panzos, for example, worker complaints led to the reinstatement of ten laid-off workers; on Finca Esquipulas the company finally agreed to rescind eighteen unfair layoffs; and on Finca Santiago they were obliged to rehire thirty people.[49] On Finca Salamá, however, the company regularly laid off people "without any motive" and got away with it. Labor inspector José Gordillo described the status quo as one of company impunity: "This is the dirty system [*el sistema cochino*] which, it is fair to say, all the foremen adopt when they want to get rid of some employee who happens to displease them . . . and without gratitude or even a moment's reflection they seize the bread [from the worker] that he has earned through the sweat of his brow in the mortifying climate of the fruit plantations."[50]

The possibilities for organized action by workers in the context of company intransigence are best illustrated by particular conflicts. An early example of a minor dispute — presumably the most daily or constant variety — emerges in a petition of labor complaints from Finca Jocotán in 1947, where workers said prices were climbing "to the clouds" in company stores while wages remained stationary. They alleged that United Fruit refused to pay overtime, thereby breaking the labor law contained in the constitution. Night workers were forced to furnish their own machetes, boots, and rubber capes though the law mandated that the employer buy these. The company provided no masks or gloves to people whose job it was to apply a chemical "mist that is so harmful it makes the head turn blue [*azulan el cerebro*] on contact," literally dusting the worker in blue powder (it continues in use today).[51] Workers also claimed there were not enough outhouses and that those that existed were so close to the yardas they endangered people's health. And in retaliation for worker organizing, the company refused to permit workers leave-time to farm their usufruct plots or space to pasture their animals. Through formal petitions such as this one, the banana workers held their foreign employer accountable for the first time since the Tiquisate plantations had been created. In this particular case, the chief company manager in effect admitted guilt by saying not *all* of the charges from Jocotán were true.[52]

A second example demonstrates how local conflicts escalated into regional crises. The setting was Finca Totonicapán, and the occasion a long-simmering dispute between plantation workers and the manager, Alfred Smith. Smith, a Guatemalan citizen, habitually harassed union members and had unjustly fired and kicked out eighteen workers, including two union representatives. Among the victims were three "humble men who don't have the spirit to fight for their rights."[53] Another union officer at Finca Totonicapán suffered a cutback in hours when he accepted his union post. Smith also evicted the wife and family of a longtime worker when the husband was in the hospital with a work injury. The eviction, with all the family's belongings thrown outside, shattered any remnant of paternalism. The police were called in to investigate and found that Smith, during seven years of service, had proved himself "a loyal adept and great sympathizer of the North American colony in that place, especially of its high chiefs."[54] Middle management such as Smith did the company's dirty work, allowing "the gringos" a certain regal distance from the nastiness of labor control. Apparently with their approval, Smith cultivated "a system of spies that infiltrated union meetings from 1944 onwards" (ibid.). He cornered individual workers and urged them to resist joining the union, "painting the future of trade unionists in Guatemala in lugubrious phrases and auguring permanent unemployment for Company workers who joined the ranks of [their fellow] workers [in the union]" (ibid.). During a union assembly in August 1947, a worker named Blas Hernandez called Smith "an enemy of the labor movement" (a fair enough description), and one of Smith's spies reported back to him. In the days that followed, Smith tried to murder Hernandez. Unions far and near heard of the incident and were outraged: "Imagine our surprise when . . . Mr. Smith with a pistol in his hand went searching for Compañero Hernandez to kill him, which created general anxiety among all the plantation workers" (ibid.). The union officers at Totonicapán, together with their members and workers from nearby fincas, wrote a letter to the president demanding Smith's removal on the grounds he was "a mortal Enemy of our union struggle as he is of our Government, for having said the Government can't order him around . . . [and that] Doctor Arévalo is communist."[55] Quite boldly, the union reasoned that, "if the workers are unjustly reprimanded and fired by the bosses, so too can [the bosses] be fired and reprimanded by petition of the organized workers."[56] In short, workers asserted a self-evident right to equality in the workplace between the employer and the employed. They carried new ideas of justice to their logical conclusion. With a resolve that cut straight through the conventions of polite society, workers in Tiquisate were applying principles of equality with far more rigor than most of the framers of the new constitution had ever intended.

A number of important points emerge from this trail of documents. First, Alfred Smith had always behaved like a tyrant, but it was only the advent of national reform and the founding of the local union that permitted a collective response. Second, Smith reacted to the union as though it were his born enemy, and tried to shut down meetings through fits of rage while taking special pains to rid the plantation of union members. Across the land, unions were met with similar tactics, and workers in those unions rose to the occasion, mounting labor struggles that reached fever pitch long before the advent of agrarian reform in 1952. Third, union organizing in Tiquisate even at this early stage achieved a brotherhood that reached across plantation boundaries; the unions were *not* atomized units battling for rights on isolated fincas. Fourth, labor struggle among company workers found natural expression in anti-imperialist sentiments. The workers justified their demand to Arévalo on the principle of shared nationalism, and their outrage over Mr. Smith's claim to immunity from Guatemalan law on the basis of his association with the North Americans. United Fruit's senior manager in Guatemala, William Taillon, laid responsibility for worker solidarity at the door of the government, saying, "Before the arrival of the labor inspectors on our plantations, the general situation of the worker was calm."[57] His analysis was probably wrong, however, which leads to the last point: Arévalo's government was extremely wary of worker organizing, especially in the countryside, and even more so among the workforce of foreign-owned companies. The workers' elegant claim to equality between employer and employed met no approval whatsoever from the chief of state.

In the following year, 1948, Arévalo sent in the army to crush a strike that had been declared illegal under the new Labor Code's corporatist provisions. As the soldiers stood by, both the company and the workers were persuaded by the head of the Ministry of the Economy and Labor to submit to government arbitration. In hindsight, President Arbenz said that the government arbitration of the year 1948 marked a distinct turning point, because it was then that United Fruit turned in a systematic way to what it called anticommunist organizing.[58]

United Fruit responded to labor militancy by drawing closer to local landowners; a new and more calculated ruthlessness on the part of the plantation elite matched the increasing strength of the Escuintla unions. The local police, for their part, as often as not arrested strikers and jailed them to restore the peace, thus siding with the planters rather than the workers.[59] But with each passing year of the revolution, new government decrees curtailed the arbitrary power of the planters, as for example in 1949 when the first official minimum-wage commissions crisscrossed the land "meddling" in affairs that had always been the planters' prerogative. The outcome of the battle between planters and workers was never a foregone conclusion. The minimum-wage commissions, for instance, were charged with reporting on current wage rates but usually failed to do so, while the administrative arm of the Labor Department often found itself powerless to compel compliance from the agrarian elite.[60] New decrees met limited success but even so, the isolation that had worked so well to the landowners' advantage was coming to an end. (To cite one measure of this, by 1950 virtually every campesino household in Tiquisate owned a radio [Interview 1 1990].)

Tiquisate was among the first unions in the country to win a contract (López Larrave 1976, 49). The union's proposed wage scale called for the largest raises for those on the bottom, which dramatically compressed the disparity between the best- and the worst-paid company employees. At a general assembly, workers of all the different company pay classifications voted on and passed this wage scale. Then, beginning in 1950 and continuing through 1951, they joined with the United Fruit Company workers of the Atlantic Coast — on the older plantations in the department of Izabal and also on the Atlantic docks of Puerto Barrios — to win a single collective pact. When they finally succeeded, the workers achieved de facto recognition as a single workforce in spite of the legal fiction that divided United Fruit into a number of different companies with the idea of dividing employees into smaller and more manageable units and also avoiding antitrust laws.[61] This unity made real the possibility of enforcing the minimum wage of 80 centavos.

The balance sheet of national revolution for company workers under Arévalo was mixed. Repeatedly during these years, demands by workers across the land for dignity or subsistence wages were answered with squadrons of soldiers "to keep the peace," as the authorities phrased it. The "view from below" suggests that the heart of the revolution lay not in the intellect and energy of a handful of progressive lawmakers but, rather, in the determination of poor people to reforge social relations through the strength of their numbers: "The union spoke for the masses, it went to court to say the law says such and such. By working hard, we could earn a little more for our children, maybe buy another piece of bread or else some medicine. We were not going against the Company, no, we only wanted it to abide by the law. The Company didn't like the union, it just wanted us all piled up on top of each other so if one of us asked for a raise, they'd give his work to another and so on. Thousands of us were in the union there, and all of us asked for a raise together" (Interview 1 1990). The union served as the vehicle that promoted the sustained participation of the workers in revolutionary change. National reform and worker initiative emerged as two faces of the same coin, or in the words of the same banana worker, "I entered the union because, as a campesino worker, one needs the support of the Constitution of the Republic. We know we're just workers, and that without some support we're worth nothing" (Interview 1 1990).

When Arbenz took office in 1951, thanks to the landslide of votes from the poor, the workers were guaranteed an untiring advocate in the National Palace. As if to test his mettle, United Fruit almost immediately raised the ante in a showdown that workers came to call the Great Banana Strike. In September 1951 a hurricane ripped through the Pacific coast and destroyed three million trees. The company seized the occasion, claiming it would cost a year of repairs and ten million quetzals to replace the groves. Then on 26 September, the company laid off 3,746 workers without pay. The workers believed the layoffs were retaliatory and meant to break the union, since in the past natural disasters had occurred constantly without interrupting employment. Lending credence to their claims, in February 1952 the company threatened to lay off over 3,000 Atlantic-coast workers on the grounds that Sigatoka had ravaged the groves in

Izabal.[62] Again the workers said the company was lying because in fact all the fincas in question had been "denounced" as partly fallow and hence subject to the agrarian reform provisions. United Fruit was prepared to dismiss almost its entire Guatemalan workforce, apparently out of spite, to show the workers and President Arbenz who was boss. It had resorted to the same draconian solution when Guatemalan workers had struck the entire United Fruit operation under President Orellana in 1923. Ten years later the company had shut down its Caribbean plantations in Costa Rica forever after the great strike wave of 1933, though United Fruit insisted that crop disease was the cause (Dosal 1993, 129–35; Chomsky 1994, 32).

In Tiquisate in 1951 the Labor Department ordered that the workers be rehired, but to no avail. Instead, the company evicted the workers. Most of them returned to the eastern provinces to work as day laborers, while the rest waited. The strike was legal in the eyes of the state, and Arbenz arranged donations of food valued at 60 million quetzals over the course of the lockout. Messages of solidarity poured in from all over the country while United Fruit did its best to divide the workers on questions of strategy and politics, with Chévez at the helm of the anticommunist faction. Finally, in March 1952, half a year after the original layoffs, the company surrendered. It consented to the court order to end the lockout and signed an agreement that promised back wages.[63] Banana workers returned to Tiquisate in force just in time to press their advantage under the Agrarian Reform.

Agrarian reform followed eight long years of organizing in the countryside. In Tiquisate, 1 May 1952 was celebrated with the largest rally in memory as a show of popular support for the bitterly contested legislation, then mired in congressional debate. Some 4,000 campesinos gathered, many of them with the proposed land reform bill in their possession. The speeches urged people to study the bill so they could immediately bring land claims on its passage (*Octubre,* 22 May 1952, "Grandes Actos de Masas," p. 4, and "Entrevista: La Ley Agraria Recoge," p. 5). On 17 June 1952 the bill finally became law. Local committees of campesino, planter, and government representatives were set up to review the specific petitions of land-poor or landless campesinos. If approved, the claims passed up a chain of committees that ended with the president himself (see Presidencia de la República 1952). Campesinos elected to the local committees were "exceptionally honest" in the judgment of the minister of the economy, Bauer Paiz. They were entrusted with achieving the most cherished dreams of the poor (Bauer Paiz 1989). By mid-July the two company zones and the department of San Marcos, the giant among coffee producers, led the nation in the number of claims filed (*Octubre,* 17 July 1952, "¡Se Entregarán las Primeras Tierra!" p. 6). Over the following months the department of Escuintla became the most hard-fought battleground between landowners and the rural poor, not least because Congressman Pellecer urged land invasions to force the hand of the agrarian-reform committees.

Events in Tiquisate during the partitioning of the land were highly combustible because the company lashed out with all its strength and guile. In mid-February 1953 the National Agrarian Committee ruled against United Fruit and in favor of the workers and smallholders of Tiquisate. United Fruit at that point controlled almost 2,700 caballerias in Tiquisate but cultivated only one-ninth of that extension. Of the 300 caballerias in use, slightly more than half (173) were sown in banana groves, twenty-two were given over to forest products, and eight were planted in African palms. The remainder housed various installations. Under the Agrarian Reform law, United Fruit was dispossessed of over two-thirds of its Tiquisate holdings and compensated at rates based on the declared value of the land according to the company's tax returns. United Fruit chose to confess at that point, with no apparent shame, that it had grossly understated its wealth for tax purposes. Of its 2,652 total caballerias (almost 120,000 hectares) on the Pacific plantations, 1,860 were awarded to an estimated 8,000 to 10,000 campesinos in Tiquisate.[64] In addition, the company had illegally taken almost 240 caballerias that belonged to the nation, and the authorities ordered that this land be returned to the state. Unfortunately, at that point some functionaries within the government also helped themselves to the bounty, which discredited the process and created a public outcry (Handy 1994, 103). Meanwhile United Fruit stalled the land transfers, moving quickly to rent vast portions of the affected land, mostly to local cattle barons (*Octubre,* 26 February 1953, "En Tiquisate, 1860 Caballerias," pp. 5–6).

A new age had dawned for campesino workers with celebrations, firecrackers, and marimbas to mark the passage. "With land we could always sow a little, which meant we knew we could eat. People could leave something to their children and even educate them, put shoes on their feet," said a campesina whose family received land (Interview 61 1995). However, not all campesinos took advantage of the opportunity: "Well, the truth is that I was in agreement with the land reform, as the campesino that I am, and though I didn't get messed up in any of it, I was in agreement with all of it" (Interview 1 1990). People were torn between the new vision of utopia and an age-old instinct for caution. "My friends said to me, 'Come on, let's go, there's land and money, come with us!' But I never did. It was like searching for a [lost] needle, I thought. Some got money [*pisto*] and some got none—who knows how that thing worked. With their money they bought cows and horses. The government gave cows to the people, maybe 25 percent of the people in Tiquisate. I heard the commotion of President Arbenz, by radio and newspaper, because everyone heard it. People said there was going to be a war and everything" (Interview 1 1990).

The success of agrarian reform in Escuintla fulfilled the worst class fears of the landowners, adding fuel to the counterrevolutionary "Reaction" that provided the fifth column for the invasion. In Tiquisate conservatives tried to unseat pro-government officials on the town council and replace them with, in their words, anticommunists (*Octubre,* 16 February 1953, "Asalto Político de la Reacción a Municipalidad de Pueblo Nuevo," p. 7). In Escuintla two landowners were in fact killed. Many more campesinos "were shot, hung, beaten, burned, and run over throughout the country" (Handy 1994, 110). Nationally, the Reaction launched a disinformation campaign that accused the government of serving as Stalin's agents in America. This internal campaign received outside assistance because United Fruit had persuaded Eisenhower that Guatemala was indeed a Soviet beachhead. By 1952 Guatemala was the target of a full-blown destabilization program directed by CIA operatives accustomed to opponents such as the Greater East Asia Co-Prosperity Sphere and the German Wehrmacht; it is a wonder that the Guatemalan people withstood the assault for as long as they did. Arms caches were airlifted from the sky onto the fincas of the most conservative planters in Escuintla (often as not ending up in the hands of the workers). Officials found weapons stockpiled all over the country.[65]

The U.S. embassy became the headquarters of coup-plotting, and United Fruit made available all its resources, anticipating the sweetness of revenge. U.S. officials made no secret of their intentions. In March of 1953, former ambassador Spruille Braden called for U.S. intervention to expel Arbenz, saying that the presence of communists in any country was a foreign-policy concern—not an internal matter—that must be met with force (Braden was on United Fruit's payroll at the time, though this was not public knowledge (*Octubre,* 26 March 1953, p. 3, various editorials; Schlesinger and Kinser 1982, 96–97, 103). Psychological warfare went on for a period of months before the invasion of Castillo Armas and his so-called Liberation Army.[66] In the final weeks before Castillo Armas crossed the Honduran border, the banana workers were among those hastily recruited and trucked to the capital for training to defend the nation. They were instructed in the rules of warfare using only sticks, machetes, and decrepit rifles. By that point it was too little too late. Virtually the entire military establishment had been won over to the aims of the U.S. embassy, leaving an administration gripped by despair and a popular base versed in the struggles for land and a fair wage, not armed defense of the nation against U.S. assault.[67]

A Guatemalan professional whose family lived in Tiquisate as office employees from the beginning of company operations there calls Tiquisate "the Macondo of Guatemala" in reference to the fictionalized town of Santa Marta, Colombia, immortalized by the writer Gabriel García Márquez in *One Hundred Years of Solitude.* Macondo emerges out of the jungle in the Nobel-winning novel, built on flights of fancy and madness. Yet in a very real way—as recognized by the native son of Tiquisate—the novel, despite its studied lunacy, accurately portrays the historical experience of United Fruit abuses and has reached millions of people, while the real town of Tiquisate was blotted out of official memory. In the aftermath of the invasion of Castillo Armas, United Fruit workers in Escuintla suffered the worst violence, and a witch-hunt on the banana plantations sent hundreds into hiding. One girl and her mother hid in complete silence when the pro-Castillo forces came armed with sticks and machetes, yelling obscenities and stoning their house to drive out her father, a trade unionist, who had already fled (Interview 61 1995). Blacklists of union organizers effectively uprooted rural leadership throughout the country, while in Tiquisate this history unfolded with particular vengeance.[68] "The invading army pulled people out of their homes, men, women and children. They bound them hand and foot with wire, tied up like iguanas, and threw them into military trucks to take to Finca Jocotán," remembers the same campesina, who was thirteen years old at the time (Daughter of Banana Worker 1990). "There they shot them into huge open trenches and they fell whichever way. There they died because they had fought for the land." In another corner of the country a former banana worker from Tiquisate said,

Rosendo Pérez was the one in charge of that, who came in with the Liberation Army. He would take one man with him and go to each finca and find out that this person or that person was a communist, and write their names in a book. Two or three days later, the people on the list were taken away to Finca Jocotán and they never returned. At Finca Jocotán you could hear the machine guns going all the time. It lasted four or five months. They were grabbing people from everywhere, not just from Tiquisate but from all over Escuintla and from Mazatenango. Finca Jocotán was the center for the whole coast.[69]

An estimated one thousand campesinos and workers were machine-gunned at Finca Jocotán (presumably their remains are still there). In the judgment of the Tiquisate campesina whose family barely escaped capture, "Without a doubt the company permitted the massacre, since it took place on their plantation and they allowed the army to seize people" (Interview 61 1995).

In 1958 a U.S. court ruled against United Fruit in an antitrust case that had grown out of the initial claims filed by the Arbenz government. The Pacific-coast plantations were sold and the Atlantic-coast plantations eventually parcelled out to United Fruit's competitors. At present, Guatemalans own the fincas that grow bananas for the U.S. market although recent scandals suggest that subcontracting is largely a fiction. Workers in recent decades have suffered kidnap and torture when they demanded the labor rights that were once protected by the government of the October Revolution.

Many Guatemalans turned to armed struggle after the failure of the October Revolution in the belief that the enemies of social justice were so powerful that only revolution could wrest freedom from their grip. In the aftermath of 1954 this conclusion permeated the Latin American left as well (Ché Guevara for one was present in Guatemala during the 1954 invasion). Today Central Americans struggle to win justice against the will of a military establishment that in Guatemala, at least, makes Rosendo Pérez look like a gentleman. Memories of mass violence remain forbidden and unresolved, like the killing ground at Tiquisate, because the perpetrators still hold power.

The story of labor struggles in Tiquisate during the October Revolution shows that the "revolution from above" only achieved real substance when met with the strength and sacrifice of those on the bottom of the social pyramid.

From the vantage of labor history, this observation is self-evident, but from the vantage of national political history, independent worker initiative has remained largely invisible. Plantation workers in the banana zone were fiercely loyal to national leaders even though the Labor Code in many ways hedged on the right to organize. Workers profoundly challenged the United Fruit Company because their demands turned the letter of the law into reality. The Labor Code made collective bargaining possible, for example, yet only years of organizing and pressure finally won a contract for all company workers. Through the union they compelled the administration of Arévalo then Arbenz to choose sides, thereby forcing the government to stand up to United Fruit. Challenging the Octopus set off a chain reaction among North Americans who shared inter-elite connections that led to the highest halls of power in Washington, D.C. The militancy of banana workers thus altered the chemistry of relations between the Guatemalan government and the United States.

Tiquisate fits the cross-national pattern of workers in banana enclaves who mounted strikes that redefined the state's relation to foreign corporations. In Guatemala, as elsewhere, these strikes forged new conceptions of national identity (see Chomsky 1994; Meza 1985). Under Arbenz, when the government supported the organizing efforts of company workers, militant company employees in Tiquisate squared off against U.S. managment with the blessing of the country's government. This ran counter to the more typical situation elsewhere in Central America, that of state cooperation with foreign capital. Thus the October Revolution offers an unusually clear picture of anti-imperialist sentiments among the workforce, since nationalism was actively encouraged by the Guatemalan government.

A number of intriguing distinctions separate Tiquisate from plantation zones on the Caribbean coast of Central America. Tiquisate's labor force was ladino and Central American from the start, not black and Caribbean, so the expression of contrary national or racial loyalties never emerged as a natural vehicle for working-class demands. Tiquisate workers lived in their own country, free to practice their own culture without attracting the attention of xenophobes or racists. Neither were they as isolated as other banana enclaves. Tiquisate cannot be called a hinterland, considering the proximity of the coffee piedmont, the huge sugarcane industry dating from colonial times, and the largest town in the Pacific-coast hot county.

Further, in the case of Tiquisate, like the Atlantic coast of both Honduras and Costa Rica, the Communist Party was rooted among banana workers at different points in time. The picture is confusing due to the fact that the communist leadership in Tiquisate may have incited illegal actions in defiance of party policy, while the competing, anticommunist labor leadership was allegedly bought for a handsome sum. (Historian Jim Handy mentions that "Pellecer admitted to fostering land invasions, and Arbenz subsequently blamed him for much of the rural unrest" [1994, 105].) Given all these differences, the fact that the labor history of Tiquisate shares fundamental similarities with other United Fruit regions argues for further comparative analysis of corporate plantation communities across international boundaries and perhaps a greater emphasis on the role of class as an explanatory factor, apart from or alongside the role of race according to each case.

In Tiquisate the revolution arrived as a promise. On the whole, management's unfettered freedom of action—and especially its ability to hire and fire at will—was curtailed but not halted by the government of the revolution. Still, this was a tremendous achievement for company laborers. Under Arévalo the state's defense of labor rights was pro forma, while under Arbenz, by contrast, the government helped strengthen grassroots structures for enforcement. In the words of one worker, "The government in those days loved the workers, and the union was the most it could be because it had the support of the government. The Company trembled when there was going to be a conflict."[70] Acting on the promise of dignity for the poor, workers were able to bring demands at the point of production that slowly but surely began to shift the balance of power in the countryside. The particular legacy of labor struggle on the Pacific-coast banana plantations nearly slips off the edge of memory because its aims and leadership were so effectively vanquished. In one respect, however, the story of Tiquisate did come full circle:

> Five or seven years after what took place at Finca Jocotán, Rosendo Pérez was murdered. A soldier who was part of the presidential bodyguard was the one who killed him, and it happened at the National Palace. The authorities were going to give Rosendo some kind of honor at the Palace because he was a participant in the government, and that was when the soldier shot him. What happened was Rosendo had killed the soldier's parents in Tiquisate.

The boy was left an orphan, and he went into the service and rose to that rank, all with the purpose of killing the man who had murdered his parents.

Rosendo was at the Palace to get his medal or whatever it was. And the military officers [at the ceremony] said, "Good. If there is anyone here who has anything to say against this man Rosendo Pérez, let him speak now." And that was when the soldier stepped forward and said, "Yes, I have something against him," and then shot him. The soldier was taken prisoner immediately and he gave his declaration and it came out in the press. When that happened I was still in Tiquisate. Many people were deeply moved when Rosendo died, because he had killed their brothers and sisters, their parents, their relatives. He was a butcher [matazón] but no one could say anything against him.[71]

NOTES

1. All interviews where the speaker requested anonymity are identified by number and date. Information about anonymous interviews follows the notes section. Socioeconomic information on the interviewee is indicated in the endnote only when it does not appear in the text. Interviews 1 and 2, banana workers for United Fruit, interviewed May 1990 in Tiquisate, Guatemala.

2. I would like to thank Tulio Halperín-Donghi, Avi Chomsky, Myrna Santiago, and the anonymous reviewers for their very helpful comments, as well as my brother, Thomas Forster, for drawing the map.

3. Mexico, Archivo Historico (hereafter AH), Secretaria de Relaciones Exteriores (hereafter SRE) III, Legajo (hereafter L.) 254–12, num. 570 (728.1–0)44–4050, Memo from the Secretary of Foreign Relations to the Mexican President Based on the Ambassador's Reports, 20 December 1944, p. 1; AH SRE III, Legajo 254–12, Expediente 728.1/0, Letter from the Ambassador to the SRE, 21 August 1944.

4. The evidence for this outrage surfaces mostly after the end of the dictatorship—in the content of the reforms of the revolutionaries, as well as in memoirs and literary treatments of the era, such as the novels of Miguel Angel Asturias and the work of Luis Cardoza y Aragon and Manuel Galich.

5. See Interviews 1 and 2 (1990) on recruitment from the point of view of the laborers. Ironically, considering its racist labor strategies, United Fruit Company often referred to its workers as "Indians," which they were not. Myrna Santiago in her research on the labor history of the Mexican oil industry reports that U.S. oil men likewise called all Mexicans "Indians" (personal communication).

6. Guatemala, Archivo General de Centroamérica (hereafter AGCA), Inspección General de Trabajo, Correspondencia (hereafter IGT-C), Sig B, L. 48751, severance form of 20 May 1947.

7. AGCA IGT-C, L. 48826, 12 March 1953.

8. AGCA IGT-C, L. 48832, 4 September 1953.

9. AGCA IGT-C, Sig B, L. 48751, 25 September 1947.

10. Interview with Carlos Manuel Pellecer, revolutionary organizer, communist party leader, and congressman during the revolution, 11 October 1990.

11. AGCA IGT-C, Sig B, L. 48751, 1947, 9/25.

12. In *The Green Pope*, Guatemala's Nobel Laureate novelist Miguel Angel Asturias put words to the same campesino memories of violence, eviction, and flight when United Fruit took over Atlantic coastlands after the turn of the century.

13. In a study of prostitution in the capital from 1880 to 1920, historian David McCreery finds that male artisans and skilled workers patronized houses of prostitution, while poorer working-class men went to "very young women . . . , prostitutes who had left the bordels because of disease, injury or age, and members of despised racial groups" (1986, 337–39). In 1887 the state took on the role of "forcible recruitment" of prostitutes, with regulations that established debt servitude in the government-regulated bordels for "any woman fifteen years or older found guilty of 'bad conduct' " (the required passbook and threats of fines and jail exactly paralleled the system of debt peonage that reigned in the countryside) (ibid. 341–42).

14. Interview 2 (1990). At present, the "trade" in Salvadoran teenagers, aggravated by decades of civil war and structural adjustment, continues to find a ready market in virtually every town in the plantation belt of the Pacific coast. One medium-sized town in the middle of the plantation belt, for instance, had over forty cantinas, and each one kept several prostitutes. Along the Mexican border and in the larger towns, there lives a huge floating population of prostitutes, many of them minors and chronic alcoholics. They dream of the chance to make it to the United States and start over again.

15. I witnessed a so-called cat fight on a banana plantation between two women competing for the same man; the fight generated great enthusiasm, with men, women, and children gathering round and cheering on the combatants. Two men broke up the fight, with some reluctance and apparently for my benefit.

16. AGCA IGT-C, Sig. B, L. 48751, 21 August 1947.

17. AGCA IGT-C, L. 48800, January 1951, n.d. from Renato Bruni.

18. The description of beach holidays arose in response to my question as to whether local religious practice included pilgrimages of any sort. Interviews 1 and 2 (1990).

19. AGCA IGT-C, L. 48751, 19 November 1947.

20. Holt notes, "The banana is not a tree but a herbaceous plant that can grow to over twenty feet and matures in thirteen to sixteen months" (1913, 351).

21. Interview 4, tour of groves, May 1990. In 1951 different piece rates applied to the following job classifications, which involved tasks from the grove to the ship's hold: "cortar, conchar, carretonear, enganchar, descargar, bueyeros, pasador, estivar, pasador cepa, encordar fruta, lavador." Fumigation workers were paid by the hour, and those who cleared the land, by the hectare (AGCA IGT-C, L. 48802, March 1951, asunto of October 24, 1951 [sic; misfiled in the archives]).

22. In coffee production, by contrast, women have always picked and hauled beans, averaging seventy to eighty pounds a day, but they transport this weight on their backs *slowly,* whereas the banana haulers are expected to practically run with the stem of bananas from the tree to their destination. Banana harvesting was not "women's work" in the modern conceptions of United Fruit

Company managers. This sexual division of labor is of course dictated by culture not capacity, insofar as the most physically demanding work in cane harvesting, for instance, was assigned to female slaves in the nineteenth-century Caribbean, while such tasks today are exclusively assigned to men (Luis Figueroa). In Guatemala race probably also shaped the division of labor by gender, considering that indigenous workers predominated in all the other agro-export harvests *except* bananas, and indigenous women always worked alongside men in the fields. Only in banana production — where the labor force was ladino or West Indian — were women excluded.

23. Today, the groves are rigged with a system of steel cables and pulleys that run the length of each row of trees. Each banana stem is hooked on the cable as if on a meat hook. Another hauler then seizes a free-hanging piece of cable designed for the purpose and pulls the whole chain of stems like a human draft animal toward the rail line or waiting cart. Next, women in packing plants on the fincas cut, bathe, and sort the bananas, treating them as tenderly as newborns, and pack them into padded Chiquita boxes that are stacked into refrigerated train cars for their journey to U.S. supermarkets.

24. See extensive documentation of complaints regarding fumigation work, for example, AGCA IGT-C, Sig B, L. 48750, June 1947, declaration of 28 May.

25. Interview 1 (1990); AGCA IGT-C, Sig B, L. 48750, 26 June 1947, also dated 3 July.

26. A modern union representative and banana worker called himself and his companions "*obreros campesinos*" or "campesino workers" (Interview 5 1990).

27. See also Ponce campaign flyer, in AGCA Hermeroteca, Hojas Sueltas (hereafter Herm/HS), 1944. López Larrave was a labor lawyer assassinated by the government in 1977 for his defense of workers.

28. AH SRE III, L. 254-12, num. 570 (728.1-0)44-4050, Memo from the Secretary of Foreign Relations to the Mexican President based on the Ambassador's Reports, 20 December 1944, p. 1; AH SRE III, L. 254-12, Expediente 728.1/0, Letter from the Ambassador to the SRE, 21 August 1944.

29. AGCA IGT-C, L. 48756, 7 April 1948.

30. AGCA IGT-C, Sig. B, L. 48751, 17 July 1947.

31. AGCA IGT-C, Sig. B, L. 48751, 12 September 1947.

32. AGCA Herm/II3 1950, flyer.

33. Antonio Obando Sánchez was a shoemaker and founder of the communist party in the 1920s, and was jailed throughout the 1930s. He helped rekindle the labor movement after 1944. As an elderly man he was seized and interrogated in the 1980s by the military establishment, and from that point forward lived underground. No one disputes that the lawyer Chévez received generous sums from union coffers to represent his campesino clients. Like Pellecer, Chévez was among the very few in his generation who have been able to live in their native country in peace since 1954, without death threats or right-wing attacks, which is viewed as guilt by omission by many of their contemporaries.

34. Arévalo shut down a union training school called Claridad six months after it first opened its doors in 1945 because many of its founders were communist. See Graciela Garcia, 62–66, 79–95, 136, 145.

35. AGCA Herm/HS 1947, "El Ministro de Gobernación Explica las Razones que Asistieron al Gobierno para Suspender Temporalmente la Actividad Sindical en el Campo."

36. AGCA Herm/HS 1945, "Se Convoca al Primer Congreso Regional de Economía."

37. Alfonso Bauer Paiz brought charges against United Fruit on behalf of the Guatemalan government in the dispute over lands confiscated by the Agrarian Reform.

38. In 1954 books and documents were burned across the land, in public pyres by the invaders and in secret by revolutionaries trying to escape retribution. Some of the correspondence of the Labor Ministry survives among the uncataloged material in the national archives, though many officials believe these records were burned (the Labor Ministry did in fact burn records from more recent decades because, they say, there was no place to store them). Many union documents were seized by U.S. officials in 1954 and shipped to Washington, D.C.

39. AGCA IGT-C, L. 48753, January 1948, SETCAG report, 31 December 1947.

40. AGCA IGT-C, L. 48753, 23 January 1948.

41. See AGCA IGT-C, L. 48756, 6 April 1948, Ministerio de Economia y Trabajo; AGCA IGT-C, L. 48753, 5 January 1948; AGCA IGT-C, Sig. B, L. 48750, 26 June 1947, United Fruit Company Declaration, also dated 3 July; AGCA IGT-C, L. 48753, January 1948, Six-month Financial Report of the Union with Dues Noted from Domestic Servants, dated 31 December 1947.

42. AGCA IGT-C, L. 48753, 3 January 1948.

43. AGCA IGT-C, L. 48773, 21 June 1950; AGCA IGT-C, L. 48774, July–August 1950, letter and response of 1 and 4 July. The Department of Inspection agreed with the union.

44. AGCA IGT-C, Sig. B, L. 48750, 22 and 28 May 1947; AGCA IGT-C, Sig. B, L. 48751, 6 August 1947; AGCA IGT-C, Sig. B, L. 48751, October–November 1947, Acta Num. 41.

45. AGCA IGT-C, Sig. B, L. 48751, 23 June 1947.

46. AGCA IGT-C, L. 48806, July 1951, 28 April.

47. AGCA IGT-C, Sig. B, L. 48751, 24 July 1947.

48. AGCA IGT-C, L. 487521, December 1947, on SETCAG letterhead. Every two weeks the company dispensed pills to prevent malaria. All the workers would line up and consume the pills as the managers watched (Interview 1 1990).

49. AGCA IGT-C, Sig. B, L. 48750, 26 June and 3 July 1947.

50. AGCA IGT-C, Sig. B, L. 48751, 21 August 1947.

51. AGCA IGT-C, Sig. B, L. 48751, 21 August 1947, "Jocotán," undated petition; AGCA IGT-C, Sig. B, L. 48750, 1947, "Hoja de peticiones," undated petition. Curiously, some of the Jocotán workers did *not* belong to SETCAG, the Tiquisate union, for reasons that are called "political" but are not further explained in the records. They felt their persecution was doubly unjust for the fact they had resisted unionization (later events at Jocotán are recounted in the conclusion to this essay). See also AGCA IGT-C, Sig. B, L. 48750, letter of 28 May 1947.

52. AGCA IGT-C, Sig. B, L. 48750, declaration of June 26 1947, also dated July 3. William Taillon headed up United Fruit Company operations nationally and lived in the capital. In charge of the Tiquisate plantations was a man who signed his correspondence Almyr Bump Lake (the union variously addressed him as Almyr Bump Lake Bump, Almyr Lake Bump Lake, or A. Bump).

53. AGCA IGT-C, L. 48753, January 1948, 7 September 1947.

54. AGCA IGT-C, L. 48753, January 1948, 29 October 1947.

55. AGCA IGT-C, L. 48753, January 1948, 31 October 1947. See also AGCA IGT-C, L. 48753, January 1948, 6 December 1947; and AGCA IGT-C, L. 48753, January 1948, 7 September 1947. On nationalism, see AGCA IGT-C, Sig. B, L. 48750, 28 May 1947.

56. AGCA IGT-C, L. 48753, January 1948, 7 September 1947.

57. AGCA IGT-C, Sig. B, L. 48750, 16 June 1947.

58. AGCA IGT-C, L. 48756, April 1948, letter of 9 March, and telegrams and letter from the union of 25 April. The company conceded the firings were arbitrary when it later provided generous severance pay to those laid off (AGCA IGT-C, Sig. B, L. 48751, letter of July 19 1947, "Audiencias," and letter of 30 July 1947; AGCA IGT-C, L. 48756, letter of 28 April and declaration of 5 April). See also López Larrave 1976, 49; "Informe de Presidente Arbenz" 1954, 17.

59. See AGCA IGT-C, Sig. B, L. 48750, 1 June 1947.

60. AGCA IGT-C, L. 48767, 5 May 1949.

61. AGCA IGT-C, L. 48804, 31 May 1951; *Octubre,* 12 May 1951, I:2, 4; and 9 July 1951, I:10, 1.

62. In 1951 the company registered 5,611 workers, though it is unclear at what point in their labor struggles the count was taken (Presidencia de la República 1954, 221).

63. Interviews 1 and 2 (1990). See also AGCA IGT-C., L. 48808, report of 19 September; AGCA IGT-C., L. 48810, letter of 12 November and telegram of 22 November 1951; *Octubre* (21 February 1952): "Obreros de la UFCO," 2; ibid., (5 February 1953): "En Izabal, 3,000 Amenazados," 7; ibid., (14 February 1952):, "Embargada la C.A.G.," 1; and ibid., (21 February 1952): "Obreros de la UFCO.," 2 and 4; AGCA Herm/HS 1952, "¡Por la Reanudación de las Labores y el Pago de los Salarios de los Obreros de Tiquisate!" On the factional struggles, see *Octubre* issues of 14, 21, and 28 February.

64. "Informe de Presidente Arbenz" 1954, 15; Guerra Borges 1986, 212. The exact figure was 83,929 hectares (*Octubre,* 5 March 1953, "Arbenz reafirmó Su Programa,"5).

65. *Octubre,* 9 April 1953, "Los Sucesos de Salamá Son un Brote," 5; "Lo de Salamá Es una Advertencia" and "Trabajadores de la Finca Concepción," 3. The U.S. Communist Party said that United Fruit funded the Salamá coup attempt (*Octubre,* 23 April 1953, "Conspiración Tramada en Washington," 8). At this point, a former attorney of United Fruit was known to be involved in the plot, while banana workers on the Atlantic-coast plantations said conspirators tied to Castillo Armas in Honduras continually slipped in and out of the country through company lands along the border (ibid., "Los Sucesos de Salamá," 5).

66. Immerman 1982, 118–43. For the paper trail left by the Reaction, see AGCA Herm/HS 1952–1955.

67. See Gleijeses 1993 on the paralysis of the Arbenz government, especially chaps. 7 and 13.

68. Ricardo Falla (1992), a Jesuit anthropologist, published interviews with internal refugees in the northern jungle that recount the 1954 massacre in Tiquisate.

69. Interview 1 (1990), corroborated by Interview 2 (1990). The United Fruit Company has steadfastly denied scholars access to company archives. Crimes of this magnitude probably would not be recorded on paper but would be more likely to enter the record through braggadocio or tormented consciences.

70. Interview 1 (1990). The contrast with succeeding decades could not be greater given the severity of labor repression since 1954. Guatemala is one of the most dangerous places in the world to be a trade unionist.

71. Interview 1 (1990). Reports of other deaths emerge as well, such as that of Fernando Blanco, a campesino who informed on his acquaintances in 1954. Many decades later he was seized, taken from his house, and executed by three grown children whose father had died at Jocotán. Interview 61 (1990).

ANONYMOUS INTERVIEWS

Interview 1 with United Fruit Company banana worker, from author's personal archive, May 1990, Tiquisate, Guatemala.

Interview 2 with United Fruit Company banana worker, from author's personal archive, May 1990, Tiquisate, Guatemala.

Interview 3 with urban trade unionist, from author's personal archive, May 1990, Tiquisate, Guatemala.

Interview 4 with United Fruit Company banana worker, from author's personal archive, May 1990, Tiquisate, Guatemala.

Interview 5 with United Fruit Company banana worker, from author's personal archive, May 1990, Tiquisate, Guatemala.

Interview 61 with daughter of union trade leader and United Fruit Company banana worker, from author's personal archive, January 1995, Tiquisate, Guatemala.

DARÍO A. EURAQUE

The Threat of Blackness to the Mestizo Nation: Race and Ethnicity in the Honduran Banana Economy, 1920s and 1930s

In 1926 the Honduran Congress voted to name the country's national currency in honor of Lempira, an indigenous chieftain who died fighting the Spaniards in the 1530s.[1] Until then, as in most countries of Central America, the Honduran national currency was simply known as the peso. Consequently, from primary school through adulthood, Hondurans studied Lempira in schoolbooks and observed his image in statues located in parks throughout the country. Why was Lempira chosen as the icon for the national currency in Honduras in 1926? To what extent did the history of the banana economy, then thriving, serve as context for understanding the Lempira phenomenon? How did the black populations on the Caribbean coast, as settled communities and as imported laborers on the banana plantations, play roles in decisions made in Tegucigalpa about the national currency?

I address these questions in the context of a reinterpretation of the history of the banana exporting region of Honduras, the Caribbean North Coast, and the role of its black populations. The Honduran North Coast's history, whose banana exports remained largely under the control of the United and Standard Fruit Companies for most of the twentieth century, has too often been interpreted within the narrow confines of a classic "banana enclave," or worse, those of the "classic Banana Republic" (Euraque 1996c; Euraque 1997). This perspective has tended to delink not only national economic and political history from the banana enclave, at least insofar as Hondurans enjoyed any autonomy in the relationship, but it also delinked national cultural history from regional processes on the Caribbean North Coast, especially in sociological analyses (Del Cid 1988).

The best way to understand how and why Lempira became the symbol of the national currency is by locating that congressional decision in the relationship between labor struggles in the banana plantations and their racial and ethnic resonance in Tegucigalpa, the Honduran capital. The existing historiography has misread key issues associated with ethnicity and the banana companies, particularly the misrepresentation of blackness, its association with imported West Indian labor in the 1910s and 1920s, and the exclusion from regional history of Garifuna blackness. Garifuna blackness, associated with a black population located on the Caribbean coast since the 1790s (Pastor Fasquelle 1998; Herranz 1994), appeared as the main local "threat" to efforts to make Honduras a mestizo nation of an Indo-Hispanic ancestry.

LEMPIRA, BLACKNESS, AND THE LABORING POPULATION IN THE BANANA ECONOMY OF THE 1910S AND 1920S

Despite the lack of evidence for Lempira's historic existence during most of Honduras's emergence as a nation-state, elite intellectuals fashioned a "national" representation of Lempira. This occurred in the context of what Benedict Anderson (1994) has called the production of "imagined political communities," fictive renderings of historic events that help imagine nations in particularly modern ways. The official nationalization of Lempira, despite his tragic death, originated in the nineteenth century and was consolidated during the second decade of the twentieth century, and it must be associated with the history of the banana enclave in those years (Alvarado 1993, 8–9; Joya 1992).

The state version of a "nationalist" Lempira in the twentieth century took place in two moments of official iconographic representation. A critical moment took place in 1928, when Dr. Precentación Centeno, then the minister of public education and a fervent patriot (Iraheta 1952), commissioned a painting of a "representative portrait of the valiant *Lempira*."[2] Another painter in 1929 fulfilled a commission for another official painting of Lempira. In this case, male members of the Lenca peoples from Intibuca posed for this effort (Castro 1929). This built on the other act, a congressional decree in 1926 that made Lempira the emblem of the national currency, thus making Lempira's image available to most humble Hondurans. In 1935 a national holiday was declared in Lempira's name (Zuniga and Zuniga Reyes 1993, 122). By the early 1940s Lempira's name was used to designate avenues, schools, stadiums, and even coffee and cigarette brand names (Castro 1940).

In 1926 months before the deputies debated the national-currency issue and two years before the Honduran state commissioned Lempira's first painting, a leaflet distributed among banana workers called for the "sons of the invincible Lempira" to defend the "land of Columbus" against the Yankees and the blacks.[3] This document displays more than the uneasy coexistence between the conqueror and the conquered as the basis of a nationalist appeal. Negotiating this polarity has always been part of mestizo cultural heroism. Here, what is important is the negotiation evidenced in the leaflet as part of an emerging mestizo narrative of localized Honduran *Indo-hispanoamericanismo*, one that also targeted blacks and blackness on the Caribbean coast. In some ways, this is a form of "subaltern nationalism against the state" but one that simultaneously draws on a state-sanctioned discourse (Lloyd 1997). This issue is best explored by locating it within the texture of racial mixture and blackness on the Caribbean coast when compared to the interior.[4]

In Honduras cultivation of bananas on the North Coast after the 1870s, which was to generate the country's main foreign-exchange earnings by the 1920s, did not directly conflict with the land tenure of Indian communities. This was different from the overall process of coffee cultivation elsewhere in Central America (Williams 1995). The laboring peoples on the Caribbean coast consisted not of proletarianized Indians but mostly of mixed-raced migrants from Honduras's interior and of peoples of predominantly African descent. In the latter case, these peoples consisted of West Indian blacks imported by the banana companies from the English-speaking Caribbean and of descendants of the Garifuna who arrived in Honduras in 1797. Between the 1910s and the 1920s, banana labor doubled in Honduras (see table 1). Equally important, by the 1920s Honduran intellectuals and wide sectors of the population as a whole viewed the blackness of some of this laboring population as a threat to the "mestizo" nation.

What kind of "threat" did "blacks" and blackness pose to Honduran Indomestizaje and the labor movement? Sadly, Honduran historiography about this period, particularly issues central to labor history, ethnic relations, and the role of the foreign banana companies on the country's Caribbean North Coast, is very poor. In the 1980s prominent Honduran scholars such as Mario Posas,

TABLE 1   Estimated Number of Laborers Employed by the Banana
Companies in Honduras, 1913–1925 (Average Monthly Employment)

Fiscal Year	Standard Fruit	United Fruit	Cuyamel Fruit	Other	Total
1913 / 1914	1,400	960	1,500*	20	3,980
1923 / 1924	1,400	5,474	4,000	—	10,874
1924 / 1925	2,450	5,474	5,000	—	12,924

SOURCES: Based on company reports submitted to the Ministry of Development. Italicized figures represent estimates of given figures for years indicated.

* This figure is estimated based on information from Dispatch 210, U.S. vice-consul in Puerto Cortés, Claude Dawson, to Secretary of State (14 November 1911), United States National Archives, Record Group 59, 815.00/1388.

Victor Meza, and Mario Argueta began to address one of the most glaring vacuums in Honduran historiography: the absence of working-class history. The working peoples of the North Coast have been notably absent from this history, including West Indian workers on banana plantations and the largest Honduran black community living on the North Coast, the Garifuna. These are issues central for contextualizing the national currency debate of 1926.

The historiography of the 1980s both narrated working-class history and linked it to broader narratives of the country's political system. Even so, major issues remain unresolved, including the social and racial history of the most important banana towns on the Caribbean: Tela, La Ceiba, and Trujillo. In Argueta's view, the following questions merit research: "To what extent did the black West Indian workers incorporate themselves into the national culture and labor unions? Did they identify more with the corporation that contracted them and transferred them to Honduras, or with their class? Did they transcend the barriers of race, language, and customs of Hondurans? Did they become Hondurans in a cultural sense? How many remained and how many returned to their places of origin or even to a third country?" (1992, 66).

Important answers to these and other questions were first systematically offered by Elisavinda Echeverri-Gent (1988; 1992). Her most important contribution lay in her analysis of the role of race and ethnicity in the early history of the banana workers of the Honduran North Coast. Echeverri-Gent challenged key issues in previous historiography, especially the influential work of Mario Posas (1981a; 1983, 30) and others, namely Murga Frassinetti (1980). In particular, Echeverri-Gent regarded Posas's explorations of the race issue as severely limited by the lack of available documentation, a problem that persists to the present day (1988, 13 n. 2). Also, according to Echeverri-Gent, "absence of co-operation between these workers went beyond a divide and rule strategy devised by the fruit companies, a position assumed by Posas" (ibid., 41). Indeed, "blatant racism on the part of the native workers and a well founded distrust towards them on the part of the blacks was equally, if not more, important in preventing any type of collective action" (ibid., 41).

Echeverri-Gent's periodization regarding race and ethnicity on the Honduran banana plantations includes the period roughly between the 1890s and the early 1920s, that is, exactly prior to the nationalist racialization of Lempira in the 1920s. In her view, during this time West Indian laborers, recruited largely by the United Fruit Company, "were the largest and most stable group" of proletarianized workers on the North Coast (ibid., 8, 43, 68). While they were rural workers, in their relation to capital and their experience and organization in the workplace, they shared many characteristics of industrial laborers (Echeverri-Gent 1992, 276) In these years, therefore, West Indian ethnic identity became the basis for "collective action" against banana company exploitation (Echverri-Gent 1988, 8).

Echeverri-Gent's most critical claim, indeed perhaps the cornerstone of her challenging new views, turned on the extent to which West Indians actually made up, or not, the "largest and most stable group" of workers between the 1890s and the early 1920s. Her evidence to support this claim, unfortunately, is very sketchy. The only statistical evidence offered involves a 1931 British estimate of about 10,000 West Indian workers on the North Coast for 1929 (Echeverri-Gent 1988, 59; Echeverri-Gent 1992, 283). These figures, of course, are for the period after Honduran and Salvadoran laborers achieved predominance as workers on the banana plantations, an issue little understood and mostly ignored by virtually all commentators.

Does this mean that between the 1890s and early 1920s the West Indian population was even higher and hence still the foundation of ethnicity as the basis of collective action during the period? Unfortunately, Echeverri-Gent's evidence for West Indian-led strikes in Honduras during this period is also very vague. Her dissertation offered only one example, in 1919, of a strike movement led by "a British office employee" of the Cuyamel Fruit Company (1988,

91). However, in her 1992 article, she confuses this strike with a 1916 movement when black strikebreakers were used (305).

Interestingly, Cuyamel was not the primary recruiter of West Indian labor to Honduras or anywhere else in the Caribbean. According to Echeverri-Gent, "the UFCO. was the most concerned with the issue of West Indian labor. The other companies mostly hired those who drifted away from the UFCO. farms" (1992, 299 n. 86). Thus, one would have expected to find more evidence for West Indian collective action on the United Fruit plantations, as was the case in Costa Rica (Harpelle 2000; Putnam 2001), and as Echeverri-Gent so well documents herself.

In Honduras the United Fruit Company began building railroads and banana plantations only in the mid- to late 1910s, because the corporation secured its important concessions only in 1912. The first banana company to build railroads on the Honduran North Coast was an early competitor of United Fruit, the Cuyamel Fruit Company. Between 1908 and 1911, Cuyamel Fruit laid tracks in northwestern Cortés, probably with Honduran and Salvadoran labor. (A U.S. consular report of 1918 reported that Cuyamel Fruit was importing 1,500 Salvadoran laborers).[5] United Fruit railroads in Honduras outdistanced Cuyamel Fruit's only after 1914 and surpassed Standard Fruit Company's only after 1918 (Euraque 1990, 145).

Thus, it appears difficult to substantiate the claim that United Fruit imported enough West Indian laborers to Honduras for them to have constituted the majority of banana plantation workers before 1920. In fact, the available historiography offers almost no evidence of coordinated, collective worker action against the companies before 1916. A review of U.S. consular reports from the North Coast between 1910 and 1917 found no evidence of strike movements at all. A 1916 strike movement led by mestizo workers against the Cuyamel Fruit Company is recorded as the first of its kind on the Honduran North Coast (Posas 1981b, 71–72).

Moreover, a review of the existing historiography and U.S. consular reports identified fifteen strike movements on the North Coast between 1916 and 1925. None of this evidence offered instances of West Indian ethnic-based leadership (O'Brien 1996). In fact, in some cases, as in the Cuyamel strike of 1916, black workers were used as strikebreakers. But even this does not emerge as a pattern.

A strike on the La Ceiba wharf in 1920, home of the Standard Fruit Company, was broken by laborers from the country's interior.

Echeverri-Gent's own evidence supports these findings. She attributed the lack of evidence for West Indian-led strikes and other forms of collective action to British officials themselves on the North Coast. For example, "the British Consuls on the coast of Honduras appear to have been less diligent at reporting workers' protests in the area [when compared to the Costa Rican case]" (1988, 100). U.S. consular officials, who might have been even more apprehensive about strikes than their British counterparts, also reported little strike activity prior to 1920. Echeverri-Gent nonetheless concludes, "It is difficult to believe that the earliest strikes on the banana plantations took place without the cooperation from the West Indians. By virtue of their considerable numbers in the plantations they were a factor that could not be ignored. In 1916 they still made up the majority of the banana plantation workforce" (1992, 305). Given the evidence suggested by existing historiographies and by consular reports, as well as evidence to follow, the tentativeness of this conclusion is difficult to sustain.

A major problem with Honduran labor historiography, especially that literature dealing with the pre–World War II period, centers on its lack of basic data on the structure of the labor force as such. Until now, few scholars have advanced even tentative estimates regarding the number of workers employed by the banana companies before the 1930s.

The great upsurge in banana labor employment occurred in the 1910s but mostly during the transition to the early 1920s (see table 1). What is more, contrary to Echeverri-Gent claims, the nearly 4,000 workers employed by the banana companies as of 1914 were mostly Honduran and Salvadoran workers, with perhaps a scattering of West Indian laborers as well. Honduran constitutions during the nineteenth century and well into the 1950s made Salvadoran access to Honduran residency and citizenship easy, which made their migration to the plantations equally simple given labor demand (Mariñas Otero 1962, 146–47). As the U.S. minister in Tegucigalpa put it in 1914, "a puzzling feature in the study of political conditions here, and in all of the Central American republics, arises from the fact that while apparently and actually each claims to be a separate and distinct entity, yet the citizens of each of the republics are

TABLE 2   British, Salvadoran, Black, and West Indian
Population in Honduras, 1887–1926

Year	British	Salvadoran	Black	West Indian
1887	1,033	2,000	N/A	N/A
1892	1,200	N/A	N/A	N/A
1906	1,500	N/A	N/A	N/A
1910	4,710	6,260	19,176	N/A
1926	3,977	13,452	N/A	177

SOURCE: Dirección General de Estadística y Censo, *Resúmen del Censo de Población de Honduras* for 1887, 1910, 1926, 1930, 1935. The 1892 and 1906 figures are from Schoonover and Schoonover 1989. The published 1926 Census did not present a West Indian (*antillano*) classification; that figure is from Carlos Zúniga Figueroa 1953, 3.

proclaimed citizens of Central America. And upon removal of residence from one country to another a simple declaration is all that is required to invest the individual immediately with all the rights and privileges of Citizenship in the country to which he has removed."[6]

Thus, what can be said about the close to 10,000 workers employed in 1924 or the more than 20,000 employed by 1930? Might not the 10,000 West Indian workers reported by the British authorities in 1929 mean that fully half of the Honduran banana labor force represented imported labor by the United Fruit Company? I doubt it. An equally significant percentage, if not more so, of the new labor force represented immigrant Salvadorans. Echeverri-Gent notes that by the end of the 1920s more than 12,000 Salvadorans resided in Honduras (1992, 301). What percentage worked on the banana plantations?

Honduran censuses offer some basis for more fully addressing that question. The census data in table 2 show a great upsurge of Salvadoran immigration to Honduras during the first two decades of the twentieth century, precisely the period that Echeverri-Gent identifies as the time of West Indian hegemony. According to a 1932 report cited by Posas, the Cuyamel Fruit Company annually imported between 5,000 and 6,000 workers to work in its plantations in Cortés (1981b, 45–46).

Given the evidence in tables 1 and 2, this figure no doubt exaggerated the numbers of imported laborers. However, there is little doubt that Salvadorans early on made up great numbers of the banana workers, especially on the

Cuyamel Fruit plantations. The censuses of 1926, 1930, and 1935 give significant basis for this assertion. In 1926, about 46 percent of Salvadorans domiciled in Honduras resided in the North Coast departments of Cortés, Atlántida, Yoro, and Colón. The 1930 and 1935 figures were even higher, 52 percent and 62 percent respectively. Finally, the department of Cortés's Salvadoran population represented more than 50 percent of the North Coast Salvadoran population as a whole.

On the other hand, table 2 indicates another interesting phenomenon: the great upsurge of British residents into Honduras between 1906 and 1910. In fact, the more than 1,000 British nationals in Honduras in 1887 might have included mostly Jamaicans reportedly imported to work on the construction of the projected Interoceanic Railroad in the early 1870s (Léon Gómez 1978, 129). The literature is rather clear that the rise of British residents on the Central America Caribbean littoral in this period meant the immigration of West Indian black colonials to labor on banana and sugar plantations or the Panama Canal (McLean Petras 1988). But if so, how was it linked to United Fruit importation if this company did not begin railroad construction until after 1912? Or might the new West Indian immigrants have been imported by Cuyamel Fruit or Standard Fruit? The available evidence does not support definitive answers to these questions. Notwithstanding these and other unresolved questions, the extant evidence suggests that West Indians probably did not make up the majority of workers on the Honduran plantations before or after 1920. Thus, the racialization of Lempira must surely be juxtaposed to the other important black population of the North Coast, the Garifuna.

GARIFUNA BLACKNESS ON THE NORTH COAST IN 1920S

During congressional debates over the currency in 1926, deputies entertained letters from different regions of the country. A letter from a number of people residing in Tela, then a major seat of the United Fruit Company, complained not only of the rapaciousness of the banana company, but of the labor preference it supposedly granted to blacks.[7] What blacks did the Tela correspondence have in mind? Echeverri-Gent's research, the most systematic on this issue up to now, implies that the Tela letter should have referred to West Indian blacks. Available evidence suggests otherwise. Indeed, the history of Tela, like one already available for La Ceiba, the seat of the Standard Fruit Company, shows that Tela's Garifuna were important pioneers in its settlement and were its early banana growers. Moreover, Lempira's racialization, as an element of Hispanic mestizaje, should be understood as an effort to exclude the Garifuna, as well as West Indian labor, from real and potential economic power.

In fact, Garifunas populated Tela as early as the 1810s, and the mixed-race population began arriving from the interior in the 1850s and 1860s, and only in the last decades of the nineteenth century did Tela come under the economic hegemony of mestizos and recently arrived Europeans (Elvir 2001). Whereas La Ceiba became the seat of Standard Fruit managerial operations, Tela became the early hub of United Fruit's administration. The Tela region saw the first imported black British laborers, officially permitted for the banana companies for the first time in 1912.

However, until very recently little was known about the Garifuna presence in the Tela region. It has been generally assumed that they resided mostly in their villages on the shore and only intermittently involved themselves in the labor market or even participated as banana growers themselves. Indeed, Garifuna as banana growers and urban and rural landowners are rarely mentioned. For example, some research suggests that originally the Tela region's best lands were owned by the Jicaque Indians but that between the 1880s and the mid-1910s, these passed first into the hands of the ladinos and then eventually into the arms of the United Fruit Company. Garifuna are missing from this narrative (Soluri 1998, 83–84).

Evidence suggests that their presence extended beyond seaside villages like San Juan, Tornabe, Triunfo de la Cruz, La Ensenada, and others (Euraque 2001; Mark Anderson 2000). Indeed, it seems that by 1900 Garifuna owned *ejidal* (community) land in Tela and that much of this land remained in Garifuna hands into the 1910s (Palacios and Sanchez 1996). Indeed, not only did a number of Garifuna own banana lands, but some, like Pascual Valerio, were considered "capitalists" in the records of the Tela municipality during the 1910s and 1920s (López García 1996, 112; Elvir 2001, 112–13).[8] Indeed, in the 1930s, the Valerios owned much of the lands occupied by Garifuna and West Indians in the only black neighborhood in Tela, Barrio Las Brisas.[9]

Also, a recent history of La Ceiba has unearthed not only wealthy urban and banana-growing Garifuna in the 1910s and early 1920s but has uncovered a history of Garifuna economic power there since the 1870s. Mestizos, many of black heritage extending to the late colonial period, and Europeans subjugated Garifuna economic power while thereafter losing the struggle to the Standard Fruit Company (Canelas Diaz 1999). In his analysis and narrative, Antonio Canelas Díaz makes Garifuna life central to La Ceiba's history, unlike existing histories of this century. In short, in Tela and especially in La Ceiba, and perhaps elsewhere on the North Coast, Garifuna blackness in the 1920s represented the "greatest threat" to an emerging Indo-Hispanic mestizaje.

Not only were the Honduran Garifuna the first stable black population employed by the banana companies, but Garifuna labor remained critical to banana-company employment much later than many commentators suggest. Finally, given their extensive settlement of rich coastal land, their "threat" was also connected to potentially cultivable lands as the banana companies and mestizo growers sought more and more land to grow more and more bananas, particularly as the first plantations fell victim to Panama Disease and other problems associated with ecological destruction in the 1910s and 1920s (Soluri 2001).

These Garifuna were descendants of a polyglot, racially mixed population that had occupied the Honduran Atlantic littoral since the late eighteenth century. Known by the British as black Caribs and by Hondurans as morenos, they were descended from formerly enslaved West Africans who had intermarried with the local Carib Indians on St. Vincent during the 1600s. Fiercely resistant to British colonization of St. Vincent, about 2,000 black Caribs were deported to Honduras in the 1790s after British forces had crushed them militarily. The British originally left the black Caribs on the Honduran Bay Islands, presumably to help them defend against the Spaniards. From there they moved to the Honduran mainland, near Trujillo, a town that in the 1910s became a major United Fruit center of operations. While not warmly received by the Spanish military outpost, then with a population of probably less than 300, the black Caribs soon dedicated themselves to cultivating rice, manioc, sugarcane, cotton, plantains, and squash. They not only met their own needs, but also sold surpluses in Trujillo.

The black Caribs also migrated east and west on the Honduran North Coast, toward Guatemala and Nicaragua, via land and on very maneuverable canoes. Nancie González, the most prominent ethnographic scholar of the Garifuna, has identified three broad periods in what she calls the evolution of the Garifuna's "work identity" as an aspect of their "ethnogenesis" between the 1790s and the 1930s (González 1988, 125–43; Mark Anderson 1997). Initially, from the 1790s and the 1820s, the black Caribs served as traders, even raiders, of tiny settlements all the way to Belize and as settlers in regions like Tela and La Ceiba.

Between Honduran independence in the 1820s and the 1870s, the Garifuna diversified their labor into smuggling, becoming temporary soldiers of fortune in the country's civil wars, but also into temporary wage work in the lumber operations established in the river valleys in the interior. Their employment in lumber operations continued into the 1870s and even 1880s, when lumber exports still represented about 10 percent of Honduran exports. Finally, between the 1890s and the 1930s, black Caribs enjoyed wage work in the banana economy, both before and after the establishment of foreign-owned plantations and railroads (Galvao de Coelho 1981, 40).

González and others familiar with the Garifuna do recognize the importation of West Indian laborers and ensuing labor competition between them and the Black Caribs and Hispanic and "Indio" Honduran migrants to the area (ibid., 43). However, González argues that the black Caribs returned to "the Coastline itself," to their traditional homes, and apparently left plantation work to the Indios, newly recruited West Indians, and mixed-race Hondurans. In González's view, "Perhaps because dock work was less regular, and also because it was on the seashore where Caribs were at home and could easily travel, they came to predominate in the labor gangs of ports such as Barrios, [Puerto] Cortés, Tela, and La Ceiba" (González 1988, 136).

González does not offer a more precise periodization of this process. Given the evidence regarding banana-company employment, the establishment of United Fruit after 1912, and the timing of the Salvadoran presence on the North Coast, the exodus of black Carib labor from the plantations probably began in the late 1910s, with a greater upsurge in the early 1920s. This is not to suggest that Garifuna laborers formed the majority of the 4,000 or so wage workers in the banana economy between the 1890s and the early 1910s (see table 1). However, we cannot discount their significant numerical presence and hence their supposed threat to Indo-Hispanic nationalism in the 1920s.

It is likely that the very high estimates of West Indian labor on banana plantations probably confused black Carib workers with the smaller West Indian population.[10] Furthermore, the banana enclave not only harbored a major transnational corporation capable of concentrating and reconcentrating capital inputs, but United Fruit transported national identities across their holdings in the Caribbean. Thus, high West Indian populations reported by British consuls in 1929 probably represented a momentary concentration of labor in Honduras in relation to company strategy elsewhere. According to Phillipe I. Bourgois, "Internal company records from the early 1920s when labor unrest among West Indians was at a peak [in Costa Rica] document how thousands of workers were transferred from one country to another in order to saturate local labor markets, reduce wages, and undermine union movements. These massive labor transfers involved complicated shuffling of peoples of different nationalities and ethnicities" (1989, 217).

How significant was Garifuna labor in the overall evolution of banana-plantation life and its surroundings before and after 1920? It is very difficult to be precise, because even the total Garifuna population is difficult to pinpoint. While only rough estimates are available, little doubt exists about Garifuna fecundity and corresponding overall population growth (González 1988, 118–20). In 1986 the Garifuna population was estimated at 90,000, less than 1 percent of the country's total inhabitants (Valencia Chala 1986, 38).[11] In 1976 a population of about 61,000 was estimated by another scholar, also less than 1 percent of the total (González 1988, 119). However, the disproportionate Garifuna population today is a function of both great immigration after World War II and very high Honduran population growth rates overall. Rough estimates for the Garifuna population between 1800 and 1935 point to a range of between 1 and 5 percent of the total Honduran population (see table 3).

Obviously, Garifuna population density was highest in the departments of the North Coast. According to censuses in the 1920s and 1930s, even though they had jettisoned the "mulatto" category of the 1910 count, slightly more than 10 percent of the North Coast population was "Black," including descendants from escaped slaves from the Caribbean (Garifuna) and West Indians imported by the United Fruit Company. What is more, 95 percent of the country's black population resided on the North Coast, and well into the second decade of the twentieth century, a majority of black labor on the banana plantations was probably Garifuna.

The estimates in table 3 provide a more approximate estimate of the overall

TABLE 3   Estimates of Garifuna Population in Honduras, 1790s–1930

Year	Estimate	% of Honduran
1797	2,000	1
1801	4,000	3
1816	8,000	5
1910	14,466	3
1930	18,092	2
1935	22,979	2

SOURCES: The 1797 and 1816 figures are reported in "Ynforme de la Provincia de Honduras" 1991, 298. The 1801 figures are from "Población de las Provincias" 1991, 289. The twentieth-century figures are explained in the text.

concentration of Honduras's black population on the North Coast. The 1910, 1930, and 1935 numbers represent the black population, minus the "British" population and the West Indian inhabitants counted in the censuses for those years.[12] Surely there is room for error here, but the pre-1910 estimates and the post-1930s estimates do not contradict the overall percentage patterns, which indicate that blacks represented a range of 1 to 5 percent of the country's total population.

Moreover, expert observers who offered estimates for the Garifuna population on the Atlantic coastal littoral as a whole generally don't contradict our projections for Honduras's share. In 1928 Edward Conzemius estimated the black Carib population then living in Belize, Guatemala, Honduras, and Nicaragua to range from 20,000 to 25,000 people (Richard N. Adams 1957, 631). Ruy Galvao de Coelho estimated their Caribbean North Coast population to range from 40,000 to 50,000 members (1981, 41). Again, Honduras's approximate share of Garifuna for those decades does not contradict Coelho's views. In short, the primary black population on the Honduran North Coast between the 1890s and the 1930s and after continued to be Garifuna. The primary "Black threat" to the nation, in the 1920s, then, was internal and local.

In the 1920s the notion of an Indo-Hispanic mestizaje represented only an emerging elite discourse. However, the 1920s effort to officially designate Lempira as the "representative" of the "other race" in "our mestizaje" involved a local racism that drew on a postindependence rejection of blackness, and especially a rejection of Garifuna blackness as a more local and immediate racial threat. This elite fear was magnified by the "threat" that non-Garifuna and non-Jamaican laborers perceived in the context of labor struggles on the banana plantations. This turned into an anti-imperialism channeled through the iconography of Lempira and via concrete efforts to deport black laborers that linked these mobilizations to a racialized nationalism from above and from below. It also included ensuring that the Garifuna were deprived of resources — that is, land and commercial opportunities in towns like Tela and La Ceiba.

Honduran elites framed their nationalist response within the limitations of an Indo-Hispanic mestizaje that excluded blacks and blackness, subjects central to the history of the banana companies but critical to the immediate postindependence period as well (Euraque 2001, chap. 5). Froylan Turcios, a committed anti-imperialist in the 1920s and an ally of Sandino until 1929, published articles in Tegucigalpa as early as 1916 denouncing blacks on the North Coast, including the "danger" of racial mixture (Euraque 1998, 160). At that time, on the eve of his recognition with a verse in the national anthem decreed in 1915, Lempira was still framed as a defender of national autonomy and sovereignty, and not necessarily racialized (Liga de la Defensa Nacional Centroamericana 1914).[13] This process began to change in the late 1910s, and especially by the mid-1920s.

In July 1916 Turcios published three long editorials in his *El Nuevo Tiempo* on "unnecessary immigrants." Turcios admitted that he lacked "exact statistics" on the issue, but he nonetheless unleashed a tirade against black immigrants, who, he argued, were causing all kinds of debauchery on the North Coast. He decried government policy, including the Immigration Law of 1906, which obstructed the government from expelling members of a race made arrogant by their "nationality" — that is, West Indian subjects of the British Empire. He also condemned the possibility that this "inferior race" might mix with the "Indian element." This, in other words, meant the "danger" presented by *sambos*.

By the early 1920s even labor leaders took up the racism espoused by Froylan Turcios and others in the 1910s (Euraque 1998). Honduran labor leaders also contributed to smearing black Hondurans, closely related to mulattos, by pushing for antiblack immigration labor laws. Early in 1923, Liberal Party deputies associated with the Federación Obrera Hondureña (FOH), established in 1921 by Tegucigalpa artisans (Posas 1981b, 85), introduced legislation that sought to prohibit "the importation into the territory of the Republic of negroes of the African race and coolies."[14]

The bill also called for the banana companies to deport, within a year, "the negroes and coolies that they have brought into the country." Finally, the deputies sought a census of all negros and coolies and the issuance of identification cards. The left-wing Federación Socialista Hondureña, established in opposition to the FOH in 1929, declared its support for racist immigration legislation and called for a campaign to get the "black element into the organization in order to discipline him and conduct him in the struggle for his emancipation" (Villars 1991, 85).

At any rate, this 1923 bill, as well as others introduced into Congress in 1924 and 1925, merited the opposition of the banana companies, the British embassy, and the U.S. embassy.[15] They failed. Nonetheless, they were important because these efforts converged with the elite racism espoused by Turcios, Valladares, and others regarding the ethnic amalgamation of the North Coast, and its relationship to race, immigration, and nationality. After 1924, powerful caudillos and various future presidents not only condoned this racism but in some cases even wrote publicly about it. For example, in 1924, General Vicente Tosta, provisional president at the time, openly opposed black immigration.[16]

During the 1925 presidential campaign, General Tiburcio Carías Andino, who would eventually be the National Party president between 1933 and 1948 and would sanction the Lempira national holiday in 1935, pledged to oppose black immigrant labor on the North Coast.[17] The National Party victor in the 1925 elections, Dr. Miguel Paz Barahona (in office from 1925 to 1928), claimed that Honduras needed "serene races," which "are essential for peace and necessary for the permanence of democracy. Blood is a commodity of utmost necessity. We must import it" (República de Honduras 1925, 7–8). A year later, in an article published in a Turcios publication, Ramón E. Cruz, a future supreme court justice (1940s) and Honduran president (1971–1972), and a confidant of General Carías, denounced the "black race" on the North Coast and argued "that the compensation received from black labor could not be compared to the incalculable damage done to our species" (1926, 700).

The elite National Party activists of the 1920s did not have a monopoly on racism and its efforts to officialize what the Honduran "species" or "race" could not be — either black or mulatto (Guillen Zelaya 1931). A 1929 Immigration Law that finally institutionalized antiblack racism, as well as other forms of racism, was signed by Liberal Party President Vicente Mejía Colindres (1929–1932), closely supported by Turcios. Indeed, in 1930 the liberals finally established the immigration office called for in the Agrarian Reform Law of 1924, enacted during the provisional presidency of General Vicente Tosta (1924–1925). The liberals complemented that strategy by contracting J. H. Komor, a British subject, to import "white immigration."[18] Paradoxically, the efforts represented not just an assault on the imported black *antillanos,* but rather had as their target Garifuna blackness, especially in urban areas like Tela and La Ceiba. Sadly, the assault on Garifuna blackness in the 1920s and 1930s has only recently begun to capture some attention, especially in the work of Antonio Canelas Diaz and in forthcoming work of my own.

CONCLUSION

In the wake of the destruction wrought in Honduras in 1998 by Hurricane Mitch, Danish-American Erling Duus Christensen published a book of essays that registers an outsider's reflections on Honduran national identity. In one essay Christensen declares, "Hondurans are generally enormously inarticulate about their deepest sources. I do not suppose that they take them for granted; it is too much of a struggle to keep them alive in the midst of so much adversity, but they lack language and concept" (1999, 19). Nonetheless, Christiansen argues, "this highly Catholic, Mestizo, culturally inundated and confused people . . . carry within them an indigenous soul" (ibid.).

His evidence? Duss informs his readers that he often likes to ask his students at the high schools in which he teaches in Tegucigalpa, "Who is the greater national hero, Lempira or Francisco Morazán?" Christensen relates that a "surprisingly high number vote for Lempira." In his mind this is a function of the Indian soul that has survived and resisted 500 years of colonialism. At work, he argues, is a "vestigial memory that functions in the collective and elusive memory of the people, some remembrance of the primeval forest of a seamless garden of life and divinity embodied in the splendor of the natural world."

In his essay, of course, what matters is less "vestigial memory" than state-sponsored memory, in this case, one closely intertwined with the cultural history of Indo-Hispanic mestizaje. In Central America mestizos achieved the full status of "cultural heroes" only in the late 1920s and early 1930s (Martin 1989, 8). Thereafter, the once opprobrious duality embedded in Indian-Spanish mestizaje became, especially in the minds of elites, more often praised than resented, contrary to what was the case in the immediate postindependence period. As Simón Bolivar put it in 1826,

> We are far from emulating the happy times of Athens and Rome, and we must not compare ourselves in any way to anything European. Our origins have been of the most unwholesome sort: all our antecedents are enveloped in the black cloak of crime. We are the abominable offspring of those raging beasts that came to America to waste her blood and to breed with their victims before sacrificing them. Later, the illegitimate offspring of these unions commingled with the offspring of slaves transplanted from Africa. With such racial mixtures and such moral history, can we place laws above heroes and principles above men? (Wright 1990, 20)

How were these issues addressed in the case of Honduras, and how does the history of the banana enclave help address these issues? In part, as herein, by looking into the official history of the cultural and iconographic representation of Lempira in the context of a rereading of blackness on the Honduran Caribbean coast. Moreover, this issue should be located in two processes, one of a longer *dureé* and another of more short-term duration. The first process involved the history of the banana economy of Honduras and its implications for the construction of the official national imagination espoused by the Honduran state between the 1860s and the 1930s. In this phase two things happened. First, intellectuals who fought for Lempira's reinvindication paralleled what Mexican colleagues have called the "reindianization" of Latin America in the nineteenth century, when that century's liberal intellectuals constructed yet another "indian" to be molded into the new nations of the postcolonial world (Reina 1997). In the case of Lempira this molding involved what John Agnew has called the "national representation of space," in particular the cultural space occupied by "indianness" in early-twentieth-century Honduran history (Agnew 1994, 253). Second, in the 1920s Honduran intellectuals who were threatened by banana and U.S.-government imperialism established a mestizo identity that originated in the latter nineteenth century. This mestizo identity initially memorialized a romantic-nationalist indigenous myth that included Lempira as defender of sovereignty and autonomy against external threat. In the 1920s these long- and short-term processes served as a context for the elite liberal exclusion of blackness from the official national identity, and especially the exclusion of Garifuna blackness (Mehta 1997). Old Lempira was then put to another task, now as a racialized icon on the national currency that revered dead Indians domesticated within Indo-Hispanic mestizaje.

In short, Lempira has been celebrated not only because of the significant numbers of real Indians who preserved access to communal lands or because of some primeval Indian soul. Rather, his equation with national identity occurred precisely as banana production became the country's leading export sector. "Depopulated" as a result of continuing conquests from the sixteenth to the nineteenth centuries of its original inhabitants, the Jicaques, the North Coast emerged during the twentieth century as the center of the country's banana sector and its most racially heterogeneous population. The economic ascendancy of a region heavily reliant on the labor of mulatto and black populations, especially the Garifuna, was viewed as a "menace" to the Indian / Spanish national identity promoted in the 1920s. The official exaltation embedded in Lempira's racialization must be understood in the context of the ethnic history of the banana enclaves.

NOTES

1. This essay draws from papers presented at conferences in 1994. A very short version of this essay was published in Spanish (Euraque 1996). Avi Chomsky deserves credit for my earliest concerns with Lempira and mestizaje. The intellectual context for this version of the original idea is grounded in a long-term interdisciplinary project called "Memories of Mestizaje," which I, Jeff Gould, Charles

Hale, Carol Smith, and other colleagues have been involved in since 1995. The last version benefited also from colleagues Maurice Wade, Michael Niemann, and Stephanie Chambers, all associated with a writing group supported by the Trinity College's Center for Collaborative Teaching and Research.

2. Oficio No. 324, Dr. Presentación Centeno, Secretario de Instrucción Pública, en "Lempira, Nuestro Cacique Legendario" 1928 and "Acta de la Sesión" 1928.

3. "¡¡El Grito Del Pueblo!! A Las Compañías del Norte de Honduras," Enclosure in Dispatch 30, Ernest E. Evans to Secretary of State, 25 January 1926, United States National Archives, U.S Department of State, Record Group 59 [hereafter USNA RG 59], 815:00/3931. The currency debate in Congress is available in Actas, *Boletín del Congreso Nacional Legislativo* 1, no. 44 (3 June 1926): 675.

4. I began exploring these issues some time ago (see Euraque 1996b). Of course, the pathbreaking work on this is Gould 1998.

5. "Paraphrase of a Message received from the U.S.S. Schurzs at Puerto Cortés," Office of Naval Operations to Department of State, 8 January 1918, USNA RG 59, 815.00/1752.

6. Dispatch 84, John Ewing, U.S. Minister in Tegucigalpa, to Secretary of State, 17 September 1914, USNA RG 59, 815.00/1547.

7. Actas, *Boletín del Congreso Nacional Legislativo* 1, no. 44 (3 June 1926): 676.

8. "Clasificación de Capitalistas," *Actas de Sesiones de la Municipalidad de Tela,* 19 February 1926, 439–44, Archivo Municipal de Tela.

9. Charles Mathews, 1999, interview by author, tape recording, Tela, Honduras, August 7. Mathews's father was a good friend of the Valerios, and he confirmed this point. Mathews was born in Barrio Las Brisas in 1929. His parents, George and Catherine McNally, emigrated from Jamaica in the 1920s.

10. A 1929 report from a subsidiary of the United Fruit Company to the Honduran minister of development declared, "Naturalmente, señor Ministro, los morenos y caribes hondureños que trabajan en la empresa, son generalmente tomados como negros, lo que quizás en la mente del pueblo da lugar a la errónea idea del gran numero de negros empleados" (Carta, 26 abril 1929, Trujillo Rail Road Co. al Ministro de Fomento, Salvador Corleto, Archivo Nacional de Honduras, Legajo, Correspondencia). I thank John Soluri for sharing this document with me.

11. A second source for the mid-1980s offers what is a probably an exaggerated figure of 300,000 Garifuna. (Chávez Borjas 1991, 204).

12. The most scholarly estimates of Garfiuna population after the 1940s are available in the excellent work of Davidson (1983).

13. In 1915 Lempira's struggle became part of the recently officialized Honduran national anthem. The third stanza of the anthem declares: "It was tragic that Lempira, Honduras's lover, assumed the struggle with anger, because in the dead of night the Indian enveloped in blood succumbed; and about this epic exploit, memory has only safeguarded a rocky hill where a sepulcher remained."

14. Dispatch 274, Franklin E. Morales, U.S. Minister in Tegucigalpa, to Secretary of State, 5 February 1923, USNA RG 59, 815.55/1.

15. Dispatch 570, Franklin E. Morales, U.S. Minister in Tegucigalpa, to Secretary of State, 12 January 1924, USNA RG 59, 815.55/2; and Dispatch 821, Lawrence E. Dennis, Chargé d'Affairs, to Secretary of State, 30 July 1925, USNA RG 59, 815.55/3.

16. Dispatch 641, Franklin E. Morales, U.S. Minister in Tegucigalpa, to Secretary of State, 23 July 1924, USNA RG 59. 815.5045/51.

17. Dispatch 52, Willard L. Beaulac, U.S. Vice-consul in Trujillo, to Secretary of State, 16 July 1924, USNA RG 59, 815.5045/46.

18. David J. D. Myers, U.S. Consul in Tegucigalpa, "Memorandum for Mr. Summerlin, U.S. Minister in Tegucigalpa," 11 November 1929, USNA RG 59, 815.5571/1.

THE CARIBBEAN 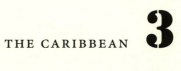 3

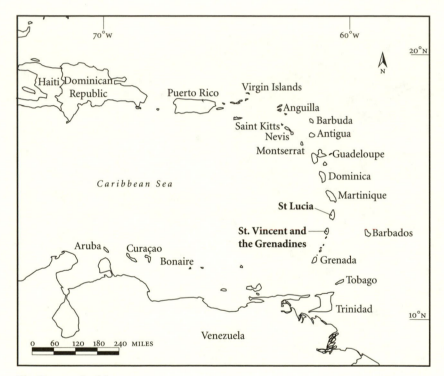

The Eastern Caribbean

KARLA SLOCUM

Discourses and Counterdiscourses on Globalization and the St. Lucian Banana Industry

For nearly a decade, international debates surrounding banana imports from the Americas to Europe have centered on the fairness of trade protections versus trade liberalization.[1] The debates are part of a larger history of competing ideas and practices regarding appropriate paths to "development." For example, preferential trade status granted to specific non–European Community (EC) producer countries (including the Caribbean) grew out of the former colonial relationship that the EC held with certain territories. As early as the 1950s, some members of the EC (particularly France and the United Kingdom) asserted that they could help postcolonial and quasicolonial countries develop, partially by providing trading links with these regions' marketing outlets. Embedded in a post–World War II notion of development (Escobar 1995; Arce and Long 2000), the policies "protected" and guaranteed the trade of specific products, including the banana. The 1990s formation of a Single European Market (SEM) in the EC and the subsequent plan to erode internal trade barriers directly affected existing and long-standing ideas about Europe's role in the development of its former colonies; changing structures around banana trade, in particular, directly brought into question the longevity of the United Kingdom's role in the development of the Caribbean (Sutton 1997; Nurse and Sandiford 1995).

As the EC proclaimed free trade as a foundation for its deeper unification, some of its member nations still upheld the earlier trade agreement and thus participated in policies that contradicted the possibilities for the liberalized flow of goods (Sutton 1997). Disagreements on this topic boiled down to responsibility toward (less-advantaged) trade partners versus full adherence to the laws of supply and demand. The internal discord within the EC left an opening for the arguments of U.S. companies that operated and / or contracted with banana farms in Latin America. Seeking to make greater inroads in the EC market, Latin Americans and the United States weighed in on the side of free trade as the correct and fair path. They subsequently entered a wrangle — a "banana war" — with EC and Caribbean supporters of trade protection over Latin Americans' right to trade goods freely with Europe.[2]

Today, debates over banana trade are situated within a larger public discourse on globalization, a discourse that has been in the making for more than a decade and that reinserts earlier "official" discourses on development (Crush 1995; Escobar 1995; Arce and Long 2000).[3] For instance, much of the mass media coverage of the issue profiles common markers and definitions of globalization by emphasizing how EC free-trade policies connect economies across the globe in ways that represent timely and fair means of economy building. Similarly, when some representatives of Caribbean governments discussed the issue, they defined free trade as part of globalization and (modern) forms of development. However, because they did not see market liberalization as natural and necessary as many mass media analysts did, they argued for trade protection. For them, protection would be a fair way to compensate for their "underdeveloped" status when compared to some of their "more developed" banana-producing counterparts around the world

Yet, there exists another analysis of the banana case. This less-profiled discourse emerged from some Caribbean banana growers organized in movement. Unlike the mass media and Caribbean states, these growers sought to uncover the root of a currently unstable Caribbean banana industry by focusing on political and social issues at a national level. They eschewed ideas about the primacy of free trade or even fragile developing countries as causal factors. In so doing, they completely ignored conventional identifiers of globalization, thus advancing a counterdiscourse.

Discussions of current changes in the Caribbean banana industry have been built around discourses and counterdiscourses about globalization. One such discussion is part of a larger and older discussion on development that centers on economic, political, physical, and infrastructural capacities necessary to achieve modernization or, at least, to survive (Arce and Long 2000).[4] While there are multiple strands within this discourse, overall it argues that "better developed" countries can, should, and will "make it" in an increasingly integrated and "modern" world. It contends, moreover, that poorer developed countries cannot make it without assistance *and* that they should not.

A counterdiscourse defies the former not only by evading specific official development topics but also by altogether ignoring the significance of conventionally accepted globalizing mechanisms. By honing in on political and social actors that shape the industry and its possible direction, it presents an entirely different way of conceptualizing problems in the banana industry. Consequently, while the first discourse is principally about economic laws guiding the current banana problem, the second centers on political and social ones. Taken further, in the first discourse global economic connections are a given, while in the second they are not acknowledged. Yet, however ideologically counterposed, the two discourses both seek to define the forces and problems behind the tenuousness of the banana industry; they also both seek solutions.

The backdrop for my discussion is the case of St. Lucia, the largest producer of bananas among the Windward Islands in the Eastern Caribbean. It also is the country frequently referred to in media accounts of the banana wars. Not only have many newspaper and magazine articles on the banana wars been written about St. Lucia, but state representatives in the country have been among the most active and vocal lobbyists for trade protection. Consequently, as an international and public discussion has developed about globalization and the banana industry, St. Lucia has been at the center of it, perhaps more so than other Windward Islands involved in the banana trade.

The public counterdiscourse also has been most loudly and more openly articulated in St. Lucia. It began in 1993, when an active farmers' movement challenged declining prices for banana sales as well as increased workloads for banana growers. Although there have been small protests in some of the other islands, none were as organized and none received as much regional attention as those of the Banana Salvation Committee (BSC), the protest group in St. Lucia.[5] What made the movement an example of a counterdiscourse was the way in which the group was publicly silent on the place of market integration and international trade policies in the current banana situation.[6] This movement's analyses of the banana situation not only confronted those made by the St. Lucian state and the popular media but ultimately challenged mainstream globalization discourses.

Since the beginning of its status as a European colony in the seventeenth century, St. Lucia's agricultural industries have been tied to a global project in which developing the economies of Europe and / or the island was a central aim. Even though dynamics internal to St. Lucia clearly shaped these industries at all times, agricultural practices and possibilities have always been constructed with a mind for events, people, demands, and tastes coming from other places. Across time, the interplay, interdependence, and competing interests of policymakers, corporate managers, plantation owners, colonial administrators, farmers, laborers, politicians, and consumers from Europe, North America, the West Indies, and St. Lucia all added to the specific way in which production, consumption, and distribution of St. Lucian agricultural goods took shape. All of these actors were involved (willingly or unwillingly) in strategies to achieve economic prosperity or at least economic "stability" for specific groups on and off of the island. This was so even if, at different moments, the various actors stood to gain or lose from specific strategies that made up the global project.

The sugar industry was at the forefront of this project. Like the rest of the West Indies, St. Lucia had a past in sugar plantations that were owned by Europeans and worked with enslaved, indentured, and / or hired labor from Africa and Asia. Most plantations were established under the French in the late eighteenth century and later maintained by the British who acquired the island in 1818 (Breen 1844).[7] Through most of the nineteenth century, the four largest were owned privately by European families and were located in the island's four valleys (ibid.). They covered over 6,000 acres of the island's 238 square miles. In their peak days of the nineteenth century, the major sugar plantations utilized approximately 2,500 to 3,000 African and Asian laborers, on an island whose population was approximately 46,000 (United Kingdom 1897, 116, 44).

West Indian plantations exported sugar to Britain and, as Eric Williams (1944) has noted, these exports helped finance European industrialization. Mintz (1985) also showed that West Indian planters' activities were part of the growing "sweet tooth" among British consumers; the eventual supply of cheap sugar rendered it an essential part of the British working-class diet, again ensuring the demand for the West Indian produced good. Thus, given the importance of sugar to the British economy and to British consumers, colonial administrators had a strong stake in how British West Indian plantations were operated while British planters were invested in profits as well. Consequently, colonial policies supported the plantation structure by backing many of planters' strategies to tie labor to the estates, such as labor coercion and debt peonage (Bolland 1992).

In the St. Lucian case, colonial administrators subsidized planters' production expenses to keep the plantations in existence (Marshall 1989). They also legislated against squatting and against giving up lands that belonged to the Crown. These policies existed to prevent a potential labor force (that planters needed) from becoming landed producers (ibid., 30). In this way, colonial administrators manipulated St. Lucian planters' and nonplanters' activities for the sake of British industries and consumers who were tied directly to West Indian producers. In the heyday of sugar, such manipulation fit well with planters' interests and profit goals. Yet, by the 1890s, administrators' and planters' activities were not as clearly in sync. Colonial officials were concerned when international free trade appeared to threaten West Indian sugar (United Kingdom 1897). Competition from Asian sugar producers led to the eventual demise of the Caribbean sugar industry, prompting West Indian policies away from recruiting labor for plantations.

Planters producing goods on a large export scale were not the only ones working within an international framework. Shortly after emancipation in 1838, a smallholder class of African-descended producers developed in St. Lucia. Like plantation owners, they became enmeshed in global events and decisions (Louis 1981; United Kingdom 1897). Although they utilized a mix of crops different from their planter counterparts and were oriented toward consumption and domestic sale, these producers also grew goods that were for international export (Louis 1981; Central Bureau of Statistics 1946). Additionally, most small-scale farmers worked as part-time, independent producers and also as sharecroppers, "contributors," or wage laborers. As sharecroppers, they produced sugarcane on lands owned by planters, keeping a portion of the cane sales for themselves and giving a portion to planters (Louis 1981; Marshall 1965). As contributors (a classification unique to the West Indies), they cultivated cane on their own or rented lands, "contributing" or selling the harvested product to plantation operators who then processed it (Meliczek 1975).[8] As wage laborers, they performed any multitude of labor tasks on plantation fields or in sugar factories. Therefore, practically all agricultural producers in St. Lucia were working within a context where external circumstances affected how and when they grew their products. As the sugar industry waxed and waned, so too did the standing of workers, small farmers, sharecroppers, and contributors, because wages, contracting, and sharecropping terms shifted with the overall status of the industry.

In the mid-1920s, as the sugar industry continued to lose ground, small-scale farmers were involved in the production and export of bananas as part of their diversified cropping system ("Rise of the Banana Industry" 1955; Development and Welfare Organisation 1951). Small-scale banana growers formed the St. Lucia Banana Association, a member institution that helped farmers market their goods internationally through British, Canadian, and U.S. shipping companies ("Rise of the Banana Industry" 1955; Trouillot 1988; Grossman 1998). Short-term contracts with these companies enabled production and distribution to North American and European markets that became key parts to the industry's development.[9] Through peasant activity, export banana production reached seven times its initial volume between 1925 and the onset of World War II ("Rise of the Banana Industry" 1955, 34; Development and Welfare Organisation 1951).

Later, in the early 1950s, as the sugar industry appeared on its last legs, colonial administrators took an interest in the preexisting banana industry that smallholders had made. The decision revealed an underlying discord between administrators and planters whose aims were not united at that time. Both sought to make up for the losses in sugar sales, but planters' responses challenged administrators' roles. In increasing numbers, planters of all production sizes abandoned their estates, which meant a decline in the island's economic activity and the loss of employment sites for labor (Meliczek 1975).

Early evidence of administrators' interest in the banana industry as a potential solution to the sugar crisis were the findings and recommendations of a 1951 study, commonly known as the Team of Experts Report.[10] Looking at the island's changing economic development and considering ways to make up for losses in international sugar sales, the reports' investigators advocated bolstering the existing banana industry by sinking British funds into it, providing technical and financial support to peasant banana farmers, and placing more of a focus on international sale of the fruit (Development and Welfare Organisation 1951). No other crop in this pivotal report received as much attention as did the banana. The idea, then, was to draw on an existing structure of production that peasants had built since slavery. In this "peasant labor process" (Trouillot 1988), peasants organized their labor uses around the production, domestic and international sale, and consumption of several crops, including bananas. The multipurpose labor strategy contrasted sharply with the plantation model of monocropping only for export. Colonial administrators' goal was to channel the parts of the peasant model that would benefit the broader colonial economy into building a banana industry.[11]

The Team of Experts' recommendations spoke to this goal. As if to transform the island's sugar monoculture into bananas, the team recommended increasing the number of large plots devoted entirely to banana production: "To organise a banana export trade it is essential to have large areas of pure stand bananas. It is from such large areas that shortfall in production by small farmers can be made up at short notice. Thus, if a contract is made to ship 5,000 stems and only 4,500 come forward from farmers . . . it is essential to get the extra 500 stems as quickly as possible and this can be done easily from large pure stands" (Development and Welfare Organisation 1951, 39). The idea of coordinating banana production with the contractual terms set by shipping companies indicated that colonial administrators saw bananas as a possible mechanism for moving beyond the sugar industry. Their formula included wedding features from the sugar industry (particularly monocropping and exporting) with "new" and borrowed ones. The latter included the use of foreign capital and peasant labor to produce and export an agricultural crop.

The team's recommendations were timely. Not only did they address the decline in sugar sales, but they also came at a time when sugar-plantation workers engaged in heavy and repeated labor strikes for better wages. Within this context of monumental economic and social pressures in the sugar industry, banana production underwent marked transformations that were sparked in part by the report's recommendations. The most significant of these transformations, perhaps, was the introduction of a new shipping company to handle banana exports. In 1954 Geest Industries, a British company, replaced the previous North American shipping companies in the export of bananas (Trouillot 1988; Grossman 1998). However, Geest took on more than a shipping role when it purchased two of St. Lucia's ailing sugar estates. The company did so by making an attractive offer to shareholders in the companies that owned the two plantations and that had liquidated two years prior to Geest's arrival (St. Lucia Government 1963).[12] By buying out all shareholders Geest became sole owner of the estates and entered direct production. This was a major shift, since previously direct production of the island's major industries had been carried out only by public companies, private planter families, or smallholders; never before had private shipping companies assumed this role. At first, Geest entered as banana shipper and sugar-estate holder. Yet, by the early 1960s, all of its sugar estates had been converted to bananas, placing the company in direct production and distribution of bananas.

Although the sugar industry had been crumbling and although one other privately owned plantation had converted to bananas before Geest did, Geest's transition into bananas sparked a conflict between the company and the colony's newly elected West Indian administrators.[13] These were a core of black West Indians who formed the island's first local government after the colony's first general elections in 1947 and 1951. This marked a shift away from Crown rule and a scaling back of direct British administrators.[14] At the core of the 1951 elections was the status of the sugar industry; those who won their seats did so, in part, by fighting on behalf of sugar workers to keep the sugar industry intact (Charles 1994).[15] Therefore, Geest's shift was politically threatening, particularly since the company's sugar estates were the only large ones remaining on the island.

Geest apparently won this wrangle with local administrators by claiming that the conversion was unstoppable. The company cited its inability to maintain sugar production due to the fall in its supply from sugar contributors who, affected by declining returns for their sugar sales, increasingly turned to bananas (St. Lucia Government 1960, 1963). Despite heated discussions between the island's chief minister and Jan Van Geest, by the beginning of the 1960s the conversion to bananas was complete on all major plantations.[16] Small-scale contributors and sharecroppers of sugar became sharecroppers and producers of bananas. Banana production, then, became both a central activity on small holdings *and* on large plantations, collapsing peasants, European planters, and corporations into the same production system for the first time (Slocum 1996).[17] All three were involved in direct production, cultivating and shipping bananas through the same structure.

The role of peasants became more visibly significant because not only were they more numerous than large planters, but, together, their yields were comparable, if not higher, than those on large estates (Meliczek 1975; St. Lucia Government, Ministry of Agriculture 1973–1974).[18] The intensification of a small-scale focus in banana exporting also was a major shift under Geest. While peasant contributors existed during the days of sugar production, their representation (as peasant producers) was not as strong as with bananas. Moreover, while previously large-scale planters set sugar production and sale terms for peasant contributors, under bananas peasant producers (with the exception of sharecroppers) could grow, harvest, and sell the crop without intersecting or deferring to European planter families. Instead, they dealt entirely with the corporation.

Geest restructured the banana industry by introducing a contract concerning the buying and selling of St. Lucian bananas. The 1970s version of Geest's contract followed a model set by the previous foreign shipping company exporting Windward Island bananas, and it also drew on the framework set by the 1967 St. Lucia Banana Growers' Act. That is, the contract bound producers into various unequal institutional relationships in which banana farmers held scant bargaining power with the shipping company, the Banana Growers' Association (BGA), and consequently the state (Trouillot 1988; Slocum 1996).[19] This was evident, for example, from the way in which the contract stipulated and mandated growers' banana-farming practices, laying out how fruit needed to be shipped as well as how it would be produced and sold. Additionally, it required farmers to be members of and sell their fruit to the BGA. By the time the contract with Geest was set the BGA had transformed into a statutory body that handled the selling of bananas.[20] The BGA was charged with selling bananas to Geest, which then unloaded them in the United Kingdom (St. Lucia Government 1967). Additionally, as banana-growing citizens, farmers were required to follow production practices recommended by the Windward Island Banana Association (WINBAN), a Windward Island agency charged with research and development activities, as stipulated in the Banana Protection and Quality Control Act of 1986. Geest was the key (and unavoidable) go-between in this setup because it represented St. Lucia's only link to a market and also to market information regarding consumer demands and market prices (Trouillot 1988). Such criteria became the justification for enforcing various WINBAN-recommended production strategies and techniques that growers, as BGA members and St. Lucian banana-growing citizens, had to follow.

By attaching growers to the BGA the contract linked producers to the government as well. Once the BGA had been transformed from a member association into a statutory body, various local government representatives gained input into the association. This included occupying high-level positions within the BGA, such as serving as members of the board of directors. Additionally, in the 1960s, new state legislation rendered certain contract clauses law, including the existence of the BGA and the duties of its members to follow specific production methods (St. Lucia Government 1967). Over time, the BGA also gradually increased its role in surveying growers' activities to ensure compliance with production, harvesting, and processing regulations. The insertion of quasistate power in the form of an overseer role and the creation of government positions within the BGA helped secure Geest's status as sole buyer of St. Lucian bananas and as the country's key link to a market (Slocum 1996). State laws and BGA / state surveillance backed Geest, ensuring that all St. Lucian bananas were available only to the company for shipping to the United Kingdom.

Placing (state) administrators directly in the local industry, and foreign capital indirectly in it, clinched strategies for controlling the labor of so-called independent banana growers. This seemed important because the production and size of smallholders far surpassed that of plantations by the 1970s. Since their output represented the vast bulk of bananas produced in the industry, small-scale growers (rather than large-scale plantations) were key to Geest's activities (Biggs et al. 1963, 11; St. Lucia Government, Ministry of Agriculture 1980, 28; Yankey et al. 1990). Their importance grew even further in the late 1970s when the plantation structure eroded amid several events that chipped away at St. Lucia's political, economic, and social foundations. These included: labor strikes, the 1978 installation of the St. Lucia Labour Party after a decade of rule by the conservative United Workers' Party, anticolonial protests (led by the Labour Party), and calls for changes in land distribution. At independence in 1979, these protests led to land reforms in which vast portions of plantations were divided into small holdings for lease or sale. Geest (and the other privately owned plantation) left direct production following these events, leasing out small portions of its lands.[21] Henceforth, distribution became Geest's major role in the Windward Islands while the banana industry was led to an even greater degree by small-scale, rural, African-descended, Creole-speaking banana growers.

Part of what made the distribution role possible and facile for Geest were several agreements that linked the Caribbean to Europe. The Treaty of Rome (1957) and the Yaounde Conventions (1964) were the first agreements that annexed former European colonies to the European Community following World War II. They did so by providing financial assistance to associated states of the EC as well as offering free trade with the EC (Frey-Wouters 1980). Later, the fourth Lome Convention, a 1975 agreement between European nations and their former colonies in Africa, the Caribbean, and the Pacific (ACP), further established a trade relationship between the parties. The stated purpose of the link was to enable economic growth in these former colonies by providing an outlet for their products, including an unlimited supply of bananas into the United Kingdom and France (Lome Convention 1989). To this end, Lome provided ACP countries with guaranteed and unlimited access to European markets for a variety of products, including bananas (Lome Convention 1989, 65). The Banana Protocol of the Lome IV accord guaranteed the "preferential treatment" of bananas from ACP suppliers.

Lome and its parallel treaties came into question especially in the late 1980s, given the conflict between the European Union's protected trade obligations that Lome mandated versus the free-trade expectations of a soon-to-be unified Europe. Making arguments that linked democracy and globalization (e.g., liberalized trade), Latin American banana-producing countries, backed by the United States and some members of the EU, objected to maintaining Lome in an argument about the disadvantage that trade protection created for Latin American producers, especially against Caribbean ones (Nurse and Sandiford 1995; Sutton 1997).[22] An initial outcome of the long-term debates was a 1993 EC ruling that prohibited *all* products from entering Europe under the *full* protection that Lome had promised. In this new provision, known as the New Banana Regime, a limited quantity of bananas from the Caribbean could enter into Europe tariff free. While some saw the Banana Regime as a victory for Caribbean bananas because it ensured partial protection, others complained about the end to unlimited trade of the fruit (ibid.). Following the EU's creation of the New Banana Regime, the newly formed World Trade Organization (WTO) challenged its legality. The challenge was supported by the United States and Latin America, again on the grounds that it violated free-trade standards.[23]

The New Banana Regime and challenges to it were the context in which St. Lucia (along with other Windward Islands) underwent major transformations of its banana industry. Not least of these was Geest's decision to withdraw as Caribbean shipping agent (and to take up direct production and shipping in Costa Rica, one Latin American "rival" in the banana wars). Following Geest's exit, the Windward Islands created their own shipping agency, the BGA privatized, and many other local banana-purchasing companies were formed. Subsequent rulings that the banana import regime contradicted goals of nondiscriminatory trade, followed by appeals for freer trade from the United States and Latin America, led to greater concern and more efforts at reorganizing local Caribbean banana industries.

DEVELOPING A PUBLIC DISCOURSE ON GLOBALIZATION

The issue surrounding global banana trade has received attention within and outside of the Caribbean, particularly through international policy discussions on trade regulations, political speeches within the Caribbean, and through media coverage. Not simply of concern to the WTO policymakers, the topic has reached into more popular, political, and public realms. The most glaring example of the crossover was when it drew the attention of a wide cross section of the American and European public, especially after the Clinton Administration applied tariffs to EC products imported into the U.S. in retaliation for trade protection policies on bananas. For a brief two to three days in 1998, this set off a firestorm of front-page and lead-story news items covering the "banana trade wars" and their impact on European and American small-business owners.

These media connected the public and various political groups in a discussion of worldwide banana trade by tapping into a growing international focus on globalization. Indeed, globalization was a word and / or concept that figured prominently in these discussions. Media analysts, politicians, and policymakers either directly mentioned globalization (or the global economy), or they indirectly referred to it by citing its commonly accepted markers: the liberalizing market, heightened competition among international producers, fairness of free-trade agreements, and the role of the wto. Yet, analysts differed in how they located globalization within the banana war, which identifiers they emphasized, and how they sized up the markers' meaning. That difference points to the presence of multiple discourses. Therefore, while the many perspectives contributed to an overall discourse on globalization (i.e., the ways that the world is now connected particularly through integrated economies and markets), they also charted out individual subdiscourses. Yet, no matter the variety of discourses, clearly the banana trade was brought into contemporary discussions about the transnational organization of economic activity.

St. Lucia was one key site where this discourse developed. Interestingly, there the word *globalization* rarely surfaced in public speeches or widely disseminated information about the banana industry. However, markers of globalization were obvious defining features for a developing dialogue on what an integrated European market would mean for St. Lucian banana farmers. For instance, "Europe 1992" was a catch phrase in official commentary, from government speeches to bga announcements to farmers. It referred to the year of European market integration and was meant to signal impending and dire consequences for St. Lucia and the other Windward Islands if their primary export product were to enter open-market competition. Concern over "Europe 1992" brought out dialogue and practices addressing what the country must do. Several studies were commissioned to look into the status and future of the Windward Island banana industries, diversification programs were proposed and started, and new methods of producing bananas were introduced to farmers, all in the name of restructuring the industry to make it competitive in the changing global market (St. Lucia Government, Ministry of Agriculture 1990; Yankey et. al. 1990; Kairi Consultants and Agrocon Limited 1993).

Restructuring was not an entirely new concept; previous decades saw many commissioned studies that looked into industry improvement and reform in the wake of several factors such as declining production, declining quality, banana disease, and management problems within the bga (Biggs et al. 1963; St. Lucia Government, Ministry of Agriculture 1980; Yankey et al. 1990; Atkinson et al. 1993; Kairi Consultants and Agrocon Limited 1993). But, in the 1990s, when the concern was about *potential* for quality to be deemed substandard in a changing Europe (rather than about actual quality decline), restructuring strategies meant new concerns for farmers. For example, the new techniques for cleaning, labeling, boxing, and transporting bananas almost always increased farmers' labor time and costs (Slocum 1996). Additionally, under the new quality-assessment system, bananas went from being classified as either acceptable or unacceptable to being ranked at four levels, three of which corresponded to different prices while the fourth entailed rejection. As a result, the new system differentiated farmers by fruit quality and income in ways that they had not before. Ironically, the new system pushed "subquality" producing growers out of banana farming in ways similar to how the European market threatened to push out the Caribbean, that is, in the name of quality and competition.

The grading and production practices presented by the BGA were mandatory for all BGA members, despite farmer complaints about rising costs of production and lower returns. Yet, when farmers came together to protest, the government responded by referring, in part, to globalization.

> Are you [protesting] against Geest? Geest is *merely* your agent to take your bananas to the market and sell them at the market price which this company does not fix. . . . [W]hether you cut bananas or not, Geest must be paid a minimum charge for his ship because that company has a contract with your Association. . . . Are you [protesting] against those who set the price in Britain? Then we must think again. The Windward islands supply only 1.9% or 2% of the bananas sold in Europe and St. Lucia's share is only 1% at most. . . . If we do not send bananas to the market, our customers will merely buy cheaper fruit elsewhere, and we may never get their custom again because we are not reliable. So we are not [protesting] against the market. (Compton 1993a, 2)

The idea, then, was that the country had no power or purpose to change or contest forces of globalization because Geest and the European market were not unapproachable and were blameless. Indeed, to the prime minister, Geest appeared as a benign and benevolent intermediary between St. Lucian farmers and the market, and "those who set the price in [the market]," as if their decisions were outside of St. Lucians' influence. Consequently, Geest and the market were presented as "just doing their job" and globalization was described as a given. Skirting questions of globalization's fairness, the prime minister suggested that the trajectory of free trade was too powerful to combat, especially for a small state like St. Lucia. Given this portrayal of the country's insignificance in a larger global scheme, the prime minister's message tapped into broader images and neoliberal discourses of development. Globalization was conceived as powerful and "right," yet surmountable through individual will and responsibility.

In the backdrop of this picture, farmers heard and saw that their own behavior was the problem. By telling banana growers that they had to produce better and package differently and that their protest response was misplaced, the prime minister sent a powerful and defining message. He suggested that both problem and solution lay with farmers, giving further rationalization for controlling farmers' labor and for raising costs of production. The further implication was that integrating into the global market was the essential path to (modern) survival, a path that would be followed even at the cost of the farmers. Indeed, integration was presented as the *only* path. Thus, new measures of banana production focused on increasing the country's competitive edge within the global market, despite industry officials' contradictory statements that the market context was exceedingly tenuous and powerful. Implementing new production and pricing policies illustrated that success could be achieved by changing farmers' behavior, not by shifting government policy and certainly not by seeking alternative selling or shipping arrangements with the EU or Geest.

Even more ironically, this message suggesting the country's capacity to survive globalization differed from what Caribbean governments argued in front of WTO officials. In this setting, by contrast, they contended that Windward Island countries could not withstand a world where trade protection did not exist. Thus, while representatives told St. Lucian farmers that the country could not survive without their productive power, they told European officials that survival rested on guaranteeing Lome's protection. Such an argument appeared in a statement made by the St. Lucian permanent secretary to the WTO.

Whilst the current dispute has been extensively analysed and commented upon often by economists and lawyers, it is for us, a matter of the livelihood of our people and the stability of our countries. . . . As . . . figures clearly show, the banana industry dominates the agricultural sector of [the Windward Islands]. It is the single most important sector of the economies of these islands and has been the main engine of growth and development, particularly rural development. . . . The production in these islands is almost exclusively on small family owned plots. . . . It is estimated that for the islands as a whole there are 27,000 farmers. This is virtually the entire rural society and is the very basis of stability. It is the most important in the employment and empowerment of women. (Statement of the Permanent Representative 1997, 1)

St. Lucia's permanent representative to the EU made clear and strong charges against globalization, contending that liberalized trade was detrimental to people of the Windward Islands. To bring the charge home, he drew specifically on ideas of underdevelopment, ideas that were not absent in the discourse to farmers but that followed a different path. For, while farmers heard that their country's minor position in the world could only be addressed through human agency (i.e., farmer's improved production), WTO officials were presented with images of a passive, dependent region in need of recolonization. References to women and rural families relying on the banana industry portrayed a region rife with poor and powerless. Calling on the WTO to maintain Lome because of these factors suggested that Europe (not farmers) could play a critical role in developing the region. This critique of European policy and the concomitant cry for help meant that the Windward Islands participated in the continuation of their own historically popular image as a region lacking human and physical resources.

The creation of Caribbean images surrounding the banana trade has also emerged more publicly through announcements and activism by particular groups in the United States, including the Clinton Administration, political activists (e.g., Jesse Jackson), small development organizations such as Oxfam, and foreign policy institutes such as TransAfrica.[24] Added to these voices has been coverage by major international newspapers and public-radio programs tracking developments in the banana-trade debate. And, while all of these voices contributed to the development of a globalization discourse on the banana trade, the media were heard and seen most often by a widespread public audience. Indeed, it was in the media that the battle motif, the idea of so-called banana wars, crystallized.

The themes emerging in media coverage of the banana-trade issue in some ways reflected those expressed by Caribbean state representatives; in other ways the media's themes departed from them. What tied the two groups together, at the very least, was participation in discourse on globalization. Media references to globalization were even more obvious, with articles sometimes appearing in sections labeled "globalization" or "global economy" and with strong emphasis on the issue of trade. Focusing on differences in opinion on trade policy between Latin America, the Caribbean, the United States, and the E.C., newspaper articles, magazine pieces, and radio programs underscored the competition between the parties.

Many pieces also made strong implications about the role of "development" in trade, particularly by differentiating the production potential of Latin American and Caribbean banana farms. This was unlike the Caribbean state representatives who, while admitting to their "underdevelopment," never seemed to state outright that farmers *could not* produce on a par with Latin America.

Regarding the notion of "development," a common media perspective was that Caribbean producers could not compete with Latin Americans, given the difference in resources between the two regions. In some instances, reporters further suggested that resource capacity should be the deciding factor and that smaller level producers should not be given protection. Most saw a Caribbean in crisis due to its Third World status and consequent inability to withstand a global trade trend. At times, reporters contended that liberalized trade was inevitable and fair and that those who could not make it are *burdened* by their (under)development status.

Interestingly, this type of argument was strikingly absent from pieces focusing on the impact of the banana disagreements on U.S. and European merchants whose items became subject to tariffs. Most of these articles lent a very sympathetic tone by profiling merchants' "plight," while not offering the same to Caribbean farmers. They described the banana war as insignificant relative to the needs of retail businesses and as senseless given its negative economic impact on such businesses.

Whether sounding sympathetic to merchants or suggesting that Caribbean farmers were noncompetitive, news analyses were largely ahistorical, apolitical, and astructural. They ignored various key pieces in the organization of the Caribbean banana industry, the crucial political and social roles that created and sustained the industry, and the dynamics that, over centuries, brought the banana industry to that particular trade juncture. As a result, there also was almost no mention of Geest Industries or the (unequal) contract it held with Windward Island producers. The role and stake of the Caribbean state in the industry were also avoided. Moreover, the history of the banana industry was typically presented as a contemporary one, thus denying farmers' role in building it. These glaring omissions and distortions made a particular case about globalization. By emphasizing economic and physical resources issues over political policies and social inequities, the mass media defined for a popular audience which features mattered in global trade issues, and which ones did not (see, for example, "Yellow Peril" 1990; "Expelled from Eden" 1997; "Banana Row" 1997; "What Bananas?" 1999; "An Outpost" 1999; "Brawl over Bananas" 1997).

A piece in the British journal the *Economist* illustrates how these features emerged in newsprint portrayals of the banana-trade case. The *Economist* is an interesting media form to consider because it caters to a corporate readership. Therefore, how the magazine displays economic events probably has much to do with the expansion and profit motives of the bulk of its readers, even if some of its themes can be found in more mainstream news sources such as the *New York Times*.

This seems clear in its December 1997 article about St. Lucia, "Expelled from Eden." The reader quickly learns that the country's banana industry is experiencing a downswing caused by European market shifts and the World Trade Organization ruling. The piece is not sympathetic to the country's case but is instead matter of fact about what the outcome will and should be. Removing trade protection, the article claims, has meant that St. Lucia has not had the cushion to render its bananas competitive and salable. For the writer, trade protection shielded St. Lucian farmers from "real" market forces, thereby masking reality: "Free trade makes losers as well as winners, losers whose fate should not be disregarded. It is true also that trade protections can prop up businesses, industries, even whole (small) countries for many years. They did so in St. Lucia, with the best of intentions. But they could not do so forever, and when the morphine is stopped, the pain of withdrawal begins. Can the little farmers of St. Lucia survive?" (35)

Not only is the writer's answer an unequivocal "no," but the piece strongly suggests that farmers *should not* survive. The writer presents trade protection as a temporary fix or an illusory paradise that (unjustly) enabled the country to stay afloat, avoiding the necessary laws of supply and demand. For the writer, paradise was lost due to the recent rise in international consumer standards, which complicated St. Lucia's possibilities for successfully competing in an international arena. Even protective trade, the article asserts, could not offset the impact of recent shifts in demand. "In recent years consumer tastes in banana have changed. Banana lovers used to be happy with anything that was vaguely yellow, curved and unsquashed. Now they want a big bright uniform, quasi-industrial product that seems untouched by dirty knives, sweaty hands, or indeed, nature. . . . [But that does] not come from St. Lucia. [It comes,] ironically enough, from the 'original banana republics'" (36).

The implication is that market forces and consumer preferences are natural and uncontrollable dynamics, unable to be influenced by purposive political, social, or historical actors. St. Lucia's marginalization is thus explained not by political or social forces but by the impact of inevitable and faceless economics. According to the article, the country lags behind Latin American banana-producing countries because it does not have the capacity (economies of scale) to compete with its neighbors farther south who are one step ahead. "If islands like St. Lucia are the corner stores of the banana business—chaotic, friendly and unreliable—the Latin American plantations are the Wal-Mart at the edge of town. They cover hundreds of square miles of ideally flat and fertile soil. They are served by railways and cable ways. . . . Productivity, at around 24 tonnes per acre, is three times as high as in St. Lucia. . . . That is how the future looks" (37).

Central to this argument is a well-known thesis on development—the notion that economic success does (or does not) result from a measure of one's resources. It supports the idea that such features as poverty, economic instability, and peasant farming all result from internal material conditions rather than from a socioeconomic, political, and historical project. Indeed, the tone of the article proposes the old idea that "the invisible hand" guides and lets things fall as they naturally should. It is no wonder, then, that the writer is critical of the

New Banana Regime and Lome because, to him or her, both created a false sense of security. They allowed St. Lucia to avoid making itself more competitive as the former prime minister warned banana growers they must do. In short, for the *Economist* writer, the country did not modernize. Behind this logic is the assumption that the implementation of, for instance, the New Banana Regime and Lome represented benevolent intentions rather than willful efforts to suppress St. Lucia's banana industry. The history of the banana industry, according to the *Economist,* is an industry *begun* by Europeans as a gesture of altruism. Thanks to such charity, bananas became the country's greatest hope for modernity. They raised rural people's living standards, converting their "shacks" into "rusty-roofed" houses, putting shoes on their feet, and giving them outhouses. Not full-fledged development, the writer admits, but large strides nonetheless for a small island like St. Lucia.

Thus, in the *Economist*'s rewriting of history, not only was colonialism pretty good but small-scale farmers had no agency. In fact, farmers are written out of the history entirely. That smallholders actually started growing and exporting bananas on their own in the 1920s, before the arrival of colonial policies for export banana production, is ignored. So too is the heavy role that Geest and the St. Lucian state played in structuring St. Lucia's banana industry with entrenched power imbalances tipped against producers. Not only is the inequality etched into the contract omitted, Geest itself is not mentioned at all. This is curious because, as a transnational company, Geest represents an uncontestable agent of global integration, even according to popular definitions that often herald the role that that transnational plays in linking up producers and markets.

In the final portion of the *Economist* article, the author considers the future of St. Lucia's place in these markets. That final section could be entitled "Helpless and Hopeless," although the author's subheading is "Tomatoes or Pot?" It is here that two photographs foreshadow the argument for a dim future. The pictures reveal men sitting on a dock, staring out blankly. In one shot, they hold their chins in their hands, appearing bored and despairing. The text corroborates the image: the country has dire socioeconomic indicators — illiteracy, poor education, a "spotty" tourist industry — and thus there are no alternatives once bananas disappear. Although the *Economist* admits that some farmers have begun new ventures, the article predicts that their efforts are worthless given the country's development characteristics, again weighed against those of Latin America. "On pocket-patches all over St. Lucia, farmers are experimenting with okra, tomatoes, and avocados grown under plastic sheets; but they gloomily acknowledge that anything they can grow will grow better in Central America, and bigger and cheaper too. Bananas are the only crop in which they come close to being competitive. A few years back they tried to make a go of plantain. . . . The Latin Americans leapt in at once and killed the St. Lucia trade stone dead" (37). So, the author announces, the islands are left to "claw their way" toward better horizons; they must weather the "cold winds of world trade."

Thus, much like the public state discourse in St. Lucia, the mass media accounts of banana trade debates link "development status" with a country's standing in the period of globalization. In both cases, however, development status is seen as a natural condition rather than an outcome of long-term social and political processes. Where the St. Lucian state and the mass media differ is in the argument over whether to continue providing support or "protection" for the country. While the state requests assistance to offset the country's physical (not historical or political) disadvantages, the writer for the *Economist* argues that if a country is underdeveloped it should live accordingly.

THE BANANA SALVATION COMMITTEE AND COUNTERDISCOURSES ON GLOBALIZATION

St. Lucian banana farmers gathered together in a protest movement, known as the Banana Salvation Committee (BSC), that had a different discourse regarding the cause and nature of problems in the banana industry. Airing concerns about specific problems befalling farmers, they reinterpreted accepted discussions on natural and unchangeable global trends as national forces of corruption and control that could be undone. They offered these interpretations through their protests against the low prices they received for banana sales, corruption within the BGA, and increasing restrictions imposed on farmers' work. While industry officials suggested that these changes (except BGA mismanagement) were a result of global market pressures, farmers in the movement argued vehemently that the problems stemmed from government control.[25] Evading discussion of the role of Geest, the BSC organized farmers to confront St. Lucian officials in charge of the local industry, and they carefully avoided rallying farmers against the market itself, Latin Americans, Europe, or U.S. policy.[26]

There were two primary features to the BSC public action. First, drawing on a strong history of labor agitation in the country's agricultural sector, they organized strikes by calling on farmers across the country to avoid harvesting and selling their fruit for a given period.[27] For more than two years, the BSC organizers called strikes each time they reached an impasse in negotiations with industry officials. Striking and failing to deliver fruit to the BGA involved several levels of liability: it meant that the BGA could not fulfill its contractual obligations to supply Geest with a predetermined quantity of bananas, and it meant that, as guarantor, the St. Lucian government was liable for all of the BGA's debt to Geest. No matter the circumstance, then, Geest would get paid while the government, the BGA, and the farmers were ultimately responsible for inadequate supply to the transnational corporation. For this reason, repeated strikes and deficits of fruit sales to Geest put economic pressure on industry decision makers and government officials to address farmers' grievances. The BSC thereby won several victories, including subsidized price increases and the overturn of a government decision to place the BGA into receivership.[28]

Mass rallies were the other public aspect of the BSC's efforts to unite farmers across the country. Due to the industry structure, banana growers rarely if ever intersected outside their forty distinct districts. However, the BSC transcended such geographic fragmentation by leading rallies that gathered growers together to air grievances and plan protest strategies. The typical rally format included platform speeches in which the BSC discussed a particular industry problem, exposed its roots, and then called on farmers to confront it with action.

Although they initially focused on money, BSC meetings became highly political and politicized events, due to both their content and their format. The BSC eventually hosted frequent speeches from the leader of the opposition party, the St. Lucian Labour Party (SLP), who endorsed their efforts. Then there was the political nature of the rally locations, public spaces such as the market steps of the capital city and the banana-buying depots alongside the island's principal highway. In contrast with how meetings are typically organized by and for rural people, BSC gatherings instead drew on methods for staging urban political rallies. Indeed, while public rallies are common in the country, they tend to be official political events, almost always conducted by the social and political elite. Rural people tend to organize meetings in rural areas but rarely cross over and convene in public urban spaces. Thus, the location of BSC meetings subverted the political rally structure by bringing farmers — a socially maligned group — into public space as prime participants *and* as meeting organizers.

The political savvy that characterized the BSC's strategy was possible, in part, due to the social and cultural capital that many BSC organizers held. The men who began the group possessed certain advantages that the majority of farmers working in the St. Lucian industry did not have. As medium-scale growers, they had access to various social and political spaces unavailable to smaller growers. The BGA Act guaranteed these privileges because, according to its terms, only farmers who produced enough (at least 500 pounds per week) were eligible to hold office within the BGA, such as delegate or board member. All BSC leaders had been delegates and some had served as board members to the BGA and to other agricultural agencies. At the same time, BSC organizers were not among the top "officials" who worked at the level of management. Their backgrounds as rural farmers, and the social and economic factors that went along with that status, most likely precluded them from occupying positions at those levels. Consequently, the BSC organizers straddled two spaces; within the institutional structure of the banana industry, they had more opportunities than most farmers, yet they were outside of many official channels wherein key decisions were made. It was this in-between status that provided fodder for their movement in both structural and ideological ways. The leaders could use their "insider" knowledge to formulate a movement that, according to them, was founded on "educating" other farmers about events and dynamics in the banana industry — events they could know about given their "privilege." Simultaneously, they also could use their marginal status as a platform from which to launch critiques of the industry structure — critiques formulated within that marginal voice. Possessing both insider and outsider status gave them tangible and symbolic materials to begin and sustain the movement, including the discourses that they built.

Publicly presenting themselves (and all farmers) as marginalized outsiders, BSC organizers structured rally themes around issues of government / BGA control and misconduct. Farmers attending the meetings received updates of recent developments regarding BSC correspondence with industry officials, and they also received analysis of those interactions. Sounding much like oral stories, the meeting discussions provided specific accounts of the government's dominance in industry decision making. BSC speeches included topics such as the exclusion of farmers from information regarding contract negotiations between BGA and WINBAN officials and Geest Industries, the legal role and primacy of the state in the BGA (resulting from the BGA Act), and BGA / state mechanisms to monitor farmers' work or provide less compensation for it. For instance, in discussing how the government continually attempted to seize control of the industry, the BSC objected to the prime minister's announcement that, due to the farmer strikes, he would appoint a new government-led board of directors to the BGA. On finding financial mismanagement within the association, he later announced plans to place the BGA into receivership. Although the stated purpose of these gestures was to enable a new, impartial body to correct BGA finances, at rallies the movement leaders interpreted the maneuver as the prime minister's attempt to completely take over a farmers' institution and to dismiss farmer input. Such control, they argued, militated against higher incomes for farmers because, as officials in the industry, government representatives would decide how much a farmer would make and why. Moreover, it would ensure an even greater degree of state power.

St. Lucian farmers who supported and participated in the BSC activity expressed particular interest in government control (along with the "price problem") as well as a disregard for the features of globalization in structuring the banana situation. In interviews with farmers residing in one of the country's largest banana-producing areas, I frequently heard that the price was the problem but that the government was to blame for the farmers' plight. Rarely, however, did I hear that Geest or European policymakers had any role to play in St. Lucian agricultural events.[29] Why not? Responses to this question ranged from descriptions of government officials as underhanded and self-serving to defining Geest and European policymakers as disconnected from and therefore not responsible for the lives of St. Lucian citizens. As one banana grower said, "[The main problem] is the money, [but the main cause] is government [and] BGA. [They are] not spending money right or organizing right to help growers. If they get $10 they take 8 and give us 2" (Banana Producer 58, 1994). Another grower laid blame in the same place but went on to explain why he did not hold

Geest responsible: "I won't blame Geest . . . because Geest is a business man. [Yet, the Prime Minister has] to see about [his] people. . . . That is why I [don't] support him" (Banana Producer 37, 1994).

Excusing Geest and blaming the state was also a BSC tactic. Indeed, once the movement was under way, concerns about unfair government practices overshadowed initial concerns about price and subsumed any possible concerns about globalization. The focus on the price paid to farmers and on financial problems within the BGA became the subtext for a larger argument about the ways that state power promoted economic, social, and political marginalization of the farmer. Discussions of government power almost always raised the issue of deeper cultural and class divisions in St. Lucia, divisions that separated farmers from government officials, rural from urban dwellers, Creole from non-Creole speakers, agriculturists from bureaucrats, and lower from upper class. Reinforcing these concerns was recurring commentary about government disregard for farmers, officials' treating farmers like dogs, and official attempts to keep farmers in the dark about their own work.

Through a focus on government-farmer relations and on government power, the BSC set out to reverse accepted dualities between farmers and elite officials in symbol and in practice. At a practical level, the movement organizers lobbied for farmer involvement in contract negotiations and for greater representation of growers on the association board to undo the government's position at the helm of the BGA. At a symbolic level, they overturned common perceptions of farmers and officials by recasting popular images of each and thereby contradicting accepted conceptualizations of each. BSC interpretations of events always placed farmers in a glowing light and government representatives in a bad light—a stark contrast to accepted understandings of their respective places in society.

Attempting to shift real structures by reworking popular representations was no more evident than when the movement leadership responded to a public address given by the prime minister on the night following the first strike. The strike had evoked an unexpectedly enthusiastic and public response from farmers and nonfarmers, a response that involved not merely refusing to harvest but also gathering in the streets to vocalize discontent, create roadblocks, and burn down structures. The deaths of two protesting farmers as a result of police gunfire prompted the prime minister to address the nation again.

In that speech, his most critical yet regarding the actions of farmers and of the BSC, he chastised the banana producers for their protests, claiming that they were harming the stability of an industry already struggling under market pressures. He substantiated his claims and reinforced ideas about farmers' low status by juxtaposing his own actions against the farmers, suggesting that he always had acted benevolently on behalf of the industry, farmers, and the country.

> Criminal elements in our society . . . blocked roads, destroyed and burnt the sheds of other farmers, attacked vehicles, molested tourists and visitors to our county, interfered with school children and in general caused a complete breakdown of civil order. . . . Speaking personally, I cannot say that I am not disappointed by these events. . . . For the past 35 years, I have devoted much time, energy and whatever intelligence God may have given me to the establishment, growth and prosperity of the banana industry. . . . All my work in this regard has been for the farmers and for St. Lucia. . . . I seek no honour, no glory, no financial reward. My only reward is the advancement and progress of this country. . . . Why do I continue to make the sacrifice? . . . Because men and women who could not own a bicycle, now have their own vehicles which they are able to purchase because of government. . . . Because of the satisfaction I get from seeing over 10,000 children now attending secondary schools when before the banana industry, secondary schools were open only to the fortunate few. (Compton 1993b)

This speech sparked a strong reaction from individual farmers and from the BSC, particularly in response to the sharp social and cultural distinctions and representations of farmers and government that it promoted. In rural regions individual farmers expressed outrage and insult at the prime minister's contention that farmers had benefited greatly from his altruism. The BSC was also critical of the prime minister's ongoing portrayal of farmers as people who had squandered their gains, and was quick to point out the irony of such a suggestion: "There is this myth . . . that the banana farmer builds a big house, buys a four-wheel drive and now he can't pay for it. . . . I'm telling you: the four-wheel drive is to take the wife to town to shop, to take you where the banana is . . . to take the farmer to church on Sunday. Meanwhile, you [officials] here have your Toyota Cressida, but because we have a four-wheel drive to bring the banana to town so *you* can sell your goods, it is a crime!" (St. Lucia Government, Information Service 1994).

The ensuing public addresses between the BSC, the prime minister, and the minister of agriculture always were rife with imaging and counter-imaging meant to reassign identities and positions to each social group. In the case of the BSC, the goal was publicly to redignify farmers and simultaneously to discredit the activities and representations of the government (and other non-farmer elites). Most interestingly, however, while chastising the extravagant behavior of government representatives and nonfarmer elites, BSC leaders also revealed the dependence of that elite lifestyle on farmers' necessary and utilitarian activities. Thus, rather than crediting the prime minister with saving the country, they claimed that farmers deserved that recognition. According to the BSC, social hierarchies and the persistent and pejorative images of farmers that informed those hierarchies had kept farmers from receiving the credit they were due.

Of course, to make their point, the BSC lumped "farmers" together, failing to refer to the distinctions of class, region, and gender that differentiated their experiences. Indeed, such differences set the BSC leadership apart from a majority of farmers, rendering the BSC's silence on the issue a failure to acknowledge their own privilege. However, the leaders' analysis was effective in emphasizing politicized misdeeds and social hierarchies at one level within the country. The silence on distinctions within the farmer population permitted them to divulge those dangerous ones between industry officials and producers.

At the same time, neither in general rally discourse nor in specific responses to government comments did the BSC emphasize the power of global market trends or the problems of underdevelopment. Never did the group respond directly to the prime minister's comment that striking against Geest or those who "set the price in Britain" was futile. While the BSC received fair criticism for this "oversight," it is important to note that their silences were part of an implicit critique of popular globalization discourses. The group's argument situated problems in the banana industry wholly outside of the accepted markers of globalization. It revealed a purposeful national, cultural, social, and political content to the downswing in the banana industry, rather than suggesting that external, natural, uncontrollable, and faceless events were at the root of the issue. Consequently, BSC discussion and action prompted a counter-globalization discourse because it drew on unconventional explanations of the status of the banana industry and employed tactics to create change solely within a national structure rather than solely *or* simultaneously within a global market structure.

CONCLUSION

Within the context of the banana industry, the concept of globalization is engaged in distinct ways through different discourses. In the opinion of the *Economist,* a representative of media and corporate interests, it seems that globalization as a form of integration refers uniquely to trade issues. As an inevitable and "normal" process, globalization's impact on St. Lucia is due purely to market dynamics that define winners and losers according to evolutionary principles. Withstanding the natural laws of market supply and demand depends on a country's stage of development.

In Caribbean state discourses, globalization's causes are not explored as much as its impacts. Citing the problems of the region's own underdevelopment, government representatives and spokespersons have argued for social policies that would impede integration processes and thereby protect the "powerless." Simultaneously, and in a somewhat contradictory message, the St. Lucian state (especially through the BGA) encouraged farmers to step up competition. This, the state argued, would allow the country to participate in globalization, the very process it argued against before WTO officials. Both state and media discourses, then, embedded notions of modernization and development, albeit from the perspective of different agendas.

By contrast banana growers in the Banana Salvation Committee argued that another, less publicly accepted, factor caused problems in the banana industry: state power. The BSC innovatively and implicitly challenged the notion that "poor" is an insurmountable condition or that one's status stems purely from resource capacity. Effacing any discussion of how wider events bore down on St. Lucia, they spoke about the cultural and class politics behind the nation's banana-production scheme. At the same time, while the BSC's protests were part of the battle over the role of globalization in the banana industry, it actively sought to shift discourse away from the primacy of the global market.

Even though these leaders did not speak directly about globalization they were part of a debate about it. First, they participated in arguments with government representatives about the nature of the banana problem, a problem that had been officially defined as market oriented. Although not speaking of the market in its public speeches, the group's ideas about the banana problem dialogued with the official discourse. Second, by critiquing the state, BSC leaders homed in on an agent of global integration. For, in its official and legal support of Geest, the state was an important force behind making (uneven) global connections happen. Therefore, the BSC's counterdiscourse challenged the notion that the banana problem is strictly about markets, by outlining how integration of the St. Lucia banana industry was a national and political project of power and control. Further, by suggesting that state power was the reason behind dilemmas in the banana industry, the BSC undermined the official position on cause and consequence of contemporary problems in the banana industry. It also undermined the suggestion that shifts in the industry structure are led by natural and unavoidable (global) events. Thus, the movement's ideas can be seen as a critique of prevailing views on globalization as a nonpolitical, purely economic event. Such a counterperspective, while typically denied, is essential to confronting and dismantling dominant discourses that suggest that there is only one path to "development" and that also ignore and downplay the exploitative practices that often are part and parcel of that path.

NOTES

1. A version of this paper was presented at the 1998 conference of the Society for Applied Anthropology. A Fulbright Scholarship and an Inter-American Foundation Dissertation Fellowship funded the research on which this paper is based.

2. Former British colonies in the Caribbean were involved in most of these arguments. They include especially the Windward Islands of St. Lucia, St. Vincent, and the Grenadines, Dominica, and Jamaica.

3. The idea of development discourses has gained currency over the past ten to fifteen years. Often informed by poststructuralist theory, supporters of the idea argue that the language and practices of development are meant to construct a deficient social reality (e.g., impoverishment) that justifies control, surveillance, and authoritative interventions (e.g., development projects). See Arce and Long 2000, Cooper and Packer 1997, Apthorpe and Gaspar 1996, Crush 1995, and Escobar 1995 for detailed discussions of development discourse. I am suggesting here that discussions of globalization can be related to development discourses.

4. The modernization thesis behind development dates back to the post–World War II period. Cooper and Packard (1997, 3), however, refer to a post-1980s "ultra-modernist" stance on devel-

opment that mirrors the modernization idea. Here, the belief is that "pure" economic laws and free market should govern and can engender efficiency. The ultramodernist perspective critiques development interventions and instead argues for the extension of free-market principles.

5. To my knowledge, there has been no coverage of the work of the Banana Salvation Committee in U.S. newspapers or broadcast media. However, regional Caribbean media and St. Lucian media covered BSC activities widely, especially between 1993 and 1995.

6. While the Banana Salvation Committee rarely if ever mentioned globalization in its public speeches, interviews and informal discussion reveal some of the participants' awareness of global trade disputes and changes in international market policies. In response to my analysis of BSC activities, one member mentioned that the decision against publicly citing the global context as a significant causal factor of changes in the banana industry was a conscious one. This paper deals, however, with the group's public presentations.

7. Over the course of two centuries, St. Lucia was under British and French colonial rule as the two countries fought successive battles over control of the island. After changing hands fourteen times, St. Lucia became a colony of Britain from 1818 until independence in 1979. However, the strength of the French legacy is noted in many of the legal, political, social, and cultural features of the island.

8. Contributing was a unique feature to West Indian sugar production. After purchasing harvested sugarcane from contributors, planters processed the crop in the sugar factory. For more information on the social and political implications of contributing (and sharecropping, also known in St. Lucia as *metayage*) see Adrian 1993 and Acosta and Casimir 1985.

9. See Grossman 1998 and Trouillot 1988 for detailed discussion of the various international shipping companies that entered the Windward Island banana industry.

10. According to Biggs et al. (1963, 6), the colonial government took an interest in the banana industry as early as the 1930s when it introduced an ordinance to establish the St. Lucia Banana Association, a statutory body. However, at that time, government intervention in the industry appears to have been minimal. In 1953 the Banana Association was replaced by a private company, but in 1967 the association again became a statutory institution, the St. Lucian Banana Growers' Association.

11. Trouillot (1988) has a lengthy discussion of colonial and corporate uses of the peasant labor process in the development of a banana industry. For him, the peasant labor process on the island of Dominica originated when African-descended slaves developed household-farming practices over which they had control and that were built on particular uses of labor and instruments of production. Labor uses were devoted to consumption and production. For Trouillot, infusing this peasant labor process into the postemancipation banana industry was key to the profiteering of the British transnational company Geest Industries, which took over the Windward Island banana industry.

12. Sugar Manufacturers was the company that owned two of St. Lucia's major plantations in the 1950s. Due to a drop in the sugar market and repeated worker strikes, Geest's offer to buy out the shareholders and purchase the company was welcomed.

13. The Barnard Plantation, on St. Lucia's eastern coast, was the first to switch from sugar to bananas in 1958. As a longstanding private-estate owner, Denis Barnard was able to make this shift without objection from local government.

14. The first general election was held in 1947; however, voters were required to pass a literacy test. In the subsequent 1951 election universal suffrage was applied (Charles 1994).

15. The 1951 election also was fueled by the growth of the island's major political parties, initially established in the 1930s. The parties supplied candidates who became the island's first African-descended chief minister and senators. Key issues in the first election campaigns were sugar workers' rights, although the issue of banana production also began to surface within campaign discourse (see Charles 1994).

16. Although Geest was not the first to convert its estates into bananas, the company's move into bananas was significant because it meant that, thenceforth, all St. Lucian plantations were covered in the fruit rather than in sugar.

17. By the time that Geest took over banana production, only one of St. Lucia's four major plantations remained in the hands of a European planter family, the Barnards. The two that Geest purchased were public companies established after private French plantation owners relinquished their ownership during the first major sugar crisis in the late nineteenth century. The other estate was turned into a U.S. Naval base during World War II. The Barnard plantation remained in family ownership until the 1970s, almost eight decades after the other three planter families had sold their operations.

18. Evidence of the uneven distribution of smallholders to largeholders is provided by Meliczek (1975, 18), who states that in 1961 close to 13,000 individuals owned 5.4 acres, whereas 23 companies owned an average of 466 acres. Further, the 1973–1974 census provides the clearest data on the differing production levels, by size of producer holdings. According to the census, smallholders with lands of five acres or less produced more than 55 percent of banana yields, whereas large growers of 100 acres or more produced approximately 21 percent (GOSL 1973–1974, 68). By contrast, Biggs et al. (1963, 11) estimate that 40 to 50 percent of banana output was met by large growers while the remainder was carried by the "middle group" and small growers. Biggs et al., however, state that clear data on this matter were not available.

19. Trouillot (1988) points out that in Dominica the 1959 Banana Act (apparently similar to St. Lucia's Banana Growers' Association Act) initiated a context for legally tying growers into a structure for banana sales over which they had no power. He argues that the 1977 contract with Geest Industries strengthened this arrangement. For Trouillot, although the Banana Act initiated this set-up, the contract with Geest was the key ingredient thwarting banana growers' bargaining power. He cites Geest as the primary agent responsible for placing growers in an unequal relationship. Elsewhere, however, I have argued that the state (in the form of the BGA) is also complicit in detracting from growers' bargaining power and autonomy (Slocum 1996).

20. The transition from the Banana Association to the St. Lucia Banana Growers' Association occurred following recommendations from a 1963 investigation into the industry's standing (see Biggs et al. 1963); Grossman (herein) gives a detailed discussion of the history and role of the St. Vincent Banana Growers Association that provides a useful comparison and contrast to the St. Lucian case and to my own analysis of it (see Slocum 1996).

21. Trouillot (1988) argues that Geest left direct production in the late 1970s after it had accumulated enough capital to finance its more lucrative wholesaling business in the United Kingdom.

While this may have been a factor in the company's move out of plantation ownership, labor unrest and anticolonial / anti-imperial protests certainly complicated Geest's possibilities for remaining a plantation owner in St. Lucia. Parceling out its land and moving out of direct production made the company less visible and thus less subject to attacks on its role in subjugating laborers through the plantation system. At the same time, while there may have been financial and other practical means by which the company could have stayed in direct production, the 1977 Lome accord, which helped strengthen access to a guaranteed market for any quantity of Caribbean bananas, certainly would have made distribution an attractive and lucrative role for Geest as well.

22. Of all of the ACP suppliers of bananas to the EU, the Caribbean countries together provide the greatest volume.

23. Documents on the WTO debates and rulings, especially regarding the Banana Regime, can be found on the Web site of the U.S. mission to the European Union (*www.useu.be/issues/bananadossier.html*).

24. Examples of the political and social action around the Windward Islands banana-trade issue include the Clinton Administration's policy supporting free trade and policies that allow more Latin American than Caribbean banana producers into the EC market; TransAfrica's critique of the Clinton policy and its economic and social impact on Caribbean farmers; and Oxfam's programs to aid Caribbean farmers in light of the impact of changing trade policies for bananas. Political and popular figures such as Jesse Jackson, Danny Glover, and Bill Cosby have been reported to speak out against the impact of the trade policies as well.

25. The formal government response to the farmers' first organized protest in 1993 was to raise prices and to investigate BGA management and financial affairs. The investigation (Atkinson et al. 1993) concluded that the BGA was in debt due to financial mismanagement and corruption. In public speeches (Compton 1993a; Compton 1993b), the prime minister laid blame on specific individuals within the BGA and on farmers as a whole, who he said had elected the BGA managers. He also countered with a decision to place the association in receivership so that the government could reorganize the mismanaged association. This response did not satisfy the BSC leaders and they protested that "solution." The issue of BGA mismanagement subsequently became less of a focus in the BSC's agenda, while the issue of government control became a larger one.

26. In 1998, while I presented my research at the Folk Research Centre in St. Lucia, a member of the BSC responded to my claim that the group's platform had not included globalization. He stated that BSC organizers felt that they should first address issues at home in order to gain changes in the industry and that they should address the global context secondarily. He firmly asserted that it was not that the BSC was unaware of the significance of global conditions for the St. Lucian banana industry.

27. Since emancipation, St. Lucia has experienced several periods of labor protests by plantation workers (see Louis 1981; Slocum 2000). Between the early 1950s and the late 1970s, there was one major strike or labor protest period per decade, almost always led by trade unions. The 1990s strike discussed here had no input from trade unions, making it the first time since the 1950s that trade unions had not been the institutional backbone to organized agricultural protests. Consequently, it was the first time that so-called independent banana growers (rather than waged sugarcane or banana laborers) withheld "labor" as a form of protest. It is my belief that noncompliance and

subtle acts of resistance were more common forms for protest by independent banana growers. Vocal street demonstrations (especially against the BGA) also have occurred.

28. Another indirect and partial result of BSC action was the 1995 victory of the St. Lucian Labour Party (SLP) in national elections. The SLP had not been in power since the early 1980s; the party backed the BSC, which may have helped it gain a widespread public profile. A few BSC organizers gained cabinet seats or official roles in the new government.

29. Farmers in this region I researched who did not support the BSC developed separate discourses that partially mirrored those ideas heard in the BSC platform. This was especially true in terms of the emphasis placed on government misdeeds and control. For more information about these individual and community discourses, see Slocum 1998.

LAWRENCE S. GROSSMAN

The St. Vincent Banana Growers' Association,

Contract Farming, and the Peasantry

B anana production destined for export to the United Kingdom has been the economic mainstay on three of the four Windward Islands in the Eastern Caribbean — St. Vincent and the Grenadines, St. Lucia, and Dominica — since the mid-1950s.[1] The large majority of growers have been peasants who cultivate bananas in small, scattered plots on rugged terrain — a pattern contrasting markedly with that in much of Latin America. Significant, widespread improvements in the quality of life on these islands have been a direct result of the growth of the industry. In 1992 the Windward Islands had almost 25,000 banana farmers producing the crop on over 41,000 acres (WINBAN 1993, 6). Since that time, however, the number of growers and the area cultivated in bananas have declined markedly because of intense market pressures associated with the Single European Market (SEM) established in 1993 and with unfavorable, United States-inspired World Trade Organization rulings (see Clegg 2001).

A key element in the history of the Windwards industry has been the banana growers' associations, which have regulated, supported, and encouraged the growth of banana production on each island. The significance of these institutions has varied considerably among the four Windward Islands (Welch 1996). The St. Vincent Banana Growers' Association (SVBGA), a statutory corporation, manages that island's industry and has the exclusive legal right to export the fruit. The SVBGA is controlled by and represents the interests of the Vincentian government and thus provides an example of the role of the state in Caribbean agriculture.

Viewed through the lens of the literature on contract farming, the association has performed the classic functions of the central buyer / coordinator in contract-farming enterprises — creating a guaranteed market, determining quality and grading standards, influencing production practices, and providing extension services, credit, and subsidized inputs. Compared to patterns associated with private capital (both national and transnational) involved in contract farming in developing countries, the svBGA has been supportive of the welfare of peasant producers in a variety of ways. Unlike private capital, the svBGA has had a dual mission of managing a business and functioning as a state institution concerned with development. Also, in its supervisory role, it has historically had much less control over the peasant labor process, calling into question the applicability of such concepts as "disguised wage laborers" that are sometimes applied to peasant growers in contract-farming schemes.[2]

CONTRACT FARMING AND THE PEASANTRY

While the Windward Islands have depended on export agriculture for their survival for well over 200 years, the emergence of the banana industry presented farmers with particular challenges, banana farming being much more labor intensive and more technologically complex than other forms of agriculture practiced previously on the islands. Moreover, the pace of technological change in the industry has accelerated over time in response to increasing demands for improvements in farm productivity and fruit quality from British capital and the British state, and, more recently, the European Union (see Grossman 1998).

Quality considerations have been paramount in the banana market, and consequently the crop must be produced in a manner that will ensure that demanding market criteria are satisfied. Harvesting must be coordinated precisely with the arrival of the banana boats that transport the crop overseas. Regularity of a guaranteed supply is also crucial, as banana-ripening rooms in the United Kingdom must continually process and deliver fruit year-round to retailers, which display the highly perishable commodity for only three or four days. Such considerations suggest that purchasers and marketers of the fruit need to achieve considerable control over the labor process during production and harvesting of the crop.

One means of securing high-quality crops on a scheduled basis is through contract farming, the use of which is growing rapidly in developing countries (Glover 1984; Minot 1986; Little and Watts 1994). Although systems of contract farming can vary considerably in their structures, two basic features are common to all such enterprises—the provision of a guaranteed market and some control exercised by capital and / or the state over the production process (Watts et al. 1988). In such systems, the purchaser—which can be a state agency, private local or foreign capital, or a public / private joint venture—usually agrees to buy the output of farmers before production begins, provides them with credit to obtain agricultural inputs, advises and supervises them through the provision of agricultural extension services, and establishes means for price determination. In return, farmers are supposed to follow the procedures for cultivating and harvesting that are established in the contract and accept the advice provided by the purchaser's extension agents. The agreements in contract farming can be either written or verbal (ibid. 1988).

Minot (1986) and Goldsmith (1985) observe that commodities produced under contract-farming arrangements are usually perishable, processed, and labor intensive; require considerable care in cultivation; have high value per unit volume or weight; and / or have economies of scale in certain phases of production—characteristics that pertain to the banana industry.[3] Contract farming is employed mostly for export, including production of both traditional commodities, such as bananas, and nontraditional ones, such as specialty horticultural crops, off-season fruits and vegetables, and flowers (Glover and Kusterer 1990; Collins 1993; Watts 1994).

Contract farming has potential advantages for both sellers and buyers. Farmers benefit from a guaranteed market and access to credit for purchasing inputs. Buyers are not burdened by the riskiest and least profitable stage of the commodity chain, and the threat of expropriation is not a concern (Goldsmith 1985). In addition, contract farmers are motivated to produce high-quality commodities, because quality influences the prices that they receive for their crops.

Most important, contracting gives buyers a degree of control over the production process, as contracts usually specify the procedures to follow in cultivation and harvesting. To facilitate control over farmers' production practices, contracting agencies establish their own agricultural extension services, which enable them to provide more regular contact with farmers compared to patterns characteristic of government agricultural extension services. For example, a study in sub-Saharan Africa reveals that ratios of extension agents to farmers in many contract-farming schemes are usually between 1:50 and 1:200, whereas ratios of government agricultural extension officers to the general farming public typically range from 1:1,000 to 1:2,000 and above (Watts et al. 1988). Such emphasis on the provision of intensive extension supervision in contract-farming schemes is intended to facilitate the production of high-quality output. Crop processors and marketers also attempt to get peasants to comply with their contractual obligations by specifying quality standards that are exacting. Their pricing schedules establish set prices for each grade recognized, sometimes incorporating wide gradients between each grade and associated price.

The resulting effectiveness of their efforts to obtain compliance and the consequent impact on the peasant labor process are relevant to current debates in the literature concerning the appropriate characterization of contract farmers. Some researchers (Clapp 1994; Watts 1994) portray them as "disguised" or "concealed" wage laborers or "propertied proletarians," in essence being more similar to wage laborers than to independent farmers. In essence, such a view portrays contract farmers as "hired hands on their own land" (Little and Watts 1994, 16). Contract farming certainly gives capital and the state some degree of control over the production process, but whether such control is so thorough and dominating that contract farmers' autonomy is reduced to a level comparable to that of wage workers requires investigation.

Contract farming can be plagued by a variety of problems. The most contentious issue between the parties is the determination of grading standards; contracts specify how commodities are to be graded, the respective price to be paid for each grade, and the criteria for rejecting substandard output (Glover 1984; Carney 1992; Watts 1994). Grading standards can often be complex and open to subjective interpretations. Indeed, arbitrary and unfair grading of commodities is the most common complaint of contract farmers (Glover 1984). Some contracting agencies apply more stringent interpretations of standards and increase rejection rates when their markets become oversupplied (ibid.; Carney 1992; Collins 1993). Indeed, in some cases, rejection rates have been over 50 percent (Glover and Kusterer 1990), and in even more extreme cases, buyers have unilaterally terminated contracts (ibid.; Carney 1992).

Growers have their own methods of evading the provisions of contracts (Daddieh 1994; Jackson and Cheater 1994; Jaffee 1994; Watts 1994). Application of agrochemical inputs obtained on credit from contracting agencies to crops not under contract is widespread (Porter and Phillips-Howard 1997). Most important, farmers are highly variable in the extent to which they faithfully follow the procedures specified in contracts and accept the advice given by extension officers.

The literature on contract farming tends to be dominated by cases focusing on the activities of private capital or public / private joint ventures. The more extreme cases of abuse of farmers by contracting agencies are typically associated with private capital involvement (see Raynolds 2000), though abuse in state-run schemes can also occur (Daddieh 1994). In contrast, the svBGA, although a state institution, has had more positive impacts on the peasantry—though recent events are changing the relation between the statutory organization and the peasantry.

A BRIEF HISTORY OF THE WINDWARD
ISLANDS BANANA INDUSTRY

Although the contemporary banana industry in the Windwards started in the 1950s, events farther back in time set the context for its emergence (Grossman 1998; Clegg 2000). Since the turn of the twentieth century, the British government had been concerned about both the Caribbean banana trade and its own banana imports being dominated by U.S.-based corporations, particularly since United Fruit gained control over the Jamaican banana trade early in this century (Trouillot 1988). Subsequently, in 1926, the Imperial Economic Committee's influential report on fruit production in the British Empire suggested that the British Windwards should become suppliers of bananas to the British market and should form producers' organizations under government auspices to encourage growth of the trade and negotiate with potential shipping companies.

But Britain was not the destination for the first sustained Windwards-wide banana export industry. In 1933 the Canadian Banana Company, under the control of United Fruit, started shipping bananas from the Windwards to Canada. Because the Canadian Banana Company refused to negotiate purchases with individual farmers, the islands established statutory corporations to manage the industry and negotiate with the shipper (Mourillon 1978, 9). These growers' associations were the forerunners of the contemporary institutions on the islands. The trade never achieved prominence in the economies of the region and finally collapsed in 1942.

It was not until after World War II that the Windwards banana industry focused its exports on the United Kingdom market. At the time, Jamaica, which was the main prewar banana supplier of Britain, was not able to produce enough fruit to satisfy the needs of the British banana market. To take advantage of this undersupplied market, the British firm Geest Industries in 1952 took an interest in Antilles Products, which had been buying bananas first from Dominica in 1949 and later from St. Lucia and shipping them to continental Europe, Ireland, and, subsequently, Britain (see Mourillon 1978; Davies 1990; Clegg 2000). Geest gained complete control of Antilles by 1954 (Clegg 2000). Like the Canadian Banana Company in the 1930s, Geest did not want to deal with individual growers. The company thus signed ten-year contracts in 1954 with all four banana growers' associations in the Windwards, guaranteeing to purchase all bananas of exportable quality. As a result, Geest became the exclusive shipper and marketer of Windwards bananas, a position that it retained until 1995. Geest's relations with the Windward Islands banana growers' associations were very controversial, with many researchers blaming Geest for unfair and inequitable contractual arrangements and dealings with the Windwards that ensured that Geest reaped a disproportionate share of profits from the trade (Thomson 1987; Trouillot 1988; Nurse and Sandiford 1995; Grossman 1998). Geest also left the burden of organizing and managing the industry in the hands of the statutory organizations, including the SVBGA.

Also critical to the emergence of the Windwards export industry were changes in British banana import regulations. To encourage banana imports from sterling areas, including the Windwards, the British government in the 1950s increased the existing import tariff on non-Commonwealth bananas and also established a quota on the importation of fruit from Latin America — so-called dollar bananas. In contrast, it allowed the importation of unlimited amounts of bananas duty free from sterling areas. Such British quotas and tariffs underwent numerous revisions in the ensuing years but remained in effect until the creation of the banana regime of the SEM. In the 1950s the British government also provided the first aid program to assist the Windwards industry; it subsequently created numerous other aid packages to support the growth of banana production, a pattern that continued until the 1980s (Grossman 1994). British initiatives to foster the growth of the industry were partly a function of self-interest. England needed to conserve scarce foreign exchange, ensure a regular supply of the fruit, and reduce the amounts of recurrent budgetary support that it provided to the Windward Islands administrations. But there was also an element of concern for reducing poverty and increasing the welfare of the peasantry in the region.

British assistance in the form of market protection and financial aid was pivotal in maintaining banana production in the Windward Islands in the ensuing years. These islands were not able to compete in an open, unregulated market with much larger banana producers from Latin America, who benefited from much lower labor costs — resulting from exploitative employment practices (see Striffler 1999) — and much more significant economies of scale based on substantially larger production units and larger shipping volumes (Grossman 1998; Wiley 1998). Also, unlike the Windwards, Latin American growers benefited from large stretches of flat terrain and a location outside the hurricane belt. Similarly, droughts have had a much more severe impact on the Windwards industry (see Grossman 1998, 63).[4]

The guaranteed market provided by Geest and the British government, market protection in the United Kingdom, and initially high prices for bananas spurred rapid growth of banana production in the Windward Islands.[5] However, except for brief periods of prosperity in the 1950s and in the latter half of the 1980s and early 1990s, the Windward Islands banana industry has often been in a precarious situation. It has been beleaguered by repeated environmental and economic crises: recurrent drought and windstorms and occasional devastating pest infestations; intense competition from Jamaican banana imports in the late 1950s and 1960s, culminating in the so-called Jamaica-Windwards banana war of 1964–1965; and Britain's successful application to join the European Community (EC) in 1973, which forced Britain to gradually eliminate its preferential tariff on non-Commonwealth fruit from both overseas territories of EC member states and ACP countries, which were the EC members' former colonies in Africa, the Caribbean, and the Pacific.

Pressures from imports from Jamaica and Latin America heightened awareness of the importance of fruit quality as a key determinant of competitive success in the banana market. Fruit quality, determined in large part by the physical appearance of bananas, affected the prices that farmers received for their crop. Unfortunately for the Windwards, the quality of their fruit has been a long-term problem. In fact, the British government threatened repeatedly to increase the quota on the amount of Latin American fruit if the Windwards did not improve the quality of their exports. Geest had also complained frequently about Windwards' banana quality. Another source of pressure for better-quality fruit in the United Kingdom has been the growing dominance of the supermarket trade and its demand for prepackaging (WINBAN 1986, 15; Nurse and Sandiford 1995, 38–39). Such influences have forced the Windwards to adopt a variety of changes in their production and harvesting practices, and it was the banana growers' associations on the islands that were responsible for ensuring that growers implemented the changes.

The most recent — and most serious — challenge to the survival of the Windward Islands banana industry has been the creation of the EU and the formation of the SEM. The EU established a uniform set of rules governing the importation of bananas, and thus the various separate preferential regimes that its member states had established previously had to be dismantled. Consequently, the United Kingdom could no longer provide the Windwards with its own preferential system of tariffs and quotas, which had been so essential for the industry's survival. The result of the creation of the SEM, whose banana import policies have worsened over time for the Windwards in response to pressures for trade liberalization (see Clegg 2001), has been lower prices for bananas and more changes in the technologies of production and harvesting on Windwards' farms.

In the context of these numerous pressures and crises throughout the history of the industry, banana production in the Windwards could never have survived without a variety of supportive structures, including market protection and aid. Indeed, dependence on aid continues with the recent EU-funded Windward Islands Recovery Plan initiated in 1998, providing approximately U.S.$55.5 million in funding to raise production and productivity and improve fruit quality. Another key supportive structure on St. Vincent has been the SVBGA.

BANANA PRODUCTION ON ST. VINCENT

St. Vincent is the largest island in the nation of St. Vincent and the Grenadines in the Eastern Caribbean. This rugged, volcanic island is small, measuring eleven miles wide and eighteen miles long. Most of the island's 102,000 inhabitants live along the coast or in inland valleys, with the largest concentration residing in or near the port capital of Kingstown on the south end of the island (St. Vincent Statistical Unit 1999). The overwhelming majority of farmers are small-scale peasant producers, as the plantation sector — long dominant in the island's history — has been declining since the latter half of the nineteenth century and has withered significantly in the post–World War II era. Both men and women are engaged in banana farming (see Grossman 2000). While bananas are the main crop, peasants also grow a variety of other crops for home consumption and for sale in local markets. Similar to the situation of many of its neighbors, the open economy of St. Vincent and the Grenadines is continually plagued by trade deficits, and in this context, export agriculture, the main economic endeavor on the island, becomes particularly important. Also, in the late 1980s and early 1990s, the banana industry employed, directly or indirectly, 54 percent of the nation's workforce (SVBGA 1994, 3).

The overwhelming majority of banana growers are peasants cultivating less than five acres of the fruit, usually in small, fragmented plots on steep, rugged land, and often intercropping bananas with local food crops. The largest holdings on the island in the mid-1990s were only between sixty and seventy acres. The numerical dominance of small-scale producers presents particular problems for the industry. Educating the large number of growers about new technologies and grading standards presents a challenge to SVBGA extension services. Farmers process and pack their harvested fruits on or near their own farms, leading to difficulties in standardizing procedures. They have to carry their harvested bananas over rugged terrain, creating conditions conducive to bruising of fruit, which lowers fruit quality. The winding roads on the island, especially the feeder roads that radiate into the banana-growing areas, have numerous ruts and potholes that further contribute to bruising of bananas while they are being transported in trucks from villages to Kingstown. In addition, the myriad production units on the island militate against achieving economies of scale.

Attempting to describe the technologies employed on banana farms is similar to trying to hit a moving target. One of the most remarkable aspects of the industry has been the rapid pace of technological change. Thus, descriptions of farming practices one year will be inaccurate the next. With this caveat in mind, I will describe briefly the situation as it existed in 1995, highlighting two separate aspects—the stages of production and the process of harvesting and packing the fruit. The latter aspect, that of harvesting and packing, has experienced the more substantial degree of change over time (Grossman 1998). The following description of practices is based on official instructions from the SVBGA; farmers, however, exhibit variability in implementing them.

Just after planting, farmers are supposed to make the first application of nematicides to control the depredations of microscopic nematodes in the soil. Three or four weeks later, they begin weed control, usually relying on herbicides. Fertilization is next. Four or five months after planting, villagers begin pruning, removing the unwanted suckers sprouting from the base of the plants; they are supposed to leave just one sucker as the "follower" that will produce the next bunch after bananas on the original "pseudostem" are harvested.[6] Soon afterward comes "pluming," in which workers cut off the yellowing and dried leaves and remove the peeling, dried outer covering of the pseudostems. Growers then turn their attention to deflowering, in which they brush off the flower growing at the end of each banana "finger" (an individual banana). Subsequently, workers have to "sleeve" the bunches, covering each one in a thin, blue translucent polyethylene bag that helps prevent pest damage and increases bunch weights. The next step of "propping"—tying the top of a plant to a wooden stake driven into the ground—ensures that the top-heavy plants do not fall over.

Harvesting, which is the most labor-intensive activity, also requires the most care. Green bananas must be harvested weekly or biweekly, because bananas ready for market one week may be unsuitable for sale the next. The system of harvesting and packing is called "cluster packing" or "mini-wet pack," having been adopted throughout the Windwards by 1993. People first cut individual hands of bananas off the bunch (each pseudostem produces one bunch, and a bunch on St. Vincent usually contains between six to ten "hands" of bananas); they then must subdivide the hands into "clusters" containing between four and nine banana fingers. Growers set the clusters on a freshly cut banana leaf resting on the ground and allow the latex oozing from the "crowns" of the clusters to drain for ten minutes, being careful to ensure that the sticky latex does not drip onto the banana fingers (which would result in unsightly staining of the peel). Then they load the clusters onto specially designed, rectangular plastic trays, which hold approximately fifty pounds of the green fruit, being sure to place soft, shredded banana leaves between clusters to prevent the peels from being scratched while in transport. Villagers carry the heavy trays on their heads to a central processing and packing area located in or near their banana fields, where villagers unload the clusters and wash them in a fungicide solution to prevent crown rot from developing later. After washing the fruit, they set the clusters on a table to allow the liquid to drain off.

Packing bananas in cardboard boxes, which comes next, is an intricate process demanding considerable skill, as improperly packed bananas can lead to bruising and rejection of the fruit. They must pack short- and regular-length bananas into different boxes and then weigh the packed cardboard boxes, making sure that each one contains the required amount (34 net pounds) — both procedures specified by regulations of the European Union. Villagers then have to "head" (carry) their packed boxes of green fruit to a road, where trucks carry the boxes to Kingstown. Here, the svbga inspects the fruit and loads the boxes onto refrigerated ships bound ultimately for the United Kingdom.

Banana production, harvesting, and packing require considerable time, care, and precision. My own research (Grossman 1993) indicated that in the late 1980s banana production consumed roughly 150 labor-days per acre per year, and, by 1995, even more effort was required. Any step performed incorrectly — applying too little fertilizer, deflowering or sleeving late, allowing latex staining, poor placement of clusters in a cardboard box, failing to pack the precise amount required — can produce defects recognizable at the inspection stage and can lead to the fruit being either downgraded or rejected as unsuitable for export.

The technologies involved in the banana industry have changed considerably over time. Such changes are relevant to debates about the nature of the peasant labor process in contract farming. Some researchers (Clapp 1994; Watts 1994) assert that contract farming entails a "deskilling of labor" (see Braverman 1974), a key dimension of which is the increasing subdivision and fragmentation of the peasant labor process into more simplified stages that require less skill over time. In the banana industry the opposite pattern has occurred, especially in the harvesting and packing of bananas. In the 1950s and 1960s the endeavor was much less complex, as farmers only had to deliver whole bunches to the svbga. In the 1970s growers began "dehanding" bananas (cutting hands off the bunch) in their fields and delivering the fruit in rectangular, plastic "field boxes" to the svbga's boxing plants, where svbga employees weighed, inspected, washed, and packed the fruit into cardboard boxes. In the 1980s a revolutionary new system, "field packing," was introduced, in which farmers had to harvest, dehand, and pack banana hands into cardboard boxes right in their fields. This was the first time that farmers themselves had to pack bananas directly into cardboard boxes. Field packing also required much more skill and time than did previous systems; it demanded precision in cutting the hands and crowns, proper timing in draining latex from the cut crowns, correct placement of a fungicide-treated pad on the cut crown, and very careful positioning of hands packed in the cardboard boxes to prevent scratching and bruising of the fruit. Field packing, adopted throughout St. Vincent by 1986, was subsequently modified in various ways in the ensuing years by the "paco pack" system. The mini-wet system followed in the 1990s, adding the tasks of clustering, carrying fruit to a central processing station, washing the clusters, packing short- and regular-length bananas into separate boxes, much more precise packing, and the weighing of boxes in the field.

Each of these successive stages became more complex and required more skill. The stages also reflected three sets of influences: the SVBGA's attempts to obtain better-quality fruit; both Geest's and the SVBGA's attempts to reduce the costs of their own operations by transferring tasks performed previously off-farm to the farmers; and the need to comply with the regulations imposed by the EU.

In the latter half of the 1990s and early 2000s banana production on St. Vincent was still undergoing major modifications, further increasing the complexity of the production process. One arena of change was in the nature of packing bananas. In 1995 farmers were exporting only two product types—those with small fruit and those with regular-size fruit. By 1999 they were exporting nine different product types, most of which were packaged according to individual UK supermarket specifications (SVBGA 2000).

Another dimension of change concerned technological innovations. New irrigation systems on the flatter areas of the island and the adoption of imported tissue-culture plants—which require improved levels of husbandry and more fertilizers (Dominica Banana Marketing Corporation 1999, 19; Clissold 2001, 6)—enabled farmers to boost productivity significantly (SVBGA 2000). Growers in 1997 also began using a ribbon-tagging system to more accurately determine the precise ages of individual plants to facilitate harvesting at optimum times. The svbga has played a critical role in managing the industry and retraining farmers during all these changes.

THE ST. VINCENT BANANA GROWERS' ASSOCIATION

The pattern of a statutory corporation managing an agricultural industry on St. Vincent has precedents dating back to the pre-World War II era. The St. Vincent Banana Association was established in 1934 as the exclusive exporter of bananas and was charged with managing and encouraging the growth of the industry.[7] The St. Vincent Co-operative Arrowroot Association, established in 1930, performed similar functions in relation to the arrowroot industry. In neither case, however, was a system of contract farming evident because the associations did not have control over the production process.

The contemporary svbga was formed in late 1953 as a public company with shares and then was transformed into a statutory organization by the Banana Growers' Association Ordinance No. 54 of 1954, which became law in early 1955. The association was granted the exclusive legal right to market and control all bananas produced for export on the island (Commission of Enquiry 1959, 2). The statute also required the maintenance of a registry of growers and the formation of district branches to give growers a voice in the industry.

The name of this statutory organization implies that it is an association run by the growers. This is true to only a very limited extent. The membership of the association is divided into sixteen district branches, and each one holds occasional meetings to discuss issues associated with the banana industry and to hear infrequent talks given by officials of the svbga. Each branch also elects its own officers and is able to table resolutions to be considered at the svbga's annual meetings. At these annual meetings, two types of growers can vote: five delegates who are elected by each district branch and those farmers who have sold a minimum amount of bananas in the previous twelve months — 62,500 pounds (to produce such an amount requires slightly more than five acres of bananas). Having district branch members elect their own voting delegates for the annual meetings imparts a small degree of democracy into the svbga; all district members can vote for delegates, and the requirement for eligibility for election as a delegate is minimal — selling 2,500 pounds during the previous year. In contrast, those who obtain the right to vote because of the volume of their sales — known as "delegates in their own right" — are a much more select group, comprising only 6 percent of the active growers in 1992, which reflects the overwhelming numerical dominance of peasants in the industry (SVBGA files).

The annual meetings serve as a public forum in which to vent complaints, ask members of the board of directors and management of the SVBGA about a variety of issues, and discuss the information contained in the SVBGA's annual financial report. Banana prices are, of course, a popular topic. The district branches also table numerous resolutions for consideration on issues ranging from testing growers for pesticide contamination to petitioning the government to reduce the export tax. However, even when resolutions are passed in a vote by those who are in attendance, they do not necessarily become SVBGA policy. But growers' votes sometimes do affect policy decisions on important issues raised by the board of directors, issues such as determining whether small- and large-scale growers would benefit equally from a new retirement scheme. In any case, the few larger growers in the industry tend to dominate most of the discussions at the annual meetings. Also, the really crucial issues affecting the lives of the growers — the prices that they receive from the SVBGA, the technologies that they are supposed to employ, the number of extension agents available to help them, the costs of their inputs — are beyond their control, being determined by SVBGA management.

Those eligible to vote at these annual meetings also elect seven of the thirteen members of the board of directors, who establish policies for SVBGA management to follow.[8] Two types of individual are eligible to be elected to the board of directors: three of the five delegates selected by each branch and those who have sold a minimum of 125,000 pounds of bananas during the previous year. Although the government appoints only six members of the board of directors, it also appoints the chairman from the seven elected directors, selecting someone whose views are sympathetic to national policy. Thus, the government is usually able to ensure that SVBGA policies are consistent with its own goals, though occasional disagreements do emerge between the chairman and the government. In any case, those elected to the board of directors are usually not truly representative of the large majority of growers, most of whom cultivate only a few acres of bananas or less. Those elected tend to be medium- and large-scale farmers.

The SVBGA is ultimately controlled by the Vincentian government. The government must approve the SVBGA budget, the price it offers to farmers, and the appointment of senior management. The government also has the power to dismiss the board of directors. Government influence over and interest in the SVBGA reflect the critical importance of the banana industry to the Vincentian economy.

Despite the fact that the state traditionally levied a 3 percent export tax on bananas (which was reduced to 2 percent in 1994), it has not used the industry as a major vehicle for state accumulation based on the exploitation of the peasantry. In fact, the Vincentian government planned to remove the export tax on bananas in 1999. In contrast, a classic pattern in sub-Saharan Africa is for statutory corporations, some of which are involved in contract farming, to keep the prices paid to farmers far below those of world-market prices and retain the difference between the two prices to fund other state operations (Daddieh 1994).

The SVBGA has a degree of independence from the government. In the management of day-to-day affairs and issues related to production goals and technological innovations the SVBGA has considerable independence. In addition, the Vincentian government cannot draw on funds held in reserve by the association.

The SVBGA performs the classic functions of the central buyer / coordinator in contract-farming schemes. However, none of the works that have been published about the Windward Islands banana industry have considered it in relation to the institution of contract farming (see Marie 1979; Thomson 1987; Trouillot 1988; Nurse and Sandiford 1995; Welch 1996). Undoubtedly, a major reason for this pattern has been the absence of formal, written contracts between purchaser and growers, though formal contracts have now been introduced in the latter half of the 1990s. However, written contracts are not the hallmark of contract farming systems (Watts et al. 1988). Rather, the two essential ingredients are a guaranteed market and some degree of control by capital and / or the state over the labor process of farmers. The SVBGA has always provided farmers with a guaranteed market, but it gained its significant degree of control over the labor process only gradually. A critical transition in relation to control occurred in the 1980s, when farmers had to deliver all bananas packed strictly according to the regulations associated with field packing. Previously, no single method of harvesting and packing had been required; before the introduction of field packing, the SVBGA encouraged the adoption of particular cultivation and packing procedures through the payment of bonuses rather than by decree. Also, the svbga's influence over the labor process has a legal basis established in regulations incorporated into various government statutes, such as the Banana (Protection and Quality Control) Act of 1984 (St. Vincent 1984). Thus, it is appropriate to consider the svbga in relation to patterns associated with contract farming.

Unlike the situation in many contract-farming schemes, the buyer / central coordinator—here the svbga—does not limit the number of growers who can participate. Membership in the svbga is relatively easy to obtain. Anyone can become a registered member of the svbga as long as they meet certain simple requirements: complete a one-page application form, be at least sixteen years old, and plant at least thirty bananas, a minimal amount. More than one person from the same household can register to become a member of the svbga, which enables both men and women, who often control separate garden plots, to participate in the industry (see Grossman 2000).

Even though each grower is supposed to register with the svbga, the association does not know the exact number of active banana farmers. SVBGA statistics (svbga files) indicate that there were 12,695 registered growers in 1992 and 13,216 in 1995, but many more people (7,855) sold fruit in 1992 than did in 1995 (5,991) (table 1). In both years a substantial number of registered growers sold no bananas. Determining the actual number of growers who sold bananas in any one year is difficult because of the practice of "multiple registration." The practice occurs when an individual grower obtains one membership in his or her own name and a second one in the name of a different household member, relative, or even fictitious individual, with such farmers selling their own fruit under both names. Although the practice has plagued the svbga since the 1950s (Commission of Enquiry 1959), the frequency of multiple registrations is unknown. Some farmers have several registrations to avoid repaying credit from the svbga or loans from banks; in such instances, they initially obtain credit under one name, then sell their bananas using only their other registration, thwarting the provider of credit from obtaining repayments. But other growers have a nonmalevolent intent. Peasants who sharecrop prefer to keep records of their banana sales from land that they sharecrop separate from records dealing with their plots that they hold under other forms of tenure to avoid possible conflicts over amounts owed to owners of the sharecropped parcels.

TABLE 1   Number of Growers by Amounts Sold, 1992 and 1995

Amount sold (tons)	Number of Growers (1992)	Number of Growers (1995)
Nil	4,840	7,225
< 1	1,201	1,070
1–2	787	667
2–3	682	567
3–5	1,077	815
5–7	781	620
7–10	937	707
10–15	941	672
15–20	524	327
20–25	289	195
25–30	172	123
30–40	227	105
40–50	107	53
50–80	89	45
80–100	15	10
>100	26	15
Total farmers selling	7,855	5,991

SOURCE: SVBGA Files; SVBGA 1996; Grossman 1998.

Despite the difficulty of determining the exact number of growers, it is clear that peasants with banana holdings of five acres or less clearly predominate in the industry. Based on the approximate yield of six tons per acre that was characteristic in the first half of the 1990s, the data in table 1 indicate that roughly 95 percent of the growers cultivated five acres of bananas or less.[9] Indeed, many had less than one acre. This distribution of banana holdings has important welfare implications; benefits from the industry that reach St. Vincent are spread widely throughout the population.

The large number of small-scale growers has critical implications for contract-farming enterprises because it places a high burden on extension services. One of the keys to successful contract farming is a high ratio of extension agents to farmers. Because banana production is technologically complex and the pace of technological change in the industry has accelerated over time, a

TABLE 2   Ratio of Extension Agents to Active
Banana Growers, St. Vincent, 1987–1994

Year	Ratio
1987	1:461
1988	1:653
1989	1:564
1990	1:717
1991	1:557
1992	1:561
1993	1:628
1994	1:558

SOURCE: SVBGA Files; Grossman 1998.

high ratio of extension agents to farmers would be expected. However, such a pattern has not been evident, as the ratios from 1987 to 1994 illustrate (table 2). In contrast, many contract-farming schemes based on labor-intensive crops in sub-Saharan Africa have had much higher ratios; for example, in British American Tobacco's scheme in western Kenya, the high ratio of 1:50 enabled extension officers to visit each grower once every two weeks to closely monitor and supervise their activities. In comparison, many Vincentian banana growers see their extension agents only once every one or two months or at even longer intervals. The inability of the SVBGA to provide adequate extension services stemmed directly from its usually weak financial condition, a reflection of the unfavorable contracts that it had with Geest, recurrent environmental problems, and frequent pricing pressures in the United Kingdom market.

Such insufficient extension assistance in the context of complex and rapid technological change in an industry in which fruit quality considerations are paramount creates two significant problems. First, it limits the ability of the buyer / central coordinator to monitor, regulate, and induce uniformity in production practices. Second, it constrains the potential for educating farmers adequately enough to foster improvements in fruit quality.

The SVBGA performs numerous other functions that are characteristic of buyers / central coordinators in contract-farming schemes. One is the provision of a guaranteed market. Unlike schemes in which the contracting agency breaches its commitment to provide a guaranteed market during times of market oversupply and low prices (Glover and Kusterer 1990), the SVBGA always fulfills its obligation. Even when the SVBGA decides not to export all bananas that farmers harvest in a week to prevent oversupplying the British market, it will still purchase all fruit of exportable quality. Also, the SVBGA pays growers promptly and on time, one week after purchasing their bananas. Long delays in making payments to growers have occurred in other contexts involving statutory corporations, especially in sub-Saharan Africa (Jackson and Cheater 1994).

Another typical function is the provision of inputs and credit. The SVBGA is the island's largest importer of agrochemicals. The Vincentian government grants the association a duty-free concession on imports of fertilizers and pesticides. The SVBGA, in turn, sells agrochemicals to farmers on a nonprofit basis and below market rates. To facilitate farmers' use of these inputs, the SVBGA withholds a "cess," or deduction, from each payment that it makes to growers and places the amounts deducted in their individual cess accounts. Farmers are supposed to use funds accumulated in their cess accounts to purchase agrochemicals every two months.[10] The association also provides credit to enable farmers to obtain additional sacks of fertilizer as well as other inputs, requiring a 50 percent deposit on such fertilizer purchases and a 25 percent deposit on the purchase of other inputs, such as pesticides, ladders, and sprayers. It charges farmers no interest on their debts and obtains repayments from them on a liberal schedule by deducting small, fixed amounts from each sale that the growers make. Such characteristics are consistent with the pattern of the Vincentian state not using the resources of the SVBGA as a vehicle for accumulation.

The SVBGA performs other usual services. Contracting agencies are often involved in pest control where significant economies of scale can be achieved. The SVBGA takes responsibility for the control of leaf-spot disease, a potentially devastating fungal infection, by providing ground crews and aerial spraying to combat infestations throughout the island.

Less widespread in contract-farming enterprises is the provision of transport to assist farmers in bringing their crops to market. The SVBGA organizes and provides transportation for shipping of harvested, boxed bananas from roadsides in rural areas to inspection stations scattered in the countryside and in Kingstown. Farmers are not charged individually for transportation; rather, the SVBGA considers the cost of providing transportation as one of its operating expenses included in its calculations when determining the overall price paid to growers. Thus, small- and large-scale growers and those near and far from Kingstown all receive the same service without direct payment — ensuring that growers do not suffer disadvantages in relation to transportation because of the size or location of their farms.

As is characteristic of buyer / coordinators in contract-farming schemes, the SVBGA is involved in quality determination; it inspects the green bananas that farmers deliver to determine whether the fruit is exportable and which quality grade best characterizes the bananas; the higher the quality, the better the price. Whereas some contracting agencies dishonestly change their interpretations of their grading standards in response to fluctuations in the availability of supplies and market prices to maximize their profits (Glover and Kusterer 1990), the association, which is a nonprofit organization, does not. Its rejection rates, which rarely exceeded 4 or 5 percent of fruit inspected from the late 1980s to 1997, were low compared to those in many other contract-farming schemes in developing countries (SVBGA files; SVBGA 1998, 12).

Nonetheless, grading standards are rigid. In 1993, the SVBGA specified twenty-five defects related to the characteristics of bananas that could lead to downgrading or rejection of fruit (SVBGA files; Grossman 1998):

1. Superficial bruises
2. Crown trimming
3. Damaged pedicels
4. Dirty
5. Finger end rot
6. Flower thrips
7. Fused fingers
8. Latex staining
9. Maturity stain
10. Misshapen / deformed fingers / units
11. Mutilated fingers
12. Overgrade
13. Peel burn
14. Pest damage
15. Residue
16. Red rust damage

17. Ripe and turning
18. Scars
19. Scruffy
20. Short finger
21. Sooty mold
22. Speckling / pin spotting
23. Stale fruit
24. Undeflowered
25. Undergrade

In addition to these defects, other problems in relation to the boxing of fruit were grounds for rejection. For example, even if the bananas packed inside a cardboard box were of the highest quality, the box of fruit could still be rejected for export if the container were dirty, wet, poorly packed, or underweight.

Contract-farming schemes employ differential pricing structures based on the quality of fruit delivered to encourage high-quality output. The SVBGA has employed a variety of pricing schedules over time (table 3). In the late 1980s and early 1990s it specified only two exportable grades, with the price difference between them being just three cents per pound; such a small price differential was of limited significance in encouraging high-quality output. In 1994 the association changed the system to include three grades. By 1996 it had introduced five different classes with even more extreme price gradients, reflecting the SVBGA's desperate need to obtain better-quality bananas from growers in the context of the severe financial difficulties in the industry and increasing pressures from the EU for better quality fruit.

A critical function of the SVBGA that is not characteristic of buyers / coordinators in contract-farming schemes is the initiation and management of numerous aid and rehabilitation schemes; without such programs of support for its growers, the industry would have collapsed due to the repeated environmental and economic crises experienced during its history. Some of the programs have been Windwards-wide and dependent on external funding, supplied mostly by the EU during the 1990s; in the past the British government has provided the external funding for such schemes (Grossman 1994). These programs usually focus on improving farm productivity, facilitating the adoption of new technologies, and enhancing fruit quality. The SVBGA also funds much

TABLE 3   SVBGA Pricing Structures in 1989, 1994, and 1996 (in EC dollars)

1989		1994		1996	
Quality	Price	Quality	Price	Quality	Price
Basic	0.30 / lb*	Basic	0.153 / lb	Basic	0.095 / lb
Premium	0.33 / lb**	75–84% UWS***	0.223 / lb	75–79% UWS	0.2175 / lb
		85–100% UWS	0.273 / lb	80–84% UWS	0.235 / lb
				85–90% UWS	0.27 / lb
				91–100% UWS	0.2875 / lb

SOURCE: SVBGA Files.

* The basic price in 1989 varied according to the season; fruit sold between April and September received 0.30 / lb, while that sold the rest of the year received 0.25 / lb, the difference in the two periods reflecting traditional variations in seasonal demand for bananas in Britain. Part of the basic price included a 0.05 / lb "bonus" that everyone received.

** To receive the premium price, 70 percent of the boxes in a shipment had to be graded as containing premium quality fruit.

*** UWS (Unit Within Specification) indicates either no noticeable defects or relatively minor flaws in relation to certain criteria (see above). Scores are based on the percentage of all clusters within a small number of boxes sampled by the SVBGA.

smaller-scale programs from its own reserve funds—though spending such reserve funds eventually affects the price that it can afford to pay to growers. These programs are usually intended for replanting and rehabilitation of fields, providing low-cost loans to farmers to help them expand the area under bananas and to make improvements to their banana plots. The SVBGA previously used its reserve funds to also provide farmers with some compensation for destruction of their banana crops resulting from tropical storms and hurricanes; since 1990, it has participated in an insurance scheme for that purpose. In very severe cases of environmental damage to growers' banana fields, the SVBGA uses its own reserve funds to grant short-term living allowances to help support affected farmers. In addition, the SVBGA occasionally props up the price that it pays to growers when market conditions are very poor, sometimes having to obtain overdrafts from banks to afford paying the elevated prices—all with the hope that when banana prices improve, it will be able to repay the banks. (Major programs initiated and / or managed by the SVBGA from 1987 to 1998 are listed in table 4.)

TABLE 4   Programs of Assistance Administered by the SVBGA, 1987–1998

Years	Name of Program	Comments
1981–1990	Banana Disaster Fund	Help farmers affected by storms and drought
1987	Replanting Program	Loans for replanting after drought
1987	Emily Rehabilitation Program	Help farmers affected by tropical storm
1989–1993	Growers' Retirement Benefit Scheme	Provide retirement benefits to growers
1990–*	Windward Islands Crop Insurance Scheme	Basic insurance to growers for storm damage
1991	Replanting Program	Loans for replanting
1994	Income Support Scheme**	Price support due to low price of bananas
1994–1995	Rehabilitation / Replanting Program**	Loans for replanting / rehabilitation
1996–*	Banana Industry Development Program**	Technological modernization of the industry
1998	Windward Islands Recovery Plan**	Fruit quality and productivity improvements; increase number of certified growers

* Still in operation in 1998

** Includes external funding, mostly from the EU.

While the association believes that such efforts are indicative of its interest in helping small farmers, many peasants hold negative views about the statutory organization. They tend to be suspicious about large organizations in general, and the SVBGA, for them, is another large institution intent on exploiting and cheating them. Many complain that personnel of the SVBGA draw large salaries while doing little work, whereas farmers do most of the work in the industry but receive very little reward for their extensive efforts. They also claim that the SVBGA listens to and helps only large-scale growers and further assert that large-scale growers receive more lenient treatment in relation to the down payments required for obtaining inputs on credit and in the scheduling of their repayments—assertions that the SVBGA denies. Indeed, one of the common complaints about the banana growers' associations in the Windwards generally is that they are biased toward helping large farmers (see Thomson 1987). While instances of favoritism toward larger-scale growers can be found, it is also true that the association's policies have been supportive of small-scale farmers and have been essential in maintaining peasant involvement in the industry.

THE SVBGA, CONTRACT FARMING, AND
CONTROL OVER THE LABOR PROCESS

Certainly, the SVBGA is not a perfect organization. For example, it has been accused of weak financial management during the period of 1992–1995 (Cargill Technical Services 1995). Nor has it provided enough extension agents to adequately monitor, train, and assist peasants attempting to cope with repeated changes in the industry. But the association also has not exhibited the abuses characteristic of buyers / central coordinators in some contract-farming schemes. It has provided peasants with numerous services, been fair in grading standards, had low rejection rates since the mid-1980s, made payments promptly to farmers, provided credit on liberal terms, and been faithful in providing a guaranteed market. Farmers do have a voice—albeit a limited one—in influencing some aspects of the operations of the association, a pattern that is very rare in contract-farming schemes (Watts 1994). Even more unique is the SVBGA's provision of aid to help farmers recover after natural disasters. Nor has the SVBGA been plagued by endemic corruption as have some statutory organizations involved in agriculture in other developing countries. And it has not been authoritarian in attempting to achieve control over the labor process of farmers. Such a pattern reflects not only a weak extension service but also a particular tradition of state-peasant relations.

The absence of a tradition of rigid control over peasant land use has been evident in other contexts. A prime example concerns the Vincentian government's soil conservation efforts in the 1930s and 1940s, the period of greatest

British colonial concern about erosion in the Empire. Whereas colonial administrations in parts of British East Africa employed authoritarian methods to force villagers to adopt conservation techniques, those in the Windwards and the rest of the British Caribbean relied on voluntary compliance by peasants, reflecting the lack of authoritarianism in state-peasant relations on St. Vincent (Grossman 1997). The SVBGA has continued that tradition.

Lack of control has been evident in the inability of the SVBGA to instill uniform farming practices. Most variations in practices occur in the various stages of production, though some deviation from official instructions can also be found in harvesting and packing. Pesticide use, for instance, often differs from official instructions. Many farmers who interplant bananas with local food crops delay application of nematicides until nine months after planting, by which time their provisions will be harvested; they worry that applying nematicides earlier—at the time of planting, as instructed by the SVBGA— would contaminate their food crops. In contrast, in other contexts, peasants misuse pesticides, for example applying "pesticide cocktails," which is against official recommendations. Patterns of applying fertilizers also vary. The association expects farmers to apply fertilizers obtained on credit from the SVBGA only on bananas, but many who intercrop bananas with food crops put the first application of such fertilizers not on the bananas at all but only on their food crops; otherwise, their bananas would grow too quickly compared to their food crops, create too much shade, and thus inhibit growth of the food crops. Weed control, too, is sometimes performed less frequently than recommended. Whereas the SVBGA asserts that only one "follower" should be permitted to survive at the base of each plant, many farmers allow two or more to remain in the belief that such a pattern maximizes output from their small parcels and inhibits weed regrowth. These examples represent only a few of the common deviations from prescribed farming practices (see Grossman 1998).

Such deviations reflect a variety of pressures experienced by farmers. Low banana prices force farmers to cut back on expenditures on agrochemicals and on the amounts of labor that they hire. There is also a shortage of household labor for agriculture, conditioned, in part, by the increasing labor intensity of banana production over time. Also, some farmers find that they can produce high-quality fruit without following all of the officially sanctioned practices. Lastly, farmers cultivate in a variety of fields that have contrasting environmental and spatial characteristics and different crop combinations—all of which they consider when determining which practices are most useful and feasible to employ in their particular situations.

The existence of such deviations indicates that in the various stages of production peasants have considerable autonomy from control by capital and the state, though autonomy is less marked in the stages of harvesting and packing. Thus, concepts such as "disguised wage labor," which suggest that capital and the state thoroughly dominate the labor of contract farmers, are not applicable in this case. Also, such concepts are inappropriate because they mask the critical significance of the complex ways in which banana farmers creatively recruit the assistance of other household members, relatives, friends, and wage workers to solve their labor needs, which are conditioned by the changing harvesting and packing requirements; such initiatives in recruitment are alien to the wage labor form (see Grossman 1998). Moreover, contract farmers are unlike wage laborers because they retain control over their own land; such control is not nominal but real (Clapp 1994), giving them an "exit option" from banana production—an option that many have already taken since the mid-1990s. The degree of control exercised by capital and the state over peasant labor in contract farming is therefore highly variable (see Jaffee 1994; Little 1994; Raynolds 2000a). Use of concepts such as "disguised wage labor" reflects the tendency in some of the literature to focus on cases that involve what Watts (1994, 64) terms "authoritarian and despotic forms of contracting"—those in which control is very effectively achieved.

THE FUTURE OF THE SVBGA AND THE PEASANTRY

The SVBGA and its system of contract farming—along with the rest of the Windwards industry—have been undergoing major transformations since the latter half of the 1990s, altering many of the long-standing patterns described herein. The decline in market protection for Windwards bananas that began with the formation of the EU has been accelerating in the wake of adverse WTO rulings and intense pressure from the United States (see Clegg 2001). Desperate to find a solution to the resulting fall in banana prices and market share as lower-cost fruit from Latin America increasingly dominates the market, the Windwards industry is attempting to reshape its structure. Additional pressure is coming from the EU, which demands "reform" as a condition for continued aid to Windwards growers. The Windwards industry hopes that the radical changes that it is implementing will enable it to become more competitive and survive as market deregulation advances to the benefit of Latin American producers. The restructuring is affecting both the banana growers' associations and their relationships with the peasantry.

Due both to pricing and marketing pressures associated with the changing EU banana-import regime and to financial mismanagement in the first half of the 1990s, the associations in the Windwards, including the SVBGA, ran up unprecedented levels of debt. An EU-inspired study of the industry by Cargill Technical Services (1995) of Britain called for increasing efficiency in the industry and for replacing the boards of directors and senior management of all the associations. The report has been accepted by the governments of the Windward Islands as a condition for future aid from the EU. The banana growers' associations are thus undergoing significant restructuring. The St. Lucia Banana Growers' Association has now been privatized, and the SVBGA views such an outcome as inevitable for itself as well (SVBGA 1998, 7–9).

Another dimension of restructuring involves the implementation of the Certified Growers Program, introduced in 1997, in which those who consistently produce, process, and package high-quality bananas in line with strict guidelines are paid a significant bonus for their bananas (ibid. 15). By the end of 1999 there were 1,486 certified growers on St. Vincent out of the total 3,761 active growers producing the large majority of the island's banana exports (SVBGA 2000). The fruit of certified growers can be sold directly to supermarket chains in the United Kingdom, but they are therefore required to pack their fruit in accordance with the specifications of the particular supermarket, thus adding new tasks to be performed on the farm (Patsy Lewis 1998) and requiring even more skill from the workers. Such a pattern is consistent with the long-term industry trend toward increasing complexity in banana production.

The program has resulted in significant improvements in fruit quality. But the International Labor Organization (1999) asserts that many small-scale producers will not be able to participate in the Certified Growers Program because they do not have adequate capital to make the expenditures necessary for certification, a point confirmed by Clissold (2001).

The Certified Growers Program involves much closer extension monitoring of certified farmers' field practices compared to previous SVBGA extension patterns. The SVBGA threatens to "decertify" growers who fail to follow the required husbandry practices, as happened to nineteen certified growers in 1998 (SVBGA 1999). Restructuring also means getting rid of less-productive individuals — so-called marginal farmers — who do not have what officials and consultants consider "economical" units of production. Unfortunately, by labeling many small-scale farmers marginal — which implies the solution of jettisoning them from the industry — attention focuses on their shortcomings rather than on the creative and intelligent ways in which they have managed to adapt and produce bananas under constantly changing requirements and circumstances. Their past contributions to the growth of the banana industry are quickly forgotten.

The SVBGA believes that an industry based on a smaller number of growers is an essential element in restructuring the industry to be on a more internationally competitive footing. Those most likely to remain in the industry are those growers with at least three to five acres or more in bananas. While such an area may appear small, the majority of banana growers have cultivated fewer acres in the past. Moreover, irrigation, which is being introduced as a major solution for increasing productivity per acre, cannot be applied in the rugged hills where many peasants have their holdings. Such changes are unfortunate, because it has been the ability of so many small-scale growers to participate in the industry that has helped spread the benefits of banana production so widely throughout the island's population. The exodus of farmers from the industry will mean increased unemployment, poverty, illegal drug cultivation, crime, and outmigration (Grossman 1999; Clissold 2001). Such outcomes are intensified by the limited potential for economic diversification on the island.

A marked reduction in the number of peasants involved in the industry is already occurring. From approximately 25,000 banana growers in the Windwards in 1992 (just before the creation of the Single European Market in bananas), the number fell to approximately 9,400 in 2001. Similarly, on St. Vincent from 1992 to 1999, the number of active growers dropped from more than 7,800 to 3,761 (table 1; SVBGA 2000). In particular, older female small-scale growers, who suffer the most from household labor shortages, were most likely to leave the industry. The downturn in banana prices and the increasing labor intensity of banana production were primarily responsible for these declines. Farmers' loss of confidence in the industry because of adverse WTO rulings and frequent drought during the 1990s also contributed to these declines. And other changes unfavorable to peasants are evident as well; for example, the association's long-standing policy of interest-free credit disappeared in 1999—it now charges 5 percent interest on outstanding loan balances (SVBGA 2000, 31).

The key to an analysis of the SVBGA is understanding its attempts to balance its dual roles as the central buyer / coordinator in a contract-farming enterprise and as an institution concerned with development. The policies of the SVBGA have been critical in supporting the peasantry through the turbulent, dynamic history of the Windwards banana industry. Its lack of rigid control over the labor process reflected, in part, the fact that profit maximization was never part of its central mission. But the pressures of restructuring that are so pervasive in the global economy are introducing a new phase in the relationship between the SVBGA and the peasantry. The association's focus on efficiency and restructuring will mean that the development dimension of the SVBGA, which has been so critical for improving the living conditions of thousands of peasants on the island over the last fifty years, will decline in relative importance— with unfortunate consequences for the island's small-scale producers.

NOTES

1. This research was supported by grants from the National Science Foundation, Geography and Regional Science and the National Geographic Society.
2. This chapter is based on long-term research on the industry. I conducted fieldwork on St. Vincent from August 1988 to August 1989. I subsequently made brief visits to St. Vincent and St. Lucia in 1990, 1991, 1992, 1994, and 1995 and conducted additional research at archives on Barbados and the United Kingdom in 1990. Thus, the discussion of the SVBGA in this paper refers primarily to patterns during this period. However, occasional reference is also made to more recent events.
3. Whether one considers bananas "processed" depends on whether artificial ripening of bananas is viewed as an example of processing.
4. Ellis (1975, 47) described the differences between Latin American producers and those in the Windwards as they existed in 1971: yields per acre in Latin America were four to six times higher, while Windwards labor costs were 50 percent higher. A recent comparative assessment (SVBGA 1998, 6–7) revealed FOB costs of production per metric ton of U.S.$523 in the Windward Islands and U.S.$303 in Latin America.
5. To further encourage developments in the industry and deal more effectively with Geest, the four

Windwards banana growers' associations in 1958 formed an umbrella organization headquartered in St. Lucia, the Windward Islands Banana Growers' Association, commonly known as WINBAN.

6. Bananas do not have a real stem, and thus it is called a "pseudostem."

7. By government statute, it was dissolved in 1948 because the export industry had long been inactive by then.

8. In 1997 the SVBGA reduced the number of directors to nine in response to the Banana Industry Amendment Act of 1996 (SVBGA 1998, 22), with growers electing five, still a majority (Patsy Lewis 1998). Also, the minimum production requirement for eligibility for election to the board of directors was increased to ten tons per year (ibid.).

9. This figure has to be accepted as an approximation because of multiple registrations.

10. The cess varied from EC$0.06 to EC$0.08 per pound of bananas sold over the period 1988 to 1995. Since 1976, the value of the Eastern Caribbean dollar has been tied to the United States dollar at EC$2.70 = U.S.$1.00.

ALLEN WELLS

Conclusions: Dialectical Bananas

Latin America's integration into the European and North American economies has been a recurring theme in the historical literature. Typically, scholarly studies have gauged the evolution of a nation's economy, a particular region's economic development, or the growth and / or decline of a specific sector of a national economy. Recently, however, historians have found that the cross-cultural study of commodities has helped them test—in ways that more traditional approaches elide—fundamental assumptions about Latin America's ties to Europe and the United States (Roseberry, Gudmundson, and Kutschbach et al. 1995; Topik and Wells 1998; Mintz 1985). Commodities were distinctive in respect to their capital, labor, and technology requirements, and that had significant implications for an export sector's vulnerability to price fluctuations, whether ownership would be foreign-owned or domestic, if ownership was highly concentrated or diffuse, and whether the product's cultivation and processing was labor-intensive or not. And, as studies like this one signal, each commodity charted a distinctive path in different settings.

At first glance, bananas appear to fit the classic pattern of food staples that first found their way from tropical plantations to European and North American dining rooms during the late-nineteenth- and early-twentieth-century export boom. High in carbohydrates, vitamins, and calories, the inexpensive banana, along with sugar, coffee, and cacao, helped satiate the industrial world's appetite and thirst for exotic foods. Like its sweet and stimulating counterparts, this seasonless fresh fruit initially sparked vigorous competition among an array of foreign competitors who marshaled their assets and invested considerable capital, technology, and know-how in the region to first obtain and then protect market share. These ambitious foreign entrepreneurs built ports, roads, and railways to get their products to market, cleared wide swaths of virgin lands in frontier regions, helped transform land and labor into monetized commodities subject to market whims, collaborated with area politicians to thwart competition and labor unrest and to secure generous concessions, relied on their home government's political muscle to persuade recalcitrant nation-states that cooperation was in their enlightened self-interest, and procured low-wage labor abroad and locally to cultivate their product.

This new monocultural regimen required significant dollops of capitalization—well beyond the means of local elites and national governments. Since banana plantations generally were located so distant from major population centers, foreign companies (such as foreign mining interests operating in remote mountainous locales in the Andes and in north central Mexico) opted to establish enclaves, or "company towns," that not only provided essential goods and services for workers but insulated company managers from the rank and file by creating what amounted to foreign islands in the tropics.

In fact, bananas and other primary products were and are so intimately associated with capitalism's growth over the last century that they sometimes appear to be integral components of "a vast impersonal machine, governed by the large scale movements of prices, complex institutional interests and a totally demystified bureaucratic and self-regulating character" (Appadurai 1986, 48). But as cultural anthropologist Arjun Appadurai notes, and as the essays herein make clear, this impersonal machine belies "complex interactions between local, politically mediated, systems of demand" (ibid.). This volume's comparative approach complicates the generally accepted understanding of the role that foreign markets, capital, the environment, social relations, culture, and politics played in bringing about the region's integration into the global economy.

Change—in some cases, radical change—has been the rule at each stage of the banana's commodity chain over the last century. Workers, managers, and marketers have had to adapt repeatedly just to survive in this highly competitive industry. It should be emphasized that such thrust and parry has not been something imposed from without. Rather, the essays in this volume document a constantly shifting, dialectical relationship at work between producers, marketers, and consumers; changes wrought by plant disease or labor unrest between companies and their labor forces, for instance, not only shaped how multinationals operated but how producers and consumers responded. Similarly, consumer preferences and jobbers' expectations in metropolitan centers had significant consequences for workers and company managers in the tropics.

The regional and national variations noted throughout the volume are as revealing as the generalizations. Yes, the cultivation, marketing, and consumption of bananas had indelible consequences for property ownership, labor regimes, and the distribution of wealth throughout Latin America and the Caribbean, but it did not do so in isolation. Banana enclaves were rarely, as depicted in historical texts and in *One Hundred Years of Solitude*, a world apart; each of these regions was linked in important ways to a budding nation-state, just as it was tied to the global marketplace (LeGrand 1998). These essays also help track how gender roles were redefined, ethnicities were mixed and recast, and culture was transformed throughout the region over the course of the twentieth century.

A number of the essays challenge assumptions about the hegemonic character of El Pulpo in Central and South America. United Fruit's story, for instance, is really a tale of two discrete half-centuries. In its halcyon first decades, the company reduced uncertainties by controlling all stages of the production process from plantation to market, acquiring vast amounts of land throughout the tropics. It was relentless in driving out competition and crushing unrest. United Fruit's ability to spread itself out throughout the region meant that it could, with some impunity, threaten to pull out and leave a country—as it did in Belize—should national politicians even consider withholding concessions or subsidies.

In other words, United Fruit acted the way that many large American corporations did during the Gilded Age. Such oligopolistic "first-movers" invested in plants large enough to capture economies of scale and scope, while embracing new technologies to increase throughput. As a result, they were well ahead of the learning curve in comparison to their nearest competitors. According to business historian Alfred Chandler, "Such advantages made it easy for first movers to nip challengers in the bud, to stop their growth before they acquired the facilities and developed the skills needed to become strong competitors. And such advantages could be and often were used ruthlessly" (1990 34–35). Although economic historians disagree on why these combinations occurred and what their relative impact was at home and abroad, they generally concur that they set the stage for a "managerial revolution" that followed—a revolution that effectively altered the way that business was conducted throughout the world. Integrating "backward," these first movers secured access to raw materials; linking "forward," they created a modern, responsive sales organization to market their goods and services efficiently.

If United Fruit's methods are familiar, what is surprising is how El Pulpo was placed increasingly on the defensive after World War II by a combination of debilitating plant pathogens that ravaged its product and reluctantly forced it to grow new species of Cavendish bananas; feisty labor unions that resisted corporate culture; neighboring peasants who refused to relinquish claims to their lands or who squatted on United's properties; opportunistic politicians stricken with pangs of populist conscience who, when it suited them, sided with workers and peasants; anxious Wall Street investors whose dampened expectations reined in company actions; and the North American antitrust courts that forced the Octopus to divest itself of a considerable portion of its Central American holdings, thereby giving competitors a new lease on life.

To be sure, the company, recalling earlier heady days, did have its moments of "success" after World War II. In Guatemala's "Macondo," United Fruit collaborated with Arévalo to stifle union dissent and then played a still-murky role in the 1954 ouster of Arbenz and the subsequent rollback of his agrarian reform. But the sum total of all of these countervailing forces pressured United Fruit to pursue a policy after World War II that Bucheli has aptly termed "vertical disintegration." Seeking to deflect risks to producers, United Fruit inked future agreements with contract farmers, gradually divested itself of its properties, and focused its efforts on marketing and distribution.

Although it was a shadow of its former, haughty self in Latin America and the Caribbean, El Pulpo's extensive reconfiguration and retooling did enable the company to maintain its preeminent position within the industry. United's (and its corporate progeny's) tale of two half-centuries demonstrates the extent to which the industry had to reinvent itself to increase productivity and maintain profitability. Each change precipitated subsequent responses at each phase of the commodity chain. Tracking these changes and adaptations reveals a great deal about the industry's contingent character and, in the process, dispels facile generalizations about bananas. It also illustrates the significant role that commodities can and do play in linking Latin America and the Caribbean to those who buy its products. What is perhaps most surprising about the banana "case," however, is the crucial role that the environment has played in shaping the industry's destiny.

IT'S NOT NICE TO FOOL MOTHER NATURE

The banana industry's "Fordist" factories in the field during its first half-century featured a genetically uniform crop. Unfortunately, the Gros Michel variety, which was increasingly popular in U.S. and European markets, had an Achilles' heel; even though United Fruit's and Standard Fruit's company managers incorporated the latest scientific advances by agronomists and technicians, the Gros Michel was susceptible to fungal infections. As additional lands were cleared for plantation monoculture, Mother Nature struck back with a vengeance, forcing United Fruit and the industry as a whole to repudiate earlier strategies and fundamentally change the way it did business.

Interestingly, a heated debate exists in the scholarly literature about the role that the Panama (*Fusarium oxysporum*) and Sigatoka (*Cercospora musae*) diseases—both accidentally imported from Asia—played in reshaping the industry. A number of the Octopus's critics believe that the company could have responded more aggressively (if it had been so inclined) to the fungal epidemics that infiltrated the plant's roots and clogged its tissues. Critics contend that United Fruit elected not to, because the disease served as a convenient pretext vis-à-vis competition and labor. More recent research, however, sustains the view that United Fruit responded aggressively, investing large sums into scientific research to curb the contagion's spread, but their range of responses fell short (Marquardt 2001).

The banana industry was not alone in fighting fungal epidemics. In fact, disease would prove as destructive to Brazilian rubber and Ecuadorian cacao as it did to Central American bananas. Unlike bananas, neither rubber nor cacao would recover from the fungi and the damage done, because neither had an industry giant able and willing to invest millions to buy up new lands and conduct research and development to contain the plague. In Ecuador two fungi struck the cacao industry in quick succession in the late 1910s and early 1920s. First,

Monilophthora roreri or *Monilia* weakened the industry and then *Crinipellis perniciosa* (locally known as Witch's Broom) delivered the coup de grâce to Ecuador's profitable cacao sector in the 1920s. Planters simply lacked the resources to invest in fungicides to treat the airborne plague. They had little choice but to abandon cacao, let go more than 25,000 workers, and shift production to new crops. A similar fate befell Costa Rican and Brazilian (Bahian) cacao in decades to come (McCook 2001).

The situation in the Brazilian rubber industry was a bit more complicated, but fungus would play its part in hampering production and discouraging investment. The Amazonian rubber industry faced stiff competition from Asian producers thanks to the British Royal Botanic Gardens at Kew. British scientists had obtained viable seeds from Brazilian rubber trees and had had them transplanted in their Southeast Asian colonies of Ceylon and Malaya. As a result, Brazil ceded its monopoly position in the rubber market, and, in relatively short order, Asian producers took advantage of economies of scale and low labor costs to drive Brazilian producers to the wall. But, as historian Warren Dean (1987) asserts, leaf blight (*Mycrocyclus ulei*) also contributed to the rubber industry's demise after World War I. It is revealing that the blight did not appear in the Amazon until Brazilian capitalists had begun to implement modern plantation production schemes. A recent study by economic historians Zephyr Frank and Aldo Musacchio (2001) have tempered Dean's findings. They argue that leaf blight alone is insufficient to understand why Brazil lost its comparative advantage in rubber production, but that the fungus discouraged producers from meeting the Asian challenge.

Banana technicians could have learned a great deal from Brazilian rubber's or Ecuadorian cacao's encounters with fungus. If monoculture meant gains in productivity, it came at the cost of ecological vulnerability. As historian Stuart McCook documents in *States of Nature: Science, Agriculture, and the Environment in the Spanish Caribbean* (2002), it was not until the late-nineteenth- and early-twentieth-century export boom triggered major changes in farming practices that plant pathogens assumed plaguelike proportions in Latin America and the Caribbean. As monoculture increasingly became the order of the day, tropical forest frontiers were cleared by planters and treated as a nonrenewable resource. In vintage slash-and-burn style, it became more "rational" for producers to burn, clear, and cultivate a tract of land and then move on to a virgin site than to invest in and maintain existing plots. The result was a depletion of biological diversity, a simplification of the region's topography that aided the fungi's diffusion, and a corresponding increase in the density of hosts for the virulent spores — in short, conditions tailor-made for an increase in the number of pathogens on the new plantations (McCook 2002). It is instructive that the Caribbean banana-industry model — smaller farms with banana crops interspersed with plantings of other crops — has proved much more resistant to disease.

Historian Steve Marquardt (2001) argues that banana fungal epidemics simply provoked an acceleration of the industry's usual and customary practices. As the disease spread, the life expectancy of plantations dropped from fifteen to less than five years, with some areas producing fruit for two years or less. Marquardt contends, "The gradual nature of this plantation life-cycle contraction may account for the company's rather slow response to the epidemic" (2001, 60). In an effort to outrun the pathogen's grasp, United Fruit turned to a slash-and-burn strategy that focused on obtaining as much land as possible, cultivating product until the telltale signs of the Panama Disease showed itself on their estates, and then moving onto to its newly acquired properties. Needless to say, this had important consequences for the industry.

It is ironic that United Fruit's scientists early on had concluded that new disease-resistant varieties of bananas offered the best solution to the problem. As early as 1922 its scientists had tested and found that the two Giant Cavendish varieties that eventually would dominate the industry after 1960 were resistant to fungus. But the company, discouraged by the fact that the experimental varieties bruised easily and that they had to be shipped and marketed in expensive boxes, bet the plantation on the disease-riddled Gros Michel varieties. Soluri herein explains that marketers, who had spent decades working assiduously to build an industry from the ground up, were skittish about disrupting consumption patterns in North America and Europe. There was, after all, a lot at stake. By the mid-1950s, the banana was the world's fourth-largest fruit crop, representing 40 percent of fruit sales internationally (Tucker 2000, 121).

Instead, the company convinced itself that it could hold the disease in check through better soil-management practices and cultivation techniques. They even had some successes. A copper sulfate fungicide, although expensive, did arrest Sigatoka in flat, open areas where low-volume aerial spraying was cost-effective; it was to prove less successful on more hilly properties in Ecuador. Placing polyethylene bags on the bunches prior to ripening controlled parasites. Yet, despite extensive irrigation, the wholesale application of chemical fungicides and fertilizers, and futile attempts to drown the spores in man-made lakes, *Fusarium* wilt would not cease and desist (Marquardt 2001). Even relocating a large percentage of its operations to the Pacific Coast did not help El Pulpo to stop the pathogen's spread. The banana industry finally conceded and switched to the disease-resistant Cavendish varieties — although the reprieve may, indeed, prove short-lived. A new *Fusarium* mutation has been attacking Cavendish fruit outside of Latin America over the last decade (Tucker 2000).

Environmental historians concur that the company's multiple strategies to fight, first, fungal diseases and, later, plagues of nematodes proved to be an ecological catastrophe of the highest magnitude for the Central American landscape. Wherever they went, banana companies poisoned water systems and reduced avian habitat. Aerial spraying to control Sigatoka affected properties at some distance from the targeted zones. Costa Rica, justifiably proud of its extensive national-parks system and its impressive record of environmental education, is a world leader in the use of pesticides, thanks, in large part, to banana monoculture.

The banana industry was not alone in its determination to fight the spread of pathogens through the application of modern scientific research. The extensive use of pesticides was part of the post–World War II "green revolution" throughout Latin America, which featured the massive application of chemical fertilizers and the introduction of new hybrid crop varieties. True to form, banana lands were not alone in reaping the deleterious ecological consequences of these new strategies. The countless consumption of acres of tropical forest, the contamination of soil and water, salinization and soil erosion, affected many Latin American exports.

If the environment has been an unfortunate casualty of the banana industry's growth, the extensive use of pesticides and fungicides has also come at a high price for its workforce. Unhealthy working conditions have just been one of the significant side effects, however. Bananas, more than many export staples, have played a pivotal role in creating a persistently peripatetic workforce, and that mobility has proved disruptive and costly for them.

ON THE MOVE

A number of forces conspired to ensure that banana workers stayed on the move during the first half of the twentieth century. Banana lands were, for the most part, located in underpopulated regions throughout the tropics, generally perceived to be unhealthy and unattractive for settlement by highlanders. That meant that workers had to be lured from the highlands by both the carrot and the stick or imported from abroad to meet the new labor demands. All had to adapt to their new surroundings. As aggrandizing companies sought out new lands for cultivation, and as the Panama Disease spread, workers — those who did not just lose their jobs — were uprooted and "enticed" to migrate to new banana zones. Indicative of such enforced mobility was the fact that United Fruit abandoned more than 100,000 acres in Central America alone during the first half of the century.

Labor migration was not unheard of in other tropical pursuits. West Indian and Chinese contract labor had been a staple of the Cuban sugar industry, for instance. But what set the banana industry apart from other pursuits where labor was concerned were its persistent impermanence and the challenges that this unstable regime posed for workers.

As the Honduran case shows, the importation of large numbers of West Indians to work in Central America and on South America's north coast was cause for concern for national elites. Even though banana workers often were located in remote areas, an intolerant combination of xenophobia and racism led to restrictive immigration laws and other discriminatory practices. Interestingly, Honduran elites viewed the native Garifuna as more of a threat than West Indian blacks, indicating that elite fears about miscegenation were at the root of the problem.

Promoting mestizaje and whitening the race was a recurrent theme in the 1920s and 1930s throughout the Caribbean and Central America and was not confined to the banana industry. In the Dominican Republic, for instance, the dictator Rafael Trujillo became so obsessed with stemming the tide of Haitian (that is, black) migration into his country that he not only ordered his army to massacre more than 10,000 Haitians during a ten-day rampage in October 1937. He also offered to admit up to 100,000 European Jews fleeing Nazi persecution in the hopes that they would intermarry with Dominicans and thereby whiten the race (Vega 1988; Vega 1995; Wells 2001).

To attract sufficient manpower, to overcome barriers created by racist politicians, and to help compensate for the constant uprooting characteristic of the industry during the century's first decades, the banana companies had to offer a relatively attractive benefits package. As Striffler herein notes, they were offered up with characteristic benevolent paternalism. The banana companies provided housing, schools, recreation facilities, and access to company stores. They also invested considerably in sanitation and public health and, to their credit, made significant strides in eradicating tropical diseases like yellow fever and malaria.

Yet if it was true that banana workers were often better paid and received benefits superior to those received by their counterparts elsewhere, those benefits came at some cost to workers. Like enclaves elsewhere, workers became "company men," with all the baggage and mechanisms of social control that that epithet carried. Moreover, being a company man did not imply job security, nor did it ensure workers' welfare. Prolonged exposure to nematicides and other forms of chemical contamination the banana companies thought essential to the care, cultivation, and marketing of a blemish-free fruit eventually caused the sterility of thousands of Central American banana workers.

The plantation workforce's constant movement and instability also meant that different ethnicities were thrown together on estates, sometimes sparking conflict. Although always a concern to company managers, they learned that such heterogeneity helped hinder worker solidarity. It is often said that plantation workers were more docile and less willing to resist management than independent peasantries, as is clear in Striffler's Ecuadorian case study. But that does not mean that resident banana workers were not active agents in shaping the terms of their own oppression. West Indian banana workers, Cuban sugar slaves, or Yucatecan henequen peons forged countervailing cultures that could deal blows, materially and symbolically, against the masters' exactions. Such quieter or "everyday forms of resistance," as James Scott (1985) terms them, might include small, self-serving acts of noncompliance, foot-dragging, shirking, and flight; or more aggressive clandestine acts of theft, arson, and sabotage (Scott 1990). Moreover, company managers and large landowners had little cause to publicize these moments of insubordination, for to do so would be to acknowledge unpopular policies and practices. Day-to-day resistance is little noticed in the official records of the state, and it is, not surprisingly, largely conspicuous by its absence in this volume. Still, such modes of resistance occurred wherever asymmetrical power relationships were the norm, and there is no reason to doubt that they were part of the fabric of everyday life on banana estates (Wells and Joseph 1996, esp. chap. 6).

These ethnic and linguistic strangers who worked on banana estates, however, were at a disadvantage when it came to organizing collective resistance. Unlike Yucatán's Maya resident peons, for example, who always made up the vast majority of the fiber estate's labor force and who possessed a distinctive culture and language that fostered community cohesiveness and solidarity, banana workers often had little choice but to rely on outsiders to organize resistance against foreign companies. Forster's and Striffler's essays herein demonstrate the problems posed for the plantation workforce when the company perceived that outside agitators provoked unrest.

Given their relative isolation, banana workers during the export economy's first half-century often were hamstrung by attenuated social and cultural ties with the rest of society. They instead had to build informal social networks among themselves—no easy task given the workforce's heterogeneous character. Workers perceived foreign ownership as their enemy and had ample reason to suspect that the state and the military served the banana companies' interests and not their own.

What motivates workers is not just grievances and perceived injustice but the "tactical mobility" that facilitates their redress. That mobility makes itself manifest when elites are divided, when the international context is altered, or when national policies have changed in their favor (Aya 1984). Leftist ideologies, a presence in the region since the turn of the twentieth century, lambasted imperialism, corporate greed, and national oligarchies with something akin to missionary fervor. Their message, with some exceptions, was relatively muted until the 1930s. But the Great Depression, so devastating economically for all of the exports trade, proved to be fertile ground for labor organizing throughout the region. As conditions worsened, banana workers found an unlikely ally in the state, which theretofore had made common cause with the banana companies. After 1930, populist politicians, seeking multiclass coalitions, at times sided with independent labor unions. This gave some banana workers the tactical mobility to demand better working conditions and to mount impressive work stoppages against their employers.

Although these efforts did not always yield success, because the state's actions did not always match its rhetoric, and in some notable cases, as in Guatemala and Colombia, political authorities actually turned against the workers, there were hard-won gains. More significantly, a prideful legacy of resistance against perceived injustice was instilled among banana workers. In Colombia the government's nefarious role in the 1928 Santa Marta banana massacre prompted criticism by the state's political opponents. A young liberal politician, Jorge Eliécer Gaitán, galvanized workers well beyond the confines of the banana enclave. In 1929 historian Charles Bergquist recounts, Gaitán, whose political assassination two decades later triggered the urban riot called the Bogotazo, came before the Colombian Congress carrying a small skull. He claimed it was the remains of a child who had been murdered by Colombian soldiers on United Fruit's Santa Marta banana plantations during the massacre (Bergquist 1986, 346). The Colombian case is particularly instructive, because even though the state came to United Fruit's defense by violently crushing the strike, El Pulpo decided to curtail its Colombian operations and focus efforts elsewhere. Sometimes success came at a high price.

As banana companies divested themselves of the means of production and switched to contract farming, workers had to be more creative about making their demands known. Slocum's essay on competing discourses uttered by workers, politicians, and the media during the 1990s banana wars in St. Lucia is illustrative of how workers were at once empowered and limited by the international context. Banana workers, under pressure from political officials and the state-run banana growers association to improve their productivity and efficiency, responded by casting the state as the problem. Interestingly, by withholding criticism of the distributors and marketers of their product and refusing to protest the European Union's controversial decision to terminate the preferential system that had been in place since the 1950s, the Banana Salvation Committee accepted at face value globalization's "rules of the game." If earlier generations of workers saw multinationals as their oppressors, contemporary workers trained their sights on state-run banana growers' associations and government officials. Their strategy suggests that workers increasingly believe that their best chance for success lies at the local and national levels and that they are powerless to contest an international system that appears more powerful and monolithic than it has in the past.

How much of this is a political ploy by the workers and how much is meant as a critique of the state's conflictive and historically compromised role in the banana industry is difficult to assess. But since states have increasingly come to play the role of mediator between international capital and local labor, the way in which they respond is monitored carefully by suspicious contract growers who have come to expect the worst.

THE STATE'S SHIFTING ASPIRATIONS

The banana companies did not impose themselves on reticent Central and South American states. On the contrary, as this collection makes evident, they were welcomed, even feted. This was as true in independent Latin American nations, like Honduras or Panama, as it was in British colonial possessions like Belize, as Moberg indicates herein. To be sure, national politicians and colonial administrators wanted a piece of the action, imposing duties on banana exports to generate revenues. In return, the banana companies received generous land grants or leases as well as concessions to build railroads and other public works projects the state thought necessary for economic development. Central American states and British colonial officers, who shared an unshakable belief in modernity's benefits, insisted that the new infrastructure not only serve the interests of the fruit companies but that it connect the export sector to other areas of the nation. In this manner, the railways, roads, and ports came to benefit national elite commercial and agricultural interests. Successive Republican and Democratic administrations in Washington encouraged such cooperation because it curbed political and social unrest and promoted stronger nation-states thought more "user-friendly" to North American capital. And that suited American strategic interests in the region.

Even regarding this early expansionist phase, it is easy to overstate the importance of the symbiotic relationship carved out between Central American and Caribbean nation-states and the banana companies. States had been weak and fragmented before bananas, since almost all had suffered serious civil wars and revolts led by competing elites throughout the nineteenth century. There is little doubt, however, that the export boom and state formation reinforced each other. States gained control over the new boom-generated resources, especially foreign loans and taxes on international trade. But these nations, as small and as weak as they were, were not monolithic. As the boom intensified, local elites scrambled to produce commodities for the world market. In a number of the so-called banana republics, coffee was, if not king, a force to be reckoned with in the corridors of state power. Sugar, cacao, and mineral interests raised their voices as well (Topik and Wells 1998, 221–26)

During the Depression, the interests of cash-strapped national governments, who were anxious to obtain larger revenues and a greater degree of regulatory control over the banana sector, dovetailed with those of the workers, who wanted higher pay and better working conditions. In addition, the across-the-board collapse of commodity prices meant that Latin American economies turned inward, promoting import-substitution industrialization. As a result, states became more assertive in their negotiations with banana companies and more solicitous of organized labor. Over the course of the next two decades, United Fruit and its competitors found that they could no longer operate with impunity. Since the fruit companies were such inviting targets for nationalistic politicians and because corporate investors expressed growing concern about conditions on the ground, banana companies decided to gradually divest themselves of their properties and work through local subsidiaries and quasi-independent growers.

But the banana sector remained under foreign control and that meant there were limits to what the state could or would do to defend its national interests. Even in Ecuador, where nationalist politicians took an aggressive stand against the banana companies, the workers had little to show for all of the state's reforms and posturing. More often than not, it was difficult to predict exactly just what would transpire next. Guatemala illustrated the difficulties that workers and management faced in gauging just how the state would act at any given moment. First, Ubico gave away the store to United Fruit, then Arévalo behaved erratically when, after initially siding with the workers, he called out the military to crush the union. Arévalo's successor, Arbenz, held out the hope of meaningful reform only to have his and the banana workers' expectations crushed bitterly by the 1954 coup. A succession of right-wing military dictatorships ensued bringing the nation's relationship with the banana companies and its workforce full circle. In 1955, despite all the political upheaval and the unpredictable oscillations in state policy, United Fruit still planted more than half of the nation's banana lands and exported three-quarters of its bananas (Tucker 2000, 167).

Unlike in Brazil or Colombia, where states took nationalistic stands against foreign coffee merchants, there would be no valorization campaigns in Central or South American banana-growing states. Nor would there be any thought of nationalizing banana interests, as in Mexico and Venezuela, where two of the world's largest petroleum producers were sent packing with little compensation. Oil, unlike bananas, was an important symbol of national progress, since it was both necessary for national defense and an internal consumption item. Petroleum occupied a much larger position in the national imagination because of its links to industrialization and its domestic applications. As Soluri wryly notes, bananas never carried that cachet. It is revealing that during the 1970s, Central American and South American banana-growing countries attempted to form an OPEC-like cartel to force banana companies to pay a one-dollar tax on every forty-pound crate of bananas. The big three companies refused to pay the tax; the banana states tried to reduce their demands, but when the companies dug in their heels, the cartel collapsed (ibid., 174).

The preferential treatment afforded Caribbean banana growers by their mother countries offers a quite different model of state engagement with the banana industry. Colonial administrators early on resisted the Octopus—and in this they were initially aided by the absence of cost-effective refrigerated shipping. Instead, they relied on the same time-tested model that had kept the beet-sugar industry afloat since the last decades of the nineteenth century when European states cobbled together an intricate protectionist system composed of subsidies and direct aid (the so-called sugar bounties). That had brought beet-sugar prices below any possible competition from rival cane sugar, preserving the European market for colonial exports (Moreno Fraginals 1986, 194; Albert and Graves 1984).

In similar fashion, British colonial authorities built tariff walls around British colonies' bananas, then contracted the business to European-based multinationals. These companies used the considerable leverage the monopoly afforded to dictate everything from prices to packaging. Since small-scale contract farming is the norm in the Caribbean, the state, which until recently had propped up prices, has sought to mediate the seemingly endless disputes between multinationals and producers. State-sponsored growers associations, like the one Grossman herein describes for St. Vincent, appear to have the producers' interests at heart. Grossman praises the St. Vincent Banana Growers' Association for granting low-cost loans and for introducing new technologies and rehabilitation schemes designed to improve productivity. Although farmers chafe at the BGA's bureaucratic character—a universal lament of farmers everywhere—there is little doubt in Grossman's mind that smallholders could not have survived the twists and turns of the market of the last few decades without government assistance.

Although the Windward Islands' governments have been consistently more helpful to their laborers than their Central and South American counterparts, they have had little success in altering market share or the terms of trade for their growers. Although much has changed in the banana industry over the course of the last century, the market's structure and its concentrated character have, if anything, solidified.

AN IMPREGNABLE MARKET

The banana's transition from a luxury good sold to upscale hotels to an everyday staple in American and European diets is a familiar pattern to those who study commodities. By World War I, a scant thirty years after its introduction to the United States and a mere fifteen years after importers had to sell the fruit with instructions on how to peel it, the banana became the first tropical fruit to become a staple in North American diets. Although supplies were disrupted by both World Wars and the Depression, American demand continued to skyrocket until the 1950s (Bucheli 2001).

The fruit's perishable quality meant that production, transportation, and distribution had to be coordinated, lest profits vanish. Perishability coupled with its seasonless character, sizable start-up costs, and the propensity of American companies to form powerful economic combinations during the Gilded Age all contributed to the industry's consolidation in the hands of a few megacompanies.

Given higher productivity, lower prices, and increasing imports after World

War II, it might be logical to assume that Americans and Europeans consumed more rather than fewer bananas. But North American and European per capita consumption of bananas actually tumbled after World War II. A shift in consumption patterns was the culprit, as bananas along with other fresh fruit had to cope with a new, formidable rival—processed foods. New technologies permitted processed fruit to reach 40 percent of the U.S. market by the early 1960s. This change in consumer preference meant that banana companies had to scramble to protect their declining markets. Bucheli has found that per capita consumption of processed baby food, for example, grew from 21 million pounds to one billion pounds in the twenty-two-year period from 1934 to 1956 (Bucheli 2001).

Change and adaptation was again the rule in the industry. Knowing a growing market when they saw one, banana companies diversified operations and expanded into the processed-food industry. United Fruits, for instance, moved into the lucrative food-processing sector when it merged with meat packer AMK-John Morrell to create United Brands in 1970.

Even though the former banana companies now find themselves as cogs in larger machines, two global commodity networks continue to dominate the banana sector—the dollar market that serves the United States and, until recently, a protected European market that gives preferential access to former colonies of European mother countries. The banana market is not really segmented the way that markets for other commodities are. While North Americans receive larger (e.g., more expensive) fruit than Europeans, except for a modest number of specialty food stores or in areas where large Latino populations reside, North Americans and Europeans think of the Cavendish varieties as "the banana." The recent growth of small niches for fair trade and organic bananas notwithstanding, most consumers do not realize that they are missing out on many delicious kinds of bananas.

These two commodity chains have not been entirely discrete, with the larger, well-capitalized dollar bananas making recent inroads into the European market. But by and large, the paths have remained remarkably consistent over the last hundred years. With some exceptions, Americans still receive the bulk of their daily supply of bananas from Central and South America, while Europeans have more options, but their principal supplier remains the Caribbean islands (Gereffi and Korzeniewicz 1994).

This is in stark contrast to coffee, for instance; there has been an extraordinary diversity in the ways the coffee sector has been organized over time. The coffee market has been marked by radical disjunctures and has become increasingly segmented over time. While most think of coffee as a necessity, more and more of us are willing to pay the kind of prices that suggest that coffee is akin a luxury good. At different moments in history, control of the coffee market has been in the hands of producers, exporters, importers, roasters, and governments. Not until the last half of the twentieth century did coffee come to be dominated by the model familiar to the banana industry—a few vertically integrated multinational firms (Topik and Kutschbach 2001). The sugar industry's consolidation, on the other hand, more closely resembles the banana market's vertical and horizontal consolidation in processing and marketing (Eichner 1969; Mintz 1985).

Despite sweeping changes in virtually all facets of production, infrastructure, marketing, and distribution, at the dawn of a new century the banana industry continues to be dominated by descendants of the "first movers." The big three companies not only control 66 percent of the market but are fighting tooth and nail—and with some success, thanks to friends in high places in Washington and to the recent actions of the WTO—to build on the one-third share of the lucrative European market that they currently hold.

Free-market rhetoric notwithstanding, bananas are, to paraphrase Appadurai, a politically mediated commodity, if there ever was one. Although the banana companies no longer cultivate product themselves, their control over all aspects of the process, including prices, is so great, that banana workers, independent contractors, and governments were and are, for all intents and purposes, powerless to object. Not surprisingly, an ever-greater share of the product's value is added on in consuming countries by an ever-smaller number of companies. Production for export created few backward linkages for the host countries that aided economic integration for the host countries. Simply put, bananas have not acted as a growth multiplier throughout the circum Caribbean (Pérez Brignoli 1989, 104).

The recent banana wars recall past debates about the costs and benefits of export-led growth, or, as it is now called, "globalization." What is qualitatively different from earlier export booms that integrated Latin America to North

America and Europe is that today capitalist ideology is hegemonic in ways that it would have been impossible to imagine in the past. For their part, many Latin Americans are still ambivalent about the purported benefits of foreign investment and view terms like "free trade" and "laissez-faire" with a healthy dose of suspicion whenever invoked by erstwhile proponents of neoliberal orthodoxy.

Taken together, this volume's essays not only illustrate the hazards of making generalizations about the contested terrain of commodities, but they demonstrate the uncanny ability of companies, states, and workers to change and adapt dialectically to the sweeping changes the industry has undergone over the course of the last century. Responding in turn to nature, technologies, market forces, and each other, producers, marketers, and political authorities have carved out a durable, if inequitable, commodity network for a perishable product that has found an enduring place at our dining-room tables. If the market's structure remains unassailable, how all those connected to the banana trade will respond and react to its vicissitudes will continue to be an open question.

BIBLIOGRAPHY

ARCHIVAL SOURCES

Archivo General de Centroamérica (AGCA), Guatemala
   Inspección General de Trabajo–Correspondencia (IGT-C).
   Hermeroteca, Hojas Sueltas (Herm/HS), bundled by year.

Archivo Historico (AH), Secretaria de Relaciones Exteriores (SRE), Mexico

Archivo Nacional, Tegucigalpa, Honduras

British Public Records Office (BPRO), Kew
   CO 123 233. Confidential dispatch from Governor Wilson to the secretary of state for the colonies, London. 3 August.
   CO 123 240. 1902a. Dispatch from Governor Wilson to Colonial Office, London. 13 February.
   ———. 1902b. Letter from Henry Keith to Governor Wilson, transmitted in dispatch to Colonial Office. 13 February.
   ———. 1902c. Letter from Fairweather, Cuthbert, and Woods, unofficial members of the legislative council, to Colonial Office. 6 March.
   ———. n.d. Colonial Office minute paper commenting on letter from Fairweather, Cuthbert, and Woods.
   CO 123 255. 1907. Confidential dispatch from Governor Swayne to secretary of state for the colonies. 19 April.
   CO 123 261. 1909. Dispatch from Governor Swayne to Colonial Office accompanying draft agreement with United Fruit Company for CO approval. February 11.
   CO 123 267. Report of the Committee on Landing Rights for Submarine Cables on the application by United Fruit Company for permission to establish a wireless telegraph station in British Honduras. Marked confidential. 10 December.
   CO 123 268. 1911a. Letter from C. H. Ellis to Governor Swayne, dated 28 February, transmitted with Swayne's dispatch to Colonial Office. 29 May.
   ———. 1911b. Confidential dispatch from Governor Swayne to secretary of state for the colonies. 29 May.
   CO 123 271. 1911. Correspondence between Colonial Office and House of Commons concerning unplanned expenditures on the Stann Creek Valley railway. 11 July.
   CO 123 284. 1916. Annual report for 1915 on the Stann Creek railway, submitted by railway superintendent. April.
   CO 123 291. Dispatch from acting Governor Walter to Colonial Office. 1 April.

CO 123 292. Dispatch from Governor Bennett to Colonial Office. 8 August,

CO 123 295a. 1918. Dispatch from Governor Hutson to Colonial Office. 24 May.

CO 123 295b. 1919. Dispatch from Governor Hutson to Colonial Office. 3 July.

CO 123 300. 1920a. Agricultural report for Riversdale by W. R. Dunlop, transmitted with dispatch from Governor Hutson to Colonial Office. 11 February.

———. 1920b. Letter from colonial secretary in Belize to United Fruit Company in Boston, dated 11 February, transmitted with Governor Hutson's dispatch to Colonial Office. 5 April.

———. 1920c. Letter from railway superintendent to Governor Hutson, transmitted with Hutson's dispatch to Colonial Office. 5 April.

———. 1920d. Dispatch from Governor Hutson to Colonial Office. 5 April.

CO 123 302. 1918. Dispatch from Governor Hutson to Colonial Office. 18 August.

CO 123 316. 1923. Telegram from Governor Hutson to secretary of state for the colonies. 16 November.

CO 123 392/2. 1928. Agricultural reconnaissance of the Stann Creek Valley, by C. L. Stocker.

Fundación Hondureña de Investigación Agrícola (FHIA), Library, La Lima, Honduras

Fruit Dispatch Company conference report, Chicago. 11–12 November. 1925.

Tela Railroad Company, *Datos de1963.*

United Brands, *Banana Operations Manual.* December.

United Fruit Company, Division of Tropical Research, *Annual Report* 1939–53, 1957–68.

United Fruit Company, Division of Tropical Research, *Research Extension Newsletter.*

Harvard University, Baker Business Library, Historical Collections, Cambridge, Massachussetts

Henry B. Arthur Papers, Banana Study

Harvard University Graduate School of Business Administration. Exhibits presented for the Harvard Advertising Awards, manuscript division, SPGD H339a.

Howard-Tilton Memorial Library, Tulane University, New Orleans Standard Fruit and Steamship Company Papers

National Archives of Belize (AB), Belmopan

Colony of British Honduras. 1890–1903. *Blue Books.* Belize.

———. 1901. *Government Gazette* (and supplement). Belize. 23 February.

———. 1937. *Sessional Paper on the Banana Industry.* SP no. 43 of 1937. Belize.

DO 123 of 1937. 1937. Dispatch from Governor Burns to Colonial Office. 23 April.

MP 3424–17. 1917. "Labouring Work Done by Contract on Banana Plantations and Remedy for Noncompliance: Letter from Stann Creek Planters." 25 October.

MP 1148–19. 1919. "Communication with the United Fruit Company in Regard to Stann Creek Railway and the Company's Interests and Obligations in that District." 8 May.

MP 3121–23. 1923. "Valuation of Middlesex Estate for Forestry Purposes." 16 November.

MP 2091–33. 1933. "Information as to History and Development of the Stann Creek Railway." 16 October.

National Museum of American History, Washington, D.C., United States
Warshaw Collection, Food.

United States National Archives (USNA), Washington, D.C.
United States Foreign Agricultural Service (Record Group 166).
United States Department of State (Record Group 59), Dispatches from U.S. consuls in
Kingston, Jamaica, British West Indies, 1876–1906, microfilm T 31, v. 28–29.

NEWSPAPERS

Clarion
Colonial Guardian
Correo del Norte
New York Times
Octubre
Wall Street Journal

PUBLICATIONS

Acosta, Yvonne, and Jean Casimir. 1985. "Social Origins of the Counter-Plantation System in
St. Lucia." In *Rural Development in the Caribbean,* edited by P. I. Gomes. New York: St.
Martin's Press.
"Acta de la Sesión Extraordinaria Celebrada Por La Sociedad de Geografía e Historia de Hon-
duras Para Emitir Opinión Sobre El Cuadro Representativo de Lempira." 1928. *Revista del
Archivo y Biblioteca Nacionales de Honduras* 7, no. 6 (30 November): 162–65.
Acuña Ortega, Victor H. 1984. *La Huelga Bananera de 1934.* San José, Costa Rica: CENAP.
Adams, Franklin. 1911. "The Banana and Its Relatives." *Bulletin of the Pan American Union* 32:
845–62.
Adams, Frederick Upham. 1914. *Conquest of the Tropics.* New York: Doubleday, Page.
Adams, Richard N. 1957. *Cultural Surveys of Panama-Nicaragua-Guatemala-El Salvador-
Honduras.* Washington, D.C.: U.S. Government Printing Office.
Addy, David. 1999. *Restructuring and the Loss of Preferences: Labour Challenges for the
Caribbean Banana Industry.* Port of Spain: ILO Caribbean Office.
Adrian, Peter. 1996. *Metayage, Capitalism, and Peasant Development in St. Lucia, 1840–1957.*
Mona, Jamaica: Consortium Graduate School of Social Sciences, University of the West
Indies.
Agnew, John. 1994. "Representing Space: Space, Scale, and Culture in Social Science." In
Place/Culture/Representation, edited by James Duncan and David Ley. London: Verso.
Albert, Bill, and Adrian Graves. 1984. "Introduction." In *Crisis and Change in the Inter-
national Sugar Economy, 1860–1914,* edited by Bill Albert and Adrian Graves. Norwich,
England: ISC Press.

Alvarado, Arturo. 1993. *Visión Panorámica del Romanticismo en Honduras.* Tegucigalpa, Honduras: Universidad Pedagógica Nacional.

Anderson, Benedict. 1994. *Imagined Communities: Reflections on the Origin and Spread of Nationalism.* London: Verso.

Anderson, Mark. 1997. "The Significance of Blackness: Representations of Garifuna in St. Vincent and Central America, 1700–1900." *Transforming Anthropology* 6, nos. 1 and 2: 22–35.

———. 2000. "Garifuna Kids: Blackness, Tradition, and Modernity in Honduras." Ph.D. diss., University of Texas, Austin.

Andreatta, Susan. 1998. "Agrochemical Exposure and Farmworker Health in the Caribbean: A Local/Global Perspective." *Human Organization* 57, no. 3: 350–58.

Appadurai, Arjun. 1986. "Introduction: Commodities and the Politics of Value." In *The Social Life of Things: Commodities in Cultural Perspective,* edited by Arjun Appadurai. New York: Cambridge University Press.

"Apples and Bananas." 1913. *New York Times,* 26 August, p. 8.

APROMA (Association des Produits a Marche). 1992. *Le Marche de la Banane.* Paris: Ministère de la Cooperation et du Developpement.

Apthorpe, Raymond, and Des Gaspar. 1996. "Introduction: Discourse Analysis and Policy Discourse." In *Arguing Development Policy: Frames and Discourses,* edited by Raymond Apthorpe and Des Gaspar. London: Frank Cass.

Arce, Alberto, and Norman Long. 2000. "Reconfiguring Modernity and Development from an Anthropological Perspective." In *Anthropology, Development, and Modernities: Exploring Discourses, Counter-tendencies and Violence,* edited by Alberto Arce and Norman Long. London: Routledge.

Arce, Alberto, and Terence Marsden. 1993. "The Social Construction of International Food." *Economic Geography* 69: 293–311.

Argueta, Mario R. 1989. *Bananos y Politica: Samuel Zemurray y la Cuyamel Fruit Company en Honduras.* Tegucigalpa, Honduras: Editorial Universitaria.

———. 1992. *Historia de los Sin Historia.* Tegucigalpa, Honduras: Editorial Guaymuras.

Armijos, Sergio. 1996. Interview by Steve Striffler. Tape recording. Tenguel, Ecuador, 6 June.

Arthur, Henry B., James P. Houck, and George L. Beckford. 1968. *Tropical Agribusiness Structures and Adjustments: Bananas.* Cambridge, Mass.: Harvard Business School.

Ashcraft, Norman. 1973. *Colonialism and Underdevelopment: Processes of Political Economic Change in British Honduras.* New York: Teachers College Press.

Ashdown, Peter D. 1979. "Race, Class, and the Unofficial Majority in British Honduras, 1890–1949." Ph.D. diss., University of Sussex.

———. 1980. "Sweet-Escott, Swayne, and the Unofficial Majority in the Legislative Council of British Honduras, 1904–1911." *Journal of Imperial and Commonwealth History* 9: 57–75.

Asturias, Miguel Angel. 1971. *The Green Pope.* New York: Delacorte Press.

Atkinson, H. V., Calixte George, David Demacque, Geoff Devaux, Richard Peterkin, Michael Joseph, Octave Fevrier, and Cyrus Reynolds. 1993. *Report of the Banana Review Committee.* Castries, St. Lucia: St. Lucia Banana Growers' Association.

Aya, Rod. 1984. "Popular Intervention in Revolutionary Situations." In *Statemaking and Social Movements: Essays in History and Theory,* edited by Charles Bright and Susan Hardings. Ann Arbor: University of Michigan Press.

"Banana Charlotte." 1897. *Boston Cooking School* 2, no. 1 (June–July): 47–48.

"Bananas." 1898. *Boston School of Cooking* 2, no. 5 (February–March): 299.

Banana Link. 1997a. "Fair Trade Bananas from St. Lucia." *Banana Trade News Bulletin* (7 July).

———. 1997b. "Massive Potential Consumer Support for EU Fair Trade Bananas." *Banana Trade News Bulletin* (1 November).

———. 1998a. "Women Workers Risk Cancer and Birth Defects." *Banana Trade News Bulletin* (4 September).

———. 1998b. "European Union Banana Consumption." *Banana Trade News Bulletin* (9 September).

———. 1999. "1998 Export Boom in Costa Rica." *Banana Trade News Bulletin* (12 February).

———. 2000. "European Union Banana Supplies." *Banana Trade News Bulletin* (3 October).

———. 2001. "Ecuador, US, and EU Agree Transitional Regime." *Banana Trade News Bulletin* (2 May).

"The Banana, or Plantain." 1832. *Penny:* 253.

Banana Producer 37. 1994. Interview by Karla Slocum. Tape recording. Morne Verte (a pseudonym), St. Lucia, 24 October.

Banana Producer 58. 1994. Interview by Karla Slocum. Tape recording. Morne Verte (a pseudonym), St. Lucia, 8 August.

"Banana Row: The Eastern Caribbean." 1997. *Economist* 343, no. 8019: 36.

Barsky, Osvaldo. 1988. *La Reforma Agraria Ecuatoriana.* Quito, Ecuador: Corporación Editora Nacional.

Bauer Paiz, Alfonso. 1989. Interview by Cindy Forster. From author's personal archive. Mexico City, 16 December.

Bergquist, Charles. 1986. *Labor in Latin America. Comparative Essays on Chile, Argentina, Venezuela, and Colombia.* Stanford, Calif.: Stanford University Press.

Berry, Riley M. Fletcher. 1911. *Fruit Recipes.* New York: Doubleday, Page.

Bethel, Leslie, ed. 1986. *The Cambridge History of Latin America,* Volume 4. Cambridge: Cambridge University Press.

Biggs, Henry Charles, Charles John, Michael Bennett, and Robert Leach. 1963. *Report of the Commission of Inquiry into the Banana Industry of St. Lucia.* Castries, St. Lucia: Government Printer at the Government Printing Office.

Bitter, Wilhelm. 1922. "Al Margen de la Industria Bananera." *Revista Económica* 9, no. 10 (August): 650–56.

Blaney, Henry R. 1900. *The Golden Caribbean.* Boston: Lee and Shepard.

Bolland, O. Nigel. 1984. "Reply to William A. Green's 'The Perils of Comparative History.'" *Comparative Studies in Society and History* 23: 561–619.

———. 1992. "The Politics of Freedom in the British Caribbean." In *The Meaning of*

Freedom: Economics, Politics, and Culture after Slavery, edited by Frank McGlynn and
Seymour Drescher. Pittsburgh, Penn.: University of Pittsburgh Press.

Botero Herrera, Fernando. 1988. "La Evolución de la Economia Bananera en la Decada de los
Ochentas: La Experiencia Colombiana." In FLACSO/CEDAL/FES, *Cambio y Continuidad
en la Economia Bananera.* San José, Costa Rica: FLACSO/CEDAL/FES.

Botero Herrera, Fernando, and Alvaro Guzmán Barney. 1977. "El Enclave Agrícola en la Zona
Bananera de Santa Marta." *Cuadernos Colombianos* 2:308–89.

Botero Herrera, Fernando, and Diego Sierra. 1981. *El Mercado de Trabajo en la Zona Bananera de Uraba.* Bogotá: Editorial Lealon.

Bourdieu, Pierre, and Löic J. D. Wacquant. 1992. *An Invitation to Reflexive Sociology.* Chicago:
University of Chicago Press.

Bourgois, Philippe I. 1989. *Ethnicity at Work: Divided Labor on a Central American Banana
Plantation.* Baltimore, Md.: Johns Hopkins University Press.

Braverman, Harry. 1974. *Labour and Monopoly Capital: The Degradation of Work in the
Twentieth Century.* New York: Monthly Review Press.

"Brawl over Bananas." 1997. *Newsweek* 129, no. 17 (28 April): 43–45.

Breen, Henry. 1844. *St. Lucia: Historical, Statistical, and Descriptive.* London: Frank Cass.

Bright, Charles, and Susan Hardings, eds. 1984. *Statemaking and Social Movements: Essays in
History and Theory.* Ann Arbor: University of Michigan Press

Bucheli, Marcelo. 1997. "United Fruit in Colombia: Impact of Labor Relations and Governmental Regulations on Its Operations, 1948–1968." *Essays in Economic and Business
History* 17: 65–84.

———. 2001. "The Role of Demand in the Historical Development of the Banana Market."
Paper delivered at the Latin America and Global Trade Conference, November 16–17,
Stanford University, Stanford, California.

Byington, Margaret. 1910. *Homestead: The Households of a Mill Town.* New York: Russell Sage
Foundation.

Cal, Angel. 1991. "Rural Society and Economic Development: British Mercantile Capital in
Nineteenth Century Belize." Ph.D. diss., University of Arizona.

Canelas Díaz, Antonio. 1999. *La Ceiba, Sus Raíces y Su Historia (1810–1940).* La Ceiba, Honduras: Tipografía Renacimiento.

Cardoza y Aragon, Luis. 1986 [1955]. *Guatemala: Las Lineas de su Mano.* México, DF: Fondo
de Cultura Económica.

Cargill Technical Services. 1995. *Proposals for Restructuring the Windward Islands Banana
Industry.* Surrey: Cargill Technical Services.

Carías Velásquez, Marco Virgilio. 1991. *La Guerra del Banano.* Tegucigalpa, Honduras:
Ediciones Paysa.

Caribbean Conservation Association. 1991. *St. Lucia: Country Environmental Profile.* Castries,
St. Lucia: Caribbean Conservation Association.

Carney, Judith. 1992. "Peasant Women and Economic Transformation in The Gambia."
Development and Change 23, no 2: 67–90.

Carroll, C. R., John Vandermeer, and Peter Rossett, eds. 1990. *Agroecology.* New York: McGraw-Hill.

Casson, Mark, ed. 1983. *The Growth of International Business.* Boston: Allen and Unwin.

Castro, Alejandro. 1929. "El Lempira del Artista Zuniga Figueroa." *Revista Tegucigalpa* no. 120: 1.

———. 1940. "Lempira." *Revista Ariel* no. 74: 1.

Censo General de la Población. 1950. Guatemala City: Departamento de Estadistica.

Centeno, Santos. 1997. *Historia del Movimiento Negro Hondureño.* Tegucigalpa, Honduras: Editorial Guaymuras.

Central Bureau of Statistics. 1946. West Indian Census, 1946, Part B: Census of Agriculture in Barbados, the Leeward Islands, the Windward Islands, and Trinidad and Tobago. Kingston, Jamaica.

Chambron, Anne-Claire. 1995. *The European Banana Market.* Trade Briefing: Bulletin of the European NGO Network on Agriculture, Trade, and Development, 1. 2–5 December.

Chandler, Alfred D. 1990. *Scale and Scope: The Dynamics of Industrial Capitalism.* Cambridge, Mass.: Harvard University Press.

Charles, George F. L. 1994. *The History of the Labour Movement in St. Lucia, 1945–1974: A Personal Memoir.* Castries, St. Lucia: Folk Research Centre.

Chávez Borjas, Manuel. 1991. "La Cuestión Etnica en Honduras." In *Honduras: Panorama y Perspectivas,* edited by Leticia Salomón. Tegucigalpa, Honduras: CEDOH.

Chiquita Brands International. 1999. Company Information. *http://www.Chiquita.com.*

Chomsky, Aviva. 1994. "The Role of West Indian Workers in Costa Rican Radical and Nationalist Ideology, 1900–1950." *Americas* 51, no. 1.

———. 1996. *West Indian Workers and the United Fruit Company in Costa Rica, 1870–1940.* Baton Rouge: Louisiana State University Press.

———. 1998. "Laborers and Smallholders in Costa Rica's Mining Communities, 1900–1940." In *Close Encounters of Empire: Writing the Cultural History of U.S.-Latin American Relations,* edited by Gilbert M. Joseph, Catherine C. LeGrand, and Ricardo D. Salvatore. Durham, N.C.: Duke University Press.

Christensen, Erling Duss. 1999. *Jesus Walks in the Garden of the Parque Central, and Other Honduran Essays.* Tegucigalpa, Honduras: Litografía López.

Clapp, Roger. 1994. "The Moral Economy of the Contract." In *Living under Contract: Contract Farming and Agrarian Transformation in Sub-Saharan Africa,* edited by Peter D. Little and Michael J. Watts. Madison: University of Wisconsin Press.

Clegg, Peter. 2000. "The Development of the Windward Islands Banana Export Trade: Commercial Opportunity and Colonial Necessity." Paper presented at the annual meeting of the Society for Caribbean Studies, Birmingham, United Kingdom.

———. 2001. "From Insiders to Outsiders: Caribbean Banana Interests in the New International Trading Framework." Paper presented at the annual meeting of the Society for Caribbean Studies, Bristol, United Kingdom.

Clissold, Gillian Gunn. 2001. *Can the Windward Islands Survive Globalization?* Caribbean Briefing Paper, no. 4. Washington, D.C.: Georgetown University.

Coatsworth, John H. 1994. *Central America and the United States.* New York: Twayne Publishing.

Colburn, Forrest D. 1997. "Shrimp or Bananas." *Journal of Business Research* 38, no. 1: 97–103.

Collins, Jane L. 1993. "Gender, Contracts, and Wage Work: Agricultural Restructuring in Brazil's São Francisco Valley." *Development and Change* 24, no. 1: 53–82.

Colombia, Departamento Administrativo Nacional de Estadística. Various years. *Anuario de Comercio Exterior.* Bogotá: Imprenta Nacional.

Commission of Enquiry. 1959. *Report of the Commission of Enquiry into the Affairs of the SVBGA.* Kingstown, St. Vincent: Government Printing Office.

Compton, Rt. Hon. John. 1993a. "Address to the Nation by the Prime Minister, 4 October." Castries, St. Lucia: Government Information Service.

———. 1993b. "Address to the Nation by the Prime Minister, 11 October." Castries, St. Lucia: Government Information Service.

Cooper, Frederick, and Randall Packard. 1997. "Introduction." In *International Development and the Social Sciences: Essays on the History and Politics of Knowledge,* edited by Frederick Cooper and Randall Packard. Berkeley: University of California Press.

Cooper, Frederick, and Ann L. Stoler, eds. 1997. *Tensions of Empire: Colonial Cultures in a Bourgeois World.* Berkeley: University of California Press.

Cross, Malcolm, and Gad Heumann, eds. 1988. *Labour in the Caribbean: From Emancipation to Independence.* London: Macmillan Caribbean.

Crawford, Michael H., ed. 1983. *Black Caribs: A Case Study in Biocultural Adaptation,* vol. 3 of *Current Developments in Anthropological Genetics.* New York: Plenum Press.

Crush, Johnathan. 1995. *The Power of Development.* New York: Routledge.

Cruz, Ramon E. 1926. "La Ley de Inmigración y el Problema de la Raza Negra en la Costa Norte." *Revista Ariel,* no. 35: 70.

Daddieh, Cyril. 1994. "Contract Farming and Palm Oil Production in Côte d'Ivoire and Ghana." In *Living under Contract: Contract Farming and Agrarian Transformation in Sub-Saharan Africa,* edited by Peter D. Little and Michael J. Watts. Madison: University of Wisconsin Press.

Davidson, William V. 1983. "The Garifuna in Central America: Ethnohistorical and Geographical Foundations." In *Black Caribs: A Case Study in Biocultural Adaptation,* vol. 3 of *Current Developments in Anthropological Genetics,* edited by Michael H. Crawford. New York: Plenum Press.

Davies, Peter N. 1990. *Fyffes and the Banana Musa Sapientum: A Centenary History, 1888–1988.* Atlantic Highlands, N.J.: Althone.

Dawdy, Shannon. 1999. "Cultivos Locales y la Comida Criolla: La Biodiversidad en la Cocina." Paper presented at Taller Bilateral Jardín Botánico de Cienfuegos, Harvard University, Cambridge, Massachussets.

Dean, Warren. 1987. *Brazil and the Struggle for Rubber: A Study in Environmental History.* Cambridge: Cambridge University Press.

Deere, Carmen Diana, Peggy Antrobus, Lynn Bolles, Edwin Melendez, Peter Phillips, Marcia

Rivera, and Helen Safa. 1990. *In the Shadows of the Sun: Caribbean Development Alternatives and U.S. Policy.* Boulder, Colo.: Westview Press.

de Jonquieres, Guy, and Maggie Urry. 1997. "WTO Puts Skids under Banana Regime." *Financial Times,* 20 March, p. 5.

Del Cid, Rafael. 1988. "Populating the Green Desert: Population Policy and Development: Their Effect on Population Distribution. Honduras, 1876– 1980." Ph.D. diss., University of Texas, Austin.

Development and Welfare Organisation of the West Indies. 1951. *The Agricultural Development of St. Lucia.* London: Development and Welfare Organisation, Great Britain.

Dole Food Company. 2000. Company Information. *http://www.Dole.com.*

Dominica Banana Marketing Corporation. 1999. *Annual Report 1998.* Roseau, Dominica: Dominica Banana Marketing Corporation.

Dosal, Paul. 1993. *Doing Business with the Dictators: A Political History of United Fruit in Guatemala, 1899–1944.* Wilmington, Del.: Scholarly Resources.

Duncan, James, and David Ley, eds. 1994. *Place/Culture/Representation.* London: Verso

ECCR. N.d. *Going Bananas?* Fareham, England: Ecumenical Committee for Corporate Responsibility.

Echeverri-Gent, Elisavinda. 1988. "Labor, Class, and Political Representation: A Comparative Analysis of Honduras and Costa Rica." Ph.D. diss., University of Chicago.

———. 1992. "Forgotten Workers: British West Indians and the Early Days in Costa Rica and Honduras." *Journal of Latin American Studies* 24, no. 2: 275–308.

Economic Commission for Latin America. 1950–1959. *Boletín Económico para América Latina.* Santiago: Economic Commission for Latin America.

Editorial Universitaria de Panama. 1975. *Panama y La Frutera: Analisis de una Confrontación Económico-Fiscal.* Panama City: Editorial Universitaria de Panama.

Eichner, Alfred S. 1979. *The Emergence of Oligopoly: Sugar Refining as a Case Study.* Baltimore, Md.: Johns Hopkins University Press.

Ellis, Frank. 1975. *An Institutional Approach to Tropical Commodity Trade: Case-Study of Banana Exports from the Commonwealth Caribbean.* London: Commonwealth Secretariat.

———. 1983. *Las Transnacionales del Banano en Centroamerica.* San José, Costa Rica: Editorial Universitaria Centroamericana.

Elvir, Rafael A. 2001. *La Villa de Triunfo de la Cruz en la Historia.* San Pedro Sula: Centro Editorial.

Enloe, Cynthia. 1989. *Bananas, Beaches, and Bases: Making Feminist Sense of International Politics.* Berkeley: University of California Press.

Escobar, Arturo. 1995. *Encountering Development: The Making and Unmaking of the Third World.* Princeton, N.J.: Princeton University Press.

Euraque, Darío A. 1990. "Merchants and Industrialists in Northern Honduras: The Making of National Bourgeoisie in Peripheral Capitalism, 1870s–1972." Ph.D. diss., University of Wisconsin, Madison.

———. 1996a. "La Creación de la Moneda Nacional y el Enclave Bananero en la Costa

Caribeña de Honduras: ¿En Busca de una Identidad Étnico-Racial?" *Yaxkin* 14, nos. 1 and 2: 138–50.

———. 1996b. *Estado, Poder, Nacionalidad y Raza en la Historia de Honduras: Ensayos.* Tegucigalpa, Honduras: Centro de Publicaciones, Obispado de Choluteca.

———. 1996c. *Reinterpreting the Banana Republic: Region and State in Honduras, 1870–1972.* Chapel Hill: University of North Carolina Press.

———. 1997. "El Imperialismo y Honduras como 'Republica Bananera': Hacia Una Nueva Historiografía." Paper presented at the annual conference of the Latin American Studies Association, Guadalajara, México.

———. 1998. "The Banana Enclave, Nationalism, and *Mestizaje* in Honduras, 1910s–1930s." In *Identity and Struggle at the Margins of the Nation-State: Identity and Struggle in the Making of the Laboring Peoples of Central America and the Hispanic Caribbean, 1860–1960,* edited by Avi Chomsky and Aldo Lauria. Durham, N.C.: Duke University Press.

———. 2001a. "Negritud Garifuna y Coyunturas Políticas en la Costa Norte de Honduras, 1940–1970." Chap. 6 in *Conversaciones Históricas con el Mestizaje Hondureño y su Identidad Nacional,* edited by Darío A. Euraque. Tegucigalpa, Honduras: Comisionado Nacional de Protección de los Derechos Humanos.

———. 2001b. "Evangelización, Civilización y Civismo como Discursos Modernizantes en Olanchito, un Pueblo Mulato de Honduras." Chap. 5 in *Conservaciones Históricas con el Mestizaje Hondureño y su Identidad Nacional,* edited by Darío A. Euraque. Tegucigalpa, Honduras: Comisionado Nacional de Protección de los Derechos Humanos.

———. Forthcoming. "Honduras." In *The Marcus Garvey and Universal Negro Improvement Association Papers.* Vol. 11, *The Caribbean,* edited by Robert Hill. Los Angeles: University of California Press.

"Expelled From Eden." 1997. *Economist* 345, no. 8048: 35–39.

Fabre, Pierre. 1997. "Competitiveness of Banana Export Systems." Paper presented at the meeting of the Research Committee on the Sociology of Agriculture and Food, International Sociological Association, August 16–17, Toronto, Canada.

Fair Trade Federation. 1999. Fair Trade Facts. *http://www.fairtradefederation.com.*

Falla, Ricardo. 1992. *Masacres de la Selva: Ixcán, Guatemala (1975–1982).* Guatemala City: Editorial Universitaria.

FAO. 1986. *The World Banana Economy 1970–1984.* Rome: Food and Agriculture Organization of the United Nations.

———. 1999a. *Banana Statistics.* CCP:BA/TF 99/3. Rome: Food and Agriculture Organization of the United Nations.

———. 1999b. *The Market for "Organic" and "Fair-Trade Bananas."* CCP:BA/TF 99/7. Rome: Food and Agriculture Organization of the United Nations.

———. 1999c. *Review of Policy Developments Affecting Banana Trade.* CCP:BA/TF 99/8. Rome: Food and Agriculture Organization of the United Nations.

———. 2001. FAOSTAT database results. *http://www.fao.org.*

Faulkner, William. 1964 [1930]. *As I Lay Dying.* New York: Vintage Books.

Fawcett, William. 1902. "La Industria Bananera en Jamaica." *Boletín del Instituto Físico-geográfico de Costa Rica* 2: 267–84.

Figueroa, Carlos Zúniga. 1953. *Estadísticas Demográficas, 1926–1951.* Tegucigalpa, Honduras: Direccion general de Estadistica y Censos.

Figueroa, Luis A. 1994. "Stirring Up the Fields: Sugarcane Workers and American Colonial Capitalism in Guayama, Puerto Rico, 1898–1923." Paper presented at the American Historical Association Meeting, San Francisco, California.

FLACSO/CEDAL/FES. 1988. *Cambio y Continuidad en la Economia Bananera.* San José, Costa Rica: FLACSO/CEDAL/FES.

Fonnegra, Gabriel. 1980. *Bananeras Testimonio Vivo de una Epopeya.* Bogotá: Ediciones Tercer Mundo.

Foro Emaus. 1997. *Bananos para el Mundo y el Dano para Costa Rica?* Limón, Costa Rica: Foro Emaus.

Forster, Cindy. 1998. "Reforging National Revolution: Campesino Labor Struggles in Guatemala, 1944–1954." In *Identity and Struggle at the Margins of the Nation-State: The Laboring Peoples of Central America and the Hispanic Caribbean,* edited by Aviva Chomsky and Aldo Lauria-Santiago. Durham, N.C.: Duke University Press.

Foucault, Michel. 1978. *The History of Sexuality,* Volume I: *An Introduction.* New York: Random House.

Frank, Zephyr, and Aldo Musacchio. 2001. "Brazil in the International Rubber Trade (1870–1930)." Paper presented at the Latin America and Global Trade conference, November 16–17, Stanford University, Stanford, California.

Fresh Del Monte. 2000. Company Information. *http://www.DelMonte.com.*

Frey-Wouters, Adele Ellen. 1980. *The European Community and the Third World: The Lome Convention and Its Impacts.* New York: Praeger.

Friedland, William H. 1984. "Commodity Systems Analysis: An Approach to the Sociology of Agriculture." In *Research in Rural Sociology and Development,* edited by H. K. Schwarzweller. Greenwich, Conn.: JAI Press. 35–58.

Friedland, William H., Lawrence Busch, Frederick H. Buttel, Alan Rudy, eds. 1991. *Towards a New Political Economy of Agriculture.* Boulder, Colo.: Westview.

Friedmann, Harriet. 1991. "Changes in the International Division of Labor: Agri-Food Complexes and Export Agriculture." In *Towards a New Political Economy of Agriculture,* edited by William H. Friedland et al. Boulder, Colo.: Westview.

FruiTrop. 1999. "Statistics: European Imports." *FruiTrop* (July–August): 1–18.

La Gaceta. 1893. Tegucigalpa, Honduras: Tipografía Nacional. 17 October.

Galich, Manuel. 1985 [1949]. *Del Pánico al Ataque.* Guatemala City: Editorial Universitaria.

Galvao de Coelho, Ruy. 1981. *Los Negros Caribes de Honduras.* Tegucigalpa, Honduras: Editorial Guaymuras.

García Buchard, Ethel. 1997. *Poder Politico, Interes Bananero e Identidad Nacional en Centro America: Un Estudio Comparativo: Costa Rica (1884–1938) y Honduras (1902–1958).* Tegucigalpa, Honduras: Editorial Universitaria.

Garcia L., Graciela. 1952. *Las Luchas Revolucionarias de la Nueva Guatemala*. Mexico: no publisher noted on photocopy.

García Márquez, Gabriel. 1970. *One Hundred Years of Solitude*. New York: Harper and Row.

Gaspar, Jeffrey Casey. 1979. *Limón: 1880–1940: Un Estudio de la industria bananera en Costa Rica*. San José: Editorial Costa Rica.

Gereffi, Gary. 1994. "The Organization of Buyer-Driven Global Commodity Chains." In *Commodity Chains and Global Capitalism*, edited by Gary Gereffi and M. Korzeniewicz. Westport, Conn.: Praeger.

Gereffi, Gary, and Miguel Korzeniewicz, eds. 1994. *Commodity Chains and Global Capitalism*. Westport, Conn.: Praeger.

Gleijeses, Piero. 1993. *A Shattered Hope: The Guatemalan Revolution and the United States, 1899–1944*. Wilmington, Del.: Scholarly Resources.

Glover, David. 1984. "Contract Farming and Smallholder Outgrower Schemes in Less-developed Countries." *World Development* 12, no. 1: 1143–57.

Glover, David, and Carlos Larrea Maldonado. 1991. "Changing Comparative Advantage, Short Term Instability, and Long Term Change in the Latin American Banana Industry." *Canadian Journal of Latin American and Caribbean Studies* 16, no. 32: 91–108.

Glover, David, and Ken Kusterer. 1990. *Small Farmers, Big Business: Contract Farming and Rural Development*. New York: St. Martin's Press.

Godfrey, Claire. 1998. *A Future for Caribbean Bananas: The Importance of Europe's Banana Market to the Caribbean*. London: Oxfam Policy Department.

Goffman, Erving. 1961. *Asylum: Essays on the Social Situation of Mental Patients and Other Inmates*. Garden City, N.Y.: Anchor Books.

Goldsmith, Arthur. 1985. "The Private Sector and Rural Development: Can Agribusiness Help the Small Farmer?" *World Development* 13, no. 2: 1125–38.

Gomes, P. I., ed. 1985. *Rural Development in the Caribbean*. New York: St. Martin's Press.

González, Nancie. 1988. *Sojourners of the Caribbean: Ethnogenesis and Ethnohistory of the Garifuna*. Urbana: University of Illinois Press.

González Casanova, Pablo, ed. 1985. *Historia del Movimiento Obrero en América Latina*. México, D.F.: Siglo Ventiuno Editores.

Goodman, David, and Michael Watts. 1994. "Reconfiguring the Rural or Fording the Divide? Capitalist Restructuring and Global Agro-Food System." *Journal of Peasant Studies* 22, no. 1: 1–49.

Gould, Jeff. 1998. *To Die in This Way: Nicaraguan Indians and the Myth of Mestizaje, 1880–1965*. Durham, N.C.: Duke University Press.

Grant, Cedric. 1976. *The Making of Modern Belize*. Cambridge: Cambridge University Press.

Green, William A. 1984 "The Perils of Comparative History: Belize and the British Sugar Colonies after Slavery." *Comparative Studies in Society and History* 26, no. 1: 112–19.

Grossman, Lawrence. 1993. "The Political Ecology of Banana Exports and Local Food Production in St. Vincent, Eastern Caribbean." *Annals of the Association of American Geographers* 83: 347–67.

————. 1994. "British Aid and Windwards Bananas: The Case of St. Vincent and the Grenadines." *Social and Economic Studies* 43: 151–79.

————. 1997. "Soil Conservation, Political Ecology, and Technological Change on Saint
Vincent." *Geographical Review* 87: 353–74.

————. 1998. *The Political Ecology of Bananas: Contract Farming, Peasants, and Agrarian
Change in the Eastern Caribbean.* Chapel Hill: University of North Carolina Press.

————. 1999. "Uncle Sam Is Going Bananas in Trade War with Europe." *Roanoke Times and
World News,* 23 March, sec. A, p. 9.

————. 2000. "Women and Export Agriculture: The Case of Banana Production on St.
Vincent in the Eastern Caribbean." In *Women Farmers and Commercial Ventures: Increas-
ing Food Security in Developing Countries,* edited by Anita Spring. Boulder, Colo.: Lynne
Rienner.

Guerra Borges, Alfredo. 1986. *Compendio Geografía Económica y Humana de Guatemala,* 2a.
Edición. Guatemala City: Editorial Universitaria de Guatemala.

Guillen Zelaya, Alfonso. 2000 [1930]. "Proteccion a los Nacionales." In *Alfonso Guillén
Zelaya: Conciencia de Una Epoca,* edited by Ramon Oqueli. Tegucigalpa, Honduras:
UNAH.

Hallam, David, and Lord Peston. 1997. "The Political Economy of Europe's Banana Trade."
Reading, England: University of Reading, Department of Agricultural and Food Economics, Occasional Paper no. 5.

Handy, Jim. 1984. *Gift of the Devil: A History of Guatemala.* Boston: South End Press.

————. 1994. *Revolution in the Countryside.* Chapel Hill: University of North Carolina.

Harpelle, Ronald. 2000. "Radicalism and Accommodation: Garveyism in a United Fruit
Company Enclave." *Journal of Iberian and Latin American Studies* 6, no. 1: 1–27.

Hernandez, Osvaldo. 1996. Interview by Steve Striffler. Tape recording. Tenguel, Ecuador,
8 August.

Hernandez, Silvio. 1997. "Banana Workers Oppose Contract with Transnational." *Interpress
News Service,* 12 December.

Herranz, Atanasio. 1994. "Los Negros Caribes o Garifunas de Honduras." *Paraninfo,* no. 5:
127–48.

Hobson, Jesse. 1959. "Research in the United Fruit Company." N.p. Unpublished manuscript.

Holt, Byron. 1913. Editorial letter to the *New York Times,* 2 July, sec. A, p. 8.

Holt, Thomas C. 1992. *The Problem of Freedom: Race, Labor, and Politics in Jamaica and
Britian, 1832–1938.* Baltimore, Md.: Johns Hopkins University Press.

Hopkins, Terence K., and Immanuel Wallerstein. 1986. "Commodity Chains in the World-
Economy Prior to 1800." *Review* 10, no. 1: 157–70.

Hord, H. H. V. 1966. "The Conversion of Standard Fruit Company Banana Plantations in
Honduras from the Gros Michel to the Giant Cavendish Variety." *Tropical Agriculture* 43:
269–75.

Humboldt, Alexander von, and Aimé Bonpland. 1852. *Personal Narratives of the Travels to
the Equinoctial Regions of America during the Years 1799–1804.* Translated and edited by
Thomasina Ross. London: Henry G. Bohn.

Humphrey, James Ellis. 1894. "Where Bananas Grow." *Popular Science Monthly* 44: 487–88.

Hutson, Sir Eyre. 1925. *The Handbook of British Honduras.* London: Colonial Office.

Hymes, Dell. 1972. *Reinventing Anthropology.* New York: Pantheon

ICTSD (International Centre for Trade and Sustainable Development). 1999. "Bananas: WTO Rules against EU." *Bridges Weekly Trade News Digest* 3, nos. 13 and 14 (12 April).

———. 2000. "European Union Seeks Reforms to Banana and Sugar Regimes." *Bridges Weekly Trade News Digest* 4, no. 38 (10 October).

———. 2001. Banana Dispute Resolved as EU, Ecuador Reach Agreement. *Bridges Weekly Trade News Digest* 5, no. 16 (1 May).

Immerman, Richard H. 1982. *The CIA in Guatemala: The Foreign Policy of Intervention.* Austin: University of Texas Press.

Imperial Economic Committee. 1926. *Report of the Imperial Economic Committee on Marketing and Preparing for Market of Foodstuffs Produced in the Overseas Parts of the Empire: Third Report—Fruit.* London: His Majesty's Stationery Office.

Informe de Presidente Arbenz al Congreso Nacional. 1954. *Revista Democracia* 2, no. 2 (10 March).

International Labor Organization. 1999. "Restructuring and the Loss of Preferences: Labor Challenges for the Caribbean Banana Industry." *http://www.ilocarib.org.tt/banana/ banana_content.html.* 22 October.

International Monetary Fund. 1968. *International Financial Statistics.* Washington, D.C.: International Monetary Fund.

———. 1970. *International Financial Statistics.* Washington, D.C.: International Monetary Fund.

Interpress News Service. 1997. "Fruit Grower to Pay Workers." *Interpress News Service,* 17 June.

Iraheta, Adriana. 1952. "Síntesis Biográfica del Doctor Presentación Centeno." *Revista del Archivo y Biblioteca Nacionales de Honduras* 30, nos. 7–8: 346–49.

Jackson, Jeremy C., and Angela P. Cheater. 1994. "Contract Farming in Zimbabwe: Case Studies of Sugar, Tea, and Cotton." In *Living under Contract: Contract Farming and Agrarian Transformation in Sub-Saharan Africa,* edited by Peter D. Little and Michael J. Watts. Madison: University of Wisconsin Press.

Jaffee, Steven. 1994. "Contract Farming in the Shadow of Competitive Markets: the Experience of Kenyan Horticulture." In *Living under Contract: Contract Farming and Agrarian Transformation in Sub-Saharan Africa,* edited by Peter D. Little and Michael J. Watts. Madison: University of Wisconsin Press.

Jenkins, Virginia Scott. 2000. *Bananas: An American History.* Washington, D.C.: Smithsonian Institution Press.

Johnston, John R. 1923. *Mosaic Disease of Sugar Cane in 1923: Diseases and Pests of the Banana.* Boston: United Fruit Company.

Jonas, Susanne. 1991. *The Battle for Guatemala: Rebels, Death Squads, and U.S. Power.* Boulder, Colo.: Westview Press.

Jordan, William James [O. Henry]. 1904. *Cabbages and Kings.* New York: McClure, Phillips.

Joseph, Gilbert M., Catherine C. LeGrand, and Ricardo D. Salvatore, eds. 1998. *Close Encounters of Empire: Writing the Cultural History of U.S.–Latin American Relations.* Durham, N.C.: Duke University Press.

Joya, Olga. 1992. "Crónica de las Crónicas: La Conquista de la Provincia de Honduras (S. XVII)." *Paranínfo* 1, no. 2: 109–44.

Kairi Consultants and Agrocon Limited. 1993. *Development of a Time-Phased Action Programme to Improve the International Competitiveness of the Banana Industry of the Windward Islands: Volume 2.* Final Report submitted to Caribbean Development Bank, Barbados, Windward Islands, April.

Karnes, Thomas L. 1978. *Tropical Enterprise: The Standard Fruit and Steamship Company in Latin America.* Baton Rouge: Louisiana State University Press.

Kepner, Charles D. 1936. *Social Aspects of the Banana Industry.* New York: Columbia University Press.

Kepner, Charles D., and Jay Soothill. 1935. *The Banana Empire: A Case Study in Economic Imperialism.* New York: Russell and Russell.

Klak, Thomas, ed. 1998. *Globalization and Neoliberalism: The Caribbean Context.* Boulder, Colo.: Rowman and Littlefield.

Kortbech-Olesen, R. 1998. "Export Potential of Organic Products from Developing Countries." Paper presented at the IFOAM Conference, Mar del Plata, Argentina.

LaBarge, Richard Allen. 1959. "A Study of United Fruit Company Operations in Isthmian America, 1946–1956." Ph.D. diss., Duke University.

Lamoreaux, Naomi. 1985. *The Great Merger Movement in American Business, 1895–1904.* Cambridge: Cambridge University Press.

Langdon, Robert. 1993. "The Banana as a Key to Early American and Polynesian History." *Journal of Pacific History* 28: 15–35.

Langley, Lester, and Thomas Schoonover. 1995. *The Banana Men: American Mercenaries and Entrepreneurs in Central America, 1880–1930.* Lexington: University Press of Kentucky.

Larimer, Brook. 1997. "The Banana Wars." *Newsweek* 129, no. 17 (28 April): 18–28.

Larrea Maldonado, Carlos. 1987. *El Banano en el Ecuador.* Quito, Ecuador: Corporacion Editoral Nacional.

———. 1988 "Los Cambios Recientes en el Subsistema Bananero Ecuatoriano." In FLACSO/CEDAL/FES, *Cambio y Continuidad en la Economia Bananera.* San José, Costa Rica: FLACSO/CEDAL/FES.

LeGrand, Catherine C. 1984. "Colombian Transformations: Peasants and Wage Laborers in the Santa Martha Banana Zone." *Journal of Peasant Studies* 11, no. 4: 178–200.

———. 1998. "Living in Macondo: Economy and Culture in a United Fruit Company Banana Enclave in Colombia." In *Close Encounters of Empire: Writing the Cultural History of U.S.–Latin American Relations,* edited by Gilbert M. Joseph, Catherine C. LeGrand, and Ricardo D. Salvatore. Durham, N.C.: Duke University Press.

"Lempira, Nuestro Cacique Legendario, Inmortalizado En El Lienzo." 1928. *Revista del Archivo y Biblioteca Nacionales de Honduras* 7, no. 6 (30 November): 161–62.

Léon Gómez, Alfredo. 1978. *El Escándolo Del Ferrocarril: Ensayo Histórico.* Tegucigalpa, Honduras: Imprenta Soto.

León, Rafael. 1996. Interview by Steve Striffler. Tape recording. Tenguel, Ecuador, 6 May.

Levenson-Estrada, Deborah. 1994. *Trade Unionists against Terror: Guatemala City 1954–1985.* Chapel Hill: University of North Carolina Press.

Levenstein, Harvey. 1988. *Revolution at the Table: The Transformation of the American Diet.* New York: Oxford University Press.

Lewis, Gordon K. 1968. *The Making of the Modern West Indies.* New York: Modern Reader.

Lewis, Patsy. 1998. "Making a Better Banana Farmer: Restructuring the West Indian Banana Industry." *Caribbean Dialog* 4: 1–19.

Lewis, R. W. B., and Nancy Lewis, eds. 1988. *The Letters of Edith Wharton.* New York: Charles Scribner's Sons.

Leyva, Héctor, ed. 1991. *Documentos Coloniales de Honduras.* Tegucigalpa, Honduras: Ediciones Subirana.

Liga de la Defensa Nacional Centroamericana. 1914. *Labor Hondureña por la Autonomía de Centro América.* Comayaguela, Honduras: Imprenta El Sol.

Lincoln, Mary J. 1900. *Boston Cookbook.* Boston: Little, Brown.

Little, Peter D. 1994. "Contract Farming and the Development Question." In *Living under Contract: Contract Farming and Agrarian Transformation in Sub-Saharan Africa,* edited by Peter D. Little and Michael J. Watts, 216–47. Madison: University of Wisconsin Press.

Little, Peter D., and Michael J. Watts, eds. 1994. *Living under Contract: Contract Farming and Agrarian Transformation in Sub-Saharan Africa.* Madison: University of Wisconsin Press.

Llivichusca, Jose. 1996a. Interview by Steve Striffler. Tape recording. Tenguel, Ecuador, 22 April.

———. 1996b. Interview by Steve Striffler. Tape recording. Tenguel, Ecuador, 17 June.

Lloyd, David. 1997. "Nationalisms against the State." In *The Politics of Culture in the Shadow of Capital,* edited by Lisa Lowe and David Lloyd. Durham, N.C.: Duke University Press.

Lobdell, Richard A. 1988. "British Officials and the West Indian Peasantry, 1842–1938." In *Labour in the Caribbean: From Emancipation to Independence,* edited by Malcolm Cross and Gad Heumann. London: Macmillan Caribbean.

Lome Convention. 1989. "The Fourth ACP-EEC Convention signed at Lome, 15 December." Brussels: ACP-EEC Council of Ministers. Port Louis, Mauritius: Silvio M. Empeigne, Government Printer, 1991.

López García, Victor. 1996. *La Bahía del Puerto del Sol y la Masacre de los Garifunas de San Juan.* Tegucigalpa, Honduras: Editorial Guaymuras.

López Larrave, Mario. 1976. *Breve Historia del Movimiento Sindical Guatemalteco.* Guatemala City: Editorial Universitaria.

Louis, Michael. 1981. "An Equal Right to the Soil: The Rise of a Peasantry in St. Lucia, 1838–1900." Ph.D. diss., Johns Hopkins University.

Lowe, Lisa, and David Lloyd, eds. 1997. *The Politics of Culture in the Shadow of Capital.* Durham, N.C.: Duke University Press.

Marie, J. M. 1979. *Agricultural Diversification in a Small Economy: The Case for Dominica.*

Cave Hill, Barbados: Institute of Social and Economic Research (Eastern Caribbean), University of West Indies.

Mariñas Otero, Luis. 1962. *Las Constituciones de Honduras*. Madrid: Ediciones Hispánicas.

Marquardt, Steve. 2001. " 'Green Havoc': Panama Disease, Environmental Change, and Labor Process in the Central American Banana Industry." *American Historical Review* 106, no. 1: 49–80.

Marshall, Woodville K. 1965. "Metayage in the Sugar Industry of the British Windward Islands, 1838–1865." *Jamaican Historical Review* 5: 26–55.

―――. 1989. "St. Lucia in the Economic History of the Windward Islands: The Nineteenth-Century Experience." *Caribbean Quarterly* 35: 24–33.

Martin, Gerald. 1989. *Journeys Through the Labyrinth: Latin American Fiction in the Twentieth Century*. London: Verso.

Martínez Cuenca, Alvaro. 1991. *Banana Libre*. Managua: Editorial Nueva Nicaragua.

Mathews, Charles. 1999. Interview by Darío A. Euraque. Tape recording. Tela, Honduras, August 7.

May, Stacy, and Galo Plaza. 1958. *The United Fruit Company in Latin America*. Washington, D.C.: National Planning Association.

Max Havelaar. 1999. *Fair Trade Banana Statistics*. Copenhagen, Denmark: Max Havelaar.

McCann, Thomas. 1976. *An American Company: The Tragedy of United Fruit*. New York: Crown.

McClintock, Michael. 1985. *The American Connection*, Volume 2: *State Terror and Popular Resistance in Guatemala*. London: Zed Books.

McCook, Stuart. 2001. "Las Epidemias Liberales: Agricultura, Ambiente y Globalización en Ecuador, 1790–1930." Paper presented at Latin American Studies Association meeting, September, Washington, D.C.

―――. 2002. *States of Nature: Science, Agriculture, and the Environment in the Spanish Caribbean*. Austin: University of Texas Press.

McCreery, David. 1986. " 'This Life of Misery and Shame': Female Prostitution in Guatemala City, 1880–1920." *Journal of Latin American Studies* 18, no. 2: 333–53.

McDonald, Roderick A. 1981. " 'Goods and Chattels': The Economy of Slaves on Sugar Plantations in Jamaica and Louisiana." Ph.D. diss., University of Kansas.

McGlynn, Frank, and Seymour Drescher, eds. 1992. *The Meaning of Freedom: Economics, Politics, and Culture after Slavery*. Pittsburgh, Penn.: University of Pittsburgh Press.

McKenney, R. E. B. 1910. "The Central American Banana Blight." *Science* 31, no. 802: 750–51.

McLean Petras, Elisabeth. 1988. *Jamaican Labor Migration: White Capital and Black Labor, 1850–1930*. Boulder, Colo.: Westview Press.

McMichael, Philip. 1997. "Rethinking Globalization: The Agrarian Question Revisited." *Review of International Political Economy* 4, no. 4: 630–62.

Mehta, Uhda S. 1997. "Liberal Strategies of Exclusion." In *Tensions of Empire: Colonial Cultures in a Bourgeois World*, edited by Frederick Cooper and Ann L. Stoler. Berkeley: University of California Press.

Meliczek, H. 1975. "Land Tenure, St. Lucia: Project Findings and Recommendations." Report prepared for the government of St. Lucia, the United Nations Development Programme, and the Food and Agriculture Organisation, Rome.

Meza, Víctor. 1985. "Historia del Movimiento Obrero en Honduras." In *Historia del Movimiento Obrero en América Latina,* edited by Pablo González Casanova. México, D.F.: Siglo Ventiuno Editores.

Minot, Nicholas. 1986. "Contract Farming and Its Effect on Small Farmers in Less Developed Countries." Michigan State University Development Papers, working paper no. 31. East Lansing: Michigan State University.

Mintz, Sidney W. 1985. *Sweetness and Power: The Place of Sugar in Modern History.* New York: Viking.

Moberg, Mark. 1996. "Transnational Labor and Refugee Enclaves in a Central American Banana Industry." *Human Organization* 55, no. 4: 425–35.

———. 1997. *Myths of Ethnicity and Nation: Immigration, Work, and Identity in the Belize Banana Industry.* Knoxville: University of Tennessee Press.

Moody's Investors Service. 1930–1970. *Moody's Stock Survey.* New York: Moody's Investors Service.

Moreno Fraginals, Manuel. 1986. "Plantation Economies and Societies in the Spanish Caribbean, 1860–1930." In *The Cambridge History of Latin America,* Volume 4, edited by Leslie Bethell. Cambridge: Cambridge University Press.

Moritz, C. F., and Adele Kahn. 1898. *The Twentieth Century Cookbook.* 10th ed. New York: M. A. Donohue.

Mourillon, V. J. 1978. *The Dominica Banana Industry from Inception to Independence 1928–1978.* Roseau, Dominica: Tropical Printers.

Muery, Henry O. 1984. "History of Standard Research, 1950–1980." N.p. Typescript, 17 May.

Mundt, Christopher C. 1990. "Disease Dynamics in Agroecosystems." In *Agroecology,* edited by C. R. Carroll, John Vandermeer, and Peter Rossett. New York: McGraw-Hill.

Murga Frassinetti, Antonio. 1981. "Economía Primario Exportadora y Formación del Proletariado: El Caso Centroamericano (1850–1920)." *Economía Política* 19: 40–78.

Murray, Douglas L. 1994. *Cultivating Crisis: The Human Cost of Pesticides in Latin America.* Austin: University of Texas Press.

Murray, Douglas L., and Laura T. Raynolds. 2000. "Alternative Trade in Bananas: Obstacles and Opportunities for Progressive Social Change in the Global Economy." *Agriculture and Human Values* 17: 65–74.

Nader, Laura. 1972. "Urban Anthropologist Perspectives Gained from Studying Up." In *Reinventing Anthropology,* edited by Dell Hymes. New York: Pantheon.

Nurse, Keith, and Wayne Sandiford. 1995. *Windward Islands Bananas: Challenges and Options under the Single European Market.* Kingston, Jamaica: Friedrich Ebert Stiftung.

Obando Sánchez, Antonio. 1978. *Memorias: La Historia del Movimiento Obrero.* Guatemala City: Editorial Universitaria.

O'Brien, Thomas. 1996. *The Revolutionary Mission: American Enterprise in Latin America, 1900–1945.* Cambridge: Cambridge University Press.

Oqueli, Ramon, ed. 2000. *Alfonso Guillén Zelaya: Conciencia de Una Epoca.* Tegucigalpa, Honduras: UNAH.

"An Outpost in the Banana and Marijuana Wars." 1999. *New York Times,* 4 March 4, sec. A, p. 4.

Palacios, Carlos, and Sánchez, Reynaldo. 1996. *Informe de Investigación Sobre Tenencia de la Tierra, San Juan de Tela.* Unpublished manuscript, Ministerio Publico, Fiscalía de las Etnias, Tegucigalpa, Honduras.

Pantin, Dennis, Wayne Sandiford, and Michael Henry. 1999. *Cake, Mama Coca or?: Alternatives Facing the Caribbean Banana Industry.* WINFA, CPDC, Oxfam, Caribbean.

Pastor Fasquelle, Rodolfo. 1998. "Historia e Identidad de los Garifunas." *Astrolabio* no. 2: 14–20.

Pellecer, Carlor Manuel. 1990. Interview by Cindy Forster. From author's personal archive. Tiquisate, Guatemala, October 11.

Pérez Brignoli, Héctor. 1989. *A Brief History of Central America.* Translated by Ricardo B. Sawrey A. and Susana Stettri de Sawrey. Berkeley: University of California Press.

Perman, J. H. 1929. "Banana Breeding." *United Fruit Company Research Department Bulletin* 21.

"Población de las Provincias de Honduras, Matrícula del Año de 1801." 1991. *Documentos Coloniales de Honduras,* edited by Héctor Leyva, 289. Tegucigalpa, Honduras: Ediciones Subirana.

Poole, Hester M. 1890. *Fruits and How to Use Them.* New York: Fowler and Wells.

Porter, Gina, and Kevin Phillips-Howard. 1997. "Comparing Contracts: An Evaluation of Contract Farming Schemes in Africa." *World Development* 25, no. 2: 227–38.

Posada Carbó, Eduardo. 1991. "Imperialism, Local Elites, and Regional Development: The United Fruit Company in Colombia Reconsidered, 1900–1945." Paper presented at the 47th International Congress of Americanists, New Orleans, Louisiana.

Posas, Mario. 1981a. "El 'Problema Negro': Racismo y Explotacion en las Bananeras." *Alvaravan* 9: 6–9.

———. 1981b. *Luchas del Movimiento Obrero Hondureno.* San José, Costa Rica: EDUCA.

———. 1983. "El Surgimiento de la Clase Obrera Hondureña." *Anuario de Estudios Centroamericanos* 9: 17–35.

Pratt, Mary Louise. 1992. *Imperial Eyes: Travel Writing and Transculturation.* New York: Routledge.

Prescott, Samuel C. 1917. "The Banana: A Food of Exceptional Value." In *Food Value of the Banana: Opinion of Leading Medical and Scientific Authorities.* Boston: United Fruit Company.

Presidencia de la República. 1952. *Reglamento para el Funcionamiento de los Comites Agrarios Locales.* Guatemala City: Tipografia Nacional, Publicaciones del Departamento Agrario Nacional.

———. 1954. *Expediente de Expropiación Seguido contra la Compañia Agrícola de Guatemala, de conformidad con la Ley de Reforma Agraria.* Guatemala City: Tipografia Nacional, Publicaciones del Departamento Agrario Nacional.

Purcell, Trevor W. 1993. *Banana Fallout: Class, Color, and Culture among West Indians in Costa Rica.* Los Angeles: University of California, Los Angeles, Center for African American Studies.

Putnam, Lara. 2000. "Public Women and One-Pant Men: Production and Politics on Costa Rica's Caribbean Coast, 1870 to 1960." Ph.D. diss., University of Michigan.

———. 2001. "Respectability, Rudeness, and Race: West Indian Migrants in Costa Rica, 1920–1938." Paper presented at the annual conference of Latin American Studies Association, Washington, D.C.

Ransom, David. 1999. "One Short of a Bunch." *New Internationalist* 317: 26–28.

Raynolds, Laura T. 2000a. "Negotiating Contract Farming in the Dominican Republic." *Human Organization* 59, no. 4: 441–51.

———. 2000b. Re-Embedding Global Agriculture: The International Organic and Fair Trade Movements. *Journal of Agriculture and Human Values* 17: 297–309.

———. Forthcoming. "Creating Alternative Commodity Systems: The Case of Bananas." *Plantation Society in the Americas.*

Raynolds, Laura T., David Myhre, Philip McMichael, Vivian Carro-Figueroa, and Frederick H. Buttel. 1993. "The 'New' Internationalization of Agriculture: A Reformulation." *World Development* 21, no. 7: 1101–21.

Raynolds, Laura T., and Douglas Murray. 1998. "Yes, We Have No Bananas: Re-Regulating Global and Regional Trade." *International Journal of Sociology of Agriculture and Food* 7: 7–43.

Read, Ian. 2000. "Reinterpreting the United Fruit Company: The Role of the U.S. Government and American Popular Perception." Stanford, Calif.: n.p. Unpublished paper.

Read, Robert. 1983. "The Growth and Structure of Multinationals in the Banana Export Trade." In *The Growth of International Business,* edited by Mark Casson. Boston: Allen and Unwin.

Reina, Leticia, ed. 1997. *La Reindianización de América, Siglo XIX.* México City: Siglo XXI.

República de Honduras. 1925. *Manifiesto del Dr. Miguel Paz Barahona al Pueblo Hondureño.* Tegucigalpa, Honduras: Tipografía Nacional.

"Rise of the Banana Industry in the Windward Islands." 1955. In *The Windward Islands Annual,* vols. 32–35. Sussex, England: House Magazine Publishing.

Roberts, Shari. 1993. " 'The Lady in the Tutti-Frutti Hat': Carmen Miranda, a Spectacle of Ethnicity." *Cinema Journal* 32 (spring): 3–23.

Roche, Julian. 1998. *The International Banana Trade.* New York: CRC Press.

Rodriquez, D. W. 1955. "Bananas: An Outline of the Economic History of Production and Trade with Special Reference to Jamaica." Kingston, Jamaica: Government Printer.

Rose, Mary Swartz. 1918. *Everyday Foods in War Time.* New York: Webb Publishing Company.

Rose, Renwick. 1999. "WTO Deals Blow to Windwards." *Banana Trade News Bulletin,* 1 May.

Roseberry, William, Lowell Gudmundson, and Mario Samper Kutschbach, eds. 1995. *Coffee, Society, and Power in Latin America.* Baltimore, Md.: Johns Hopkins University Press.

Rowe, Philip, and D. L. Richardson. 1975. *Breeding Bananas for Disease Resistance, Fruit Quality, and Yield.* La Lima, Honduras: Tropical Agriculture Research Services.

Salomón, Leticia, ed. 1991. *Honduras: Panorama y Perspectivas.* Tegucigalpa, Honduras: CEDOH.

Sampson, H. C. 1929. *Report on the Development of Agriculture in British Honduras.* London: His Majesty's Stationery Office.

Sanchez, Arturo. 1996. Interview by Steve Striffler. Tape recording. Tenguel, Ecuador, 3 June.

Sanchez, José P. N.d. [1988–1992]. *En el prisma de la historia.* N.p. Unpublished manuscript.

Sanders, David. Forthcoming. "One Hundred Years of Solidarity: Development and Democracy in Honduras," Ph.D. diss., Yale University.

Sauve, Eric. 1999. "The Global Market for Organic Bananas." Paper presented at the International Workshop on the Production of Organic and Environmentally Sustainable Bananas, Montpellier, France.

Schlesinger, Stephen, and Stephen Kinser. 1982. *Bitter Fruit: The Untold Story of the American Coup in Guatemala.* Garden City, N.Y.: Doubleday, 1982.

Schoonover, Thomas, and Ebba Schoonover. 1989. "Statistics for an Understanding of Foreign Intrusions into Central America from the 1820s to 1930." *Anuario de Estudios Centroamericanos* 15, no. 1: 108.

Schremp, Gerry. 1996. *Celebration of American Food: Four Centuries in the Melting Pot.* Golden: Fulcrum Publishing.

Schwarzweller, H. K., ed. 1984. *Research in Rural Sociology and Development.* Greenwich, Conn.: JAI Press.

Scott, James C. 1985. *Weapons of the Weak: Everyday Forms of Peasant Resistance.* New Haven, Conn.: Yale University Press.

———. 1990. *Domination and the Arts of Resistance: Hidden Transcripts.* New Haven, Conn.: Yale University Press.

Sealy, Theodore, and Herbert Hart. 1984. *Jamaica's Banana Industry.* Kingston: Jamaica Banana Producers Association.

Silver, Frank, and Irving Cohn. 1977 [1923]. "Yes, We Have No Bananas." In *Songs of the Twenties.* Milwaukee, Wisc.: Hal Leonard Corporation.

Simmonds, N. W., and Robert H. Stover. 1987. *Bananas.* London: Longman.

Slocum, Karla. 1996. "Producing under a Globalizing Economy: The Intersection of Flexible Production and Local Autonomy in the Work, Lives, and Actions of St. Lucian Banana Growers." Ph.D. diss., University of Florida.

———. 1998. "Challenges to Globalization: St. Lucian Banana Growers and Notions of Freedom and Control." Paper presented at the University of North Carolina, Chapel Hill, Department of Anthropology.

———. 2000. "History, Class, and Culture in St. Lucian Banana Growers' Protests against State Power." Paper presented at the University of Wisconsin, Madison, Department of Afro-American Studies.

Slutsky, Daniel, and Esther Alonso. 1980. *Empresas Transnacionales y Agricultura: El Caso del Enclave Bananero en Honduras.* Tegucigalpa, Honduras: Editorial Universitaria.

Solberg, Helena, and David Meyer. 1994. *Carmen Miranda: Bananas Is My Business.* International Cinema. Videocassette.

Solidaridad. 1995. *Yellow Fever: Proposal for Quota Allocation for Fair Trade Bananas.* Utrecht, Netherlands: Solidaridad.

Solórzano F., Valentín. 1977. *Evolución económica de Guatemala.* Guatemala City: Editorial José de Pineda Ibarra.

Soluri, John. 1998. "Landscape and Livelihood: An Agroecological History of Export Banana Growing in Honduras, 1870–1975." Ph.D. diss., University of Michigan.

———. 2000. "People, Plants, and Pathogens: The Eco-Social Dynamics of Export Banana Production in Honduras." *Hispanic American Historical Review* 80, no. 3: 463–501.

Southey, Caroline. 1995. "EU Banana Rules Backed as U.S. Exports Slip." *Financial Times,* 11 September, p. 4.

Spring, Anita, ed. 2000. *Women Farmers and Commercial Ventures: Increasing Food Security in Developing Countries.* Boulder, Colo.: Lynne Rienner.

Standley, Paul C. 1931. "The Flora of Lancetilla." *Field Museum of Natural History–Botany* 10: 8–49.

"Statement of the Permanent Representative of St. Lucia to the WTO at a Press Conference on the Occasion of the Meeting of the WTO Dispute Settlement Body." 1997. Eastern Caribbean News and Views on Organisation of Eastern Caribbean States, *http://www.caribisles.org/news-01a.htm),* 16 October.

Stephens, Clyde S. 1987. *Bosquejo Historico del Cultivo del Banano en la Provincia de Bocas del Toro (1880–1980).* Panama City: Impretex.

Stevens, Wallace. 1972 [1929]. "Floral Decoration for Bananas." In *The Palm at the End of the Mind.* Edited by Holly Stevens. New York: Vintage Books.

Stewart, Watt. 1964. *Keith and Costa Rica.* Albuquerque: University of New Mexico Press.

St. Lucia Government. 1960. *Proceedings from Discussion with Government Representatives and Geest Industries Representatives Concerning the Sugar Industry.* Castries, St. Lucia. 6 February.

———. 1963. *Government Announcement Regarding Sugar Industry.* Castries, St. Lucia. 12 August.

———. 1967. St. Lucia Banana Growers' Association Act of 1967. Castries, St. Lucia. 23 August.

———. 1986. Banana Protection and Quality Control Act of 1986. Castries, St. Lucia.

St. Lucia Government, Information Service. 1994. *Mount Coubaril Summit Meeting on the Banana Industry.* Videotaped recording of proceedings. Government Information Service. March.

St. Lucia Government, Ministry of Agriculture, Lands, Fisheries, and Cooperatives. 1973–1974. The Agricultural Census of St. Lucia, 1973–1974. Castries, St. Lucia.

———. 1980. *Inquiry into the Banana Industry, Final Report.* Commissioned by the Government of St. Lucia. Castries, St. Lucia. 26 August.

———. 1990. *Comprehensive Audit of the Ministry of Agriculture, Lands, Fisheries, and Cooperatives: Diversification and Extension.* Castries, St. Lucia.

Stover, Robert H. 1962. *Fusarial Wilt (Panama Disease) of the Banana and Other Musa Species.* Kew, England: Commonwealth Mycological Institute.

Striffler, Steve. 1999. "Wedded to Work: Class Struggles and Gendered Identities in the Re-structuring of the Ecuadorian Banana Industry." *Identities: Global Studies in Culture and Power* 6, no. 1: 91–120.

———. 2002. *In the Shadows of State and Capital: The United Fruit Company, Popular Struggle, and Agrarian Restructuring in Ecuador, 1900–1995.* Durham, N.C.: Duke University Press.

St. Vincent. 1984. Banana (Protection and Quality Control) Act, 1984. Act No. 33 of 1984. Kingstown, St. Vincent.

St. Vincent Statistical Unit. 1999. *Digest of Statistics for the Year 1997, No. 47.* Kingstown, St. Vincent: Central Planning Division.

Sutton, Paul. 1997. "The Banana Regime of the European Union, the Caribbean, and Latin America." *Journal of Interamerican Studies and World Affairs* 39, no. 2: 5–36.

SVBGA. 1994. *Annual Report 1993.* Kingstown, St. Vincent: St.Vincent Banana Growers' Association.

———. 1996. *1995 Report and Statement of Accounts to the 42nd Annual General Meeting.* Kingstown, St. Vincent: St. Vincent Banana Growers' Association.

———. 1998. *1997 Report and Statement of Accounts to the 44th Annual General Meeting.* Kingstown, St. Vincent: St.Vincent Banana Growers' Association.

———. 1999. *1998 Report and Statement of Accounts to the 45th Annual General Meeting.* Kingstown, St. Vincent: St.Vincent Banana Growers' Association.

———. 2000. *1999 Report and Statement of Accounts to the 46th Annual General Meeting.* Kingstown, St. Vincent: St.Vincent Banana Growers' Association.

Sylva Charvet, Paola. 1987. "Los Productores del Banano." In *El Banano en el Ecuador,* ed. Carlos Larrea Maldonado. Quito, Ecuador: FLACSO.

Thomson, Robert. 1987. *Green Gold: Bananas and Dependency in the Eastern Caribbean.* London: Latin American Bureau.

Thompson, Grace Agnes. 1915. "The Story of a Great New England Enterprise." *New England* (May): 17.

Thrupp, Lori Ann. 1991. "Sterilization of Workers from Pesticide Exposure: The Causes and Consequences of DBCP-induced Damage in Costa Rica and Beyond." *International Journal of Health Services* 21, no. 4: 731–57.

"The Timeing of Bananas." 1905. *Journal of Jamaica Agricultural Society* 9 (February 1905): 58.

Tomich, Dale. 1990. *Slavery and the Circuit of Sugar: Martinique and the World Economy, 1830–1848.* Baltimore, Md.: Johns Hopkins University Press.

Topik, Steven C., and Allen Wells. 1998. *The Second Conquest of Latin America: Coffee, Henequen and Oil during the Export Boom, 1850–1930.* Austin: University of Texas Press.

Topik, Steven C., and Mario Samper Kutschbach. 2001. "The Latin American Coffee Commodity Chain." Paper presented at the Latin America and Global Trade Conference, 16–17 November, Stanford University, Stanford, California.

Toussaint, Mónica, ed. 1988. *Guatemala: Textos de la Historia de Centroamérica y el Caribe.* Distrito Federal, Mexico: Universidad de Guadalajara, Nueva Imagen.

Trouillot, Michel-Rolph. 1988. *Peasants and Capital: Dominica in the World Economy.* Baltimore, Md.: Johns Hopkins University Press.

Tucker, Richard P. 2000. *Insatiable Appetite: The United States and the Ecological Degradation of the Tropical World.* Berkeley: University of California Press.

Tyrell, Ian. 1999. *True Gardens of the Gods.* Berkeley: University of California Press.

"The Undervalued Banana." 1912. *Journal of the American Medical Association* 58: 276.

United Brands. 1970. *Banana Operations Manual.* Boston: United Brands.

———. 1972. *Annual Report to the Stockholders.* Boston: United Brands.

United Fruit Company. 1939–53, 1957–68. *Annual Report to the Stockholders.* Boston: United Fruit Company, Division of Tropical Research.

———. 1917. *Food Value of the Banana: Opinion of Leading Medical and Scientific Authorities.* Boston: United Fruit Company.

———. 1936. *Nutritive and Therapeutic Values of the Banana: A Digest of Scientific Literature.* Boston: United Fruit Company.

———. 1958. *Problems and Progress in Banana Disease Research.* Boston: United Fruit Company.

———. 1961. *Unifruitco* 20.

———. 1969. *Unifruitco* 27 (30 May): 4–5.

———. N.d. *Research Extension Newsletter.* Boston: United Fruit Company, Division of Tropical Research.

United Kingdom. 1897. *Report of the West India Royal Commission.* London: Her Majesty's Stationary Office.

United Press International. 2000. "WTO Approves Ecuador's Punitive Trade Sanctions." *UPI News,* 18 May.

United States Department of Agriculture. 1957. *Consumption of Food in the United States, 1909–1952.* Washington, D.C.: United States Department of Agriculture Marketing Service.

Urra Veloso, Pedro. 1975. *La Guerra del Banano: De la Mamita Yunai a la UPEB.* Buenos Aires: Tierra Nueva.

Valencia Chala, Santiago. 1986. *El Negro en Centroamérica.* Quito, Ecuador: Centro Cultural Afro-Ecuatoriano, Editorial Abya-Yala.

Valeriano, Enrique Flores. 1987. *Explotación Bananera en Honduras.* Tegucigalpa, Honduras: Editorial Universitaria.

Valles, Jean-Paul. 1968. *The World Market for Bananas, 1964–72.* New York: Praeger.

Van de Kasteele, Adelien. 1998. "The Banana Chain: The Macro Economics of the Banana Trade." Paper presented at the International Banana Conference, May 4–6, Brussels, Belgium.

Vandermeer, John, and Ivette Perfecto. 1995. *Breakfast of Biodiversity: The Truth about Rain Forest Destruction.* Oakland, Calif.: Institute for Food and Development Policy.

Vega, Bernardo. 1988. *Trujillo y Haití, 1930–1937,* Volume 1. Santo Domingo, Dominican Republic: Fundación Cultural Dominicana.

————. 1995. *Trujillo y Haití, 1930–1937*, Volume 2. Santo Domingo, Dominican Republic: Fundación Cultural Dominicana.

Villars, Rina. *Porque Quiero Seguir Viviendo . . . Habla Graciela García*. Tegucigalpa, Honduras: Editorial Guaymuras.

Waddell, D. A. G. 1961. *British Honduras: A Historical and Contemporary Survey*. Oxford: Oxford University Press.

Wardlaw, Claude W. 1935. *Diseases of the Banana*. London: MacMillan.

Watson, Hilborne A., ed. 1994. *The Caribbean in the Global Political Economy*. Boulder, Colo.: Lynne Rienner.

Watts, Michael J. 1994. "Life Under Contract: Contract Farming, Agrarian Restructuring, and Flexible Accumulation." In *Living under Contract: Contract Farming and Agrarian Transformation in Sub-Saharan Africa,* edited by Peter D. Little and Michael J. Watts. Madison: University of Wisconsin Press.

Watts, Michael J., and David Goodman, eds. 1997. *Globalising Food: Agrarian Questions and Global Restructuring*. London: Routledge.

Watts, Michael J., Peter D. Little, Christopher Mock, Martin Billings, and Steven Jaffee. 1988. *Contract Farming in Africa*, Volume I: *Comparative Analysis*. Binghamton, N.Y.: Institute for Development Anthropology.

Welch, Barbara. 1996. *Survival by Association*. Montreal: McGill-Queens University Press.

Wells, Allen. Forthcoming. "Altruism's Cost: General Trujillo, FDR, and the Dominican Republic Settlement Association." In *Against Oblivion: Latin America and the Holocaust,* edited by Ilan Stavans and Leo Spitzer. Berkeley: University of California Press.

Wells, Allen, and Gilbert M. Joseph. 1996. *Summer of Discontent, Seasons of Upheaval: Elite Politics and Rural Insurgency in Yucatán, 1876–1915*. Stanford, Calif.: Stanford University Press.

Wharton, Edith. 1988. *The Letters of Edith Wharton*. Edited by R. W. B. Lewis and Nancy Lewis. New York: Charles Scribner's Sons.

"What Bananas! Tariff Fight Baffles Europe." 1999. *New York Times,* 5 March, sec. A, p. 1.

Wheat, Andrew. 1996. "Toxic Bananas." *Multinational Monitor* 17, no. 9: 9–15.

White, Judith. 1978. *La United Fruit Co. en Colombia: Historia de una Ignomia*. Bogotá: Editorial Presencia.

Wiley, James. 1998. "Dominica's Economic Diversification: Microstates in a Neoliberal Era." In *Globalization and Neoliberalism: The Caribbean Context,* edited by Thomas Klak. Boulder, Colo.: Rowman and Littlefield.

Wilkins, Mira. 1970. *The Emergence of Multinational Enterprise: American Business Abroad from the Colonial Era to 1914*. Cambridge, Mass.: Harvard University Press.

————. 1974. *The Maturing of Multinational Enterprise: American Business Abroad from 1914 to 1970*. Cambridge, Mass.: Harvard University Press.

Williams, Eric. 1944. *Capitalism and Slavery*. Chapel Hill: University of North Carolina Press.

Williams, Robert G. 1995. *States and Social Evolution: Coffee and the Rise of National Governments in Central America*. Chapel Hill: University of North Carolina.

Willis, Susan. 1987. "Learning from the Banana." *American Quarterly* 39, no. 4: 587–92.

Wilson, Charles Morrow. 1947. *Empire in Green and Gold.* New York: Henry Holt.

WINBAN. 1986. *WINBAN Annual Report.* Castries, St. Lucia: Windward Islands Banana Association.

———. 1993. *1992 Annual Report and Accounts.* Castries, St. Lucia: Windward Islands Banana Association.

Wright, Winthrop. 1990. *Café con Leche: Race, Class, and National Image in Venezuela.* Austin: University of Texas Press.

Yankey, Bernard, et al. 1988. *Review of the Banana Industry of St. Lucia.* Castries, St. Lucia: Prepared for the Government of St. Lucia.

"Yellow Peril." 1990. *Economist* 317, no. 7678: 72.

"Ynforme de la Provincia de Honduras . . . por el gobernador." 1991. In *Documentos Coloniales de Honduras,* edited by Héctor Leyva, 298. Tegucigalpa, Honduras: Ediciones Subirana.

Zuniga, Alma Briceno de, and Hernán Zuniga Reyes. 1993. *Antología de las Fiestas Escolares Hondureñas.* Tegucigalpa, Honduras: Quiñonez Editorial.

Zúniga Figueroa, Carlos. 1953. *Estadísticas Demográficas, 1926–1951.* Tegucigalpa, Honduras: Dirección General de Estadística y Censos.

CONTRIBUTORS

PHILIPPE BOURGOIS is Professor and Chair of the Department of Anthropology, History, and Social Medicine at the University of California, San Francisco. His most recent book, *In Search of Respect: Selling Crack in El Barrio* (1995, Cambridge University Press), won the C. Wright Mills Prize and the Margaret Mead Prize, among others.

MARCELO BUCHELI has a Ph.D. in History from Stanford University, where he currently lectures.

DARÍO A. EURAQUE teaches Latin American History at Trinity College in Hartford, Connecticut.

CINDY FORSTER has worked with immigrant-rights groups and labor unions in San Francisco and teaches Latin American History at Scripps College in Los Angeles County.

LAWRENCE S. GROSSMAN is Professor and Head of the Department of Geography at Virginia Tech. He has conducted research on peasants and agrarian change on St. Vincent in the Eastern Caribbean, in Kenya, and in Papua New Guinea.

MARK MOBERG is a Professor of Anthropology at the University of South Alabama and has conducted research in the banana industries of Belize and St. Lucia.

LAURA T. RAYNOLDS is Associate Professor of Sociology at Colorado State University. Her research focuses on globalization, agrarian restructuring, alternative trade networks, and gendered labor forces in the Caribbean and Latin

America. Recent publications appear in *World Development, Gender and Society, Human Organization,* and *Agriculture and Human Values.*

KARLA SLOCUM is Assistant Professor in the Department of Anthropology and holds a joint appointment in the Department of African and Afro-American Studies at the University of North Carolina, Chapel Hill. Her current work centers on the intersection of globalization and resistance in the Caribbean.

JOHN SOLURI is Assistant Professor in the History Department at Carnegie Mellon University.

STEVE STRIFFLER is Associate Professor of Anthropology and Latin American Studies at the University of Arkansas.

ALLEN WELLS is Roger Howell Jr. Professor of History at Bowdoin College.

INDEX

Honduras, 3, 5, 13, 17, 18, 26, 46 n.9, 53, 67, 69, 70, 72, 75, 95, 108, 151, 193, 229–47, 324

Imperialism, 5, 15; U.S. government and, 6, 26, 41, 192–93. *See also* United Fruit Company

Jamaica, 10, 11, 13, 26, 27, 35, 52, 53, 59, 118, 120, 121, 126, 127, 149, 150, 152, 158, 163, 291, 292

Keith, Minor, 4, 5, 10, 81, 156, 158
Kepner, Charles, 9, 15, 96

Lome, 29, 46 n.18, 263, 267, 268

Miranda, Carmen, 62–63, 73

Panama, 5, 10, 13, 29, 32, 38, 95, 105, 106
Panama Disease, 11, 12, 13, 14, 26, 49–50, 67–71, 76, 150, 162, 165, 171, 172, 173, 179, 180, 185, 186, 202, 322, 324
Peasants. *See* Smallholders
Plantations, 7, 8, 10, 11, 12, 13, 14, 33; foreign-owned, 14, 150, 197, 325–26
Preston, Andrew, 9, 81

St. Lucia, 3, 11, 29, 253–81, 327
St. Vincent, 2, 11, 239, 286–314
Santo Domingo, 10, 13
Smallholders, 3, 5–6, 11, 14, 18, 35–36, 153, 159, 163, 174–83, 197, 257, 258, 261–81, 283 n.18, 286–90, 294–314
Standard Fruit Company, 3, 5, 10, 13, 26, 32, 33,

37–40, 41, 42, 46 n.9, 49, 67, 69, 70, 72, 73, 74, 169 n.5, 228, 232, 238
State, 175–79, 191–223, 253–81, 288, 290, 328–31; relations with foreign capital, 3, 4, 5, 90, 107, 145–70, 175–91, 195, 197, 204–5, 221, 316–17
Stevens, Wallace, 61–62
Sugar, 25, 195, 203, 256–60, 282 n.12, 316

United Fruit Company, 2, 3, 5, 7, 10, 11, 12, 13, 17, 19 n.4, 32, 33, 37–40, 41, 42, 46 n.9, 54, 58, 60, 71, 72, 73, 74, 76, 80–100, 145–70, 171–90, 191–223, 228, 232, 233, 234, 237, 238, 241, 290, 318, 320; agricultural research and, 67–69; antitrust and, 26; documents of, 103–44, 189 n.3; emergence of, 25–27, 49, 81, 173

Vertical integration, 2, 26, 32, 37, 67, 80, 81–98

Wharton, Edith, 60–61
Windward Islands, 11, 13, 18, 28, 32, 35, 38, 40, 45 n.6, 46 n.13, 255, 264, 265, 268, 270, 286, 287, 290–93, 311–13, 331
Windward Islands Banana Development and Exporting Corporation (WIBDECO), 6, 32
Workers, 4, 107, 170, 171, 172, 174, 179–89, 191–223, 228, 232–47, 284 n.27, 324–25; communism and, 137, 138, 194, 203, 222, 225 n.33; divisions among, 5, 107, 108, 324
World Trade Organization, 14, 23, 41, 42, 46 nn.18, 19, 169, 267, 268, 270, 280

Library of Congress Cataloging-in-Publication Data

Banana wars : power, production, and history in the Americas /

edited by Steve Striffler and Mark Moberg.

p. ; cm. — (American encounters/global interactions)

Includes bibliographical references and index.

ISBN 0-8223-3159-4 (cloth : alk. paper)

ISBN 0-8223-3196-9 (pbk. : alk. paper)

1. Banana trade—South America—History. 2. Banana trade—

Caribbean Area—History. 3. United Fruit Company—History.

I. Striffler, Steve. II. Moberg, Mark. III. Series.

HD9259.B3S683 2003   338.1′74772′098—dc21   2003008347